SHAPING STRATEGY

SHAPING STRATEGY

THE CIVIL-MILITARY POLITICS
OF STRATEGIC ASSESSMENT

Risa A. Brooks

PRINCETON UNIVERSITY PRESS

PRINCETON AND OXFORD

Copyright © 2008 by Princeton University Press
Published by Princeton University Press, 41 William Street,
Princeton, New Jersey 08540
In the United Kingdom: Princeton University Press, 3 Market Place,
Woodstock, Oxfordshire OX20 1TW
All Rights Reserved

Library of Congress Cataloging-in-Publication Data
Brooks, Risa A.
Shaping strategy : the civil-military politics of strategic
assessment / Risa A. Brooks.
   p.   cm.
Includes bibliographical reference and index.
ISBN 978-0-691-12980-8 (hardcover : alk. paper)
ISBN 978-0-691-13668-4 (pbk. : alk. paper)
1. Civil-military relations—History—20th century.
2. Strategy—History—20th century. I. Title
JF195.B76 2008
355.02—dc22   2007043392

British Library Cataloging-in-Publication Data is available

This book has been composed in Janson

Printed on acid-free paper. ∞

press.princeton.edu

Printed in the United States of America

10 9 8 7 6 5 4 3 2 1

CONTENTS

Acknowledgments vii

Introduction • The Significance of Strategic Assessment 1

Two • Explaining Variation in Strategic Assessment 15

Three • Egypt in the Mid-1960s 62

Four • Egypt in the 1970s 102

Five • Britain and Germany and the First World War 143

Six • Pakistan and Turkey in the Late 1990s 195

Seven • U.S. Postconflict Planning for the 2003 Iraq War 226

Conclusion • Findings and Implications 256

References 275

Index 303

ACKNOWLEDGMENTS

Throughout my academic studies I have been fascinated by military organizations and their relations with political authorities. As a graduate student, that interest was sparked by a puzzling divergence in the study of civil-military relations in comparative politics and international relations. In the former, militaries were characterized as political actors, with clear agency and influence in domestic politics, yet who primarily focused on intraregime outcomes. In contrast, in the latter tradition, militaries appeared often as myopic bureaucracies oriented internationally, toward military doctrine and security strategy. This disciplinary divide would inspire my dissertation's motivating question: What happens when military leaders exercise political influence in the formulation of a state's security strategies?

As I began to answer that question, I observed that when security strategies and other corporate matters were in dispute, military and political leaders would often argue about procedures for analyzing and deciding these issues, not just about their specific substance. They would disagree about when to share information and would try to conceal it at times; or views would diverge about the format of advisory processes, such as who would be present and what role participants would play, as well as other apparently mundane organizational details. I realized that, especially when they had the political power to do so, each side would try to promote routines and structures that would advantage its preferred substantive outcomes. In turn, the processes that emerged would have larger consequences for the state. In the event of an international conflict, they would constitute the institutional environment in which the leaders engaged in strategic assessment: how they would exchange and analyze information and make decisions. From this insight I began to think more broadly about how variation in the balance of power between political and military leaders and the intensity of their conflicts might shape this competition over process and affect strategic assessment. The fruits of that inquiry fill the eight chapters of this book.

Throughout the writing of this book, and the dissertation from which it originated, numerous individuals and institutions have provided essential support. My doctoral adviser, David Lake, has been a central source of guidance, always providing the right mix of enthusiasm and critical engagement of my ideas. As a graduate student I benefited from generous funding from the University of California's Institute on Global Conflict and Cooperation. I spent a stimulating year interacting with colleagues at Harvard's Olin Institute for Strategic Studies, and then in London at the International Institute for Strategic Studies. Subsequently, Stanford's Center for International Security and Cooperation, under the leadership of Scott Sagan and Lynn Eden, proved an especially congenial place for a postdoctoral fellowship year. I thank my alma mater, Mills College, and especially my undergraduate mentor, Fred Lawson, for allowing me to get my feet wet teaching before I joined the faculty at Northwestern.

I also am grateful to the universities and centers that hosted me for talks and the audiences in their seminars that provided valuable feedback. These include the Olin Institute for Strategic Studies and Stanford's Center for International Security and Cooperation (both during and following my stays), Duke University's New Faces in International Security Conference, Georgetown University's 2003 Junior Faculty Workshop, University of Chicago's Program on International Political Economy and Security, MIT's Security Studies Program, Columbia University's International Politics Seminar, University of Texas at Austin's International Affairs Specialization Colloquium, and UCSD's Project on International Affairs seminar series. In addition, many individuals have played a part in the development of this project, by providing comments on text or on particular empirical sections or analytical issues. These include Karen Alter, Debbi Avant, Nora Bensahel, Dick Betts, Steve Biddle, Mike Desch, Alex Downes, Lynn Eden, Nisha Fazal, Peter Feaver, Scott Gartner, Sumit Ganguly, Eug Gholz, Peter Gourevitch, Steph Haggard, Paul Kapur, Ron Krebs, Jim Mahoney, Ben Page, Scott Sagan, Liz Stanley, Hendrik Spruyt, Kathy Thelen, Steve Van Evera, and Barb Walter. I also thank my IR colleagues at Northwestern University and the University of Chicago, who, especially in a meeting of our "North-South" seminar, provided feedback at an important moment in this book's development.

Above all, my friends and family have provided the love and encouragement to sustain me as I wrote this book. With tremendous grace they have endured the many stresses inevitable to any project of this magnitude. My husband Chris, with his strength of character and ever-present support, has been truly a best friend throughout. He and my son, Willem, whose exuberant spirit and infectious laughter always bring a smile to my face, are a constant source of inspiration.

Finally, throughout this long journey, one person stands out: my mother, Susan Wondrasek. From this project's beginning to its end, she has provided wisdom and perspective, encouraging me to persevere in the face of challenges, while always celebrating my successes. It is to her that I dedicate this book.

SHAPING STRATEGY

One

INTRODUCTION: THE SIGNIFICANCE OF STRATEGIC ASSESSMENT

IN MAY 1967 EGYPT'S President Nasser initiated a crisis with Israel that would end in a war he was bound to lose. The crisis began when Nasser received a report that Israel was sending forces to its border with Syria. Despite soon learning the report was false, Nasser nevertheless escalated tensions by requesting the United Nations withdraw its forces stationed in the Sinai Peninsula to make way for deployments of Egyptian troops.[1] Shortly thereafter, on May 22, Egypt's president took the even more dire step of closing the Straits of Tiran to Israeli shipping. On the morning of June 5, Israel attacked Egypt's airfields. Egypt's role in the ensuing war ended just a day and a half later in a devastating defeat that changed the complexion of Middle East politics forever.

Curiously, despite the potential stakes involved, Egypt's decisions to initiate and later hold firm to its demands that spring were taken in an internal environment ill-prepared for the gravity of the situation. Decision making was reportedly sorely lacking on Egypt's political and military situation. Historical accounts reveal that Nasser was competing with his military chief for control of military policy. Intelligence was politicized, and coordination between political and military authorities inadequate. As a result, and by his own admission, Nasser went to war with a poor assessment of how miserably Egypt's military would fare in the conflict and the devastation his regime would bear as a result.

In striking contrast, Nasser's successor, Anwar Sadat, was able to plan and implement a series of political and military initiatives in the 1970s aimed at achieving his security goals. He developed, in consultation with military authorities, a sophisticated, limited war plan based on analysis of Egypt's strategic situation. He was able repeatedly to overrule his military chiefs and implement unpopular plans, including the controversial plan for the October 1973 war, subsequent disengagement agreements, and a peace treaty with Israel. Unlike Nasser, Sadat appeared to benefit from a decision-making environment that allowed him and his military leaders to eval-

---

[1] The area had been under United Nations oversight since the 1956 Suez conflict.

uate critically Egypt's strategic and military options and their consistency with political objectives.

Why are some leaders, at some times, able to assess their capabilities and reconcile their political and military objectives? Why are others prone to poor estimates and disintegrated policies? In sum, why do some states excel at strategic assessment while others fail miserably?

A major reason is the nature of states' civil-military relations. Domestic relations between political and military leaders shape the institutional processes in which leaders evaluate their strategies in interstate conflicts. Those processes affect how leaders appraise their state's military options, plans, and the broader diplomatic and political constraints that bear on them. In short, civil-military relations affect how states engage in strategic assessment.

Strategic assessment is vital to state security and to international peace and stability. Egypt provides a vivid illustration why. Nasser's poor assessment of his capabilities and his devastating loss in the ensuing war in 1967 exposed to the world the failings of his regime and its military. Nasser's claim to regional leadership was irrevocably damaged. The war the leader precipitated also ended with Israel occupying critical areas of Syria, Palestine, and Egypt—areas today, with the exception of the latter, that remain the subject of dispute and a catalyst for tensions in the region. In the 1970s, in contrast, Egypt's strengths in strategic assessment proved an enormous advantage to Anwar Sadat. Egypt got the Sinai back, repositioned itself in the Western camp, and in the process signed the first peace treaty between Israel and an Arab state.

Today the United States must contend with the results of its own debacle of strategic assessment: the failure to evaluate adequately the postwar security environment and prepare accordingly for the 2003 Iraq War. Many analysts focus on rivalries between the State Department and Pentagon or on Secretary of Defense Rumsfeld's abrasive personality to explain weaknesses in postwar plans. Less understood are how civil-military relations predisposed the country to poor strategic assessment. As I argue in chapter 7, the underlying structure of power and preferences in U.S. civil-military relations was a major cause of inadequate planning for the security vacuum after the fall of Saddam Hussein's regime. The absence of comprehensive contingency plans and the ensuing breakdown of security alienated the population and fueled a nascent insurgency against American forces.

In these cases, as in the other empirical studies in this volume, failures of strategic assessment had enormous consequences for the states involved. In this book I explain why these failures occur and discuss the conditions under which we are likely to get better strategic assessment.

The Argument in Brief

In its approach to studying strategic assessment, this book bridges the disciplines of comparative and international politics. It begins with insights from comparative politics about the importance of the military's domestic relationship with political leaders. Comparativists have long recognized that the balance of power and intensity of substantive disagreements between political and military leaders can differ significantly across and within states, over time. These moreover can affect the military's bargaining power within ruling regimes and consequently the institutional features of states, broadly defined and specifically in security-related areas.[2] Civil-military relations are vital from this perspective in understanding the internal features of states.

Janus-faced, civil-military relations also have a significant international dimension. During interstate conflicts, military leaders provide advice to a country's political leader about the state's relative capabilities. They guide him or her in assessing the utility of different military plans and options. Military leaders have important informational advantages about these issues, both as a result of their expertise in "the management of violence" and because of their regular contact with the military organization. Political leaders are in charge of a much broader array of policy concerns—not just military and security issues—and therefore even if they, for personal or professional reasons, are well versed in military matters, must rely on those who run the armed forces on a daily basis for information and analysis.[3]

A state's processes for strategic assessment intersect these domestic and international facets of civil-military relations. Clashes over security and other corporate issues and the balance of power between military and political leaders affect the routines through which they share and analyze information, consult with one another, and make decisions at the apex of the state. These processes, in turn, constitute the environment in which political leaders evaluate and select their strategies in interstate disputes—the institutions in which they engage in strategic assessment.

---

[2] See, for example, Stepan (1988), Pion-Berlin (1992), Aguero (1995), Ulrich (1999).

[3] By political leader I refer to the individual or individuals who occupy the chief executive office in the state and are in charge of the broad panoply of economic, social, and foreign policies (and who may or may not be elected or wear a military uniform). Military leaders are the individuals who run the military on a daily basis. Note that this is a definition that differentiates among individuals according to their functional roles; by this definition all states, even those run by people in uniform, have both political and military leaders.

This book explores the causes and consequences of these institutions for strategic assessment. Theoretically, it seeks to explain why states' assessment institutions vary, in the process drawing on the insights of comparative and other scholarship on civil-military relations. In turn, empirically, in each of eight case studies, the book demonstrates how these processes mattered for understanding outcomes of critical importance to international relations.

As I elaborate in chapter 2, in developing this book's theory about how civil-military relations affect strategic assessment, I rely on what I term a "distributional approach": an approach that emphasizes the effects of individuals' and groups' distributional conflicts on the features of institutions. Institutions in this view emerge from the interactions of actors, with varying resources and interests, competing to advance rules and structures that advantage their preferred outcomes. In the current context, I anticipate that studying underlying conflicts between political and military leaders and how these are shaped by their preferences and relative power will illuminate the processes through which they interact in strategic assessment.

Specifically, two variables are key to my theory. The first, the intensity of preference divergence over corporate, professional, or security issues, determines military and political leaders' underlying incentives to contest processes essential to strategic assessment. The second causal variable, the balance of civil-military power, shapes how these conflicts are resolved. Both variables interact, generating particular "logics" that drive the emergence of institutional features in assessment within the state at any given time.

In my theory, I disaggregate strategic assessment into four constituent attributes, or sets of institutional processes: routines for *information sharing* between political and military leaders about military capabilities and plans, which vary in whether they facilitate fluid exchange or compartmentalize information; *strategic coordination*, or the structures in existence for assessing alternative political-military strategies, and whether or not they promote rigorous debate about costs and risks and help to coordinate military activity with political and diplomatic objectives and constraints; the military's *structural competence* in monitoring its own internal activities and procedures for evaluating foreign militaries and the degree to which these promote self-critical analysis about the state's capabilities and sound analysis about its adversaries' forces; and the *authorization process*, or the mechanisms for approving and vetoing political-military strategy and activity, which vary in whether they promote clearly defined, coherent decision-making processes or contested, ambiguous procedures. Each category reflects formal as well as informal processes; in fact, the "institutions" associated with assessment are much more likely to be unwritten patterns of interaction, conventions, and routines than formalized or legislated phenomena.[4]

---

[4] This informality is important because it renders these institutions especially susceptible to shifts in power and preferences. See chapter 2 on this conceptual point.

In chapter 2 I hypothesize about how various configurations of power and preference divergence affect these four attributes and therefore the overall quality of strategic assessment in the state. I anticipate, for example, that when political leaders dominate and preference divergence is low, such that divergences over security and corporate issues are not entrenched and profound, important obstacles to strategic assessment are absent. Both political and military leaders lack incentives to contest assessment processes. This allows relatively functional institutions to emerge. Consequently, information sharing should be relatively fluid. Strategic coordination is eased as political dominance facilitates the integration in advisory processes of the military with the political offices of the state. The authorization process is also clearly defined, providing structure to decision making. Overall, in these environments debate between political and military leaders can flourish, without risk of it devolving into disputes over control of decision making, or being undermined by mutual alienation born of deep-seated and enduring differences over corporate or security issues: civil-military relations provide the structural preconditions for the sort of rigorous deliberation essential to assessing state strategy. These are the best conditions for engaging in strategic assessment.

The worst conditions occur when political and military leaders are sharing power and their preferences diverge. Assessment institutions become implicated in underlying substantive disputes between political and military leaders and themselves become objects of competition; each side tries to ensure that routines and conventions of interaction protect their preferred strategies or policy outcomes. Military leaders guard access to their private information and favor institutional processes that allow them to do so, compromising routines for information sharing. The authorization process also becomes convoluted as political and military leaders vie for the right to approve and veto military plans and strategy. Strategic coordination deteriorates as military leaders grow wary of participating in joint forums with political representatives and engaging in open-ended analyses. Intraregime competition also corrupts the military's organizational processes for intelligence and internal monitoring. Consequently, in interstate disputes capabilities estimates are apt to be poor, and the analysis of military options and their integration with political objectives superficial. Leaders also struggle to make authoritative decisions about state strategy and ensure they are implemented. These states are devastatingly unprepared to manage their international relations.

I anticipate strategic assessment will be also be poor—but not quite as atrocious—when power is shared and preference divergence is low. Although military and political leaders have few incentives to try to control access to their private information about security issues, and therefore information sharing is relatively unproblematic, the military's autonomy from the diplomatic apparatus of the state weakens joint consultative entities, undermining strategic coordination. Civil-military relations also generate ambiguities in authorization processes, as ultimate rights of veto and approval over military activity remain ill-defined. Together these weaknesses complicate both the quality of deliberation and clarity of decision making about state strategy in international disputes.

Other civil-military relations generate divergent trends and, overall, fall between the extremes in their competencies in strategic assessment. For example, political dominance and high preference divergence generates clarity in the authorization process and provides tools to political leaders that mitigate problems in information sharing. Improvements in structural competence are also possible. However, the oversight methods leaders employ in this setting to protect their interests can truncate dialogue with military leaders and therefore compromise strategic coordination. The balance sheet for the four attributes of assessment is therefore mixed in these states: we should observe clear strengths in three critical areas essential to gathering and sharing information and making decisions, but also notable weaknesses in one—in the comprehensiveness and rigor of debate in advisory forums.

Finally, cases in which the military dominates politically also exhibit strengths as well as notable weaknesses. Here, regardless of the intensity of preference divergence with political leaders over substantive issues, much of the evaluative and decision-making process is internalized within the military organization. This clarifies the authorization process, giving the military ultimate control over political-military strategy. One negative byproduct of this setting, however, is that analysis of these strategies may be insulated from the political apparatus of the state, which impairs strategic coordination. In short, a specific pattern in assessment should be observed in these settings: flaws in how military and political considerations are integrated in deliberative processes, but strengths in the capacity to decide and implement strategy in interstate conflicts. See figure 1.1 for an overview of these hypotheses.

In chapter 2 I develop the theory and explain these hypotheses in greater detail. Before proceeding, however, I elaborate on the importance of studying strategic assessment.

The Problem of Assessment: Why Study It?

Why should scholars study strategic assessment? The main reason is to understand why states sometimes succumb to strategic failure. Analytical completeness requires studying successes as well as failures, but the latter are especially important if we are to understand the causes of war and con-

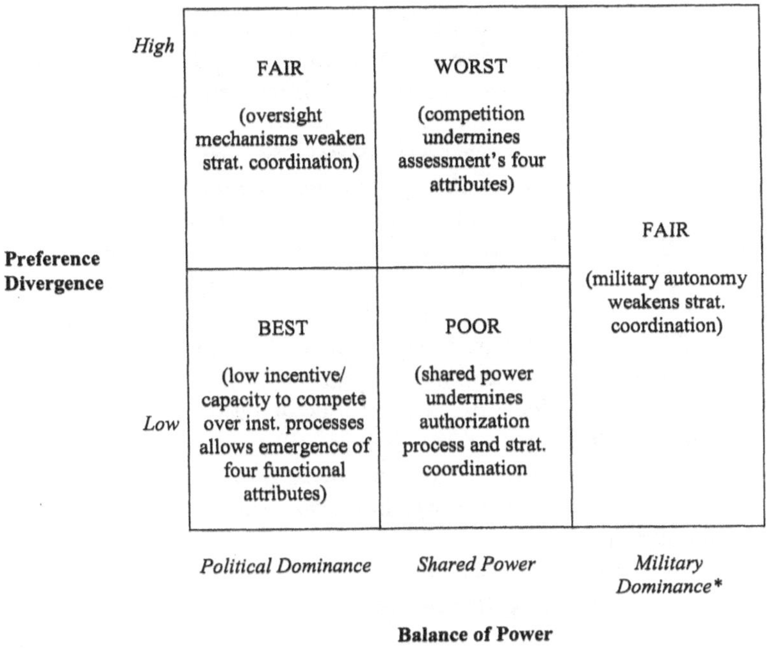

STRATEGIC ASSESSMENT'S SIGNIFICANCE

	Political Dominance	Shared Power	Military Dominance*
High (Preference Divergence)	FAIR (oversight mechanisms weaken strat. coordination)	WORST (competition undermines assessment's four attributes)	FAIR (military autonomy weakens strat. coordination)
Low	BEST (low incentive/capacity to compete over inst. processes allows emergence of four functional attributes)	POOR (shared power undermines authorization process and strat. coordination)	

Balance of Power

Figure 1.1. Variation in Strategic Assessment. *See chapter 2 for why high/low preference divergence is not consequential when military is dominant.

flict in the international arena. Accordingly, in this section I highlight a number of particularly dangerous weaknesses in strategy and pathological international outcomes that may result from poor evaluation and decision making at the civil-military apex.

First, poor strategic assessment can generate failure by undermining states' estimates of their relative military capabilities. In crises and wars, leaders are often tasked with comparing their military capabilities with their adversaries' and allies' resources. They rely on these estimates to judge the likely outcome of armed confrontation, and therefore to evaluate the utility of alternative political strategies they might adopt in the dispute. Such capabilities estimates are complicated endeavors and involve comparing everything from a state's own and its adversaries' material resources (weapons and equipment), communications, logistics, and other systems to intangibles such as training and leadership. Given this complexity, no assessment structure can provide complete and infallible information about a state's capabilities. The precise outcomes of war are never fully knowable a priori. But estimates can be better and worse. Some can be based on more complete and comprehensive information and intelligence, and more rigorous and open-ended analysis. In particular, where military and political leaders withhold private information from each other, fail to analyze that information, or have poor information about their own and adversaries' capabilities in the first place, these capabilities estimates are likely to be seriously flawed.

These capabilities misestimates are important, in turn, because they can predispose leaders toward destabilizing strategies in international conflicts. Following the logic of bargaining models of war, for example, if political leaders overestimate their capabilities and make unwarranted demands in a dispute, their opponents must choose between granting those undeserved concessions or fighting a war in which they anticipate they will perform relatively well.[5] In effect, the intransigent state pushes its adversary over its threshold for war. As this and other theoretical literature that stresses the importance of "miscalculating" capabilities suggests, when states misjudge their military power they put themselves at risk for war. Because civil-military relations and states' assessment institutions can affect their propensities to misestimate their capabilities, they are implicated as a cause of those risky strategies.

Second, poor strategic assessment can create problems in anticipating the political constraints that govern the use of force in an international dispute. One attribute of assessment in particular, strategic coordination, reflects how much the broader international political, diplomatic, and economic context is incorporated into evaluations of a state's military strategy and capabilities. Where strategic coordination is poor, leaders may discount the regional repercussions and other possible political side effects within a target state of using military action, or a particular strategy, to resolve a dispute. Take, for example, a case in which a state is contemplating launching a military offensive in a highly polarized and competitive region of the world. Although feasible militarily, the plan also threatens to destabilize the region or inspire third parties to intervene. If the military and political apparatus of the state is poorly coordinated, these broader strategic responses by other states may be discounted or poorly analyzed. The technical/operational details of implementing the military action may trump its political ramifications in the analytical process. The state consequently risks provoking unanticipated hostility from its competitors. It risks finding itself in a longer or costlier war than originally anticipated.[6]

Third, a state's process of strategic assessment can compromise its ability to translate political goals into supportive military strategies and activities. The two pathologies discussed above—capabilities misestimates and disin-

---

[5] On bargaining models, see Fearon (1995), Wagner (2000), Reiter (2003). On the importance of estimating capabilities, see Blainey (1973), Gartner (1997), Levy (1983).

[6] In other words, the integration of political goals and military means suffers. On this theme see Posen (1984), Van Evera (1991), Avant (1994).

tegration due to neglect of political constraints on military action—stem from weaknesses in information sharing and strategic coordination, and therefore the deliberative dimension of strategic assessment. This third problem originates in weaknesses in its decision-making component; it derives from ambiguities in the authorization process—from deadlock over the processes for choosing among alternative military options in interstate disputes.

At the end of the day, when the deliberative process has been exhausted, state leaders need to make definitive decisions about strategy if the state is going to pursue a clear course of action. When military and political leaders disagree and neither can overrule the other—neither can outvote nor outveto the other—they may revert to a least common denominator compromise, or simply react to events on the ground without ever articulating a principled course of action. In sum, where the authorization process is contested, states may be unable to pursue coherent strategies in international crises.

Last, ambiguity in a state's processes for strategic assessment can complicate the peaceful resolution of disputes by increasing the chance that *other states* will miscalculate its priorities in an interstate conflict. Where a state's preferences are hard to read—perhaps because competition between political and military leaders makes it difficult to monitor how decisions are being made in the security arena—its adversary may misjudge its resolve and make overly ambitious demands in a dispute. The crisis may escalate. Conversely, if a state has an extremely clear authorization process, in which the decision-making process is "readable," it might bolster the credibility of its threats and promises in a dispute: adversaries can assess for themselves the level of commitment a state has to an issue or course of action. In short, through their effects on the information they supply (or fail to supply) about its goals, a state's own strategic assessment processes can shape its adversaries' strategies in international disputes and therefore the outcomes of their strategic interactions (see table 1.1).

The Role of International Outcomes in the Causal Chain

The primary focus of this book is explaining why states vary in their processes for strategic assessment. These assessment institutions are important, as I articulate above, because they can lead to strategic failure; they generate poorly informed and executed military strategies and activities in a state's international relations. In turn, the state risks its own security, it allies' safety, and potentially the stability of the international arena.

To underscore the international importance of these internal processes, in each empirical case study, after exploring the effects of civil-military

Table 1.1
International Implications of Strategic Assessment (Examples)

Nature of Strategic Failure (due to poor strategic assessment)	*Potential Adverse International Outcomes*
Overestimating/underestimating the state's military capabilities	Bargaining failures that lead to crisis escalation and war; failure to terminate war
	Or appease adversary with unwarranted concessions
Adopting military strategies and activities that neglect diplomatic and other constraints posed by the international/regional environment	Inciting external hostility and intervention in conflicts by third parties
Failing to modify military capabilities in support of political objectives	Defeat in war; long and costly wars
	Commitment problems (e.g., poor capacity to commit to war effort, alliance, peace treaty) leading to failed international agreements, crisis escalation, and war
Obscuring signals sent to others of the state's preferences (due to ambiguities in the state's internal authorization process)	Bargaining failures due to misread by adversaries of the state's preferences; crisis escalation and war

politics on strategic assessment, I discuss how those processes shaped the state's strategy and international relations in a significant interstate dispute. Once again, I do not expect that poor process *always* yields pathological policy and poor international outcomes. States can and do get lucky in muddling through conflicts even when they make tremendous mistakes in internal assessment. Their adversaries, for example, may make mistakes that compensate for a state's own strategic failings, rendering a happy ending to an otherwise precarious situation. Alternatively, even states with solid assessment and well-informed strategy can lose wars and fail in their international ambitions. Good strategic assessment does not render a state infallible. It just lessens its chances of making large strategic errors.

In fact, in nearly every case in this book there is a clear correlation between the quality of strategic assessment, the incidence of well-informed and well-executed strategy, and international success or failure. In those cases in which the causal link between assessment, strategy, and outcomes is weak, intervening factors often shaped internal or international develop-

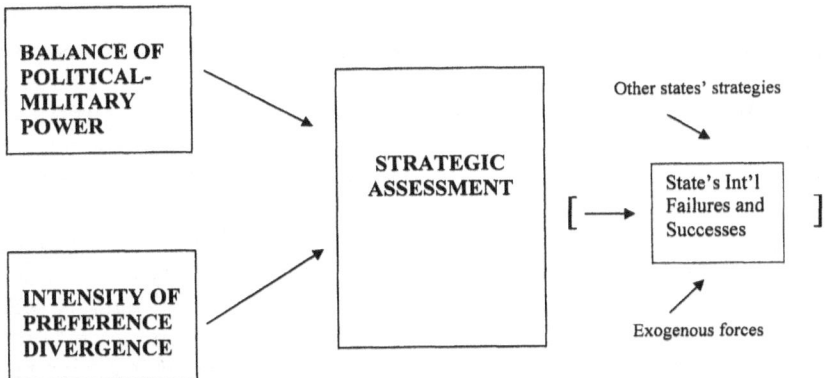

Figure 1.2. The Causal Chain

ments in ways that neutralized the advantages and disadvantages afforded by strategic assessment. In short, this book suggests that pathologies in how states evaluate and choose their strategies merit our attention if we want to understand the sources of conflict and stability in the international arena. Understanding when states are prone to weaknesses (and strengths) in strategic assessment is critical (see fig. 1.2).

The Study of Strategic Assessment in Political Science

In advancing a theory of civil-military relations and strategic assessment, this book makes several important contributions to scholarship in both areas. First, it underscores the importance of states' civil-military relations for understanding their international relations. Of course, scholars have long recognized that interaction between political and military authorities is vital to the management of interstate conflicts. Nevertheless, most studies analyze military doctrine and activity as the principal outcomes of civil-military relations (Snyder 1991a; Posen 1984; Sagan 2000; Avant 1994; Kier 1997; Biddle and Zirkle 1996; Legro 1995; Van Evera 1991, 2001; Belkin 2005; Zisk 1993). In contrast, this study links those relations to a relatively unexamined, yet critical, outcome: the processes through which political and military leaders consult and choose their state's strategies in international disputes.[7] It identifies the conditions under which civil-military relations produce better and worse processes for strategic assessment. Moreover, it

---

[7] For some exceptions, see the seminal book by Betts (1991), Cohen (2002), and Gibson and Snider (1999). While important works, none develops a theory for strategic assessment in a comparative context, as I do here.

does so in a comparative context. The book analyzes strategic assessment in a variety of historical and contemporary cases, representing diverse regions and regime types.

In the process the book also speaks to a central debate in international relations: whether democracies as a class of states are inherently better than others at evaluating their international environments. Recent scholarship argues that democracies should trump autocracies in strategic assessment (Reiter and Stam 2002; also see Peceny et al. 2002). This book is skeptical of that finding. Democracies too can regularly succumb to strategic failures. The reasons have to do with the nature of their civil-military relations. As I elaborate in chapter 2, even when political leaders clearly dominate their militaries, as is commonly observed in democracies, intense, underlying conflict over substantive issues can truncate debate in advisory processes and invite serious strategic failure.

While questioning the inherent advantages of democracy, this book also challenges the corollary of the democratic-supremacy thesis: that autocracies are necessarily inferior at strategic assessment. In fact, autocracies should, at times, perform perfectly well at strategic assessment. When political leaders are solidly in charge and their preferences converge with those of military leaders on security issues, as, for example, in North Vietnam during the Vietnam War, they can cooperate in advisory processes: Civil-military relations pose no obstacle to sound strategic assessment.[8] Holding all other factors equal, these states are quite capable of evaluating their international environments and military capabilities.

In fact one contribution of this study is to demonstrate how states can vary in strategic assessment with shifts in their civil-military relations *independent of their regime type*. The empirical studies show, for example, how the quality of strategic assessment varied considerably in Egypt in the mid-1960s and early 1970s with changes in the civil-military balance of power, despite the fact that the regime remained autocratic throughout the period. The case study of Britain exhibits similar variation: Civil-military relations generated major differences in strategic assessment prior to and then during the First World War in the democratic state.

Finally, the book speaks to scholars interested in how variation in executive advisory processes affects foreign policymaking or crisis decision making. The extant scholarship generally points to psychological phenomena and leaders' personalities to explain why consultative processes vary. For example, one strand of theorizing found in studies of American foreign policymaking emphasizes how a president's personal style affects how that president manages foreign policy advisors in international conflicts.[9]

---

[8] On the North Vietnamese case, see Biddle and Zirkle (1996).

[9] For an excellent review, see Haney (2002: 3–9). For samples, see Burke and Greenstein (1989: 4), George (1991).

This study stresses an alternative cause of strategic assessment: states' civil-military relations. It argues that relations between political and military leaders shape consultative processes, independent of a leader's personal proclivities in managing his or her subordinates. Leaders may "want" a particular advisory system—one that provides them with comprehensive information and affords them definitive decision-making power—but political realities may militate against it.[10] This was certainly true for Egypt's president Nasser in the mid-1960s.

A second strand of theorizing focuses on how cognitive, emotional, and other psychological stimuli affect how leaders process incoming information and decide strategy in crisis.[11] These approaches often assume that information is objectively available to leaders and the obstacle to good strategic assessment resides in the individual's processing of it. But information may not be so readily available to leaders in the first place because of domestic political factors, like states' civil-military relations. In turn, even the most well-adjusted, seasoned, and lucid leader is going to have problems judging his options when he has poor information and analysis at the start. Conversely, a sound assessment process could help counteract leaders' tendencies to resist new data, react emotionally, or otherwise compartmentalize and interpret information through preexisting cognitive schema.[12] Strategic assessment processes in fact may be an important remedy to these psychological pressures in decision making. Variation in assessment institutions may, moreover, explain why the cognitive and emotional problems highlighted by the literature in international relations often seem more acute in some cases than others.[13]

Plan of the Book

In the next chapter I elaborate the theory of civil-military politics and strategic assessment introduced above. I begin by orienting the argument theoretically, explaining my "distributional approach," and then discussing the causal variables, power and preference divergence, as well as the dependent variable, strategic assessment. Hypotheses about how strategic assessment

---

[10] On the importance of political context in studying psychological and biological influences on policy, see McDermott (2004: 197, 204), Rosen (2005).

[11] See Brecher (1975), Stein and Tanter (1980). For an overview of key themes in this literature, see Lebow (1981: 101–19), McDermott (2004).

[12] Some studies do include bureaucratic processes as a source of "bias" (see Lebow 1981: 101–228; also see McDermott's [2004] discussion of Allison's model III). But the sources of individual motivation and therefore the causal forces through which they affect behavior are quite different for political/bureaucratic and psychological phenomena.

[13] Once again, see Lebow (1981).

varies in five civil-military settings follow. I conclude chapter 2 with the study's research design. Especially crucial, there I lay out the rationale for choosing the empirical cases on which I focus in this book and explaining how these control for alternative explanations and provide coverage for all the major hypotheses introduced in chapter 2.

Chapter 3 begins the first of two comprehensive studies of Egypt's civil-military relations and strategic assessment that constitute the empirical core of this book. It analyzes the period under Gamal Abdel Nasser in the early and mid-1960s, before the 1967 Arab-Israeli War. Chapter 4 picks up the story with the accession of Anwar Sadat as president in 1970 and examines strategic assessment in Egypt in the ensuing decade. In the next three chapters I undertake a series of six briefer studies, which are intended to complement my research on Egypt. I focus in chapter 3 on three cases: Britain and Germany before the First World War, and Britain during the war. Chapter 6 contains two studies of Pakistan and Turkey in the latter 1990s. Chapter 7 applies my theory to U.S. war planning for the 2003 Iraq War, explaining how civil-military relations contributed to inadequacies in strategic assessment, especially in preparing for the war's postconflict phase. Finally, chapter 8 concludes the analysis, first with a summary of the book's empirical findings, and second with a discussion of some of its key implications.

Two

EXPLAINING VARIATION IN STRATEGIC ASSESSMENT

WHEN WILL LEADERS have access to the best information and analysis about their military and strategic situations? When are they best able to translate political initiatives into supportive military capabilities and plans? To answer these questions, this book argues that one must assess how information is analyzed and how authority is exercised in policymaking at the political-military apex. More fundamentally, one must understand why and when processes for strategic assessment vary across states and within them over time. Exploring these issues are the central tasks of this chapter.

Theoretical Orientation

This book begins from the premise that the process of deliberation and decision making is crucial to understanding the strategic and policy choices leaders make in international conflicts. Yet why focus on strategic assessment? Why is the process of decision making likely to be important to the choices leaders make?

One set of answers comes from insights from institutional theory.[1] Broadly speaking, this analytical tradition is interested in how the structures within which individuals and groups interact condition their behavior, interests, strategies, and ultimately the outcomes that result.[2] By implication, it suggests that examining actors' decision-making environments will help illuminate the outcomes that emerge from them. The informal and formal "rules" that structure interaction, the authority of those represented, and the information available to actors affect how interests combine in the processes of policy formulation. Different rules and structures privilege different outcomes.

---

[1] "Institutional theory" is an umbrella term that encompasses a range of approaches. See, for example, the discussion in Orren and Skowronek (1994: 311–12).

[2] In some cases, institutional theorists are interested in how structures affect strategies and actions; others also explore the effect of institutions on actors' preferences. For discussion, see Steinmo, Thelen, and Longstreth (1992). On sociological institutionalism, see Powell and DiMaggio (1991).

Other bodies of scholarship too emphasize the impact of the policymaking environment on a leader's choices, albeit often less formally. For example, the literature on presidential management emphasizes the effects of the advisory system on an executive's policy choices.[3] Implicit in Betts's (1991) discussion of the impact of military versus civilian advice in Cold War crises is the idea that the nature and quality of information available to leaders affect their choices.[4] Eliot Cohen's (2002) recent study suggests that the way in which a political leadership engages military leaders affects the quality of wartime policies adopted by the state. Everyday politics also provides examples. Witness debates about the Bush administration and the quality of deliberation and analysis involved in assessing planning for the postwar period in the 2003 Iraq conflict.[5]

This study shares with those noted above an emphasis on the importance of decision-making processes. It argues that insight about why a leader pursues a particular approach in an external conflict can be gleaned from studying the internal environment in which that leader came to the decision. Through studying these processes we can better understand the rationale underlying leaders' strategic choices in interstate conflicts. For example, studying how leaders evaluate their capabilities illuminates why they sometimes overestimate their military power and, in turn, make demands or pursue ambitions in the international arena they cannot back up with force. Similarly, the way military and political activity is coordinated in a state reveals how diplomatic consequences weigh in the assessment of options. Consequently, it may explain why leaders sometimes fail to anticipate the political fallout of military plans and strategies. Finally, studying the way decisions are made reveals when political leaders are vulnerable to military pressure in selecting security strategies. It explains why even the most determined political leaders sometimes prove incapable of developing military plans that support their goals.

Put simply, this book explores the process in which leaders make decisions in order to comprehend their strategic choices.

A Distributional Approach

My approach to explaining variation in strategic assessment emphasizes the effects of "distributional conflict" on how institutions emerge and evolve. The approach is motivated by a central premise: Because institutions shape

---

[3] For a review, see Haney (2002: 3–9); on the importance of studying decision making and foreign policy, see Burke and Greenstein (1989: 4). See also chapter 1.

[4] On advice, also see Gibson and Snider (1999).

[5] See chapter 7.

outcomes, conflict over desired outcomes should revert to conflict over the institutions that support the emergence of one outcome over another.[6] Institutions are the product of actors' seeking to create routines and processes that advantage their preferred policies. Analyzing institutional outcomes entails examining relations among actors vested in their properties.

The nature of those relations and their ultimate effects on institutions are shaped by the configuration of actors' power and preferences. Preferences affect the degree of overt disagreement over processes—they affect individuals' incentives to contest how policy is evaluated and decided. The balance of power affects the resources those individuals bring to bear in that conflict, the tactics each employs and whose interests prevail in institutional formation. Together actors' power and the intensity of their preference divergence shape the properties of the policymaking environment that emerges from their interactions.

In this book I apply this approach to the study of states' institutions for strategic assessment: I examine the interactions of military and political leaders, conditioned by the configuration of their power and preferences, to explain the attributes of a state's security policymaking environment. Yet, why should institutions for strategic assessment be understood as political outcomes, as the distributional approach implies? Why should political and military leaders, in particular, be so invested in the processes through which they coordinate, consult, and make decisions?

The answers have to do with how these structures affect the policies that result: how they affect how a state prioritizes threats and organizes and prepares for war. Whether for altruistic reasons (safeguarding national security), to sate corporate interests, or for private reasons, when military leaders disagree with political leaders over how force should be organized or used on behalf of the state, they have a stake in the processes through which these critical decisions will be made.

Take, for example, the rules governing *who* has access to *what* sort of information about a state's military capabilities, *when*. As long as political and military leaders' priorities are aligned, both sides have an interest in maximizing the availability of information to ensure that they attain the best possible outcome. In other words, where distributional conflict is absent, sharing information is relatively conflict free. However, where it persists, each side has an incentive to selectively share information and its implications for the efficacy of a particular course of action it is proposing.

---

[6] See, for example, Riker's 1980 notion of inheritability; also Schepsle (1989). This point also parallels Moe's (1989, 1995) and Knott and Miller's (1987) studies of bureaucracy when they argue that because institutions have consequences for outcomes, they are objects of political competition. More broadly, my approach perhaps most closely parallels Knight (1992).

Each has an interest in the quantity and presentation of information shared and hence in the rules governing its disclosure.[7]

Accordingly, when preferences over policy outcomes diverge and military leaders are empowered to influence institutional processes, they will try to do so in ways that allow them to present information in a light most favorable to their preferred outcomes. In the event of an international conflict, for example, militaries seeking to avoid combat may seek to structure their briefings in ways that emphasize the costs and risks of intervention; those more receptive to action are likely to structure the agenda for discussion in a way that minimize those costs and risks. Political leaders too will try to structure assessment in ways that maximize their access to information; this is especially likely if their fundamental views about the merits of intervention diverge from their military leaders' preferences. In this way, conflict over policy outcomes reverts to efforts to finesse processes essential to information sharing.

Similar dynamics can be observed in the way that advisory councils and coordinating bodies can become controversial in civil-military relations. When preferences over policy diverge, both political and military leaders have an incentive to ensure that consultative forums advantage the airing of their viewpoints. Military officials may be wary of forums that they fear will truncate conversation and minimize opportunities to express their perspectives. Alternatively, political leaders may marginalize military advice by excluding key individuals from meetings, limiting their participation, or prejudging the value of their commentary.

Finally, controversy can emerge over processes for approving and making decisions about key military strategy and policy objectives. This does not mean that military leaders will openly contest the formal authority of a political leader to issue a decision (although in some circumstances they will), but that, when they are empowered to do so, they may resort to more subtle tactics that de facto enhance their behind-the-scenes influence over how decisions are made. They may, for example, try to exercise informal vetoes, or control the options from which a political leader can choose.

In short, because process affects outcomes, conflict over outcomes is often expressed in disagreement over the processes that privilege different outcomes. Military and political leaders often have good reasons to invest time and energy in shaping the policy process to protect their priorities. The specific nature of that competition depends on the intensity of preference divergence as well as the power each brings to bear in relations with the other. As I explain in detail later, different configurations of military and

---

[7] On the value of information in shaping outcomes, and the consequent politicization of information sharing, see Morrow (1994), Fearon (1995), Bendor et al. (1987).

political power and preferences yield different policymaking environments; these "types" create alternative logics that shape strategic assessment.

Civil-Military Relations and Institutional Theory

While my "distributional approach" is tailored to the study at hand, it also builds on established traditions in institutional analysis. It borrows from rational choice the assumption that institutions are the aggregate outcomes of goal-seeking behavior—in this case, that of military and political leaders. At the same time, in common more with historical institutionalist approaches, the resources and interests military and leaders employ in the course of that goal seeking are contextualized and often rooted in historical and structural conditions.[8] In my approach, assessment institutions are also presumed to be mutable and shift with underlying structural conditions: Different institutions for strategic assessment are sustained by particular configurations of political-military power and interests. I assume that these interests and power vary across time and country for historical and other reasons. However, when those configurations change, we should also observe changes in informal routines of behavior and how actors employ and interpret rules, if not in formal structures at the political-military apex.[9]

Unlike some applications of institutional theory, my approach departs from the tendency to view institutions as stemming from their efficiency-enhancing properties.[10] It focuses as much on the generation of pathologi-

[8] For overviews, once again see Steinmo, Thelen, and Longstreth (1992), Thelen (1999).

[9] Note that this approach assumes that institutions are mutable and not heavily fixed by stickiness or sunk costs. There are several reasons I think this assumption is appropriate for my issue area. I am interested in a fairly discrete set of mostly informal institutional processes, which are rarely codified in law and involve a small group of actors within the executive realm of the state; only in the broadest sense are they determined by legislative or constitutional processes. For this reason, I expect these insular processes to be responsive to informal reinterpretation and changes in function as a result of shifts in power and interests. Other studies focus on formal, legally defined structures for defense organization; institutions in those instances, because of the formalized nature of these structures, are often more subject to other constraints (see Zegart 1999).

[10] For example, in some rational choice accounts of institutional formation, especially as they have often been conceived in international relations, actors impose institutions on themselves to facilitate efficient exchange and cooperation. Inferences about institutional origins are often made on the basis of the functions they fulfill for actors seeking to coordinate their activities. Thelen (1999: 368) nicely captures this tendency when she refers to "rational choice's emphasis on institutions as coordination mechanisms that generate or sustain equilibria." Often this literature builds on the new economics of organization and views institutions as remedies to market failures; institutions emerge to solve collective action problems and satisfy the prerequisites of efficient coordination (see Williamson 1985; also see Moe 2005; Weingast 2002). Note that some rational-choice approaches do deal more directly with

cal institutions for strategic assessment as on the origins of efficient outcomes; suboptimality is a central prediction of the theory, not a residual category. Accordingly, the study begins with the relations of military and political leaders with variable resources and interests, without assuming a priori that the institutions that emerge will be "efficient" and satisfy the requirements of the state for strategic assessment.[11] At times, these relations do yield functionally efficient structures. At other times, efforts by military and political leaders to protect their individual interests yield institutional environments that undermine efficient coordination between them, and the quality of strategic assessment for the state as a whole.[12]

Note, finally, that this approach does not imply that institutions are simply projections of power and interests. Institutional outcomes will only at times clearly map to either political or military preferences. In my view, institutions are strategic outcomes and are the byproducts of the interaction of political and military leaders whose power and interests may vary considerably. In fact, many of the institutional pathologies I discuss in this book are rooted in their strategic quality. This is notable in two cases I

---

suboptimality. For example, scholars of bureaucracy in American politics often emphasize the effects of politicians' desires to get elected, and other political forces, on inefficiencies in the oversight of public entities. See Moe (1989, 1995), Knott and Miller (1987). See also Knight (1992).

[11] More broadly, the approach here resonates with Moe's (2005) call for greater emphasis on power in shaping institutions.

[12] This point does, however, raise the question of what an "efficiency"-oriented approach would predict for the establishment of these institutions. Microeconomic models suggest that actors should be able to agree on an efficient "contract" governing their relations and that they will then distribute gains from efficient production according to their market power (Krasner 1991). By implication, military leaders should agree to the creation of institutions that promote functional strategic assessment and then use their power to extract side payments; they should acquiesce in the structure that produces an "efficient" national security policy as long as politicians pay them off. The problem is that in the area of national security policy, the outcomes are qualitative, not quantitative. Dividing the gains of efficient production according to power resources and thereby resolving distributional conflict makes sense where the spoils of cooperation—profit, wages—are divisible and divorced from the means of production. Separating the division of the good from the way it is produced is more problematic when they are not. After all, security/military policy is a choice between competing visions of the state of the world. It includes overarching questions about what the state's national security interests are, what the principal threats to those interests are, and how state leaders can best organize their forces to protect against them. The answers to these questions often have direct implications for the welfare and interests of military leaders and their organizations in the short and long term (whether those interests are motivated by corporate desires, the private interests of military leaders, or the desire to protect the public interest— see the discussion of preferences below). Military personnel care about policy outcomes (Feaver 2003: 63). This means they are vested in the institutions that formulate these policies, and not just in an unrelated side payment they could receive if they divested themselves from policy processes.

discuss below, which I note briefly here, to illustrate this point. First, take a case in which politicians are politically "dominant" but face military leaders with divergent policy preferences. Political leaders often create structures of oversight to safeguard their interests. This logic seems relatively straightforward. I observe below, however, that political leaders' efforts to protect their individual interests in the face of a recalcitrant military can yield structures that are pathological for strategic assessment as a whole. For example, one common strategy of political oversight is to appoint military leaders with similar preferences to key posts. Yet, in so doing, politicians may preempt search and the introduction of competing perspectives that illuminate complex or unforeseen issues in debates about military plans and policies. This undermines a state's advisory or consultative bodies. Thus, individually rational behavior (politicians' desire to protect their policy priorities) can contribute to a counterproductive outcome in the aggregate (less rigorous joint political-military debate).

The strategic, and pathological, quality of institutional outcomes is also evident in states where military and political leaders both are politically powerful and compete over rules and procedures. Here the tactics they employ to protect their respective interests can yield a cumulatively incoherent and unwieldy assessment environment. This dynamic is evident in my case study of Egypt in the 1960s, in which I argue that President Nasser and his military chief, Abdel Hakim Amer, were actively competing for control of military affairs. In the mid-1960s Nasser pushed to have his ally, General Mohammed Fawzi, appointed chief of the General Staff, to increase his own access to information and control of military affairs, which Amer was then seeking to dominate. Amer acquiesced in the appointment. However, he then proceeded to alter the command structure by creating a new entity in the chain of command, Ground Forces Command, which usurped Fawzi's responsibilities as chief of staff and tried to undercut the latter's influence over the armed forces. Both Nasser's and Amer's efforts to protect their private interests therefore yielded an outcome that reflected neither actor's preferred outcome. More importantly for Egypt's sake, they yielded a convoluted command structure, which greatly undermined the implementation of military policy.

Finally, in allowing the relative power of political and military leaders to vary in decision making, this approach differs from other institutional approaches that have been usefully applied to the study of civil-military relations—notably principal-agent approaches.[13] These approaches may assume a hierarchy of power (i.e., usually civilian dominance) and seek to explain how the act of delegation and efforts to constrain military authorities affect

---

[13] See Feaver (2003) and Avant (1994) for examples.

the structure of civil-military relations.[14] This variety of principal-agent theory generates important insights. It highlights the dilemmas inherent in overseeing the military when politicians are dominant. The present study, however, is interested in exploring the impact of variation in the relative power of civilians and political leaders (not assuming a hierarchical relationship); the delegation metaphor has more limited applicability in this broader domain of cases. For example, when power is shared, assessment institutions emerge from implicit negotiation or bargaining between political and military leaders, not from the delegation of one to the other. Since many states in which strategic assessment is likely to be poor are precisely those in which politicians are not dominant, this broader theoretical framework is necessary to capture these variations in power. Hence while employing some insights from principal-agent theory when discussing particular institutional environments, this study forgoes explicit use of that framework.

In fact, by allowing variation in power, this approach builds on the prevalent view of civil-military relations in comparative politics. In that scholarship, militaries are commonly portrayed as political players whose relative resources vary and shape state development and government institutions in important ways.[15] This study shares the basic premise that the military's political power can and does vary across time and place, and that this should be consequential for its impact on governmental processes. Yet, it departs from the comparative literature by focusing on internationally focused se-

---

[14] See Feaver (2003: 54–55). Other conceptualizations allow for agents to exercise more influence in the principal-agent relationship. For example, Miller (1992: 77–86) and White (1991: 208–9) both point out that agents can gain influence over organizational forms because the principal comes to rely on their expertise and informational advantages in deciding how to structure production of a good. Nevertheless, power to affect institutions that originates in an agent's expertise is still contingent on the principal's ongoing delegation of prerogatives to the agent: for example, if a political leader detects inefficiencies or that his or her goals are being compromised because of the agent's decisions about how to structure the organization, the principal can still retract those prerogatives and reform the organization (i.e., the principal/civilian retains rights of residual control). The kind of power on which this book focuses, which derives from the military's influence in domestic politics, imbues its chiefs with independent resources to bargain over institutions for assessment and is not contingent on the ongoing consent of the political leadership to play a role in institutional creation. The consequences for strategic assessment should be far-reaching and potentially much more difficult to remedy.

[15] The vast literature on coups and on democratization in comparative politics commonly characterizes the military as a political agent, not just a bureaucratic entity. For examples, see O'Donnell, Schmitter, and Whitehead (1986), Huntington (1993), Przeworski (1991). For an explicit discussion of thinking about civil-military relations in terms of power balances, see Aguero (1995: 11). While comparativists have not focused on strategic assessment, some work does discuss institutions and the issues related to military policy (budgets, doctrine). See Ulrich (1999), Pion-Berlin (1997), Stepan (1988).

curity policymaking structures; most comparative literature is concerned with dependent variables associated with regime change, consolidation, and domestic governance. At the same time, this study contributes to the international relations literature by emphasizing the military's role as a political actor in shaping security policymaking. Much of the prominent literature in this area views the military as a (frequently troublesome) bureaucratic actor, often neglecting the independent power that militaries sometimes enjoy over how policy is made and decided.[16] In short, this study attempts to bridge comparative and international relations concerns. It emphasizes the effects of the domestic politics of civil military relations (a comparative politics issue) on strategic assessment (an international relations issue).

The Causal Variables

In the following section I introduce my two independent variables—power and preference divergence—and discuss how I measure them. These two variables interact to produce different "types" of civil-military relations. As I explain in greater detail when I introduce the study's central hypotheses, in each setting military and political leaders have variable incentives and resources to contest how information is shared and decisions are made, which in turn yields distinct strengths and weaknesses in states' processes for strategic assessment.

Preference Divergence

If there is one shared point of departure in the civil-military relations literature, it is that the political-military divide invites friction. Military and political leaders are apt to disagree about any number of issues, from the grandest, such as the threats and challenges facing the country, to the most mundane, such as the efficacy of a particular weapons system. So common, in fact, are disagreements that much of the extant civil-military relations literature assumes a relatively constant degree of preference divergence.

In reality, however, while disputes may be common, the intensity and scope of disagreement between a state's political leaders and its military

---

[16] In contrast, many scholars working in security studies treat the military as a bureaucratic actor, ultimately subject to civilian control, and not as an independent political agent capable of challenging civilian prerogatives. Militaries, in these studies, primarily respond to civilian initiatives and direction. For a critique of this assumption, see Farrell (2001). An earlier set of scholars of civil-military relations recognized the importance of variation in the military's power in policymaking. See Finer (1962) and Perlmutter (1977). For exceptions to the tendency to treat militaries as apolitical, see Desch (1999), Snyder (1991b), Belkin (2005).

leaders vary considerably over time and country.[17] Most notable are conflicts when they are at their most intense and consequential: between Charles de Gaulle and his generals, or Hitler and his military commanders during the mid-1930s. Yet, there are also periods when military and political friction appears to decrease, as it appeared to in the United States during the early 1990s between George Bush and his commanders, only to be followed by the "crisis" in civil-military relations under Clinton.[18]

Rather than assuming a particular level of preference divergence, I allow the degree of conflict to vary. I then examine how it affects strategic assessment. As the logic of the distributional approach suggests, I expect underlying conflicts over policy issues to affect the incentives leaders bring to the development of processes for strategic assessment. These conflicts affect political and military leaders' willingness to share information readily, coordinate with one another, and contest how decisions are made. They affect how much political and military leaders become vested in different ways of organizing their relations at the decision-making apex. This intensity of conflict then interacts with political and military leaders' resources to shape the overall assessment environment.

Specifically, there are three main areas in which I anticipate military and political preferences could diverge. First are the state's security goals, which include everything from identifying and characterizing international threats and prioritizing foreign policy and security objectives, to more specific issues of participating in multinational interventions and international arms control treaties. Second are the country's military strategies and plans, which includes broad questions of military strategy, as well as, at times, issues associated with operational plans and tactical activity. Many conflicts over the latter may stem from differences in philosophies about how to organize and use force on the battlefield. Third are corporate issues.[19] This includes military budgets, as well as professional norms of behavior, codes of conduct, conscription, and other demographic issues.[20]

---

[17] On variation in the intensity of military and civilian preference divergence, see Feaver (2003: 58–59).

[18] See, for example, Kohn (1993: 3–17), Feaver (1995). See also Colin Powell's opinion piece on Bosnia in the *New York Times* (9 October 1992, A35), and Powell (1992/93).

[19] On corporate interests, see Nordlinger (1977: 65), Finer (1962), Farcau (1994).

[20] Note that my argument assumes that conflicts in one issue area will affect the overall assessment environment, and therefore conventions of assessment over other issues. Thus, if military and political leaders disagree profoundly about corporate issues, efforts to protect their interests can result in dynamics that affect assessment over operational plans or military strategy. I make this assumption for two reasons: first, because advisory bodies are not necessarily established by issue area, I expect military and political leaders' incentives to protect their interests in one area will affect how conventions emerge for consideration of other issues; second, conflict in one area fosters mistrust (or, alternatively, uncertainty about preferences), which corrodes assessment in other areas. Note also that, empirically, because conflicts

Measuring Preference Divergence

In principle, the degree of conflict observed between political and military leaders could assume any value: "Preference divergence" is a continuous variable. For analytical clarity, however, I focus on specific levels or intensities of divergence, which I anticipate will be important to the features of a state's institutions for strategic assessment. I divide these into two levels: low and high preference divergence.

Low Preference Divergence: Preference divergence is low when the historical or contemporary record reveals little evidence of recurring, systematic cleavages over security goals, military strategy/policy, or corporate issues. *Note that low preference divergence does not imply the total absence of friction.* Episodic disagreements are to be expected. But while military and political leaders may disagree about the details of an issue in the security or corporate domain, they are not so far apart in their perspectives within the broader category as to preclude some basic overlap of views.

High Preference Divergence: Preference divergence is high when deep, enduring cleavages over issues related to security goals, military policy, or corporate issues are observed. Within the historical or contemporary record there is evidence of ongoing, recognizable disputes in preferred policy outcomes.

To measure the level of preference divergence, I use an inductive approach—one based on observation. This differs from simply assuming a high level of conflict or deducing it from some preexisting theoretical argument (as does the scholarship that derives premises about military preferences from organizational theory).[21] The advantage of this inductive approach is that it permits me to measure variation in the intensity of conflict over corporate or security issues to see how it affects assessment institutions.

To guide the analysis, as I elaborate below, I draw from existing scholarship on civil-military relations in political science, which suggests a variety of reasons why differences over security goals, military strategy and plans, or corporate issues might emerge. I use this literature as a template for helping me to more readily identify instances in which conflict between political and military leaders is more and less likely to be observed as I undertake the empirical case studies. Regardless of its source, it is essential

---

in corporate issues are often linked to disputes over military strategy (and vice versa), there is usually conflict in more than one issue area anyway.

[21] See Frieden (1999) for a discussion of different ways to measure preferences.

that this conflict be chronologically prior to, and independent from, assessment institutions. I assume that these conflicts over policy outcomes—over strategic, corporate, and strategic issues—are distinct from military and political leaders' (implicit and explicit) disagreements over process: These are the underlying divergences that drive conflict over process.

One important potential source of conflicting or complementary interests noted in the civil-military relations literature is the class, regional, or ethnic composition of the officer corps and military leadership relative to the political leadership and its civilian allies.[22] In Jordan, for example, the dominance of Bedouin tribes in the military bureaucracy, and the king's ties to prominent families, is often viewed as the basis for a substantial overlap of preferences over many security matters between the Hashemite regime and the armed forces (Brooks 1998). In historical Germany, evocative of what Morris Janowitz called the aristocratic-feudal model of civil-military relations, the overlap between the Junker aristocratic class and Prussian officer corps is viewed as key to understanding the harmony of interests among the landed classes, emperor, and army.[23]

The internal/external threat environment is a second possible source of civil-military conflict or agreement (Desch 1999; Posen 1984) The presence of external threat might, for example, provide the basis for unity of purpose between the military and its political counterparts, and this could promote convergence over security goals (Desch 1999). However, international threats might also heighten conflict over military strategy and operational plans by heightening the stakes involved in the nature of those plans.

Differences can also emerge from the distinctiveness of military "culture," which may be at odds with political or civilian beliefs, values, or priorities. These cultural differences can stem from global norms that shape military professionals' beliefs about "appropriate" structures and methods of fighting, which put them at odds with civilians, who are less attuned to these normative pressures;[24] organizational biases inherent in military bureaucracies (Snyder 1991b; Posen 1984; Sagan 1996–1997; Van Evera 1991, 2001);[25] the unique, historically determined development of a military organization's culture (Kier 1997; Legro 1995); or differences in socialization and the professional experiences of military personnel and their civilian counterparts (Betts 1991; Feaver and Gelpi 2004; Feaver and Kohn 2001; Huntington 1957).

---

[22] On social structure, see Rosen (1996).

[23] Also see Finer (1962: 40–47) for discussion of how class origins affect officer preferences.

[24] On the impact of global norms on militaries' ideas about the "appropriate way to organize and fight," see Farrell (2001).

[25] On differences in how analysts characterize organizational preferences, see Feaver (2003: 316, n. 16).

Regardless of why military and political preferences vary, however, I assume that both sets of leaders will have a vested interest in the nature of a state's security goals, military strategy, and corporate issues.[26] Whether military leaders are concerned about them because of their desires to safeguard "national security" or for more parochial reasons, I assume that the content of these policies matters to them. Similarly, political leaders care about military and security issues.[27]

The Political-Military Balance of Power

The level of preference divergence interacts with a second variable—the balance of civil-military power—to affect strategic assessment. The balance of power between political and military leaders varies with their underlying domestic relationship. It depends on the military's influence in a political leader's coalition—on how unified is the military leadership and central its position relative to other social groups that provide a leader support for his or her position in office.[28]

The intuition here is that when the military occupies a pivotal position in, or indirect influence over, a leader's ruling coalition, it can threaten his or her tenure in office by undermining his or her support base. In turn, I

---

[26] On this assumption, also see Feaver (203: 63).

[27] There is one potential measurement issue that warrants discussion before proceeding. In my analysis, I treat the level of preference divergence as exogenous; it is the product of external factors distinct from a state's institutions. But the intensity of preference divergence can be partially endogenous if, for example, the political leader is dominant: The political leader can replace dissenting individuals and appoint more like-minded military leaders. As a result, cases of high preference divergence can at first glance look like examples of low preference divergence. I deal with this in two ways. First, despite this dynamic, I do not expect all preference divergence to be endogenous: Leaders may try to appoint like-minded individuals, but preference formation is complex and external events can still promote different views. It is unlikely that any military leader will be totally divorced from prevailing opinion within the organization. Hence there is only so much a leader can do to manage the preferences of military subordinates. On these points, see Feaver (2003: 59). As a result, I look for more subtle evidence of recurring differences and for evidence of underlying discord to gauge preference divergence. Second, I am also mindful of the endogeneity factor and, if there appears to be preference alignment, but the leader is constantly removing people to maintain it, use that as an indication to look deeper into the case and at the underlying rationale for appointments. For an example of an argument in which preferences are endogenous to institutions in the civil-military context, see Sechser (2004).

[28] For other coalitional approaches, see Solingen (1998), Snyder (1991b), Rogowski (1989), Lobell (1999), Trubowitz (1998).

assume that leaders prioritize retaining office.[29] Therefore, a leader who relies on military support faces significant pressure to defer to military leaders in disputes over substantive policies or procedural issues to secure that leader's position in office. This translates into bargaining power over processes essential to strategic assessment: into leverage over how relations between political and military leaders in security matters should be structured. The more influential the military in the coalition, the more power its leaders exercise over their political counterparts in deciding how they share information, coordinate with one another, and make decisions at the apex of the state.

The impact of the balance of power on a state's institutions for assessment is perhaps most intuitive when preferences diverge. Divergent preferences over policy create incentives for leaders to invest time and energy in shaping institutional outcomes; they create incentives to haggle over institutional processes as each side wants to promote structures that privilege its position. In turn, the relative power of political and military leaders affects how and in whose favor those conflicts are resolved.[30]

Less intuitive, but equally significant, are the effects of the balance of power on strategic assessment when preferences do not diverge. In this case, power affects the "default" institutional setup for strategic assessment that emerges at the apex of policymaking when leaders do not disagree. In any situation there are multiple ways of functionally organizing relations between political and military leaders at the decision-making apex. If preferences do not diverge, the choice among them may be uncontroversial, but it is unlikely to be random.[31] Rather, it will be influenced by the distribution of power of the actors involved. For example, if the military is dominant in civil-military relations, I expect the mechanisms for consultation and decision making about military policy to reflect the military's power position. These processes may be internalized within their bureaucracies or closely tied to them (if not formally, than in informal routines and conventions of behavior); strategic assessment occurs within the military's own entities—in

---

[29] In particular they prioritize short-term, credible threats to their position in office, like those posed by the withdrawal of support by a key constituency (such as the military). As noted above, I also assume that they, like their military chiefs, care about security policy, not least because failings in this area can also jeopardize their position in office (Bueno de Mesquita and Siverson 1995). This motivates them to try to retain control over processes for strategic assessment and fuels conflicts over such processes with military leaders. Nevertheless, an immediate threat to their positions should trump the more uncertain and longer-term challenge to their tenure posed by strategic failure in the state's international relations.

[30] This accords with what David Pion-Berlin (1997: 14–15) reminds us is a defining quality of civil-military relations: who has the power to decide what roles the military will play in the formulation of military policy. Also see Feaver (1995: 113), Welch (1987: 13).

[31] This insight is akin to the idea in Krasner (1991) that power affects the default institutional setup that emerges between actors.

the conference rooms and offices of uniformed officers—independent of the broader political bureaucracies of the state.[32] Conversely, when political leaders dominate, consultation and decision making are more likely to be integrated with the political apparatus of the state. Military analysis is more likely to be tied to other political and diplomatic offices of the state, over which a political leader (by definition) has daily oversight. In this way, power conditions assessment institutions even in the absence of overt conflict.

Measuring the Balance of Power

In evaluating the military's relative influence in the coalition—and therefore the balance of political-military power—I focus on three factors: (1) the military establishment's position in domestic society and its ties to influential constituencies; (2) its senior officers' internal unity; and (3) the expansiveness of the political leader's own base of civilian support. In general, the more prominent the military's ties to important segments of domestic society, the more united a front it can present to the political leadership, and the weaker the political leader's own civilian base, the more influence the military has in that coalition and therefore the more bargaining power it wields at the apex of the state.

In emphasizing the importance of the military's ties to domestic society, this study builds on the general insight, common within comparative studies of civil-military relations, that the military's power in the state depends on its capacity to cultivate and maintain social allies or influence mass opinion.[33] The reasons why militaries may be able to do so are diverse and may depend on the particularities of political development in a country, societal values about the appropriate role of the military in the state, as well as the military's own normative organizational beliefs.[34] For example, in places like Pakistan and Turkey, and historically in large swaths of Latin America, where the military has consistently intervened in politics, analysts and citizens associate the military with an influential role in politics.[35]

---

[32] For a similar argument, see Schofield (2000).

[33] Many studies link relations between the military and key social groups to the military establishment's power in the state. See O'Donnell (1973), O'Donnell, Schmitter, and Whitehead (1986), Remmer (1989: 4–6), Farcau (1996). The theme is also pervasive in the literature on military interventions, where the military's support from society is seen as a key motivation and source of success. See Luttwak (1968), Farcau (1994), Koonings and Kruijt (2002: 23), Perlmutter (1977: 100–102), Kebschull (1994: 571), Welch and Smith (1974: 27), Janowitz (1977: 160). On the evolution of scholarship on military interventions, see Pion-Berlin (2001: 4–9). Also see Koonings and Kruijt (2002: 16–19), Taylor (2003: 20–21).

[34] On the latter, see, for example, Fitch (1998), Loveman (1993).

[35] Koonings and Kruijt's (2002: 1) notion of political armies may be useful here. They suggest that some militaries are common participants in political coalitions for historical and structural reasons.

Even where a military has long played a prominent role in internal politics, however, its relative influence in society is not necessarily constant and can fluctuate over time. The military's sway at any given time, for example, may depend on its ties to other politically salient constituencies, or support from the masses. Militaries that enjoy substantial prestige within society are often formidable political forces. Similarly, a military that allies with a politically salient economic group (e.g., the aristocracy, middle class, or workers; or industry or sector), a religious or ethnic group or other salient constituency also gains influence. Conversely, even a historically prominent military can lose influence in a coalition if it loses the esteem of the population, or the support of pivotal groups with which it is allied.

In states in which the military is not a direct actor in politics, these ties to groups and masses can provide an indirect channel of military influence in a leader's coalition. In a democracy, for example, the military establishment's ties to important special interests or its mass popularity can elevate its standing in domestic society; public appeals by esteemed military leaders or lobbying by its civilian allies within the political establishment can be powerful sources of influence. In these ways a military can, under particular circumstances, come to exercise significant influence over a leader's political coalition, even if it never directly participates in domestic politics. At times, these indirect channels of influence can prove very important.[36] For example, in the case study of Britain during the First World War in this book, I show how the army leadership's ties to the conservative political establishment and media and its influence over popular opinion interacted with weaknesses in Asquith's and Lloyd George's coalition governments to afford them substantial leverage in negotiating with the prime ministers. Less pronounced, but also provocatively, in the early 1990s in the United States, scholars warned that the military was gaining inordinate influence over the Clinton administration in part because of the popularity of the military establishment and the overt public appeals of key military leaders (notably Colin Powell).[37]

In short, in some cases, the military plays a direct role in a political leader's coalition and at other times it has substantial, indirect influence over pivotal constituencies within it. The latter may be a less potent means of influence, but conceptually it matters for the same reason as the former:

---

[36] A word on the "scope" of my argument might be beneficial here. I am interested in the military's power to the extent that it affects its influence in security policymaking. Hence I am not suggesting that in democracies leaders will necessarily use their influence in a coalition to intervene in domestic politics more broadly. Scholars such as Ben Meir (1995: 5) and Colton (1990) make an important distinction between the military's involvement in security policy arenas and its intervention in governance issues and other areas of domestic policy.

[37] See Kohn (1993), Snider and Carleton-Carew (1995). On pathways of military influence in democracies, see Brooks (2002). On military influence in the United States, see Feaver (2001).

It means the military can affect a political leader's tenure in office. In either case, military leaders can influence the coalition and threaten the support base that keeps the political leader in power.

To evaluate the military's standing in society and therefore evaluate the influence it gains from these ties, I look for evidence of links between the military, the mass population, and key social constituencies, as reported in historical studies, biographies, and other documents and analyses of the country in the time period in question. Of special significance are trends in popular opinion that indicate the military's social prestige.[38] Ties to political parties, the media, legislative or other institutions, or relations with key social, economic, or other constituencies in the state are also crucial. In historical Latin America, for example, many analysts have highlighted the military's ties to working classes or the bourgeoisie as a source of influence for military organizations and their leaders.[39] In historical Germany, ties between the landholding aristocracy and the Prussian Army have also commonly been cited as an indication of the military's position in society. In general, close contextual analysis and knowledge of the case is essential to assessing these relationships, which is facilitated by my use of qualitative methods (see the research design at end of this chapter).

A second factor that affects the military's influence in the coalition is the cohesion of the top military leadership. The intuition here is that the more united a front military leaders can present, the more pressure they can exert in the leader's ruling coalition. By cohesion I am interested in the degree to which the military leadership is internally unified around a person, position, or ideology either within a dominant single service (often the army), or across services.[40]

To measure the degree of unity in the military leadership, I examine relations between individuals occupying top positions in the military establishment. While not all must be allied for an influential group to be present, for unity to be high the chiefs in key commands and positions (e.g., the top commanders and heads of an influential service branch—in many countries, the army) should share a common bond, based on branch of service,

---

[38] See the discussion of mass public opinion and support for militaries in Latin America's authoritarian era of the 1960s and 1970s in Geddes and Zaller (1989: 329). On the mass "popularity" of the military more broadly, see Finer (1962: 80), Brooks (2002).

[39] One example is scholarship on the middle-class military coup in Latin America, which linked the military's power to its alliance with a particular social class. See Nun (1967). Also see O'Donnell (1973).

[40] On the cohesion of the officer corps and its propensity for collective action, see Farcau (1994: 102), Janowitz (1977: 143–50), Welch and Smith (1974: 14). The importance of military cohesion/unity is also prominent in the democratization literature in its discussion of factions (Przeworski 1991; Haggard and Kaufman 1995; O'Donnell, Schmitter, and Whitehead 1986; Huntington 1993).

ideological belief systems, corporate interests, or other related issues.[41] Relations in the leadership core conversely are divided when there is evidence of clear internal rivalries or factions within the top leadership.

Finally, the power a leader derives from his or her own social allies weighs against that of the military. A substantial civilian support base allows political leaders to reduce the degree to which they rely on military support in their coalition. The more expansive a leader's support base, the more that leader can draw on it in negotiating institutional prerogatives with military leaders. The underlying logic here is that a leader's influence with any one group in the coalition (such as the military) is strengthened by the degree of support he or she draws from others. As Hunter notes, "The greater the mandate a given government enjoys, the less likely military elites will aggressively counteract civilian attempts to diminish their political role" (1995: 430). At the extreme, when a leader has consolidated support among multiple constituencies, the leader can float on top of all them.[42] The leader can balance one (e.g., the military) against the others in the equivalent of domestic balance of power politics. Alternatively, the absence of social support or fractures within the civilian base can enhance the military's relative position. In sum, one has to look at the entire coalition—the military's position as well as the extent of social support enjoyed by a political leader—to determine the balance of power between political and military leaders.[43]

To measure the political leaders' social allies, I once again draw on the judgments and analyses of historians, participants, and other observers (as well as primary sources in some cases) about the political leader's position in civilian society and support bases among key constituencies. In this regard I look to public opinion, votes and seats won in elections (where relevant), and events such as mass demonstrations to indicate the support or opposition of a group to a leader.

I also focus on the specific policies a leader pursues as indications of his or her support base. The intuition here accords with a general political

---

[41] For a list of reasons why military officers might develop such ties, see Farcau (1994: 62–83); also see Janowitz (1977).

[42] Roeder's (1993: 30–33) description of "directive" leadership evokes a similar logic.

[43] This approach allows for examination of variation in the balance of power between political and military authorities independent of a state's regime type (e.g., I do not assume a particular civil-military balance of power in democracies). This does not mean that political structures are not important; they can act as a prior factor that affects the values of the variables I examine here. For example, democratic political structures can affect the size of the civilian mandate: democratic leaders, because of electoral constraints, rule with a broad civilian coalition. For this reason, it is probably less likely that a military will gain substantial power in states with democratic electoral institutions. However, my approach allows for the possibility that under particular conditions (e.g., when popular esteem for the military is unusually high and a politician's civilian base is narrow or factionalized), the military can become an important political constituency even in democracies.

economy approach to modeling politics.[44] In this view every political leader relies on support from some coalition of societal actors for which the leader trades policy concessions. This can include some major subset of the masses, prominent economic classes (subsistence farmers and urban workers; large landholders and private capital), clerics and religious groups, ethnic groups, religious interests, party apparatuses, and elements of the state bureaucracy (including the security services and police, aside from the conventional armed services), public sector, and civil service. As Waterbury puts it, "all systems of rule have coalitional underpinnings, and they typically contain constituents that spread across formal state agencies and dependencies into civil society . . . public resources are used to maintain these coalitions and hence to ensure political survival" (1993: 190). The overall *pattern* of concessions indicates the coalitional underpinnings of a regime. Hence one can make inferences about a leader's social base from the policies he or she pursues.

Three Configurations of Power

Like "preference divergence," power in my argument is in principle a continuous variable.[45] However, in my analysis I focus on three particular distributions of power, each of which provides leverage on explaining variation in strategic assessment.

Political Dominance: This occurs when either the military is not an influential constituency in domestic society or its support base is internally factionalized and the political leader rules with an expansive social base within civilian society. In these cases the military operates as one of many special interest groups and has marginal influence in or over the political coalition. The political leader retains the upper hand.

Military Dominance: This occurs when the military is a prominent constituency in domestic society, and either the political leader lacks a significant social base or that base is extremely factionalized such that it provides the leader little practical support. The military leadership is also cohesive. In these situations, the political leader has no alternative source of support to draw in relations with the military chiefs, who themselves present a relatively united front. Military leaders wield substantial influence in the coalition. They retain the upper hand over a political leader in this setting.

---

[44] For an example of a political economy approach that assumes that policy outcomes reflect the variable political influence of different groups, see Becker (1983).

[45] On conceptualizing the military's power on a continuum, see Dekmejian (1982: 29), Finer (1962: 86–87), Perlmutter (1977: 94–95).

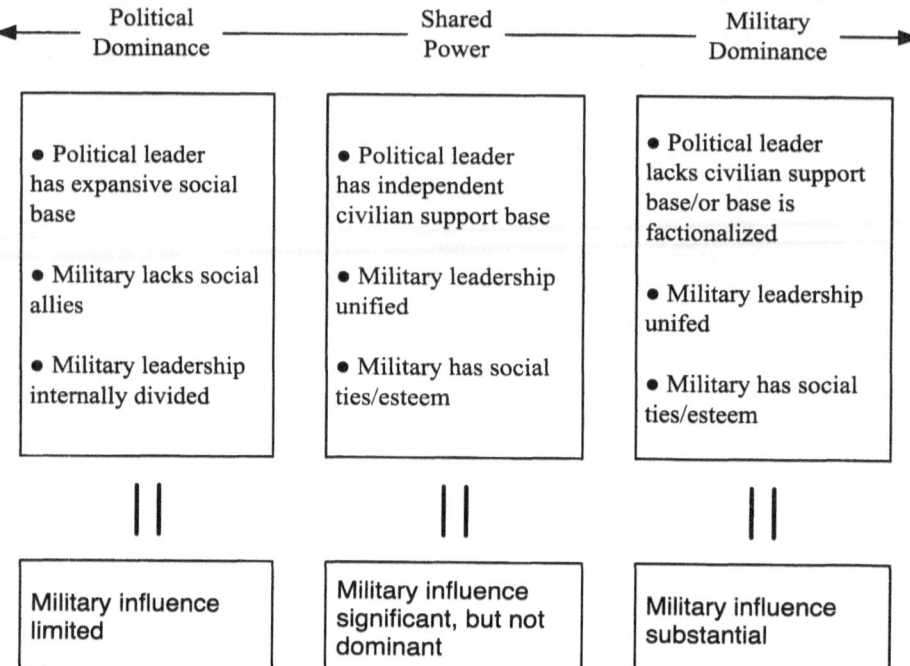

Figure 2.1. The Political-Military Balance of Power

Shared Power: This occurs when the military is an important constituency in domestic society, either because of its position in the social structure or because it has cultivated powerful allies in civilian society. The military leadership is also unified. However, the political leader also has a solid social base outside the military. In this situation both political and military leaders have their own resources on which they can draw in relations with one another. The military is an important, but not sole, player in the coalition. See figure 2.1 for an overview.

Strategic Assessment

Above I discussed the two main determinants of the quality of strategic assessment: the balance of power and intensity of civil-military preference divergence. In this section I explain more fully what I mean by the concept of strategic assessment.

Strategic assessment is the process through which relations between a state's political goals/strategies and military strategies/activities are evaluated and decided. Central issues encompassed in strategic assessment include evaluating a state's operational plans and how they support political and military objectives; evaluating the likely international consequences of modifying military activity or undertaking particular military missions; and assessing a state's relative capabilities and how they bear on the efficacy of its alternative political strategies in a crisis or war. In short, as the concept is employed in this book, the variety of issues that concern the interaction of military and political activity fall within the realm of strategic assessment.

As I elaborate below, I divide strategic assessment into four key sets of processes: information sharing, structural competence, strategic coordination, and the authorization process. Many of these processes are informal and unwritten.[46] When formal structures exist, how these entities operate in practice is crucial.

Information Sharing

A first key attribute of strategic assessment is what I term *information sharing*: the routines and conventions of dialogue associated with the exchange of information at the political-military apex.

By definition, I expect military leaders to have private information about military matters, not only as a result of their occupational specialization in the use of force, but because of their daily exposure to the military organization.[47] This information includes evaluations of the state's own and adversaries' capabilities as well as the costs, risks, and probability of success of alternative military plans in an international conflict. As a state confronts a threat or pursues its ambitions, military leaders are uniquely positioned to supply information to the political leadership about the state's military options. Similarly, a political leader can have private information that bears on these military assessments. Foreign governments may supply intelligence, or other, nonmilitary intelligence agencies or governmental agencies within the state may provide information to a political leader relevant to the assessment of capabilities and military plans.

Evaluating Information Sharing

Information sharing is "good" when both political and military leaders convey their private information to each other. Military leaders present information without withholding or prejudging the value of that information (this does not mean that military officers refrain from opinions, but offering judgment is a separate enterprise from laying out the respective capabil-

---

[46] See note 9.
[47] On political-military information asymmetries fostered by the military's specialization in the use of force and the importance of military advice, see Betts (1991) and Feaver (2003).

ities and feasibilities of military options). Of course, some passive "bias" in reporting is probably inevitable because, like many individuals engaged in a profession, military leaders will likely have views colored by their service affiliation and career path. But, that aside, military leaders can be more and less forthcoming with the internal information available to them and transparent about the predispositions they bring to the consultation table; they can be more and less activist in seeking to alter the presentation of information. Evidence, for example, that military leaders are consistently and knowingly altering or omitting information in ways that privilege their preferred policy outcomes, at the expense of a comprehensive survey of alternatives, signals a pathology in information sharing. Evidence that politicians are actively withholding pertinent information is similarly revealing.

Key to measuring the quality of information sharing are the briefings, reports, and verbal communications exchanged between military and political leaders. When information sharing is good, the accounts of analysts, historians, and other relevant observers should reveal that military leaders made a substantial effort to survey and evaluate a full range of alternatives. Military leaders should offer concrete and documented assessments of the costs, risks, and feasibility of each, without unilaterally minimizing or dismissing some options as unviable.

Conversely, evidence that military leaders are misrepresenting information includes overt distortions or falsification of data and, in the most egregious cases, the deliberate refusal to share information about military activity. Misrepresentation can also have subtle forms, which include the manipulation and omission of data to present them in a light supportive of military leaders' preferences. Regardless of its form, if information is shaped to conform to preexisting policy priorities, then information sharing is compromised.

Strategic Coordination

A second critical dimension of strategic assessment is *strategic coordination*. It refers to the overall structure and mechanisms in peacetime and war for assessing alternative military strategies and more specific plans (how force is to be organized and used in the event of armed conflict), and coordinating military activity with political and diplomatic objectives and constraints.

Strategic coordination is important because of the deliberation and airing of alternative perspectives it introduces into security policy formulation. As noted above, information sharing affects what private information military leaders provide to their political counterparts about military capabilities and plans. Strategic coordination affects how well those assessments and alternative courses of action are then probed and analyzed. Thus even if military leaders are fully forthcoming in what they know, strategic coordination helps ensure that key assumptions and uncertainties in that information are exposed and debated.

Strategic coordination also helps integrate political and military considerations in the making of military strategy and policy in international disputes. It helps "politicize" military activity and "militarize" political judgments about the use of force. Military strategy, operational plans, and (at times) tactical activity can have political implications, just as political goals have implications for military activity. Strategic coordination works to offset disconnects in political and military considerations. A joint civilian-military advisory process can help heighten military personnel's sensitivity to exogenous, environmental, or political constraints that bear on the efficacy of force, while heightening civilians' sensitivities to military constraints. It helps ensure that political and military leaders are aware of developments in their respective spheres and analyze their implications jointly. It helps expose faulty assumptions, logic, and evidence about the efficacy of force and its integration with political objectives.

Evaluating Strategic Coordination

Ideally, a state should have routine, established forums for interaction among military chiefs, political leaders, and representatives of other offices of the state. Such joint entities can come in a variety of forms, whether in a national security council-style apparatus or a less formalized entity. Regardless, when strategic coordination is "good," military chiefs should regularly be represented, as should diplomatic and political authorities.

Also critical is how these entities operate. Even if meetings are routinized and representative, if they lack analytical substance and conventions that favor systematic and comprehensive review and debate, then strategic coordination is poor. Norms and patterns of conversation are critical.[48] Within these meetings, one should see concerted efforts invested in search and analysis of confirming and disconfirming information about alternative military plans and options, including the solicitation of multiple perspectives and viewpoints. Political leaders, for their part should not "cherry-pick" for information that supports their views, while a priori discounting other disconfirming data. Especially crucial is assessing how alternatives to military action (or to particular military courses of action) are canvassed and how political and diplomatic developments that could affect military

---

[48] On the importance of these and other activities in advisory processes, see the discussion in Haney (2002). Haney provides an extensive literature review and lays out key components of a "rigorous" advisory structure.

outcomes are integrated into the discussion. Also key is how assumptions and concepts about military plans themselves are analyzed. As such, when strategic coordination is "working," dialogue across the political and military divide may become heated and even conflictual at times; critical is that one viewpoint does not hijack the conversation and shut down dialogue. The airing of competing views within executive conference rooms, private meeting spaces, or palace rooms is thus a good thing. It is one of the hallmarks of effective strategic coordination.

Structural Competence

A third category of institutional features I group under the rubric of the *structural competence* of the military. Structural competence captures the quality of organizational structures and conventions devoted to "self-critical" analysis and evaluations of a military's own activities—what I term internal monitoring. It also refers to the quality of effort devoted by the military to intelligence gathering and analysis of foreign armies.

One reason structural competence is important is that it affects a military's capacity to assess its own capabilities relative to its adversaries' and allies' forces. Assessing relative military capabilities is a complicated endeavor and requires significant organizational competency. It entails looking beyond calculations of numerical strengths in personnel, weapons, and equipment to intangible factors—such as the skill and quality of troops, morale, and the rigor of training, leadership, and doctrine—that allow a military to translate its material strengths into military power on the battlefield.[49] The latter are among the more difficult aspects of military activity to measure, which is why a military's capacity to monitor its own activities and to assess foreign militaries is so critical to the accuracy of its capabilities' estimates.

Evaluating Structural Competence

When a military is competent in self-evaluation it should have tools for assessing its internal strengths and weaknesses. Organizational forms may vary across states, but observable, systematic mechanisms for assessing military activity and communicating the information up the chain of command are essential. Also crucial are the conventions and value the military organization places on self-critical analysis, and how it rewards and punishes members who report critical information. The criteria for officer promotions and appointments can influence this organizational ethos. Where, for

---

[49] On the intangible determinants of "military effectiveness," see Biddle and Zirkle (1996), Brooks (1998), Brooks and Stanley (2007), Pollack (2002), Reiter and Stam (2002), Biddle (2004).

example, appointments reward merit and skill, military personnel are likely to be more competent in assessing their unit's performance and face fewer incentives to distort information. In contrast, promotion criteria that reward partisanship and political loyalty tend to discourage the impartiality of information exchange; at the extreme, disincentives to report bad news can encourage a "yes-man" phenomenon, in which subordinates withhold unfavorable information in reporting to their superiors.[50]

The structural competence of the military also depends on its military intelligence functions. Competition among entities in a zero-sum bureaucratic environment, absorption of intelligence resources in internal regime competition, and heavy emphasis on political criteria in promotions versus merit all impede the effectiveness of military organizations in gathering and evaluating intelligence about adversaries' capabilities (Handel 1985: 262–63).

Of course, many things beyond a state's civil-military relations are likely to affect a state's competence in internal monitoring and intelligence. States may exhibit different levels of structural competence in these areas for historical or cultural reasons, or because of the state's level of economic development and access to technology. This study is interested only in the effects of relations between military and political leaders at the apex of decision making on the priorities and activities at lower levels of the military organization. Dynamics at the top can filter down through the organization in a number of ways, especially through their effects on the criteria for officer appointment and promotions, organizational norms, and the priorities of intelligence agencies. As I explain below, these effects are most likely to occur under a particular configuration of power and preference divergence—where power is shared and preference divergence is high. This environment politicizes military activity with adverse effects on the military organization. Because I anticipate that only under particular conditions will civil-military relations affect structural competence, my hypotheses about this attribute tend to be more limited than predictions about the other three institutional attributes of strategic assessment.

Authorization Process

A fourth and final dimension of strategic assessment I refer to as the *authorization process* at the political-military apex. It captures variation in how state leaders select among the military strategies and activities available to them in their interstate relations—in how decisions are made at the civil-military apex.

---

[50] On the politicization of military advice, see Heller (1996), Handel (1989: 203–4), Betts (1991: 53).

The authorization process is critical to strategic assessment, but in a somewhat different way from the informational mechanisms I describe above. The latter affect how political leaders evaluate their relative capabilities and plans and therefore the quality of the information that informs their decisions about what political-military strategies to adopt in an interstate dispute. The authorization process, in contrast, affects the capacity to choose that strategy and translate it into practical actions in support of it. Evaluating a course of action is a critical component of any decision-making process. But at the end of the day, a state's leaders have to be able to act on the fruits of that analytical process: a clear choice of one course of action over another has to be made and implemented. All the deliberation in the world does not matter if there is no clear decision-making mechanism in operation in a state during an international dispute.

Essential is the degree to which a state exhibits a clearly defined versus an ambiguous authorization process: that is, whether decision-making prerogatives are allocated such that domains of responsibility and lines of accountability are clearly drawn, discernable, and coherent. When the authorization process is clearly defined, prerogatives such as veto rights, rights of final approval, and appointment privileges (discussed below) are concentrated in the hands of either the political or military leadership: These leaders may delegate the exercise of particular rights to their counterparts on a daily basis, but they retain ultimate rights of residual control over them (in effect, this means they can reclaim them at will). One side is the ultimate decision maker.

When a state has an ambiguous authorization process, the allocation of decision-making prerogatives is poorly defined. Rules governing decision making may be idiosyncratic, context specific, or simply difficult to discern. At times, this ambiguity manifests itself in overt competition over these prerogatives; political and military leaders compete for the right to veto or approve policies. In other cases it is expressed more passively (or less contentiously) in a set of routines or conventions that do not clearly confer prerogatives on one side or the other. Neither side is clearly the decision maker.

In the absence of a clearly defined authorization process, states may adopt incoherent strategies or experience rapid cycling and erratic shifts among strategies. It is difficult to translate political initiatives into supportive military strategies or capabilities.

Evaluating the Authorization Process

Measuring the authorization process requires looking at key decision-making prerogatives and how they are allocated. When these rules are codified in legislation, the country's constitution, or regulations, and where formal dictates accord with actual practice, measuring the authorization process may be relatively straightforward.

However, when rules are vaguely formulated, laws are not codified, or formal structures are ignored, one must discern actual practices. What matters is not what the rules say, but what happens on a day-to-day basis. Take, for example, the various ways that states' national security councils (NSC) function. Some entities, like the National Security Council in the United States, are purely advisory bodies; the uniformed military plays a minimal role within the body. In Brazil, in contrast, in the years immediately following the transition to democracy, the NSC was headed by a general officer, and its many subdirectorates were controlled by active-duty military, which allowed the military "significant agenda-shaping power" in decision making (Stepan 1988: 141). In Turkey, the National Security Council has traditionally been seen as the primary decision-making body in military-security affairs and has been dominated by active-duty military officers. In short, despite the institutional isomorphism, how NSCs operate in practice and allocate decision-making prerogatives within them varies considerably. Evaluating the authorization process requires attention to these subtleties.

Specifically, among the prerogatives essential to analyzing the authorization process are rights of veto and approval. Key questions and issues here include: Do military leaders retain the capacity to veto initiatives by the political leadership? Who has a practical "vote" in decision-making forums, and who is represented in those entities? Are decisions made by consensus, or do choice rules afford the political or military leadership substantial "votes" in decision making?

One empirical incarnation of these decision-making prerogatives is the chain of command in the armed forces: the rules governing the division of rights and responsibilities within the military establishment, who answers to whom, and whose approval is required for what initiative. When authorization processes are clearly defined, chains of command in practice have clearly delineated lines of accountability and responsibility. When they are ambiguous, who actually exercises command responsibilities tends to be more idiosyncratic and difficult to discern in the abstract.

Also important in assessing the authorization process is the allocation of rights of appointment, promotion, dismissal, and punishment of senior military officers—whether they are retained by the political or military leadership or contested. Although perhaps less obvious than other indicators, these rights are powerful means of influence over military activity (Nordlinger 1977: 74). Senior officers shape their services' peacetime planning and wartime administrative and combat activities; they set the tone and establish standards of behavior for the enlisted ranks and influence the norms of a military organization. Appointing officers with particular personalities, leadership styles, command experiences, or strategic perspectives therefore can have a powerful effect on the internal activities of a military establishment. Similarly, disciplining officers for undesirable or "aberrant" behavior helps reinforce prevailing conventions and attitudes within the military organization.[51] For this reason, the allocation of prerogatives associated with officer advancement and promotion is essential to assessing the authorization process in military-security matters (see table 2.1 for a summary of the attributes).

Hypotheses on Strategic Assessment

What civil-military relations are most likely to produce the best environment for strategic assessment: When will political and military leaders share their private information fluidly and comprehensively; joint political-military consultation be well established, representative, and rigorous; the military organization exhibit competencies in intelligence and internal monitoring; and a clear process for authorizing military activity be present? In short, when will a leader be best prepared to manage the state's international relations? When will a leader be worst prepared?

Below I outline several hypotheses about when strategic assessment should be better or worse, depending on variation in its civil-military relations. Specifically, the hypotheses reflect predictions about the values for each of the four attributes of assessment in five alternative civil-military settings. However, I also frame the discussion with "best-to-worst" categories to provide some intuitive traction on the hypotheses.

The "Best" Civil-Military Relations for Strategic Assessment

The best environment for strategic assessment is observed when preference divergence is low and political leaders are dominant. These civil-military relations are most conducive to the emergence of functional structures that facilitate the sharing and analysis of information and authoritative decision making. They facilitate healthy dialogue and debate between political and military leaders.

Information sharing is fluid in these settings. Neither political nor military leaders have good reason to withhold information about capabilities or military plans. In briefings and oral communications, military leaders provide detailed analysis that surveys all options and lays out risks and costs without prejudging outcomes. Conversely, there are no concerted efforts

---

[51] For examples of variation in these methods, see Pion-Berlin (1992: 199).

Table 2.1
Four Attributes of Strategic Assessment

	Information Sharing	Strategic Coordination	Structural Competence	Authorization Process
Indicators	Briefings, reports Informal dialogue	Advisory forums Representation in meetings Procedural conventions of dialogue and interaction in meetings	Internal evaluative processes/self-monitoring in military organization Intramilitary structures for intelligence gathering on foreign militaries	Decision-making processes: rights of veto/approval/voting Process for senior officer appointments Chain of command
Varies with	Degree information is freely exchanged between political and military leadership Degree of omissions and bias in language and format of presentations and analyses	Existence/frequency of meetings Participation of military leaders Involvement of chiefs of other diplomatic/political/economic functions of the state Solicitation of multiple perspectives and viewpoints in advisory processes Evidence of efforts to limit scope and domain of options for discussion Critical analysis of "unpopular," "unlikely" options or outcomes	Degree military intelligence resources allocated to external targets Rigor and objectivity of analytical processes Degree to which organizational conventions (e.g., as promoted by appointment criteria) encourage self-critical analysis and systematic reporting of information	Allocation of prerogatives: hierarchical and concentrated in military or political leadership versus divided Clarity of selection processes: clear versus ambiguous lines of accountability and responsibility

by military leaders to distort or omit information; nor do political leaders intentionally mislead military leaders and withhold any information they might have gleaned from private sources that bears on the efficacy of military activity.

Strategic coordination is also relatively routinized, representative, and rigorous. Advisory bodies include representatives from both the political and military apparatus of the state. The intuition here is that because the political leader is dominant and, by definition, directs the broader economic and other arenas of the state, he or she is more likely to bring together diplomats and military officials than if the military was autonomous from the political state. These civil-military relations facilitate interaction between the political and military arenas of the state.

Within consultative entities, conversation is relatively unguarded. These environments provide the structural basis for productive conflict and debate; those conflicts may be intense in the moment. But the hierarchical nature of these environments and the absence of more fundamental policy cleavages between political and military leaders means episodic disagreements are unlikely to devolve into open disaffection and alienation. Open debate can flourish. This healthy dialogue—and not necessarily the wholesale absence of friction—is essential to strategic coordination.[52]

These environments also facilitate improvements in the military's structural competencies in intelligence and internal monitoring. Because power is concentrated in the political leader, he or she can stress meritocratic and "professional" standards in critical appointments. The political leader can also change personnel and promote organizational reforms that improve intelligence activity and enhance internal monitoring. This does not guarantee that the military will achieve some absolute benchmark of proficiency; rather, civil-military relations pose no obstacle to major improvements in organizational activity. At the least, relations between political and military leaders should not create pressures that worsen any extant organizational deficiencies.

Finally, the authorization process is clearly defined. Political leaders retain ultimate rights of approval and veto. The mechanisms for making choices about military and security issues are unambiguous. Political leaders also retain the power to hire and fire military leaders and restructure the chain of command.

In summary, these settings exhibit the following dynamics: few active efforts to withhold information; consultation forums that bring together political and military apparatuses of the state; and clearly defined lines of responsibility and accountability in making decisions about military related

---

[52] For a return to this theme, see the discussion of "ideal civil-military relations" in this book's conclusion.

issues. These states are best equipped to evaluate their relative capabilities and integrate political and military considerations in their strategic choices. They should also be able to commit the state to a military strategy or coherent course of action in an international dispute.

HYPOTHESIS 1 When political leaders are dominant and preference divergence is low, *ceteris paribus*, strategic assessment is good: States exhibit fluid information sharing, well-developed strategic coordination, the potential for improvements in structural competencies in intelligence and monitoring, and clear authorization processes.

The Worst Civil-Military Relations for Strategic Assessment

When political and military leaders are sharing power and their preferences diverge, states exhibit the worst strategic assessment. Both political and military leaders have the means and motive to compete over how decisions about sensitive military and security issues are made. Underlying disputes about substantive issues devolve into open competition between political and military leaders over how they will share information, coordinate with one another, and make decisions at the civil-military apex. This competition introduces institutional pathologies in strategic assessment.

Specifically, information sharing is extremely poor in these settings. Military leaders hoard information and shape its presentation in ways that privilege their goals and interests. Political leaders also withhold private information when it helps them protect their goals from efforts by military leaders to subvert them.

Strategic coordination is also dysfunctional. Military and political leaders are estranged from one another, and consultation between them degrades. Military leaders are wary of participating fully in advisory forums and resist coordinating with other political and diplomatic authorities of the state, especially if the latter are allies of the political leader. Where meetings remain routine, military leaders are reluctant to engage in analyses that might compromise their interests and rigorous and forthcoming review of the country's military strategy and plans is unlikely.

Competition at the civil military apex is also destructive to the military's structural competence in intelligence and internal monitoring. The reasons have to do with how competition for control of military activity and policy affects the incentives of political and military leaders to elevate personal loyalty in officer appointments and promotions. Political leaders will appoint allies to key positions, sometimes at the expense of more talented and skilled officers. Military leaders will resist those appointments and try to secure the positions of their loyal colleagues. Over time, norms favoring meritocracy break down. As a result, officers' and their bureaucratic units' incentives and capabilities to think rigorously and self-critically about the military's organizational strengths and weaknesses decline. This undercuts the quality of internal monitoring. It also undermines the efficacy of foreign intelligence gathering efforts. In addition, as a result of internal regime competition, entities in the military usually devoted to evaluating external adversaries become absorbed in gathering intelligence about the political leader, his or her allies, and their activities. As resources are redirected, there are fewer devoted to studying foreign militaries and less emphasis within the organization on such efforts.

Finally, states with these civil-military relations have an ill-defined and ambiguous authorization process at the civil-military apex. Neither the political nor the military leader retains key decision-making prerogatives: Both actively compete for final rights of veto and approval, as well as control of senior appointments. Although a political leader may retain public control, he or she faces significant pressure behind the scenes to cede prerogatives to the military. Both sides will likely engage in creative tactics to enhance their leverage in decision making.

The cumulative effects of these pathologies complicate reasoned analysis and decisive implementation of a state's political-military strategy in an international dispute. Along every dimension—from the exchange of information, consultation, and debate about policy options to the selection and implementation of strategy—strategic assessment is flawed. Leaders in these states are at a huge disadvantage in managing their international relations. They have a hard time accurately assessing their capabilities and military options in an international dispute. Political considerations that bear on military activity will get short shrift. And it is difficult to commit the state to a coherent political-military strategy or set of military activities. Incoherent strategies or cycling is likely, while outsiders struggle to interpret the ambiguous information about goals and priorities emanating from these states' contested authorization processes.

HYPOTHESIS 2 When military and political leaders share power and preference divergence is high, strategic assessment is highly dysfunctional. Intense political-military competition undermines all four attributes of strategic assessment.

Poor Strategic Assessment

Strategic assessment should be poor—but not the worst—when military and political leaders share power and preference divergence is low. Despite the fact that the military retains substantial power in the ruling coalition, civil-military relations are stabilized by an underlying coincidence of interests between political and military leaders; the absence of conflict mutes the inherently divisive effects of shared power. Political and military leaders are not actively competing with one another for control of military policymaking.

Consequently, both political and military leaders lack strong incentives to withhold or deliberately misrepresent the information they exchange with one another about military related issues. Information sharing is not especially problematic. Nor is the structural competence of the military necessarily undermined: In these settings, political and military leaders lack incentives to politicize appointments (as compared with cases in which they are actively competing with one another for control of military affairs).

These states, however, do exhibit serious weaknesses in strategic coordination. Consistent with the logic discussed earlier in this chapter, even where preferences do not diverge, the military's power in the coalition affects the default institutions that emerge. They afford the organization's leaders substantial autonomy in managing its affairs. In this way, these settings contrast with those in which a political leader dominates and preferences align. In the latter case, although converging preferences mitigate the need to invest heavily in oversight (see below for this logic), the political leader still has some baseline incentive to coordinate activities with the military establishment and establish oversight infrastructure to facilitate that process; hence, where political leaders dominate, by default the military is more likely to be integrated with the activities of the political apparatus of the state. The military's autonomy here complicates that effort, by making it structurally more challenging to establish such coordinating mechanisms. The military operates outside the boundaries of the political and diplomatic edifice. As a result, consultative entities will be less representative and are less likely to encourage critical debate and review of military activity. There are fewer sources of external information and nonmilitary perspectives represented in advisory processes. Thus, while the exchange of information between political and military leaders about military plans and activity is uninhibited, this information is less likely to be subjected to rigorous analysis in context of broader political considerations within joint consultative bodies.

In addition, these states lack a clearly defined authorization process. The worst dynamic—open competition between political and military leaders over decision-making prerogatives—is absent. But how those rights are actually allocated and who enjoys ultimate capacity to approve or veto policy is ultimately poorly defined. Practically this means that decision making can periodically assume a decidedly ad hoc or idiosyncratic nature. It will be difficult to infer, and therefore to monitor, from the outside who has the ultimate capacity to make decisions about military activity in these states and the processes through which they do so.

In sum, states with these civil-military relations exhibit pronounced pathologies in strategic coordination and their authorization processes. They will have a difficult time integrating military activity with political objectives and international constraints. Authorization processes that are ultimately ill-defined also make it difficult to commit the state to a particular strategy or course of action in an international dispute.

HYPOTHESIS 3 Strategic assessment is poor when military and political leaders are effectively sharing power and preference divergence is low. Weaknesses in strategic coordination and the authorization process are pronounced.

Fair Strategic Assessment

Strategic assessment should exhibit mixed strengths and weaknesses in states with three civil-military configurations: (1) political dominance and high preference divergence; (2) military dominance and high preference divergence; (3) military dominance and low preference divergence. In these cases, civil-military relations have mixed effects on the four attributes of strategic assessment. They promote relatively functional processes in information sharing and the authorization process, with positive or neutral effects on the military's structural competencies in intelligence and internal monitoring. At the same time, albeit for different reasons, they all promote problems in strategic coordination. The cumulative effect of these mixed tendencies for the state's capacity to evaluate information and make decisions in interstate conflicts should vary across empirical cases: In some cases pathologies in strategic coordination may prove a major impediment as a state formulates its international strategies, while in others institutional strengths may prove more consequential.

POLITICAL DOMINANCE AND HIGH PREFERENCE DIVERGENCE

In this setting, political dominance helps ameliorate the most divisive effects of political and military leaders' diverging preferences; these settings have structural advantages over those in which leaders disagree, but the military is politically powerful. For example, although military leaders may have strong incentives to withhold or misrepresent information, political leaders have access to tools that mitigate their incentives to bias information. They can impose forms of oversight on military subordinates, which enhances their access to information.⁵³ For this reason, information sharing is not especially problematic.⁵⁴

In addition, the authorization process is clearly defined. Political leaders retain rights of approval and veto and ultimate control of senior officer appointments. A leader has final say over military policy and activities and can use military appointments and impose oversight to ensure that his or her initiatives are implemented. The dominance of the political leadership also allows the leader to structure advisory processes in conformity with its interests. The political leader can bring along representatives of the political apparatus of the state and "require" military participation in consultative entities, although the tendency to marginalize military chiefs often undercuts the effectiveness of these joint-coordinating bodies (see below).

Civil-military relations also facilitate improvements in the military's structural competence. These settings allow for greater emphasis on talent, merit, and attention to duty in promotions and key appointments. Intelligence resources can be reformed and redirected toward external sources. While no guarantee that the military will achieve an objective standard of efficiency, relative to other settings, there is room for significant strengths in the military's structural competencies in intelligence and internal monitoring in these environments.

These states nonetheless exhibit serious weaknesses in the consultative processes essential to strategic coordination. The problem originates in the oversight methods political leaders may employ to mitigate bias in information sharing and to ensure military compliance in the implementation of their preferred initiatives. Two tactics merit emphasis here. First, political leaders may manage dissent by marginalizing military leaders in consultation processes: Knowing their military leaders disagree with their priorities and perspectives on military strategy and activity, political leaders may circumscribe their chiefs' participation in advisory processes, a priori discount their opinions, and instead privilege other sources of information. These tactics limit politicians' vulnerability to what they perceive as military lead-

---

[53] These dynamics are nicely captured in the principal-agent literature, which discusses the procedural mechanisms available to political leaders in their efforts to create incentive compatible behavior. See Kiewiet and McCubbins (1991), Feaver (2003), Avant (1994).

[54] Information sharing, however, should not be as fluid as in cases where military and political leaders' preferences are closely aligned. In part, this is because even if political leaders retain the capacity to impose oversight that mitigates bias in information sharing, there is often some slippage or "agency-loss," as military leaders seek to protect their priorities with more passive forms of resistance (i.e., they resort to more subtle tactics to try to color the information they share in conformity with their preferences). Although reporting requirements and other forms of external monitoring can go far to ensure that the political leader has good access to information, it is impossible to ensure perfect information exchange.

ers' "biased" views.⁵⁵ Second, in tactics akin to "screening" procedures, political leaders appoint like-minded officials to key posts—they replace dissenting officials with individuals that tend to agree with them on strategic, security, and corporate issues. Political leaders put people in charge who will follow through on their directives and engage them in consultation processes.

Although it is not inevitable that leaders will employ these two tactics, they face strong incentives to do so.⁵⁶ These are powerful techniques that help promote what White (1991: 189–90) refers to as "operational control": they help ensure "definiteness and predictability" in military activity and thus "are essential to gaining the scope for the action" preferred by the leader. These tactics protect a political leader's interests in the process of formulating and implementing political-military strategy.

However, they have downsides for the process of strategic assessment for the state as a whole. Marginalizing military leaders out of anticipation of receiving biased evaluations and promoting likeminded officers truncates conversation and reduces critical dialogue and therefore undermines strategic coordination. The problem in part is akin to the tension between operational control and, once again as White characterizes it, strategic control: in promoting the former, leaders set up conditions ill-suited to the "flexibility and attentiveness" essential to the latter (1991: 189). Officers who agree with a leader are less likely to offer fresh perspectives and dissenting views. Ultimately this undermines the debate and rigor of analysis. The result is a less demanding evaluative process overall. In this way, efforts to "fix" the problem created by intense civil-military conflict can actually introduce other weaknesses into strategic assessment.

As I note above, it is difficult to weigh in the abstract the magnitude of these competing tendencies in strategic assessment and therefore to gauge a state's overall fitness to manage its international relations—to know whether the strengths in information sharing, structural competence, and the authorization process will outweigh any pathologies introduced into strategic coordination, or alternatively, whether weaknesses in the latter will overshadow strengths in the former. Empirically, however, one should see particular patterns in strategic assessment. These states should not have an especially difficult time estimating their relative capabilities or devel-

---

⁵⁵ Although these tactics have not necessarily been theorized as forms of oversight in the principal-agent literature, they might be considered in that category of methods. They help a leader circumvent obstruction by avoiding naysayers who might stymie debate, rehash old issues, and set the conversational agenda against analysis of particular options. They help leaders avoid getting "bogged down" in the analytical process.

⁵⁶ On other tactics leaders might employ with less counterproductive results, see the discussion of "ideal" civil-military relations in the conclusion.

oping and committing the state to particular military strategies or courses of action in interstate conflicts. They may have problems, however, in detecting internal weaknesses in those strategies and in anticipating how broader political objectives might bear on their efficacy. In short, these states are not doomed to major strategic failures in their international relations. But they are also far from invulnerable to them.

HYPOTHESIS 4 Strategic assessment exhibits competing strengths and weaknesses when preference divergence is high, but political leaders dominate in relations with the military leadership. Information sharing is relatively fluid, the authorization process is clear, and improvements are possible in structural competence. Pathologies nonetheless occur in strategic coordination.

MILITARY DOMINANCE AND HIGH DIVERGENCE / MILITARY DOMINANCE AND LOW DIVERGENCE

When the military is dominant and preference divergence is high or low, strategic assessment also exhibits mixed tendencies. Recall that by military dominance I do not mean that the military runs the state or has taken over the government.[57] Rather, because of the more subtle features of domestic politics described above, the military leaders who run the organization on a daily basis wield the upper hand in relations with the political leader as they compete over processes essential to strategic assessment.

In practice, when the military dominates in this sense, it may face a political leader whose preferences over substantive strategic, corporate, and security issues coincide or diverge: Both are logically possible and potentially observed empirically. However, I collapse these two cells for analytical reasons.[58] As long as the military dominates, I expect the consequences for assessment institutions to be relatively similar: The intensity of preference

---

[57] That is, I mean something more subtle than if the leader of the country wears a uniform or came to power through a coup d'etat. The country does not need to be ruled by the military for the military leadership to be dominant; military dominance describes a power relationship between the political and military leader at the apex of decision making. A military may be highly cohesive and socially esteemed and have the upper hand in those relations without running the country. Conversely, just because the individual in charge of the country wears a military uniform, which is sometimes referred to as a "military regime," does not mean that the officers who run the services on a daily basis are dominant at the civil-military apex.

[58] By collapsing the predictions of my typology, I am engaging in what Elman (2005: 300) refers to as pragmatic compression, or "collapsing contiguous cells if their division serves no useful theoretical purpose." Because these combinations predict the same outcome for strategic assessment (the difference in preference divergence is inconsequential when the military dominates), I merge them together in one hypothesis.

divergence has few practical implications because the military effectively internalizes strategic assessment within its own corridors. Whereas in the types of civil-military relations discussed above, both political and military leaders may be empowered in the creation of assessment processes, here the military can dictate the terms of these institutions. Moreover, and especially important to understanding the logic of these settings, when it dominates, the military controls both the actual capacity to make military strategy and operational plans as well as to implement them; in contrast, when a political leader dominates and makes key decisions, he or she must still contend with his or her military counterparts in order to get them implemented. In other words, the military does not need to engage the political leadership when it dominates (unlike the political leader who always must do so because of a lack of crucial information about day-to-day military activity and a need for military chiefs to implement any decisions).

Consequently, while information sharing may be poor in these environments (as the military controls access to information and decides when and whether to share information with the political leader), these deficiencies are practically inconsequential. Whether or not information passes freely to the political leader is ultimately trivial because the military tends to incorporate much of the actual process of strategic assessment into its own organizational machinery.

As might be expected, the authorization process is unambiguous in these civil-military settings. Military leaders retain rights of veto and approval over military and security policy. They also retain de facto control over senior appointments and promotions and decide who will occupy top posts. Structural competence will not be significantly influenced, positively or negatively, by civil-military relations at the apex; it will largely depend on factors beyond the present analysis, such as internal norms and conventions within the military organization.

Despite the clarity of the authorization process, these states should exhibit weaknesses in strategic coordination. As noted above, the leaders of the "dominant" military retain the autonomy to define their relations with the political leader and the broader apparatus of the state. As a result, the military establishment is likely to operate outside the boundaries of the political state. The shift of the locus of decision making to within the military organization reduces its leaders' interface with the political apparatus of the state, which limits the interaction of other representatives of the state and military leaders in strategic assessment.

In sum, states with these civil-military relations should exhibit particular strengths and weaknesses in strategic assessment. They should not have an especially difficult time evaluating their capabilities or committing to coherent strategies. However, they are less likely to incorporate broader

Table 2.2
Civil-Military Relations and Four Attributes of Strategic Assessment

	Low Preference Divergence (PD), Political Dominance	*High PD, Shared Power*	*Low PD, Shared Power*	*High PD, Political Dominance*	*High/Low PD, Military Dominance*
Information sharing	+	−	+	+	+
Strategic coordination	+	−	−	−	−
Structural competence	+	−	=	+	+
Authorization process	+	−	−	+	+

+ Relatively good
− Relatively bad
= Civil-military relations at apex have no major positive or negative implications; no theoretical prediction

political considerations into assessments of military activity.[59] Political objectives and military activity are apt to be poorly integrated.

Hypothesis 5 Strategic assessment also exhibits competing strengths and weaknesses when military leaders dominate in relations with the political leadership and preference divergence is high or low. The authorization process is clear, and although information sharing is poor, it is practically inconsequential because of the internalization of decision making within the military. The worst problems are observed in strategic coordination.

Predictions for the values of the four attributes in different civil-military settings are summarized in table 2.2.

---

[59] When states lack peak entities for strategic assessment, the military leadership often gains de facto influence in deciding issues of national security, especially those related to the use of force (Stepan 1988: 141). Also on the idea that the military's isolation from the political leadership and apparatus of the state will minimize the integration of political considerations in the making of military policy, see Sagan (1996–1997) and Schofield (2000).

Research Design

The goal of this book is to analyze the effects of one potential variable—civil-military relations—on strategic assessment. I engage in what Imre Lakatos refers to as a two-cornered test: I test against the null hypothesis (the hypothesis of no causal relationship between civil-military relations and assessment).[60] Ultimately, I expect that any comprehensive understanding of the causes of strategic assessment will require considering civil-military relations. That is, to understand why strategic assessment assumes a particular value in any given case, we need to look at the state of civil-military relations and evaluate how it contributes to the observed outcome: Civil-military relations are a necessary cause of strategic assessment processes.[61]

Nevertheless, other variables too could potentially influence strategic assessment. These (potential) alternative explanations have important implications for my research design, which I discuss below. Note, however, that while this study at times generates insight into the utility of other explanations, in the text that follows I do not aim to disprove systematically any alternative theories for assessment that one might formulate. In addition, my theory analyzes strategic assessment as it pertains to issues most likely to be within the expertise of military leaders—those concerning conventional military capabilities and strategies—not in other policy domains.[62] In short, my objective is straightforward: to demonstrate that civil-military relations have a significant and consistent effect on the processes through which political leaders engage in strategic assessment in international disputes. Below I explain how I go about pursuing this goal.

Method and Case Selection

I assess the explanatory power of my theory and test its central hypotheses with qualitative methods that utilize both cross-case comparisons and within-case process tracing. Specifically, the study couples two comprehensive case studies of Egypt in the 1960s and 1970s, which form the empirical

---

[60] For discussion of two- versus three-cornered tests (which test theories against other theories), see Van Evera (1997: 38).

[61] See Goertz and Starr (2003) and Mahoney (2003) on the concept of necessary causes.

[62] The four sets of processes I discuss in the text are all relevant for policymaking on conventional military issues, plans, and options, and the political factors that may bear on them—not necessarily for the array of other foreign policy concerns (e.g., trade policy) or domestic issues (human rights, economic policy) facing states, even those in which the military plays an important role. For a general discussion of other domains in which militaries may have influence, see Colton (1979).

core of the book, with six more focused studies involving a variety of cases from different regions and time periods.

Qualitative methods are well suited for evaluating this book's theory of civil-military relations and strategic assessment. Central to the argument is that institutions for assessment often become implicated in substantive policy conflicts as leaders seek to privilege their preferred outcomes in decision-making processes. Alternatively, these pressures are mitigated and institutions are shaped by efforts to promote "functional" efficiency. Either way, this book is often studying a process of institutional contestation and evolution as much as it is analyzing institutional outcomes, both of which require close attention to the interactions of political and military leaders.[63] Analytic process tracing, in particular, affords this level of consideration. By employing it, I can evaluate whether events unfolded consistently with the logic of the theory.[64] Cross-case comparisons also allow me to evaluate whether the causal relationships hold in a variety of states and settings.

The benefits of focusing the empirical analysis on Egypt are multiple. First, from the mid-1960s through the 1970s, Egypt exhibited significant variation in its civil-military relations. In the early and mid-1960s, political and military leaders shared power and preference divergence was high. In the aftermath of the 1967 Arab-Israeli War, changes in the military's social status and internal cohesion along with shifts in the political coalition altered the balance of power. In the late 1960s and 1970s, civil-military relations were characterized by political dominance and high preference divergence. These differences in Egypt's civil-military relations facilitate testing two central hypotheses of the study.

Second, Egypt in the 1960s and 1970s has been relatively understudied by theorists in international security, especially, for example, compared with European states during the world wars, which appear as cases in many prominent books in security studies.[65] There is benefit to expanding the range of empirical cases with which scholars are familiar, especially for periods with such enormous historical consequences as Egypt under Nasser in the 1960s and Sadat in the 1970s—which witnessed consequential wars and, in the latter case, an unprecedented peace with Israel. Third, the cases control for the effects of several alternative variables that could potentially influence my findings. I elaborate on this last point below.

The Egypt studies rely on a large volume of secondary material on the country and on the 1967 and 1973 Arab-Israeli wars. I also undertook interviews in Egypt (May 1996, June 1998), Israel (June 1998), Washington,

---

[63] On the utility of qualitative methods for studying a "process," see Odell (2006: 37).

[64] On "analytic" process tracing and the concept in general, see George and Bennett (2004: chap. 10).

[65] For studies on Egypt, see the literature reviews in chapters 3 and 4 for each case.

DC (March 1998), and London (1997-1998) with former government officials and politicians from Egypt as well as academic and policy experts on the periods under consideration. In some cases these interviews are directly cited in the text that follows, but in other instances I relied on them as background material to check my understanding of events.

SUPPLEMENTARY STUDIES

I supplement the Egypt studies with six brief cases: Britain before the First World War (1902-1914); Germany before the First World War (1890-1914); Britain during the First World War (1914-1918); Turkey during and immediately following the tenure of the country's first Islamist prime minister, Necmettin Erbakan (1996-1999); Pakistan under Prime Minister Nawaz Sharif (1997-1999); and the United States in the months prior to its March 2003 war against Iraq (2002-2003). For reasons of space these studies are shorter and less comprehensive than the Egypt chapters, and they focus on those attributes of strategic assessment that are especially salient in the given case. Although necessarily less detailed, they nonetheless make an important contribution to the empirical analysis: They provide analytical completeness to the study by allowing me to examine each of the theory's core hypotheses in at least one case study, and some in multiple studies. In selecting these cases, my use of typological theory helped me identify the configurations of my causal variables, or "types," that should be present in the candidate cases.[66] Accordingly, these cases provide maximum variation on my independent variables and capture all relevant types (see fig. 2.2).

Two additional criteria motivated the selection of these cases. First, the cases allow me to control for other variables that could confound my analysis. As noted above, my goal is to evaluate the effect of civil-military relations on assessment. But to the extent other variables might also affect strategic assessment, I need to address them. Similar to the effects of an omitted variable, an alternative cause that is correlated with civil-military relations with similar predicted effects on assessment could magnify my results, making it appear that those relations were far more consequential than actually justified by the empirical record. Alternatively, a factor correlated with my independent variables but inversely related to assessment could partially nullify my results, lessening the apparent effects of civil-military relations on assessment. My principal strategy to deal with the potentially confounding effects of alternative causes, as I explain in detail below, is to choose cases in which these variables are held constant, even while civil-military relations vary.[67]

---

[66] For an overview of typological theorizing, see George and Bennett (2004: chap. 11). For a recent example in international security, see Elman (2005).

[67] King, Keohane, and Verba (1994: 169-70) draw the analogy of omitted variables bias from quantitative analysis and recommend controlling for its effects through case selection.

VARIATION IN STRATEGIC ASSESSMENT   57

	Political Dominance	Shared Power	Military Dominance*
High	Egypt, 1970-1981 U.S., 2002-2003	Pakistan, 1997-99 Egypt, 1962-67 Britain, 1914-1918	
			Turkey, 1996-99
Low	Britain, 1902-14	Germany, 1890-1914	

Preference Divergence (vertical axis) / **Balance of Power** (horizontal axis)

Figure 2.2. Variation in Empirical Cases

One potential alternative explanation is suggested by realist theories of international relations: that the level of threat that the state faces in the international arena will shape the quality of strategic assessment. Realist logic suggests that states facing threats should rationalize assessment because they want to protect their interests. Alternatively, we might also expect states harboring international ambitions to have incentives to generate functional routines for assessment. I address these arguments by choosing states primarily that have different civil-military relations but that all face threats or harbor ambitions (i.e., I control for international stimuli by maintaining them at a high level). This is true for both Egypt cases,[68] the

---

On the theme of comparing qualitative and quantitative research, also see Brady and Collier (2004), Sprinz and Wolinsky-Nahmias (2004), Mahoney and Goertz (2006).

[68] Realists might contend that Egypt did not face a real "threat" from Israel in the 1960s. Therefore Egypt had few incentives to rationalize its policies prior to 1967 and was simply caught off guard in the May/June 1967 crisis that preceded the Six Day War (thereby explaining its poor political-military coordination). However, even if Israel was not a "threat" before 1967, with the onset of a serious crisis in mid-May (a crisis the Egyptians initiated and escalated), Egypt faced substantial incentives to rationalize its decision-making structures. My analysis below shows that despite the very real possibility of war, international incentives did not alleviate, and instead exacerbated, the pathologies of Egypt's institutions. That the threat was "low" is in itself debatable. Egypt was engaged in a fierce contest for influence in the region with the Arab monarchies (Kerr's "Arab Cold War"), including actually fighting a proxy war against the Saudis in Yemen. Its ally, Syria, had also had several serious run-ins with Israel. This was an extremely tense period in the region.

United States,[69] Germany,[70] Pakistan, and Turkey.[71] From the perspective of realist theory these states might be considered "least likely" cases for my theory: international incentives should trump the domestic dynamics I point to in every instance (Eckstein 1975; George and Bennett 2004: 121). If I find, despite the rationalizing incentives posed by international stimuli, that the domestic imperatives of civil-military relations often override them, it lends important support to my theory.

Other research on civil military relations suggests that divisions within the civilian elite could also influence assessment institutions. Deborah Avant (1994) for example, demonstrates how splits within the civilian leadership induced by political institutions affect oversight of military activity; Elizabeth Kier (1997) explores how conflict within the civilian sphere over normative conceptions of the armed forces' role in the state shapes the parameters whereby militaries develop doctrine. These studies suggest that when civilians disagree over strategic or policy outcomes it might also influence processes for strategic assessment. Intra-civilian preference divergence could generate incentives for politicians to compete to structure assessment in ways that advantage their favored outcomes (just as it does for political and military leaders when they disagree).

One rationale for choosing the Egyptian cases is that in neither instance are divisions within the civilian elite apt to be a major cause of assessment; these divisions are held constant at a low or absent level. Egypt's political leadership was relatively unitary by the late 1950s and there were no independent, political bodies within the state empowered in the process of foreign and security policymaking. Gamal Abdel Nasser concentrated political power in his own hands initially as a leader of the Revolutionary Command Council after the July 1952 coup, and after 1954 as president. Anwar Sadat marginalized his opponents seven months after coming to power; in May 1971 he purged Egypt's powerful leftist constituency in

---

[69] Regardless of whether the United States went to war against Iraq to confront a threat or it was an ideological war of choice, military and political leaders had incentives to rationalize strategic assessment to ensure a successful political-military strategy and international outcome. For part of the reason they failed to do so, see chapter 7.

[70] There is of course a debate about what exactly German preferences for war were in 1914. However, most historians agree that, at the least, it favored a limited war in the Balkans. Moreover, regardless of the magnitude of its ambitions, Germany wanted to keep Britain out of any continental war that might occur. These international ambitions might have encouraged rationalize assessment, but they did not. For discussion of the literature on Germany and the case analysis, see chapter 5.

[71] In contrast to the six cases listed here, one could make the argument that Britain did not face a threat or harbor ambitions in the first decade of the twentieth century (because the German threat had not yet manifested), but this actually renders it all the more surprising that it still rationalized civil-military assessment (as I argue in chapter 5). Conversely, if one accepts that Germany was a growing threat, the fact that it rationalized assessment cannot be wholly explained by its international environment. See chapter 5, where I make this latter point.

his so-called corrective revolution, eliminating his major competitors from power. In the other cases, the civilian leadership is unified or unitary,[72] civilian divisions are inconsequential for assessment because of the particularities of the case and issues I investigate, or I deal with the issue explicitly in the empirical analysis.[73]

Interservice rivalry is a third potential cause of assessment institutions.[74] Service competition over budgets, other corporate issues, or war-fighting philosophy, for example, could generate incentives for military leaders to resist sharing damaging information or engaging in forthcoming debate in order to insulate themselves from attacks by their sister organizations. Services might also collude in support of procedures that mutually benefit their organizational interests but undermine the quality of assessment as a whole. Conversely, interservice rivalry might promote better assessment by prompting the services to report information about each other, thereby indirectly advancing information sharing (Sapolsky 1997: 51). To isolate the effects of interservice rivalry, I chose cases in which one service dominates and therefore is in a position to interact with the political leadership relatively unburdened by competition from other branches. This is true, for example, in the Egyptian cases. In addition, in all the cases I focus primarily on one service—the army—and its relations with the political leadership; in many cases I am interested in issues related to ground wars and armed conflicts and the military strategies and operational plans associated with them, where the army is the relevant actor in assessment. Interservice rivalry might still complicate army-civilian relations at times, but I am sensitive to this possibility in my empirical analysis and address it if it becomes an issue.

The literature reviewed in chapter 1 about presidential advisory systems and crisis decision making suggests that a leader's psychological state could also affect strategic assessment: problematic institutions, for example, might be established by leaders with personality disorders or deficiencies in character. In most of the cases studied here, the political leaders do not exhibit psychological attributes that might render the state especially vulnerable to poor assessment. In two cases, however, a leader's psychology/personality does emerge as an issue: in the United States under Defense Secretary Rumsfeld and Germany under Kaiser Wilhelm II. In a literature review that precedes each case I address these issues, arguing that

---

[72] Arguably Wilhelmine Germany also represents a case of a unified political leadership, at least in regard to matters of "international security." Although the Reichstag retained crucial budgetary prerogatives, responsibility for all matters of defense and foreign policy lay with the kaiser. This interpretation of the kaiser's prerogatives in security policy is consistent with the historical literature. See chapter 5.

[73] Intracivilian divisions emerge, for example, as an important issue in my analysis of Britain in the decade before the First World War. See chapter 5.

[74] The importance of interservice rivalry (and collusion) is a key theme in Snyder (1991b).

personality is insufficient to explain assessment and masks deeper structural dynamics of civil-military relations.

Finally, my case selection deals with a fifth possibility—that regime type determines assessment—in two ways. First I undertake diachronic comparison of assessment within authoritarian and democratic states. This "before and after" approach allows me to hold constant regime type while studying the effects of changes in civil-military relations on assessment.[75] In the two British cases, for example, I explore whether changes in civil-military relations affected strategic assessment despite the fact that political institutions remain relatively unchanged (this, for example, in part motivated the decision to extend the prewar study of Britain into the world war). In Egypt, conversely, I analyze whether changes in the authoritarian regime's civil-military relations correspond with changes in strategic assessment. Second, I undertake synchronic comparisons across different cases to show that despite wide variation in regime type, changes in strategic assessment correlate with changes in civil-military relations.[76]

In this respect, and more broadly, my study approximates one that relies on Mill's method of agreement and method of difference (or what is sometimes referred to, using Przeworski and Teune's terminology, as a most different, and a most similar research design, respectively).[77] I employ a method of difference when I analyze the longitudinal cases of Britain and then again with the two cases of Egypt. In each set of cases, I examine the effects on the dependent variable (assessment) of differences in the independent variable (civil-military relations) while holding constant culture, political institutions, and other contextual variables. I also rely on a method of difference in the studies of Egypt, Turkey, and Pakistan. These states have a shared tradition of military involvement in politics. Therefore I examine whether more subtle variations in their civil military relations (i.e., not just the military's historical prominence in state and society) such as the balance of power and preference divergence actually cause differences in strategic assessment. Finally, I employ a method of agreement when comparing Egypt in the mid-1960s, Pakistan in the latter 1990s, and Britain during the First World War. I predict that similar dynamics in civil-military relations should produce parallel effects on strategic assessment. Following the logic of Mill's approach, equivalent findings in these cases, despite the broad variation in underlying conditions, would lend support to the theory.

In short, I have been conscious in my case selection to minimize the effects of known variables that might confound the analysis and to test

---

[75] On "before and after" research designs, see George and Bennett (2004: 166).

[76] For an example of diachronic and synchronic comparison as a basis for a research design, see Spruyt (2005: 34–35).

[77] On approximating Mill's methods, see Odell (2006: 39–40). Also see George and Bennett (2004: 153–61), Mahoney (2003: 341–43).

the theory in cases with substantial contextual differences and similarities. Nevertheless, it is difficult to control for every potential alternative explanation in every case. Fortunately, one of the best ways to compensate for this potential problem, as George and Bennett discuss (2004: 159, 214), is through within-case process tracing. By tracing the actual process through which civil-military relations affect assessment, I can confirm (or disconfirm) that my variables were causative in each case. I can also isolate the effects of other variables and address any possible implications they have for the analysis.

Here it may be helpful to note an additional strategy I employ in the empirical chapters. Before beginning the analysis, in each chapter I provide a survey of the country-specific scholarship as it pertains to issues of civil-military relations and strategic assessment. In these sections I trace alternative arguments about what caused assessment in the *particular* empirical case, as opposed to exploring broader themes about what causes assessment in general as I do here (although, as we might expect, there is overlap between the two). This allows readers to see what others have argued about the case and understand what I hope to explain and contribute to the empirical record with my theory of assessment.

In summary, two major reasons motivating case selection are achieving variation on my independent variables and controlling for alternative causes of assessment. A final reason motivating case selection relates to what Stephen Van Evera refers to as the "intrinsic human or historical importance" of the cases (1997: 86–87). Several of the cases have paramount contemporary importance: the United States, Pakistan, and Turkey. Others, like Britain and Germany, as well as the Egypt studies, have had profound historical consequences. In the instance of Germany, I also wanted to include a case with which scholars are highly familiar to provide common intellectual ground for judging my analysis. Conversely, I included Britain because, of the major protagonists in the First World War, it is among the least studied by scholars of international security; in addition, the decade leading up to the war in Britain, with a few exceptions, has been virtually unstudied by political scientists (the case, of course, also meets the selection criteria discussed above). Admittedly, there are other cases that I could have chosen to test my theory. The theory, in principle, has broad applicability to cases where the varieties of civil-military relations I highlight occur. But reasons of space and the complexity of some of the empirical material require limiting the number of case studies in the book; nevertheless the number (eight) still meets or exceeds that in many comparable monographs in international security.

Three

EGYPT IN THE MID-1960s

FOR SUCH A BRIEF and localized conflict, the June 1967 Arab-Israeli War remains one of the most consequential wars of modern history. For diplomats, the Six Day War represents a benchmark in their efforts to bring peace to the Middle East. In less than a week, Israel captured Jordan's West Bank, East Jerusalem, the Golan Heights, the Gaza Strip, and the Sinai Peninsula—areas that today, with the exception of the latter, remain the subject of dispute and sometimes fretful negotiations. For military analysts, the 1967 war demonstrated the remarkable inefficacy of the Egyptian and Syrian militaries—puzzles to be resolved.

Perhaps most striking, for academics and informal observers alike, however, is the phenomenon of the war itself. In the spring of 1967 no one—Egyptian, Israeli, American, or otherwise—anticipated an Arab-Israeli war. Nevertheless, from mid-May through the beginning of June, Egypt's President Nasser took a number of increasingly provocative actions that inflamed tensions with Israel, ultimately precipitating a preemptive strike and ending in Egypt's disastrous defeat on the battlefield.

Why would Nasser pursue a strategy with a high probability of ending in war? Why would he pursue a war he was bound to lose? More broadly, why, if "no government plotted or intended to start a war in the Middle East in the spring of 1967," did war, nonetheless, occur?[1]

Analysts commonly attribute the war to a shortfall in rationality, due either to Nasser's personality or to the fever and confusion of crisis decision making. Others explain the war as the result of regional pressures on Nasser or the outcome of a failed bluff aimed at securing a political victory without resort to force. However, as I explain below, none of these arguments fully explains a central puzzle of the war: why Nasser, a seasoned and pragmatic leader, held firm in provocations of Israel in the final days of a crisis that would culminate in Egypt's humiliating rout on the battlefield.

In this chapter I examine the Egypt 1967 case in the context of this book's argument about the causes of strategic assessment. Specifically the case evaluates a central hypothesis of the study: When military and political leaders are sharing power and have divergent preferences over policy and strategic issues, assessment will be extremely poor.

---

[1] Statement is from Charles Yost, a former adviser on Middle Eastern affairs to the State Department and former ambassador to Syria (Yost 1968: 319).

As I describe below, although Egypt's President Nasser is often perceived as a formidable leader in the region, at home by the mid-1960s he was effectively sharing power with his military chief, Abdel Hakim Amer, with whom his preferences over a variety of issues increasingly diverged. In this setting I expect political-military competition to undermine information sharing and yield a convoluted authorization process. The military's structural competence in intelligence and evaluating its capabilities degrades as the leaders elevate partisan criteria over skill in promotions and appointments. In addition, strategic coordination suffers as military leaders resist forthright coordination with the political leader and diplomats. In every respect these states should be poorly equipped at strategic assessment.

The analysis that follows confirms the devastating impact of Egypt's civil-military relations on strategic assessment. In the process it illuminates Nasser's confrontational strategy in the May/June 1967 crisis and helps explain why the state precipitated a war that would lead to its own military destruction. Although poor assessment predisposed Egypt to numerous problems, one emerges as especially significant: These processes limited the quality of information available to Nasser about the state of his military capabilities, which led him to overestimate Egypt's capacity to hold its own in a war against Israel. He then maintained a provocative strategy in the final days of the crisis, precipitating Israel's attack. Nasser's intransigence, based in part on a flawed evaluation of Egypt's capabilities, foreclosed the possibility of a peaceful settlement to the crisis.

I begin by providing some background and then situate the argument in existing explanations for the origins of Nasser's strategy in the 1967 crisis. Discussion of the theory's causal variables, power and preference divergence, follows. I then discuss the effects these civil-military relations had on strategic assessment in Egypt, focusing in particular on the May/June crisis. The chapter closes with a discussion of Nasser's strategy in the crisis, Israel's reaction, and the origins of the 1967 war.

Background to the 1967 War

The 1960s were a tense time in the Arab world, referred to by Malcom Kerr (1965) as "the Arab Cold War." The conservative Arab monarchies, and Saudi Arabia in particular, were engaged in fierce competition with the progressively oriented Arab nationalist states for influence in the region. In the ideological battle Nasser was a chief antagonist. His early foreign policy successes, including his political victory during the 1956 Suez conflict, helped elevate him to that position.

By the mid-1960s, however, Nasser had endured some serious blows to his reputation as regional leader. The first was the dissolution of Egypt's short-lived union with Syria (the "United Arab Republic") in 1961. That was followed by Egypt's long and inconclusive involvement in Yemen's civil war (1962–1967) (Nutting 1972: 338–57; Rahmy 1983). Nasser had also laid low during several skirmishes between Israel, Syria, and Jordan (Stein 1991; Oren 2002; Parker 1993; Gawrych 2000: 5). By 1967 his standing with his Arab allies and competitors was suffering (Shamir 1998: 74).

It was in this tense international environment that in mid-May 1967 the Soviet Union (falsely) reported to Nasser that Israel was mobilizing forces and planned to attack Syria.[2] This was the spark that would ignite the 1967 Arab-Israeli War.

Hoping to bolster his flagging campaign for ideological leadership of the Arab world, Nasser responded to the report on May 14 by ordering forces into the Sinai Peninsula. On May 16 Egypt followed up with a request for a redeployment of United Nations Emergency Forces (UNEF) stationed in the Sinai to make way for Egypt's military deployments.[3] The crisis might have ended there, much like an earlier incident, the Rotem crisis, had in 1960.[4] But, in a controversial decision, the UN secretary general refused the request for a partial redeployment of UNEF forces.

Subsequently, on May 18, the Egyptians sent a letter to the UN command requesting the full withdrawal of UN forces from the area, and the United Nations complied. Egypt then escalated deployments to the Sinai, including to the strategically sensitive area at the tip of the Sinai Peninsula, Sharm al-Sheikh. The occupation of Sharm al-Sheikh opened the door to an even more ominous potentiality: the closure of the Straits of Tiran to Israeli shipping. On May 22, 1967, in a speech to the Air Force Command at the Bir Gifgafa airfield in the Sinai, Nasser announced the decision to close the straits.

Notably, despite its devastating end, the Israelis had not been especially alarmed by Nasser's provocations at the start of the crisis. Many viewed Nasser's initial deployments and his request for UNEF redeployment as "political gestures" intended mainly for inter-Arab consumption (Bar-

---

[2] Why the Soviets passed an inaccurate report remains a mystery. See Parker (1996: 15–27, 35–53). For an especially provocative interpretation of why they did, see Ginor and Remez (2007).

[3] In 1951 Egypt closed the straits to Israeli ships and those carrying strategic materials bound for Eilat (Parker 1993: 40). The straits remained closed until the 1956 Suez war; opening them had been one of the concessions granted Israel in exchange for its withdrawal. In 1957 UNEF forces were stationed in the Sinai.

[4] In 1960 Nasser sent troops to the Sinai, asked for a redeployment of UN troops, claimed that he had deterred Israel's purported aggressive designs, and then withdrew. On the "Rotem crisis," see Bar-Joseph (1996: 547–66), Eban (1992: 357), Stein (1991: 130).

Siman-Tov 1987: 92, 94; Brown 1991: 128). But the closure was an altogether different matter. As Israel's foreign minister Abba Eban put it, "among Egypt's provocative acts, the concentration of troops heightened tension, but the blockade of the Straits was 'the most electric shock of all'" (cited in Brecher 1975: 343). Although Israel had been deliberately oblique in its early responses to Nasser's actions, it had long stated publicly that closure of the straits would constitute cause for war (Bar-Siman-Tov 1987: 98, 100; Hammel 1992: 32).[5] Most analysts agree that Nasser could not fail to know that closing the Straits of Tiran was a serious escalation of the crisis (Stephens 1971: 484; Parker 1993: 61; Bailey 1985: 30).[6]

Equally significant, on June 1 the Israelis reshuffled their cabinet in a sign of resolve for war. Although the dovish Levi Eshkol retained the prime ministership, Moshe Dayan was given the post of defense minister, and Menachem Begin and Joseph Saphir, prominent members of right-wing parties, were brought in as ministers without portfolio.[7] The establishment of a "war cabinet" resolved any lingering doubts about Israel's willingness to fight (Parker 1993: 56; Eban 1992: 403). As one observer put it, "the appointment of Dayan was a decision in itself—to take up Nasser's challenge" (Bar-Zohar 1970: 173). Nasser himself viewed the cabinet change as an important signal. As he later put it, "the political changes in Israel at the beginning of June and our close following of what was happening inside Israel made us feel that the war was certainly going to take place" (Draper 1967: 243; Gawrych 2000: 12).[8] On June 2, in a meeting with military commanders, he told them that he was certain that the Israelis would strike within forty-eight to seventy-two hours.[9]

---

[5] After 1956, closure of the straits was the most frequently stated casus belli in Israeli strategic doctrine (Stein and Tanter 1980:105–6).

[6] By Nasser's own admission, closure upped the probability of war. According to Nasser's confidant, Mohammed Heikal, he put the odds that the crisis would culminate in war at 50 percent; Egypt's vice president, Zakariya Mohieddin, put the figure at 80–100 percent (Parker 1993: 73; Stephens 1971: 477; Sadat 1978: 172). For a view that closure did not inevitably lead to war, see Abu-Lughod (1970: 53).

[7] Prior to this, Prime Minister Levi Eshkol had been defense minister.

[8] He reports as much in a newspaper interview on June 3. For a summary of the interview, see Mansoor (1972, June 3 entry); see also Stephens (1971: 477, 487) and Kimche and Bawle (1968: 111).

[9] There are several accounts of this meeting by first-hand participants. The accounts differ slightly as to what time-frame he gave. Sadat reports that Nasser said to expect an attack on June 3, 4, or 5 (Sadat 1978: 172). Mahmoud Riad said June 5; General Fawzi, June 4 or 5 (Parker 1993: 57). Nasser himself said he warned the high command to expect an attack in forty-eight to seventy-two hours (Draper 1967: 242; Oren 2002: 158; Hinnebusch 1985: 12). Despite these statements, a few observers still question whether Nasser was wholly convinced that war was imminent. Among these is the British journalist Anthony Nutting: On June 3 Nasser gave an interview to him stating that "as far as he was concerned the Middle East crisis had eased and that he planned no further escalation." Nasser also mentioned to a fellow Free Officer that he thought war would not come soon (Brown 1991: 126–27). However, also

Herein lies a central puzzle of the 1967 war. After the cabinet change, by his own admission, Nasser thought war was inevitable. If he truly wanted to avoid war, no matter what, now was the time to temporize. Yet he stood firm, ultimately acquiescing in Israel's attack and inviting his own military destruction. Three days passed between his June 2 meeting with his military commanders, when Nasser had by his own words admitted that war was inevitable, and the Israeli attack on June 5. Yet Nasser took no action to signal he intended to back down during this period.

Moreover, he stood firm despite two opportunities to indicate a softening of his position. On May 31 former U.S. treasury secretary Robert B. Anderson met with Nasser in an unpublicized meeting, and then on June 1 former ambassador Charles Yost met with presidential adviser Mahmoud Riad in Cairo.[10] Neither Yost nor Anderson left their visits with the impression that the Egyptians would "undo their actions."[11] Nasser indicated no flexibility on the deployments in the Sinai, or on the blockade (Quandt 1992: 42–46; Stein and Tanter 1980: 231; Parker 1993: 56; Oren 2002: 144). Rather, throughout the meetings, Nasser repeatedly expressed his confidence in his military capability, telling Anderson, for example, that "he was confident of the outcome of a conflict between the Arabs and Israelis" (cited in Quandt 1993: 516, n. 65). As one observer put it, "[Nasser] was well aware of what the stakes were."[12] Despite the profound consequences of his strategy, Nasser stood firm in the face of imminent war.[13]

---

on June 3, Nasser gave a second interview with the London *Observer* in which he stated that given the "comeback" of Moshe Dayan as defense minister, he feared a surprise attack by Israel. Overall, Nasser's reactions to the June 1 cabinet change, conversations with foreign officials, statements at the June 2 meeting with his military command, which are reported by multiple observers, and the specificity of the information he conveyed all suggest he was indeed convinced an attack was highly likely. Given the stakes involved, even a strong expectation of an attack warranted serious action on his part to avoid war. See Nutting (1972: 408–9), Oren (2002: 159); the press reports appear in Mansoor (1972: June 3 entry). On why some might have had a different take on Nasser's view, see Brown (1991: 132).

[10] There is some ambiguity about whether Anderson met with Nasser on the evening of May 31 or the following day; Anderson's diplomatic correspondence does not specify the time (Parker 1993: 252, n. 37).

[11] Remarks by Donald Bergus, in Parker (1996: 191). See Parker (1993: 233–39) for copies of the telegrams sent to Washington by Anderson and Yost expressing their pessimism about the chances of Egypt changing its position on the straits or the deployments.

[12] Remarks by Ephraim Evron (in Parker 1996: 129).

[13] Some observers, especially those sympathetic to Nasser's plight, have pointed to the fact that the president had agreed to a variety of small measures as evidence that he was seeking peaceful settlement (Nutting 1972: 411; Abu-Lughod 1970: 53; Heikal 1973: 243; Lacouture 1973: 307). He had agreed to send the dispute to the International Court of Justice and to allow his vice president, Zakariya Mohieddin, to travel to Washington to discuss the issues. In addition, when the United Nations secretary general, U Thant, visited in late May, Nasser acquiesced to a proposal that Egypt would not enforce the blockade of the straits if Israel agreed not to send any ships through to test it (Nutting 1972: 404; Heikal 1973: 243) However, seen in context of a potentially imminent military strike, all of these actions fall far short

The resolution of the crisis is well known: on the morning of June 5, Israeli forces launched a series of airstrikes that decimated the Egyptian air force. Egypt did not fare much better in subsequent ground operations. Most military analysts agree that the Egyptian military had been poorly prepared for war.[14] Its command and control was poor, quality of generalship and tactical leadership weak, training deeply deficient, and logistics poor. By midday on June 6, Amer ordered a complete withdrawal of Egyptian forces, precipitating a chaotic exodus from the Sinai. At the end of the war, Israel occupied Egypt's territory in the Gaza Strip and Sinai Peninsula, as well as the West Bank, East Jerusalem, and Golan Heights.

The Context of the Egyptian Case

Why did Nasser put Egypt on a collision course for war, maintaining an intransigent strategy in the final days of a crisis that would end in the military's devastating defeat? Within the voluminous literature on the 1967 crisis and war, four themes on the origins of the war are pervasive. The first is that Nasser stumbled into war in 1967. Cognitive blinders (Lebow 1981: 284–85, 243–44, 253–54; Stein 1980), a flash of impulsiveness (Parker 1993: 79), or Nasser's innate personality,[15] in combination with the pathologies endemic to decision making in crises in general, precluded the president from effectively pulling Egypt away from the brink of war.

The problem with these explanations is, as Mor (1991) cogently argues, much of the presumption of irrationality is a product of post hoc analysis: The outcome was irrational (provoking a war one is unprepared for), and therefore the decisions themselves are presumed to be irrational.[16]

---

of any truly concerted and urgent effort to avert war in those final few days. In the meeting with Anderson, Nasser himself belittled the possibility that the International Court of Justice could successfully arbitrate the dispute (Oren 2002: 144). The sending of Mohiedden was not accompanied by any other indication of softening in his position. Moreover, if he was seeking a peaceful solution, the fact that Nasser deliberately announced the decision to close the Straits of Tiran before U Thant's arrival (so that the latter could not head it off) is puzzling (on this issue, see U Thant's memorandum in Nassif 1988: 89). Even if these were concessions, they fell far short of what would be required to avoid war; therefore, why Nasser so drastically underestimated what was necessary still needs to be explained (here I argue it is because he overestimated his capabilities).

[14] See Gawrych (1991, 1996, 2000), Dupuy (1978), Pollack (1996), Brooks (1998; 2006), Hammel (1992), Insight Team (1974), Cordesman and Wagner (1990). For background on Egypt's "war preparation," financial, and production strategies, see Barnett (1992).

[15] According to Parker (1993: 79), Zakariya Mohieddin, Egypt's vice president, attributed Nasser's behavior to a flare-up of his diabetes. Nutting (1972) attributes the war to Nasser's personality traits.

[16] For a summary and critique of "nonrational" approaches to the 1967 war, see Mor (1991: 361).

Certainly Nasser was "reacting" to the manifest actions of Israel and the expressed interests of his neighbors, but this does not mean that he was not also assessing his options and calculating their likely consequences, albeit under conditions of uncertainty. In fact, there is much evidence to suggest that Nasser was systematically evaluating his options and updating his beliefs about the likely outcome of the crisis; as many observers report, he was even phrasing his evaluations in terms of probabilities, and in particular the probability that the crisis would culminate in war (Stephens 1971: 477; Sadat 1978: 172; Parker 1993: 73; Oren 2002: 83; Stein 1991: 134; Gawrych 2000: 8).[17] To the extent the process of evaluation was flawed during the crisis, this is something to be explained. As I argue below, this was due to the nature of strategic assessment in Egypt at the time.

A second interpretation of the crisis suggests that, far from stumbling into it, Nasser was deliberately seeking war in May 1967.[18] For those in Cairo at that time, for example, the military deployments had the striking air of premeditation; to the U.S. Embassy staff in Cairo, the initial deployments "looked as though Nasser and Amer had decided their army was ready to take on Israel and were looking for a pretext" (Parker 1993: 38). Moreover, especially after the closure of the Straits of Tiran, in their internal debates Israeli cabinet members sometimes characterized Nasser as seeking war (Segev 2007: 234, 256, 257, 258; Stein and Tanter 1980: 168; Hammel 1992: 40; Stein 1980: 140, 118; Oren 2002: 97–99).[19] If, however, the events of May/June 1967 were the result of a deliberate campaign by the Egyptians to incite war, Nasser's willingness to do so when his military was so inadequately prepared for battle with Israel is mysterious. Why would Nasser pursue a war for which he was so poorly prepared?

A third theme that emerges in the literature is that Egypt was pressured into going to war by its Arab neighbors (Brecher 1975: 324; Kerr 1969; Eban 1992: 401–2; Yost 1968: 310, 316; Amos 1979: 58–59; Gawrych 2000:

---

[17] Cited here are reports by observers of what Nasser was calculating at the time of the crisis. For self-reports of how he was evaluating the probability of war throughout, see Nasser's Revolution Day speech of July 23, 1967. A transcript appears in Draper (1967: 238–44). As for Nasser's demeanor in the crisis, the president did not appear confused or emotionally distraught to outside observers; that is, like a man who had lost his capacity to reason. For example, Robert Anderson reported that, in their June 1 meeting, "Nasser was relaxed, in sport clothes, and seemed confident both in his intelligence and in his military capability" (quoted in Parker 1993: 237).

[18] This theme is examined in detail in Brown (1991: 128–30).

[19] After the closure, the Israelis became increasingly convinced that Nasser was planning a first strike and was committed to war (Stein 1980: 140; 118; Stein and Tanter 1980; Oren 2002: 97–99; also see Ephraim Ephron's comments in Parker 1996: 126–36). It was especially the case with Israel's military leaders, who increasingly warned that Nasser might be planning to attack. See Segev (2007: 234, 256–58).

6; Brown 1991: 125–26).[20] Nasser, caught in the rhetorical cross-fire, was impelled to confront the Israelis; retreating from his provocations would have provoked the criticism of the conservative Arab states and his nationalist allies, severely damaging his regional reputation. Admittedly, the external pressures on Nasser were severe. But they alone cannot explain Nasser's strategy in May/June 1967. After all, backing down, although costly, would ultimately have proven less harmful to his reputation than the revelation that his regime and its "vanguard" military—the basis for Nasser's claim to Arab leadership—was bankrupt as a fighting force; it is hard to see how a well-choreographed retreat, perhaps under the auspices of the superpowers, would have proven less damaging than the war's actual outcome. As it was, the war and the forces it unleashed "paved the way for the undoing of Nasserism as a foreign policy" (Hinnebusch 1985: 36; Nutting 1972: 424). Hence, if Nasser was acting to protect his reputation, why did he not work harder to avoid a war that would end in a degrading military loss and devastate his standing in the Arab world?

The fourth argument about the origins of war in 1967 is that Nasser, knowing the poor state of his military and his inability to successfully take on the Israelis, was trying to bluff his way into a political victory.[21] This explanation makes sense to a point. A bluff depended, in part, on Israeli preferences or "resolve" in the face of the Egyptian challenge. In the initial phase there was some uncertainty about Israeli preferences, given divisions in the Israeli cabinet. Prime Minister Eshkol's dovish tendencies were well known (Eban 1992: 362).[22] Moreover, as noted above, prior to the closure the Israelis had been deliberately oblique in their responses to Nasser's provocations. Equally important, Nasser could have thought that the Americans would restrain the Israelis.

There are two problems with this argument. First, in public and private statements, there is no indication that Nasser was knowingly mounting a

---

[20] There is also a variant that combines the regional pressure and cognitive arguments. Stein (1996: 132) asserts that Nasser knew before the war that he could not win, but, because of regional pressures, he experienced psychologically motivated bias that led him to overestimate his capabilities. For a critique, see Lieberman (1995: 876–84). Also note that, in context of a total war against Israel, he may have anticipated a loss but thought he would perform well in a war of short duration (see below).

[21] This theme is explored in detail in Brown (1991). At the time some in Egypt assumed Nasser must have been bluffing, including Sayed Marei, deputy prime minister in the National Assembly, and Ahmad Hassan al-Feki, undersecretary of foreign affairs. See Parker (1993: 80, 82).

[22] Israeli Foreign Minister Abba Eban notes that, according to Israeli intelligence reports, the Soviet Embassy in Tel Aviv was telling the Egyptians that "the Eshkol government did not have the domestic authority for a decision involving war" (1992: 362). On divisions and debate in the cabinet and Levi Eshkol's concerns about launching an attack, see, for example Oren (2002: 122–24, 149), Eban (1977: 333–34), Rabin (1979: 86–89), Nutting (1972: 405).

campaign of deception. Of course, it makes sense that publicly he would affirm his capabilities (it was essential to the bluff), but privately he did not communicate any intention to mislead the Israelis, even to his close confidante Mohammed Heikal (Parker 1993: 81–82; Haykal 1973: 241–45). Second, and more important, if Nasser was trying to bluff his way to victory, why, if he knew the true state of his military, did he not back down even when he believed war was a near certainty? If Nasser anticipated a devastating defeat, he faced tremendous incentives to defuse the crisis once he knew of the Israelis' intention to attack. Instead, rather than indicate a softening of his position, in the final days before the war Nasser remained intransigent over the key issues that might have averted war.[23]

In sum, none of the extant scholarship alone offers a complete explanation for why Nasser provoked a war in which Egypt was doomed to defeat: It cannot explain why he maintained an intransigent strategy even in the final days of a crisis that would end in his devastating defeat on the battlefield. Below I show how Nasser's strategy in those final days is best explained by Egypt's civil-military relations. Specifically, I argue that those relations generated pathologies in assessment such that Nasser overestimated his military capabilities. Hence, he believed that Egypt had the wherewithal to hold its own and fight well against Israel, even if it would not ultimately win in a conflict of long duration. Armed with this inflated estimate of Egypt's capabilities, Nasser had incentives to maintain his confrontational strategy in the final days of the crisis—a strategy to which Israel's best response was war.

Note that in making this argument I am not the first to observe that Egypt's civil-military relations were contentious; the literature is riddled with references to the rivalry between Nasser and his military chief, Abdel Hakim Amer, as we might expect given the seriousness of the conflict between them. Nor am I the first to suggest that Nasser had an inflated sense of his military capabilities (see Laqueur 1969; Parker 1993; Lebow 1981; Nutting 1972; Stein 1991). Rather, this study contributes by situating the Egypt case in a broader theory of strategic assessment. It explains why, on analytical grounds, we might expect civil-military relations in Egypt at the time to have yielded such profound flaws in strategic assessment.

Before analyzing these problems of strategic assessment, however, let us step back and look at the state of civil-military relations that caused them. I begin with a discussion of Nasser's political coalition.

---

[23] One additional theme in the literature suggests that Egypt in 1967 was the victim of a conspiracy by the Syrians, Soviets, American, or Israelis. For example, observers argue that the United States conspired to take out Nasser by pressuring him to hold firm while Israel attacked, or that Israel deliberately "trapped" Egypt in 1967 (Lacouture 1973: 301; Nutting 1972: 397–98). Parker (1992b) reviews these arguments but finds little empirical support for any of them. For an argument that the Soviets were responsible, see Ginor and Remez (2007).

Egypt's Civil-Military Relations in the Mid-1960s

The Political-Military Balance of Power

Gamal Abdel Nasser first came to power in July 1952 as part of the Free Officers coup that removed the corrupt King Farouk from power. Although initially just one among several prominent figures in Egypt's Revolutionary Command Council, Nasser soon sidelined opponents to his rule, including the regime's first president, General Nagib.[24] By the spring of 1954 Nasser had become the unchallenged leader of the regime and consolidated power in his own right.

Like many coup leaders who seek to secure civilian support after their takeovers, from the start Nasser and his fellow Free Officers moved to create a social base for their rule (Hinnebusch 1985: 13; Baker 1978: 25–84; Stephens 1971: 109–39). In the early days they experimented with a variety of policies and approaches, courting a diverse group of constituencies (Baker 1978: 49; Barnett 1992: 83; Abdel Malek 1968: xiv).[25] However, by the early 1960s a particular approach emerged within the regime. Nasser cultivated his civilian base by appealing to the urban industrial working and middle classes as well as the rural middle class. A snapshot of the broad initiatives pursued by the regime in the 1950s and early 1960s reveals this coalitional pattern. For example, the regime advanced moderate land reform and revisions in the land tenure system. It established price controls on the rental of housing and agricultural land as well as for essential foodstuffs, cooking oil, gasoline, and electricity. The regime subsidized local transportation, provided free education and health care (the latter included immunization campaigns and the creation of seven hundred rural healthcare clinics). It also established minimum wage laws and labor welfare legislation.[26] In turn, "by enabling the [urban worker and rural middle] classes

---

[24] There was a struggle between Nagib, Nasser, and other officers in the Revolutionary Command Council over which direction the new regime would take. For a detailed account, see Mohi El Din (1995: 150–76), Beattie (1994: 86–98).

[25] Initially, for example, the regime adopted polices advocated by private capital (Baker 1978: 49). However, one goal to which the regime was committed from the start was breaking the hold of the landed aristocracy through land reform (Be'eri 1970: 107; Baker 1978: 61; Binder 1978; Vatikiotis 1971: 205; Sadowski 1991: 57).

[26] For these initiatives, see Kerr (1969), Beattie (1994), Rahmy (1983: 104), Hansen (1969: 243), Stephens (1971: 366), Hinnebusch (1985: 24). At the same time, Nasser also moved decisively against private capital. A series of nationalizations in 1957 signaled the trend, which continued with the socialist decrees of 1961 (see Abdel Malek 1968: 139–42; Rejwan 1974: 99; Waterbury 1983: 73–79; Kassem 2004: 93; Perlmutter 1974: 121–24; Barnett 1992: 94–95). These measures expanded the public sector and appealed to the interests of labor. Under the decrees, all banks and insurance companies were nationalized, as well as all manufacturing companies with a "national character"; others were forced to accept limits on shareholding, capital participation, and directorships, mandatory representation of workers on company boards, and profit redistribution to workers.

to achieve varying degrees of social gains . . . the regime gained the support of these groups" (Rahmy 1983: 104). Urban workers, in particular, were especially important to Nasser's support coalition; even as he sought to consolidate control over trade unions' organizational structures, he promoted a variety of policies to serve workers' interests (Nutting 1972: 64–65; Kassem 2004: 90–92; Baker 1978: 33; Hinnebusch 1985: 27).[27] In addition, the regime's policies also advantaged small landholders and the rural middle class, such that the "peasantry" also tended to support Nasser, "provid[ing] an unstructured popular underpinning, a diffuse but important approbation" for the regime (Baker 1978: 50; Podeh and Winckler 2004: 21; Binder 1978: 376–77).[28] The "masses" overall benefited from price controls on basic foodstuffs and commodities, such as cooking oil, bread, and textiles (Hinnebusch 1985: 28).

Nasser also took pains to ensure the complicity of the educated, urban middle class in the maintenance of his regime. In 1962 he decreed that all secondary school students would be admitted to universities; from 1950 to 1970 there was a sevenfold increase in the number of university students (Podeh and Winckler 2004: 22). Laws were also implemented guaranteeing every university graduate a job in the bureaucracy or public sector. As a result, the ranks of the bureaucracy and public sector swelled from 350,000 at the time of the 1952 coup to 770,000 in 1962, 1.0 million in 1965–66, and 1.2 million in 1970, a rate that surpassed growth in population and in national employment.[29] Offering guarantees of state employment and skewing salary schedules in favor of high administrative positions, which were reserved for the well educated, meant that by the mid-1960s the re-

---

[27] Within the literature on Egypt there is a debate about Nasser's "revolutionary" project and whether and how much it represented a "socialist" transformation (see, for example, Baker 1978; Abdel-Malek 1968: xvi; Rejwan 1974; Binder 1978: 1–10). In the present context my focus is less on the degree to which Nasser's policies represented a cohesive ideological program that transformed Egyptian society and more on their general thrust and how they served the interests of the social constituencies that formed the base of the regime.

[28] The agrarian middle class (the "rich peasants") was the main beneficiary of the regime's policies, in that its political influence increased significantly (see Binder 1978: 36; Sadowski 1991: 59–60; Ansari 1986: 6). However, the lower levels of "peasantry" also benefited. The percent of rural poverty fell between 1958 and 1965 from 35 percent to 26.8 percent of rural families. As a result of the establishment of cooperatives, the productivity of land increased (Sadowski 1991: 61, 65). The number of landholders also increased, from 35.4 percent in 1954 to 54.8 percent in 1964, although many still remained landless (Podeh and Winckler 2004: 21; Hinnebusch 1985: 27).

[29] In the period from 1962 to 1970, employment grew in the bureaucracy and public sector by 70 percent, despite the fact that neither national employment as a whole nor the increase in population exceeded 20 percent (Ayubi 1980: 224). During this same period, salaries in the bureaucracy increased at a rate much higher (by 102 percent) than in the economy as a whole (Ayubi 1980: 250–52).

gime was employing 60 percent of university graduates, including nearly 100 percent of the country's engineers and scientists.[30] The waves of nationalizations and sequestrations associated with Nasser's socialist decrees provided ever more access to healthy sinecures for this technocratic elite. With these measures Nasser was able to wed the professional classes to the regime (Hinnebusch 1991; Kerr 1969: 20; Podeh and Winckler 2004: 22).

Despite these initiatives to civilian society, the military remained an important constituency in Nasser's Egypt. Not only did the army play a central role ideologically in the "revolutionary" regime, it was also a powerful domestic actor in Egypt at the time (Baker 1978: 48; also see below). However, Nasser was also steadily building a solid civilian base for his rule. Hence, "while the army provided the primary prop for Nasserite control in the early years of the revolution, gradually the regime amassed a significant degree of popular legitimacy" (Dekmejian 1982: 35). The president, however, was not alone in trying to establish a constituency to support his rule. As I explain below, the military leadership was equally ambitious in crafting its own independent political base.

Military Cohesion and Civilian Ties

During this period, the top leadership core within the military coalesced under Abdel Hakim Amer, who had been appointed chief of the military in 1953 (Mohi El Din 1995; Baker 1978: 51–55). An ambitious and charismatic figure, from the start Amer sought to establish a loyal constituency in the officer corps. Ultimately his efforts would reap substantial rewards. By the 1960s the military had become increasingly unified around his leadership.

One way Amer cultivated his officers' loyalties was to supply them with substantial privileges and perquisites. As Parker describes it, "[Amer's] officers enjoyed a wide variety of *nomenklatura*-type privileges—importing cars and refrigerators for themselves in defiance of currency regulations, and leading a life considerably more luxurious than that of their civilian colleagues" (1993: 84; see also Beattie 1994: 125). In general officers lived comfortable and sometimes lavish lifestyles, with access to expensive cars, nice homes, and social clubs.

In addition, under Amer's leadership there was a steady enlargement of the officer corps, with all its attendant perquisites, which also helped to secure the loyalty of his followers. Although jumping ranks was not prac-

---

[30] According to Ayubi (1980), the remaining 40 percent of university graduates not employed in the bureaucracy consisted of "housewives," retired people, foreigners educated in Egypt but who later returned to their own countries, and individuals employed in the private sector. Professionals, especially doctors and engineers, were well treated by the regime, receiving access to housing and other perquisites unavailable to the average Egyptian.

ticed under the regime, promotions were accelerated, which "enhanced the prospects of advancement in rank, pay and social standing of each individual in [the officer corps]" (Be'eri 1970: 323). The average officer born at the turn of the century attained the rank of colonel twenty-six years after being commissioned. The average officer of Nasser's generation, born at the end of the First World War, became full colonel after less than twenty years of service, at forty years of age. In the mid-1960s there were some officers who were brigadier-generals at age forty-two (Be'eri 1970: 323).

One of Amer's allies, Shams Badran, eventually became the daily administrator of Amer's patronage network (Beattie 1994: 126; Dekmejian 1971: 239; Gawrych 2000: 13). Badran acquired the power to make job assignments, allocate funds for loans for officers, supply homes and villas, rank officers in priority for automobile acquisitions, and provide exceptional retirement and travel permits. Indeed, officers in general were made to feel that Badran, as Amer's agent, could provide them with whatever they desired, which in turn strengthened the power of Amer within the military. Many of the chief beneficiaries of the patronage network were, in fact, Badran's war college cohort (Beattie 1994: 126). Amer, who graduated with Nasser, resisted appointing their contemporaries, preferring to recruit from younger graduating classes, especially Badran's, whose reliance on Amer for their positions could not be questioned (Springborg 1975: 99). The result of these efforts was to create a constituency within the officer corps whose interests were closely tied to Amer's. In the current context this is significant because it underscores Amer's growing support base within the military during this period.

Amer, however, was not content to rely on military supporters. He also sought influence within civilian constituencies, colonizing the bureaucracy and public sector with military officers in order to channel patronage to his allies and to secure his influence over these civilian bodies. In 1961, for example, Amer was appointed president of the Supreme Council of Public Organizations, which he used as a vehicle for allocating jobs to his allies. Land reclamation projects provided an especially rich source of sinecures for his clients (El-Sherif 1995: 213; Springborg 1979). By extending his influence over the civilian bureaucracy, he was also able to enhance his influence over the civilian constituencies that populated them (el-Sherif 1995: 213).

The Situation in the Mid-1960s

Throughout the 1960s, both Amer and Nasser devoted considerable energy toward strengthening their respective power bases. Amer continued to extend his reach into areas outside the military, bringing key civilian constituencies within his sphere of influence. Among the titles Amer carried by 1967 were first vice president of the regime, president of the Higher Economic Committee, president of the High Dam, chairman of the Committee for the Liquidation of Feudalism, executive within the soccer federation, and executive in the fishing and transportation industries (Beattie 1994: 196). These responsibilities afforded Amer ever increasing access to resources for patronage. They also allowed him to shape the composition and activities of key organizations, sideline potential opponents, and reward loyal forces.[31] These initiatives concentrated power into the hands of the military and, more specifically, Amer himself (Oren 2002: 41).

In response to Amer's growing power, Nasser also sought to shore up his social base. The Arab Socialist Union (ASU) was important in this regard. Established in 1962 as the successor to the Liberation Rally and National Union, the ASU brought together representatives of the regime's key bases of political support and, in theory, consisted of five main functional categories: workers, peasants, intellectuals, national capitalists, and soldiers. Although far from a representative party apparatus, the ASU mobilized and penetrated key civilian constituencies in order to strengthen their bond with the regime. It "represented the regime's determination to mobilize constituencies that had always been on the margins of political life and that could be expected to support the regime" (Waterbury 1983: 315).

Beyond its mobilizational capacity, the ASU provided a focal point for Nasser's leftist allies to coalesce in opposition to their conservative opponents, such as Amer (Waterbury 1983: 323). Within the ASU, Nasser created a "vanguard organization," which consisted of a secret network of personally controlled supporters (Stephens 1971: 374). Established in 1964 as the ostensible ideological nucleus of the regime, the vanguard was to act "as a makeweight to the competing rival power cliques and [to] eventually constitute the new Nasser equivalent of the Old Free Officer cabal in the army" (Vatikiotis 1971: 183; Waterbury 1983: 336; Baker 1978: 97). Under the leadership of Ali Sabri, who took control of the organization in 1965, the ASU expanded its activities, including establishing a militant Youth Organization (YO), which in part originated in a desire to build new bases of support for the regime outside the military (Beattie 1988: 210; Auda, 1986: 103). As such, the Youth Organization existed "as a mass body that could serve as an alternative to the military's vanguard role and as a mobilizational weapon to counter the military's strength" (Beattie 1994: 179). Between July 1966 and May 1967, some 220,000 young people were

---

[31] For example, as head of the Committee for the Liquidation of Feudalism, which endeavored to crush "counterrevolutionary" forces, "Amer got rid of opposition and appointed and dismissed whoever he wanted in all public institutions and government departments—even sporting club boards. The complaints of individuals and the public establishment alike were referred to the armed forces for adjudication" (Sadat 1978: 167).

trained; by 1967 YO membership exceeded 250,000. Intriguingly, one of the organization's activities was "coup-theater": role-playing about how to react in the event of a military coup (Beattie 1994: 179). As testament to the efficacy of the ASU as a counterweight to the army, by 1965 Amer had begun to grow suspicious of the organization, viewing it as a challenge to his authority; he refused to have his soldiers join the organization, where they would be subject to the influence of Nasser and his allies.[32]

In addition to courting popular constituencies and his ties to the left through the ASU, Nasser maintained links with the right, represented by figures like Zakariya Mohieddin, the longtime head of the Interior Ministry (Baker 1978: 75). Mohieddin, for example, was appointed prime minister in 1965 but lasted only a short time in the post, when it appears that Amer pressured Nasser to replace him. When Nasser resigned in the aftermath of the June 1967 war, it was Zakariya Mohieddin whom he suggested succeed him (see chapter 4).

The Balance of Power in the Mid-1960s

In sum, by the mid-1960s both Amer and Nasser had powerful bases from which they drew support for their leadership (Beattie 1994: 161). Amer was the head of a pervasive and influential faction within the military. Nasser drew support in varying degrees from the professional classes, small rural landholders, and urban workers and had created a powerful constituency within the Egyptian Left and, to a lesser extent, the Right. Each had a separate and competing power base. As one astute observer put it, "Amer had the army, but Nasser had the people."[33]

The situation reflected many of the elements of "shared power": a political leader, with his own civilian base, faced a relatively unified military leadership that also exercised influence within civilian society. Power was divided between the political and military leadership. Neither Nasser or Amer was in a position to dominate the other; rather, both had resources they could bring to bear in their relationship. As one analyst put it, "it is clear in retrospect, that even Nasser, whose authority people thought was absolute, was ... in fact sharing power with Amer, and neither was in total control" (Parker 1993: 84; Springborg 1979; Gawrych 2000: 73). After 1962 there was a "duality of authority" between the president and the military chief.[34]

---

[32] Eventually, perceiving the YO as "a burgeoning rival," Amer also sought control of the organization. As evidence of Amer's growing power in the regime, Nasser ultimately acquiesced in his appointment to the directorship of the Youth Organization. However, the 1967 war intervened and this decision was never implemented (Beattie 1994: 179–80). On Amer's suspicion of the ASU, see Baker (1978: 109–10).

[33] Discussion with Arab journalist and commentator, London, spring 1998.

[34] Mohammad Heikal, cited in Dawisha (1976: 116).

Preference Divergence

Complicating the situation, Nasser's and Amer's preferences over several corporate and security issues diverged. Prior to the early 1960s, the leaders had in fact long been close personal friends (Stephens 1971: 49; Oren 2002; Parker 1993). As mutual planners and executors of the July 1952 coup, they shared a similar political perspective and a commitment to rebuilding the country after King Farouk's dissolute regime (Baker 1978: 25; Mohi El Din 1995). Amer was the only person besides Nasser to know the complete list of men in the Free Officers' network of secret cells complicit in the July 1952 coup. Nasser and Amer also had family ties and a close personal relationship. Nevertheless, by the early 1960s a rift had emerged between the men.

The catalyst was the withdrawal of Syria from the United Arab Republic in 1961. In 1958 Amer had been sent to Syria to oversee the administration of Syrian military and political affairs. However, rather than subduing an increasingly turbulent political situation in Syria, Amer exacerbated the tensions, allowing his officers to run rampant over the Syrian military.[35] Although other factors were important, Amer's subjugation of the Syrian armed forces helped fuel their 1961 coup and the country's subsequent secession from the union with Egypt. As a sign of the Syrians' contempt for Amer, for example, he was sent home on a plane in his pajamas on the night of the coup.

The dissolution of the union inspired "deep dissatisfaction" between Amer and Nasser (Sadat 1978: 157). The leaders' relationship deteriorated rapidly in the aftermath of the Syrian withdrawal (Farid 1994: 72). Substantively, those tensions and disagreements manifested in three areas: corporate issues, security goals, and military strategy. First, sparked by Amer's actions in Syria, the leaders increasingly disagreed about professional codes of conduct in the Egyptian military. As noted above, Amer's efforts to expand his influence within the officer corps led him to privilege personal loyalty and partisanship in promotions at the expense of meritocratic criteria. Nasser saw this as potentially harmful to the skill and competence of the officer corps (Stephens 1971: 361). He also became concerned about Amer's lackadaisical attitude in administering military affairs, problems sometimes attributed to Amer's personality and his hedonistic lifestyle in the 1960s.

---

[35] They removed Syrian officers from responsible positions, sending them to Egypt and, in general, treating the Syrian officer corps with little professionalism and respect (Abu Izzeddin 1981: 327). At the time of the dissolution, there were apparently some 800 Syrian officers in "exile in Egypt" (Palmer 1960: 57). Ironically, Nasser had originally "intended the integration of the Egyptian and Syrian armies to serve as a binding force" (Baker 1978: 57).

Amer's organizational biases, as chief of the Egyptian military, also seem to have played a role in exacerbating conflict between the leaders.[36] This manifested itself in differences over security goals and the merits of confronting Israel, in particular. Amer was especially upset about the "dishonor" of having United Nations Emergency Forces stationed on the Sinai Peninsula. As noted above, the forces had been placed there after the Suez conflict to provide a buffer between Israel and Egypt (Israel had refused to have the forces put on its own territory). Since that time they had been a thorn in Amer's side. He viewed them as a violation of Egypt's sovereignty.[37] Amer repeatedly urged Nasser to call for the withdrawal of the UNEF. In December 1966, for example, on a state visit to Pakistan, Amer wired Nasser with a proposal to expel the UNEF;[38] he had made a similar proposal the year before (Oren 2002: 39). During the May/June 1967 crisis he vehemently lobbied in favor of such a move (Oren 2002: 57–58; Stein 1991).

Nasser too disliked the UNEF presence in Sinai. However, as political leader, he paid greater heed to the diplomatic and political ramifications of military action than did his military counterparts. All things being equal, he would have liked to see the forces withdrawn, but he was wary of provoking Israel, which risked inciting the Americans, without first preparing the diplomatic ground (Oren 2002: 39–41, 57–58; Parker 1993: 75).

During the May/June 1967 crisis the leaders' preferences also diverged over Egypt's military strategy and operational plans. During the crisis, Amer favored the adoption of an offensive war plan: from Amer's initial May 14 deployment order, in which he advised his military officers to be prepared for an offensive, to the dissemination of orders for a full-scale military operation (Operation Dawn) on May 25, Amer repeatedly pushed for a first strike.[39] Scholars employing organizational theory to explain military preferences note that militaries will often favor offensive war plans or preemptive strikes because it allows them to structure the battlefield and minimize uncertainty. This seemed to be a key rationale for pursuing the offensive, as evident in discussions between Amer and his military chiefs.[40]

---

[36] On the military's organizational biases as a source of preference divergence, see chapter 2.

[37] The Jordanians and Syrians taunted Egypt, for example, for allowing the UNEF to be stationed on Egyptian territory (Stein 1991: 128 and 150, n. 8; Oren 2002: 28; 117).

[38] Israeli intelligence intercepted this message as well (Stein 1996: 120).

[39] Oren (2002: 57) mentions several of these informal instructions and plans. For details on Operation Dawn, see below and Oren (2002: 92–93, 95, 97). For a prior offensive plan, Operation Lion, and other plans, see Oren (2002: 66). On Amer's preferences to launch an offensive attack, also see Parker (1993: 252, n. 25) and Amos (1979: 60).

[40] Parker reports, for example, that the reason military chiefs wanted to strike first was that it would give them an operational advantage in fighting the war (Parker 1993: 61). Mahmud Sidqi, the commander of the air force, was especially insistent on the necessity of a first strike in order to prepare the battlefield. See Stein (1991: 139), Perlmutter (1974: 177).

Amer also seemed to be responding to popular opinion within the officer corps and increasingly seemed to identify with "the particular interests of the military" (Baker 1978: 54). Certainly Egypt's officers were itching for action.[41] Frustrated with the challenges of fighting a counterinsurgency in the Yemeni civil war, Egypt's soldiers were hoping to prove themselves in a conventional war with the Israelis where they could try out their new Soviet-supplied weapons (Kerr 1969: 15).[42] Nasser, for his part, resisted adopting an offensive war plan. He was prone to moderation on the issue, once again mindful of the international repercussions of striking Israel (Kerr 1969: 15, 17).

By the mid-1960s the compatibility of interests characteristic of the early relationship between Amer and Nasser gave way to discord over corporate issues, security goals, and military strategy. The leaders clashed over the administration of the military and placed different weight on the value of confronting Israel and the risks of taking offensive action in a confrontation with the Jewish state. Over time these tensions between the leaders contributed to an atmosphere of mutual suspicion and mistrust. As Anwar Sadat describes the degrading effects of their clashing perspectives, both powerful in their own arenas, by the mid-1960s Nasser and Amer "each now lay in wait for the other almost daily" (1977: 167). Preference divergence was high.

In summary, in analytical terms, Egyptian civil-military relations in the 1960s were characterized by high preference divergence and shared power. Nasser had a strong civilian base from which he drew support, and Amer was the head of a unified faction in the military, which also was gaining influence over civilian constituencies. The leaders' preferences over military and security issues diverged. In this civil-military environment I predict that strategic assessment will be seriously flawed: These states exhibit profound weaknesses in all four attributes of strategic assessment.

Strategic Assessment

Below I examine strategic assessment in Egypt during the 1960s. Throughout the discussion I emphasize how the four attributes of assessment were manifested during the country's May/June 1967 crisis with Israel. Not only does the nature of strategic assessment during the crisis bring into relief the pronounced pathologies apparent in the Egyptian case, it helps explain Nasser's strategic choices. As I explain in the final section of this chapter,

---

[41] On the army's eagerness for action, see Oren (2002: 56), Parker (1993).

[42] Egypt had entered the Yemeni civil war in 1962; in May/June 1967 over a third of its army was deployed there.

flaws in strategic assessment within Egypt during those fateful weeks help explain why the crisis escalated to war.

Information Sharing

Upon first reflection, it might seem natural to assume that Nasser as a former military man and leader of the July 1952 coup would have had more access than the average leader to information about military affairs.[43] While this may have been true in the regime's early days, over time relations between Amer and Nasser politicized information sharing between the leaders. As competition between them escalated, Amer became fiercely protective of his capacity to control the flow of information to Nasser. As a result, by the mid-1960s Nasser had been effectively insulated from information about internal military affairs. Information sharing was poor. Specifically, as Nasser's secretary reports, after 1962 Nasser was limited to three sources of data about military activity: (1) the reports that were passed to him through Amer's office under the military chief's discretion; (2) information gleaned through contacts with Shams Badran, who worked in Amer's office and later became minister of war (recall he was a close confidant of Amer's);[44] and (3) the scripted training maneuvers and exercises to which Nasser was invited by Amer.[45]

Other sources of information were foreclosed to the president. The intelligence agencies, Military Intelligence and General Intelligence, were administered by allies of Amer, frustrating Nasser's attempts to get uncensored information about intramilitary affairs (el-Gamasy 1993; Beattie 1994: 126). Nasser could not rely on these entities to provide independent information and analyses (Beattie 1994: 126). In response, Nasser established his own intelligence network in his presidential offices to monitor Amer and happenings within the Egyptian armed forces (Dekmejian 1971: 183). The ASU, and Nasser's leftist-leaning allies who led it, also developed an intelligence capability to counter Amer's dominance of Military and General Intelligence (Beattie 1994: 126; Vatikiotis 1978: 159).

Nasser also sought out ex-officers on his staff and asked them to establish informal contacts with their friends and acquaintances then serving in the Egyptian armed forces. He instructed them "to visit colleagues in the military and sound them out on the readiness of the forces." However, when

---

[43] Parker (1993) makes this point.

[44] When Badran was originally appointed minister of war he was viewed as a compromise candidate—one who was trusted by both Nasser and Amer (Auda 1986: 103–4). It later emerged that he was much more solely aligned with Amer and shared Amer's preferences on strategy.

[45] Interview, Abdel Majid Farid, London, November 1997. Also see Auda (1986: 103).

Amer learned of Nasser's effort, he confronted the president, "demanding that it stop immediately, because it was contrary to a secret agreement between them that Nasser would not attempt to use his ex-officers in this fashion" (Parker, 1993: 89). Amer was referring to an agreement the leaders reached in 1962 when they battled over control of military appointments and promotions (see below). At that time, Nasser had agreed, under pressure from Amer, that he "would refrain from establishing contacts with the army through those of his aides who had originally been military officers" (Farid 1994: 72). As Abdel Majid Farid summarized Nasser's lack of access to information, the Egyptian president "lost day to day touch with military affairs except to the extent and in the manner allowed to him by Marshal Amer" (Farid 1994: 72).

Many of these dynamics are evident in the May/June 1967 crisis. During those events, Nasser was forced to rely on the information Amer was willing to share about Egypt's forces and activities. As noted above, moreover, during the crisis Amer exhibited a consistent preference for confrontation with the Israelis. Hence, Amer was motivated to bias information in ways that privileged an assertive military policy. Within the 1967 crisis this meant that any information Amer had—about Egypt's allies, its adversaries, and, even more seriously, its own military activity and internal capabilities—would be carefully rationed and framed in ways that supported his preferences.

Take, for example, how Amer and his allies conveyed critical information about the Soviet Union's preferences to Nasser during the May/June crisis. One of Egypt's vital concerns in 1967 was judging the Soviet Union's potential political and military support for Egypt in the event of war with Israel (Stein 1991: 130). How this assessment took place is instructive.

In late May Shams Badran, one of Amer's allies, was sent as head of an Egyptian delegation to the Soviet Union along with officials from the Foreign Ministry to assess Soviet intentions. At the meeting the Soviets conveyed that they were reluctant to intervene to support Egypt. They "redoubled their efforts to persuade Cairo to desist from further provocative action" (Nutting 1972: 407). Amer, however, used this as an opportunity to present information in ways favorable to his preferences. Thus, rather than conveying Russian misgivings, Amer and Badran allowed Nasser to believe that the Soviets would "intervene directly and decisively" and that they had "made a pledge of active military support" if there was a risk of Arab defeat (Bailey 1985: 30–31; Oren 2002: 125; Gawrych 2000: 8). In fact, these claims hinged on the departing words of the Soviet minister of defense, Marshal Andrei Grechko, whose statements could loosely be interpreted as an expression of unconditional support. The Egyptian delegation's summary brief reports Grechko as saying that "if something happens and you need us, just send a signal. We will come to your aid immediately in the [Egyptian city of] Port Said or elsewhere" (the memorandum appears in Haykal, *Al-Infijar* [The Explosion]; it is translated and cited in Parker 1992a: 183). The Soviets later denied that Grechko's remarks were more than a passing statement. In fact, an Egyptian Foreign Ministry official reports that he was told to alter the summary brief on the trip to reflect a forthright Soviet commitment to come to Egypt's aid, despite the fact that he and others recognized Grechko's statement as a mere rhetorical expression of support (remarks by Bassouiny, former Egyptian Foreign Ministry official, in Parker 1996: 44).[46] As it was, Badran "was not going to report anything which might create despondency in Cairo" about Egypt's provocative strategy (Nutting 1972: 407).

Subsequently, officials from the Foreign Ministry reported to Nasser their misgivings about the prospect of Soviet assistance. But Amer, armed with the doctored report from Badran's visit, remained impassive and continued to support an optimistic interpretation of the Soviet Union's commitment (Bassouiny, in Parker 1996: 44). The day after Badran's return to Cairo, Nasser made a speech to the National Assembly indicating that the "Soviet Union supports us in this battle and will not allow any power to intervene until matters [are] returned to what they were in 1956" (quoted in Parker 1992a: 182; Bailey 1985: 31).[47] He also communicated the same message to three of his top political advisers (Parker 1992a: 182; Oren 2002: 125).

Taken as a whole, the routines and processes associated with information sharing in the 1967 crisis reflect a disturbing pattern: Information was heavily compartmentalized and subject to heavy-handed manipulation by Egypt's military leader. In Nasser's efforts to assess Egypt's military and political situation in the crisis, this would prove a major problem. Unfortunately, as I describe below, this was not the only difficulty facing the Egyptian president at the time.

Strategic Coordination

The structures for strategic coordination magnified the problems endemic to information sharing in Egypt in the 1960s. In fact, by the time of the 1967 crisis, severe weaknesses in advisory processes were already entrenched. Throughout the period, analysis of Egypt's political and military

---

[46] In reality, there may have been some divisions in the Soviet position. But what is notable is that Badran did not report that there were mixed messages and basically ignored the negative comments. Instead he only conveyed Grechko's passing statements.

[47] For a transcript, see Draper (1967: 232–37).

strategies took place in an environment that afforded few opportunities for informed and systematic review of alternative courses of action. None of the bodies officially charged with reviewing policy decisions—including the cabinet and National Assembly—constituted an effective forum for review and analysis of policy decisions (el-Gamasy 1993: 28; Parker 1993: 88).[48] Nor did the competitive relationship between Amer and Nasser allow for informal interaction among political and military leaders, which might have substituted for the activities of formal joint advisory and decision-making bodies. As one observer frames the problem: All of the military command was removed from the "political discourse which shapes a military strategy. The reason for this complete break lies at the most senior level of the political and military leadership. There was a divergence of thought between the political leadership and military leadership and the armed forces of the state" (el-Gamasy 1993: 85). As another put it, "the links between President Nasser and the Armed Forces were so exclusive as to have made the by-passing of the prime minister and of the whole government machinery an established practice" (Nassif 1988: 73). The army operated largely independently from the state's political machinery.

These dynamics would create serious problems for strategic assessment in the May/June crisis. As a result, Egypt did not have the benefit of a functional advisory body in which military and political considerations could be jointly and comprehensively considered. The National Defense Council, for example, played little if any role in major decisions and "consequently was not able to contribute its specialized services or suggest alternatives and options" (el-Gamasy 1993: 81; Nutting 1972: 410). Nasser met with and consulted his political advisers. However, he did so in isolation from Amer and the military. After receiving the initial report from the Soviets on May 13 that Israel was concentrating forces on the Syrian border, for example, Nasser met with Amer and the high command to survey Egypt's options; he also consulted his foreign minister, but he did so alone.[49] In fact, political officials were so marginalized from the military command that they were often left in the dark about key decisions even when they had profound diplomatic implications. Thus, even as Egypt's forces were being deployed to the Sinai in mid-May in response to the Soviet report, diplomats in the Foreign Ministry had little insight about Egypt's actions and purported objectives. "There were no briefings, no appraisals, only what diplomats had read in the papers" (Oren 2002: 59).

---

[48] In theory, the NDC, a civilian-based organization composed of the ministers of foreign affairs, war, planning, economy, and interior in addition to the chief of national intelligence, acted as the primary coordinating body between the armed forces and political offices of the state (el-Sherif 1995: 27). In practice it did not perform these functions.

[49] See Oren (2002: 57) for a discussion of how these events unfolded.

Like the public at large, they relied on the popular press to learn of these major developments.

Even worse, not only was there poor coordination among Nasser, the diplomatic apparatus, and the military, there was also poor harmonization within the upper echelons of the high command itself, which further inhibited critical analysis of Egypt's military strategy during the May/June crisis. Amer resisted coordinating with officers within his own command structure whom he viewed as sympathetic to Nasser. Nasser had, for example, succeeded in getting one of his allies, Mohammed Fawzi, appointed chief of the General Staff in 1964 (Amer's response, discussed below, was to try to neutralize Fawzi's influence in the chain of command); in addition, there were several officers in the operations staff that Amer mistrusted because of their allegiance to Nasser (Oren 2002: 64; Gawrych 1987: 545). Repeatedly during the 1967 crisis, these officers attempted to offer advice to Amer and engage him on key strategic and military issues, including the decisions to close the Straits of Tiran, to pursue offensive action during the war, and to issue a withdrawal order the day after hostilities began (see Nassif 1988: 75; Parker 1993: 75–76, 95; Dupuy 1978: 267; Hammel 1992: 244). However, Amer had long marginalized these officers. He tended to treat their advice and concerns selectively (Nassif 1988: 74–75; el-Gamasy 1993: 37). He purposely circumvented them during the crisis, further truncating dialogue about and analysis of Egypt's strategic and military situation.

The result of these dynamics was that political-military coordination at the civil-military apex became increasingly idiosyncratic. During the crisis it devolved into a completely unstructured and undisciplined process. As one observer describes the environment, "both Nasser and Amer seemed to be influenced by the remarks of the last person they talked to. There seems to be no organization or functioning command structure that can come up with an objective assessment; everything appears to be politicized and unsystematic" (Parker 1993: 98). This was true despite the dangerous international situation in which Egypt found itself in May 1967.

Finally, Nasser's June 2 meeting with the military command illustrates the deficiencies in strategic coordination at the time. As noted above, at the meeting Nasser warned of an impending attack within forty-eight to seventy-two hours and advised Amer and the commander of the air force, Mahmud Sidqi, to implement protective measures for Egypt's aircraft (Parker 1993: 57; Sadat 1978: 174). Amer, however, was skeptical. His own private intelligence sources had been playing down the imminence of an Israeli attack (el-Gamasy 1993: 46; Parker 1993: 85). That the political and military leaders had different priorities and ideas is not unusual, in principle. However, they did not sit down and analyze the possible significance of this contradictory information, as a rigorous process of strategic coordination would entail; instead, consultation broke down. Amer simply dismissed Nasser's information as incorrect. Asked later why he ignored Nasser's warnings rather than engage them, "Amer is reported to have replied that he did not know that Nasser was a prophet or that heavenly inspirations had descended on him" (Parker 1993: 85). No protective measures were consequently taken. Egypt's aircraft were aligned wing to wing on their tarmacs when Israel attacked on June 5. In less than three hours, in seventeen waves of strikes, the Israelis destroyed hundreds of aircraft on the ground.

In sum, Egypt suffered from a glaring vacuum of political and strategic analysis during the May/June crisis. Nasser and Amer were alienated from one another, while Amer distanced himself from officers within his own command whom he believed were allied with the president. Diplomats were left on the sidelines and did not take part in meetings where crucial decisions were evaluated. Reviewing Egypt's political options and how its military situation and capabilities would bear on them in the 1967 crisis would prove to be a major problem.

Structural Competence

Even had Amer and Nasser been better engaged with one another in analytical processes, however, the information available to them about Egypt's military situation would have been seriously deficient. Intraregime competition had also taken a severe toll on the military's structural competence, undermining its capacity to evaluate the country's capabilities and potential performance in battle against Israel.

Specifically, competition had two deleterious effects on Egypt's external intelligence and internal monitoring functions. First, it absorbed resources and distracted Egypt's intelligence bureaucracies from gathering information about Egypt's adversaries, especially Israel (el-Gamasy 1993). Both Military Intelligence and General Intelligence were controlled by Amer's close allies. Military intelligence resources were consequently mobilized to watch Nasser and the activities of the political regime as well as to monitor the officer corps and ensure its ongoing loyalty to Amer. Consequently, on the eve of the war, Egypt lacked even basic information about the doctrine, weapons, equipment, or leadership of the Israeli military; there were profound lacunae in intelligence gathering and assessment about Israeli plans, deployments, and capabilities (el-Edroos 1980: 418–19). Especially egregious was the shortcoming in intelligence about the Israeli air force: "Military intelligence was . . . unable to collect any genuine information about the Israeli air force, estimate its real capabilities, or provide details on the expected air attack" (el-Gamasy 1993: 46; Haykal 1975: 241).[50]

In fact, so inadequate was the intelligence effort that when the Egyptians tried to gather information about Israeli deployments during the crisis, aircraft sent to photograph the Israeli port of Eilat ended up with pictures of the Jordanian port of Aqaba (el-Sherif 1995). Even when information was available, the personnel and procedures required to evaluate it were lacking. For example, Amer was reportedly so confused by contradictory reports about Israel's military deployments from his intelligence bureaucracy that he asked the Soviet ambassador if the Russians could supply Egypt with intelligence about Israeli deployments (Bailey 1985: 31).[51] Without sound data and systematic analysis that might attest to the qualitative and quantitative strengths of the Israeli military, Egypt's intelligence bureaucracy significantly underestimated its adversary's military proficiency (Oren 2002: 56; Stein 1991: 135; Gawrych 2000: 14). As one of Egypt's prominent military leaders later described the root of the problem, "it can be said then that the energy and efforts required to ensure security within the armed forces effectively prevented adequate information-gathering on the Israeli enemy, the main task at hand" (el-Gamasy 1993: 47).

Second, civil-military competition undermined self-monitoring and conventions of critical evaluation of Egypt's *own* military activity. Put simply, the Egyptian military was ill-equipped to evaluate its capabilities. Key here is how competition affected appointments and the qualifications of military leaders and officers within the Egyptian military. To advance his influence within the officer corps, and therefore strengthen his position vis-à-vis Nasser, Amer sought to appoint loyal individuals to key positions. As noted above, in personnel matters Amer delegated substantial responsibility to Shams Badran, who built their clique of loyal supporters at the expense of the officer corps' professional competence. Dedication to mission was not the primary criterion for advancement under Badran's regime (el-Gamasy 1993: 46; Beattie 1988: 212). In fact, at the time of the 1967 war, the same service commanders who had performed poorly in 1956 still occupied their posts (Gawrych 2000: 13). In addition, although once an accomplished officer, by the mid-1960s Amer was himself no longer qualified to run the military (Stephens 1971: 361; Mohi El Din 1995: 158). Over time he became less interested in military affairs and ever more absorbed in his activities in civilian institutions, rarely attending the pro forma military exercises and training that were undertaken (Gawrych 2000: 13). From 1962 to 1967, Amer himself visited units in the Sinai only three times;

---

[50] The Israelis, in contrast, had excellent intelligence about the deployments and doctrine of the Egyptian armed forces (Dupuy 1978; el-Edroos 1980: 419).

[51] On other intelligence failures, see Gawrych (2000: 19–21).

"under these circumstances it would have been difficult to assess their combat readiness or their fighting skill" (el-Gamasy 1993: 40).

Partisanship in appointments and promotions in turn eroded the quality of leadership and internal organizational processes in the Egyptian military. In an environment in which leaders were rewarded for political loyalty, the impartial exchange of information about military affairs was discouraged. Systems of accountability and responsibility for military functions fragmented. Internal assessments and reviews were lackadaisical, altogether absent, or treated as formalities by Amer's clique of service branch commanders. This was not a military that had an organizational ethos devoted to critical self-evaluation.

Evidence for this weakness in internal monitoring can be seen in the failure to track and analyze basic data about Egypt's capabilities. As it was, only after the 1967 war was much of the data indicating potential shortcomings in Egypt's military capabilities systematically analyzed and reported. For example, figures compiled after the war revealed a shallow training regimen in the mid-1960s. For the infantry only 26 percent of munitions allocated to training were actually consumed in those exercises. The figures were worse for the other combat arms: 15 percent of munitions allocated for armor were used; 18 percent for artillery; 16.3 percent for light anti-aircraft guns; 11.8 percent for heavy anti-aircraft guns. Each howitzer (122 mm) in the Egyptians' arsenal fired an average of 1.5 shots for the entire 1965–66 period; every 120 mm Bazooka, 1.0; every 82 mm Bazooka, 15.0; every tank, 1.0. (el-Sherif 1995: 142–43). Despite the alarming implications of these data for Egypt's military effectiveness, there was not an emphasis on systematic reporting of these lapses in the mid-1960s. Nor was there systematic tracking of the readiness of tactical units and breakdowns in essential military activities. This made it difficult to register and account for weaknesses in Egypt's preparation for war. In large part, this inadequacy was due to the standards the senior leadership set and the messages their own lack of emphasis on internal monitoring and critical self-evaluation sent to their subordinates. Amer himself set a poor example for his chiefs (el-Gamasy 1993: 40).

In sum, intraregime competition undermined military intelligence and internal monitoring in Egypt during the 1960s. Military intelligence functions were absorbed with monitoring Nasser and the political regime; this inward focus lessened the attention paid to external adversaries. Competition and the desire to project influence into the armed forces also placed a premium on loyalty in appointments. This shaped routines and organizational conventions within the military in ways inimical to critical analysis.

Combined, these failings created a military that was unable to accurately assess its adversary's capabilities or evaluate its own strengths and weaknesses. Egypt's military did not have a good sense of Israel's doctrine, equipment, and weapons. It was also structurally incompetent to evaluate the extent of its own capabilities, especially in qualitative areas, such as leadership, training, and doctrine, which are typically harder to measure than weapons systems capabilities (yet, as discussed in chapter 2, vitally important to the ability to project force on the battlefield). Combined with problems in information sharing and strategic coordination, weaknesses in structural competence would worsen the assessment environment in the May/June 1967 crisis. Nasser was unlikely to get information he needed about Egypt's military capabilities from his chiefs and lacked a rigorous joint political-military process in which to evaluate it, and any information the military did supply would likely be wrong in the first place.

Authorization Process

Finally, as if these problems were not enough, Egypt also lacked a clear authorization process. Competition over decision-making prerogatives between Amer and Nasser was once again the central culprit.

Take, for example, Nasser's efforts in the early 1960s to win control from Amer over officer appointments and promotions—a significant lever of control over a military organization and manifestation of decision making in the military context. In late 1961 Nasser sought to claim Amer's control of appointments by reorganizing the government and establishing the Presidential Council, a new, collegial decision-making body in which decisions would be taken by the majority (for accounts, see Sadat 1978; Beattie 1994; Stephens 1971; Nutting 1972; Farid 1994; Auda 1986: 107).[52] Nasser appointed several of his colleagues from the Revolutionary Command Council to sit on the entity, as well as Amer. Amer, however, was told that as a member he would have to relinquish day-to-day command of the armed forces. Although Amer initially acquiesced, when reports that Amer's supporters in the officer corps were ready to mobilize if the chief was removed from command, Nasser withdrew the initiative (Beattie 1994: 43; Sadat 1978: 158).

Not to be deterred, a few months later Nasser engineered passage of a bill by the council placing control over appointments, promotions, transfers, and pensions in its hands, rather than allowing them to be left to Amer and his staff's discretion (Farid 1994: 71; Auda 1986: 107). Upon receiving word of the initiative, Amer left Cairo. Eight days later he reappeared and

---

[52] My account is based on these texts as well as on interviews with former Nasser officials in Cairo May 1996 and with Abdel Majid Farid (Nasser's longtime secretary) in London in the fall and spring of 1997–98. These accounts differ in some of the details, but on the major events they are consistent.

submitted his resignation to Nasser. He also started passing out letters calling for the restoration of democracy (a measure aimed at heightening his popularity and also a shrewd attempt to undercut Nasser's position). Amer then mobilized support from his high-ranking officers, who began to speculate that there was a "political plan to intervene in military affairs and to strip them all, including the general commander, of power" (Farid 1994: 71–72). Reports filtered back to Nasser that pro-Amer *kulat* (coteries) were coalescing, threatening to move against Nasser if he ousted the military chief (Beattie 1994: 161). On December 11, 1962, Nasser and Amer met for nine hours to arrive at a compromise (Beattie 1994: 161). Although Amer subsequently agreed to resign as commander-in-chief (and assume the position of deputy commander) and allow a new commander to be chosen for his professional credentials, he later blocked the appointment (Sadat 1978: 159–60).

Despite the failure of these initial efforts to secure control over appointments, Nasser continued to press for the appointment of his chosen candidates to key positions. In March 1964 he succeeded, for example, in having Mohammed Fawzi, an able administrator and disciplinarian as well as a Nasser loyalist, appointed chief of staff. In theory Fawzi's appointment was important because of the pivotal role the chief of staff plays in training and in the peacetime integration of the service branches. Amer agreed to the appointment. However, subsequently he finessed the command structure to ensure that Fawzi had little actual influence in decision making by forming a new entity, the Ground Forces Command (GFC), to act as a coordinating body for all the ground forces in the army, navy, and air force.[53] The GFC's broad mission made it the largest command in the military. It also put it into direct competition with the General Staff. In effect, Amer bypassed Fawzi with the establishment of the GFC, neutralizing Nasser's efforts to project influence into decision making by inserting an ally into the army's command structure.[54] As these examples illustrate, control over decision-making prerogatives was a controversial issue between Nasser and Amer in the 1960s.

During the 1967 crisis these conflicts would come to a head, manifesting themselves in arguments over rights of final approval and veto, and agenda-setting powers. Competition between Nasser and Amer wreaked havoc on the authorization process. By examining several events in the crisis, we get a sense of the haphazard way in which major decisions escalating the crisis were made in May 1967.

[53] According to Gawrych (1987), the GFC was unprecedented in Egypt and was not consistent with current Soviet conventions.

[54] For a detailed account of these effects, see Gawrych (1987).

Response to the May 13 Soviet Report

Egypt's initial decision to deploy forces to the Sinai underscores these ambiguities in the authorization process. Nasser publicly reported that the decision had been made by his cabinet the same day Egypt received the report from the Soviet Union that Israel was deploying forces on the Syrian border (Rikhye 1980: 159; Parker 1993: 63–64). However, according to Heikal, Nasser's public account was incomplete at best. As Heikal put it, late into the evening of May 13 Nasser and Amer met to discuss how to respond to the Soviet report and assess alternative courses of action. Although the leaders agreed that Egypt must respond to the report, *no decision to mobilize and deploy forces was made*. Instead, the men agreed to convene the General Staff and continue the consultation process before issuing a decision the following day (Oren 2002: 55; Parker 1993: 64–65).

The next morning, however, Amer convened a meeting with his military chiefs and announced that Egypt was sending forces to the Sinai. At the time, Nasser was meeting with his foreign minister (Oren 2002: 57). Nasser heard from Amer only after the meeting when the latter told him, "in his capacity as deputy commander in chief he and the high command had decided to send units to Sinai" (Parker 1993: 62). Members of Amer's staff later reported that the leader effectively had made the decision alone.[55] In short, rather than a clear, deliberate decision to escalate, Egypt's first steps in the crisis emerged from a contested and problematic authorization process.

The Request for UNEF Redeployment

Similar dynamics are evident in how the decision was made to ask for a redeployment of UN forces to make way for Egyptian forces in the Sinai. Recall that a letter was sent to the commander of UN forces in the Sinai, General Rikhye, requesting that UN forces be moved to make way for deployments of Egypt's forces. Nasser's goal at that point was to seek a limited redeployment, not to request a total withdrawal of UN forces from the Sinai. By limiting the request and sending it to the commander in Sinai rather than to the UN secretary general, Nasser hoped to control the escalation of the crisis (Oren 2002: 58; Stein 1991: 131).[56]

---

[55] According to General Murtagi, the May 14 meeting focused purely on the implementation of Amer's orders; the deputy commander passed them a briefing that had been prepared during the night. These events are recounted in Heikal's major work on the 1967 war, *al-Infijar* [The Explosion] and in Murtagi's memoirs. For summaries, see Parker (1993: 62–63, 42–43).

[56] The letter was purposely sent to the local UN commander in Sinai rather than to the secretary general to emphasize the "practical" nature of the request: to ask that UN forces be relocated, rather than to suggest Nasser was recommending their expulsion (Oren 2002: 58).

Amer, however, had very different preferences. He had pushed for a total withdrawal of UN forces from the beginning of the crisis (Parker 1993: 71).[57] Subsequently, on the morning of May 16 Nasser received a draft of the letter that was to be sent to the UN commander. Nasser was first given the letter in Arabic and had to request a copy of the English translation. The translation was nearly exact, with one important exception: the English version referred to *all* the UNEF forces in requesting force changes, whereas the Arabic version omitted the word "all." Nasser then crossed out the word "all" and asked Amer also to change the wording so that the word "withdrawal" was replaced with "redeployment" to clarify that the Egyptians were not requesting a complete termination of UNEF operations. Amer later told Nasser he had been unable to intercept the letter in transit to make the changes (although, in principle, there was sufficient time to reach the envoy because the letter was not delivered to the UN command until late that evening).[58]

The ambiguously worded letter had enormous implications. As Parker argues, had the Egyptians clearly requested a limited redeployment, perhaps the "impression that they were hell-bent on a military confrontation would have been softened," and Egypt's position at the UN made more tenable (1993: 66). Instead the head of the UN operation, General Rikhye, asserted that the letter requested his withdrawal from Sharm al-Sheikh (Bailey 1985: 178).[59] What exactly the letter implied remains controversial, which in itself testifies to the ambiguity of the text. Once again, weaknesses in the authorization process meant that Egypt was escalating the crisis in a haphazard manner.

Closure of the Straits

If the withdrawal of UN forces and reoccupation by Egyptian forces was an alarming development, of greater portent was the decision to close the

---

[57] Nasser told Mahmoud Fawzi, one of his advisers, that, while he supported a redeployment, he did not want to terminate the work of UNEF completely. An account of this conversation (which appears in Arabic in Heikal's *al-Infijar*) can be found in Parker (1993: 64–65); also see Oren (2002: 57–58).

[58] For accounts of this incident, see Oren (2002: 67, 73), Hammel (1992: 31), Sicker (2001: 221–22), Parker (1993: 66). Text of the letter appears in Rikhye (1980: 16). Also see Nassif (1988: 74).

[59] Speaking in 1992, Sir Brian Urquhart, UN deputy undersecretary general in 1967, noted that in retrospect he was not sure whether the Egyptian officials were operating on the premise of a redeployment or withdrawal in their initial communications with General Rikhye. He notes, however, that at the time, UN officials were operating on the word "withdrawal" (remarks by Urquhart in Parker 1996: 83). In contrast, accounts more sympathetic to Nasser, such as Nutting (1972: 399) and Heikal (1973: 241), report that the request was for a limited redeployment.

Straits of Tiran. Considerable confusion exists regarding when and by whom the final decision to close the straits was taken, which is indicative of the fragmentation of decision making in Egypt at the time.[60] Political sources, including Zakariya Mohieddin, the vice president, Anwar Sadat, and Mohammed Heikal all say the decision was made on May 21 (the day before Nasser announced the closure in his speech at Bir Gifgafa airfield) at a meeting with other political officials (Sadat 1978: 167; Parker 1993: 71–76; Stein 1991: 134). Interestingly, military sources, including the accounts of generals Fawzi and Murtagi, chief of staff and commander of the Sinai, respectively, say the decision was made much earlier, on May 16 or 17 at a meeting of the military high command without consultation with Nasser (Stein 1991: 153, n. 51).

Regardless, through his actions, Amer had already set the agenda in favor of closure by deploying forces to Sharm al-Sheikh on May 21 before a final decision on the Straits of Tiran had been announced. After Egyptian forces had been deployed, Amer then refused to delink the deployment from the decision to close the straits (Oren 2002: 83; Parker 1993: 75). For his part, once Egypt's forces were at the tip of Sinai, Nasser faced a choice: He could tell the Egyptian Army to sit on its hands and watch ships travel up the gulf to the Israeli port of Eilat or go ahead with the closure. Amer had stacked the deck against moderation. Nasser ordered the closure (Bailey 1985: 15; Bar-Zohar 1970: 167).[61]

Operation Dawn

Amer's pursuit of Operation Dawn provides a final and especially disturbing example of competition over decision-making prerogatives and how they undermined the authorization process during the crisis. As noted above, during the crisis Amer lobbied to initiate hostilities with a first strike against Israel. On May 25 he went so far as to disseminate an operations order for Operation Dawn, which called for such an offensive to begin on May 27. To this day, sources conflict as to how much Nasser knew about the plan when it was formulated. Regardless, Nasser eventually did find out about it and countermanded the plan before it was implemented.[62]

---

[60] Parker (1993: 71–76) reviews the various accounts of when and how the decision was made.

[61] For an overview of these decisions, see Oren (2002: 57–58).

[62] See Oren (2002: 92–93, 95, 97) on the conflicting arguments about what Nasser knew. Mohammed Heikal says Nasser first learned of the order on the May 26 and pressed Amer to cancel it the next day. See Parker (1993: 252, n. 25), Amos (1979: 60). Gawrych (2000: 18) notes that the offensive was scheduled for May 28 and was canceled by Nasser on May 25. Israeli intelligence apparently intercepted these orders. See Stein (1991: 139–41), Parker (1996: 142), Oren (2002: 118).

• • •

Ultimately, as the theory predicts, when political and military leaders' preferences diverge and both are empowered to compete with one another, their conflicts over substantive policy manifest in clashes over decision-making prerogatives. The result in this case was a poorly defined authorization process. The crisis escalated, not always in a preconceived, deliberate fashion, but in a series of decisions in which both political and military leaders were vying for control of military activity.

International Implications

If ever a state was ill-prepared for an international crisis, it was Egypt in 1967. Yet, how exactly did poor strategic assessment contribute to the May/June crisis and Egypt's actions that fateful spring? Weaknesses in deliberative processes and decision making rendered Egypt vulnerable to a variety of problems. Not least was its tendency to produce incoherent, often haphazard, political and military strategies. At numerous points and in a myriad of ways in May and June 1967, Egypt fell prey to inconsistencies and a lack of clarity in political actions, military strategy, and operational plans.

Yet, above all, one consequence of poor strategic assessment would prove especially significant in 1967: As a result of poor assessment, Egypt suffered from a void of reliable information about how long realistically it could last in a war against Israel. Consequently, Nasser was forced to make critical decisions about Egypt's strategy based on a poor estimate of his military capabilities.

All the problems in strategic assessment cited above interacted to put Nasser in this unenviable position. First, due to weaknesses in its structural competence, the Egyptian military lacked information about the limits of its capabilities. In the highly polarized civil-military environment, there simply was not the rigorous evaluation of Egypt's military activities that would have exposed the depth of the military's handicaps. This was especially problematic given the nature of its weakness in capabilities, which were largely qualitative in leadership, training, command, and control—weaknesses that are more ephemeral and hence inherently harder to measure than conventional numerical indices of capabilities.[63]

The second problem compounded the first: Due to weaknesses in information sharing, the military lacked incentives to make any information

---

[63] On problems with states miscalculating their capabilities because of the intangibilities of military effectiveness, see Brooks (2007a).

about capabilities it *did* have available to the president, especially if it would have discouraged Nasser's assertive policy in 1967. When reporting to Nasser, military leaders tended to extrapolate from the information they had about Egypt's capabilities relative to Israel's in ways that supported their preferences. For example, although military intelligence had spotty data about the state of Israel's equipment and air force, they tended to adopt positive views in their communications with Nasser, arguing that "the Arabs were superior to the Israelis in the main classes of equipment" (Bailey 1985: 30; Nutting 1972: 409).[64] The Egyptian air force commander was highly optimistic in reporting about his capabilities and underestimated the range of Israel's aircraft; the capabilities of Egypt's ground forces, including its tanks and missile defenses, were also overestimated (Stein 1996: 126–27; Gawrych 2000: 14).

Third, because of weaknesses in strategic coordination, Nasser lacked the kind of rigorous analytical process that might have forced more sober and comprehensive analysis of Egypt's capabilities and precipitated debate about how precisely to measure the state's military effectiveness. In sum, Nasser faced a myriad of problems in strategic assessment—the lack of good information about his military capabilities, the military's disincentives to supply what was available, and its disinclination to participate in an open-ended evaluation of Egypt's military and political position in the crisis.

These problems in evaluative structures would only be worsened by deficiencies in the authorization process. The latter meant that Nasser would find himself in a precarious position in late May 1967 with the prospect of an imminent war hanging over him. Competition over decision making at key moments had helped push the crisis to a critical point. Nasser would be forced to make hugely consequential decisions about Egypt's strategy with limited information about Egypt's capabilities. In turn, as I explain below, these poor capabilities estimates would have devastating effects on Nasser's strategic choices, fueling an extremely destabilizing political stance in the final days of the crisis.

Nasser's Strategy in the 1967 Crisis

Despite the obvious problems with the arrangement, throughout the May/June 1967 crisis Amer remained Nasser's primary conduit of information and advice about Egypt's military situation. Moreover, predictably, he tended to put a positive spin on the country's capacity to perform well

---

[64] These officers were later criticized for their flawed analyses (Amos 1979: 83).

should the crisis end in war. On the fateful day when the decision to close the straits was taken, for example, Amer publicly assured Nasser that the military would be ready in the event of war. As the military chief reportedly put it, "On my neck be it, boss! Everything is in tip top shape."[65] Subsequently, in the June 2 meeting when Nasser warned that he anticipated an Israeli attack and inquired whether the air force could withstand a first strike, Amer and his air force chief assured Nasser that they could weather it with only 10–15 percent losses (over 90 percent of Egyptian aircraft were subsequently lost in the June 5 raid).[66]

Of course, Nasser, an intelligent and savvy politician, was likely cognizant of his military's biases and incentives to paint a rosy picture of Egypt's military capabilities (Brown 1991: 134). Yet even if he discounted the analyses of Amer and his subordinates, lacking independent, comprehensive evaluations, it was unclear exactly how much they might be off in their estimates. Nasser was still left with the task of assessing his capabilities and the likely outcome in the event of war.

To do this Nasser reportedly resorted to the one source of information that was available: quantitative figures. He relied on laundry lists of weapons, equipment, and manpower and was forced to evaluate Egyptian capabilities "by means of mechanical, and not qualitative, intelligence" (Sadat 1978: 136). Moreover, those figures suggested that there was an objective basis for moderate, if not overwhelming, optimism. Egypt had a substantial number of men and equipment. Over the prior decade the Soviets had steadily supplied Egypt with substantial equipment and weaponry.[67] There had also been a dramatic increase in defense spending, and Egypt was producing new weapons and equipment (Barnett 1992: 81; Stein 1996: 123). Thus Nasser "compared the manpower figures, the number of tanks, the firing power of artillery, the size of the two forces, and saw that—on paper—his forces enjoyed considerable superiority" (Sadat 1978: 136).[68]

Quantitative increases such as these, in particular, seemed to weigh heavily in Nasser's calculations and played into his reasoning that Egypt's military

---

[65] Several participants independently report this statement. See Parker (1993: 72) for accounts of the meeting.

[66] Sadat, interview with Ms. Himmat Mustafa, October 6, 1977, *FBIS*, October 25, 1977. Quoted in Amos (1979: 291). Others report this estimate as well (see, for example, Hinnebusch 1985: 14). On Amer's tendency to report favorably about the military, see Oren (2002: 56).

[67] As Stein (1996: 123) notes, the military was spending $200 more a year on defense by 1966 than it had in 1960.

[68] As we might expect given the dearth of critical analyses, the Egyptian military also relied heavily on quantitative indicators, comparing the number of planes and weapons to support the conclusion that Egypt could easily prevail over Israel (Oren 2002: 56).

capability had improved throughout the 1960s. In a speech to the Damascus-based Arab Workers Conference on May 26, Nasser referred to this steady buildup of Egyptian military capability, arguing forcefully that Egypt was "ready to enter a general war with Israel. . . . I probably could not have said such things five or even three years ago. Today, some eleven years after 1956, I say such things because I am confident" (cited in Stein and Tanter 1980: 190; see also Draper 1967). Moreover, the combined command of Jordanian, Syrian, and Egyptian forces, although hastily constructed, yielded a military force that had twice as many tanks as Israel had, more than one-third more planes, and ample personnel. These considerations all seemed to favor optimism in estimating how Egypt would fare on the battlefield.

It is worth noting that, for their part, the Israelis had a more realistic view of the limits of Egypt's capabilities and the likely outcome of war (el-Edroos 1980: 419). In addition to its own internal estimates, Israel had access to American intelligence, which estimated that Egypt could be defeated by the Israelis in a matter of days and certainly in less than a week (Quandt 1993: 37–39; Stein 1996: 127). As Yigdal Allon, a member of the Israeli cabinet, said, " 'I have no shadow of a doubt as to the final outcome, nor the outcome at each stage. . . . It is in our power,' he concluded on 2nd June, 'not only to check the enemy, but to obliterate him' " (Brecher 1975: 348). As Yitzak Rabin, chief of staff, stated, "We have it in our power not just to check aggression, but also to be decisive over the enemy armies in their own land" (quoted in Brecher 1975: 348).[69] Hence, while "Nasser was misled by his own military experts . . . Israeli and Western intelligence services thought that if war came, the Arabs would be defeated in a manner of days" (Bailey 1985: 30).

Unfortunately, Israel was in no position to share intelligence about the balance of capabilities; doing so would have exposed information about its own military capabilities and impaired its capacity to attack first, which was considered crucial to keeping the costs of fighting the war down. Although most were not concerned about the capacity to prevail, keeping the number of casualties down was an important consideration.[70] Moreover, if the Israelis or Americans had passed intelligence, given their incentives to misrepresent the military situation, it is unlikely that Nasser would have taken it at face value. The Soviets also had an exaggerated sense of Egypt's military

---

[69] The head of Mossad, Meir Amit, estimated that the war with Egypt would last two days (Oren 2002: 147).

[70] Indeed, some, like David Ben-Gurion, felt the costs of fighting were prohibitive. For the most complete account of various views of Israel's political and military leaders, see Segev (2007).

capabilities and therefore could not have been much help to Nasser (el-Edroos 1980: 418; Parker 1993: 28–30; Oren 2002: 118).

In short, competition in civil-military relations and the flaws in strategic assessment they engendered limited the quality of information available about Egypt's relative capabilities that fateful May and June 1967. Nasser was forced to rely on superficial indicators, which, he would soon learn, significantly overstated his military's capacity to perform in war.

In turn, this overestimate would severely compromise Nasser's calculations about Egypt's political strategy in the crisis. To see how, once again we have to return to a central puzzle of the 1967 crisis: why, after Nasser knew that Israel was highly likely to attack, he maintained his confrontational strategy in the final days of the crisis. The answer suggested by the analysis above is that Nasser appears to have had an overly optimistic picture of what he could accomplish on the battlefield, and therefore incentives to maintain his strategy even if it would lead to war. Given the overestimation of his capabilities, the costs and risks of fighting Israel appeared much less than they actually proved to be in 1967; at the time Nasser appeared to have less to lose by holding his ground than would ultimately be the case. Hence even if he anticipated an attack by Israel, the Egyptian leader could reap the international and domestic benefits of standing firm and giving what he anticipated would be a respectable performance in battle against Israel.

In this regard, it is important to note that although Nasser often used the rhetoric of victory, he did not necessarily expect to prevail in a war of extended duration against Israel; nor did he necessarily need to. In the Cold War atmosphere, it was expected that both superpowers would keep a lid on the conflict and rush to impose a cease-fire. Nasser had been told by his military leaders that he could last two weeks, more than enough time to "check Israeli action and promote a diplomatic solution" (Perlmutter 1974: 179–80; Amos 1979: 59). Interestingly, on June 1, just days before Israel's preemptive strike, Egypt's foreign minister Mahmoud Riad mentioned such a potentiality in a meeting with former American ambassador Yost in Cairo. Yost reported in his telegram to the State Department on June 2, "Perhaps the only way out of the impasse, [Riad] declared at one point, may be a short war, appeal to UNSC [United Nations Security Council], which would then call for a cease fire with which the UAR [United Arab Republic] would at once comply. Thereafter more realistic settlement might be possible."[71] Also telling is Parker's report that, at least

---

[71] U.S. Embassy Cairo telegram no. 8349 to Department of State, June 2, 1967; appears in Parker (1993: 233). On May 26, 1967, Heikal (long considered a spokesman for Nasser's views) published an editorial in *al-Ahram* that suggests this was the president's reasoning. As L. Carl Brown describes the press report: "The most plausible interpretation of this editorial

to some observers, one of the major question marks within Egyptian diplomatic circles was when the United States would intervene to assist the Israelis if war occurred (Parker 1992a: 193–94).[72] In short, in estimating his options in June 1967 and the merits of fighting versus standing down, Nasser did not necessarily anticipate that he would be fighting a war of long duration.

The historical record suggests that Nasser indeed placed substantial weight on the state of his military in formulating his strategy—that his assessment of his capabilities was a crucial calculation in his decision to maintain his confrontational strategy. Nasser was concerned about the relative capabilities of Egyptian and Israeli forces and repeatedly sought assessments about the readiness of his forces (Amos 1979: 290; Oren 2002: 83). He premised the closure of the straits on an inquiry into the state of his armed forces (Sadat 1978: 172; Stein 1991: 134). At the last meeting of the military command before the war, Nasser warned the military of the imminence of an Israeli strike and again queried Amer on the military situation (Amos 1979: 291).[73] In short, Nasser repeatedly linked his political decisions to overly optimistic assessments of the military balance. As one observer frames it: "Why did Nasser decide to broaden the aim of his operations from the deterrence of attack against Syria to a revision of the political status quo[?] . . . Probably the main reason is that, trusting in the assurances from his military commanders, he re-assessed and over-estimated his military bargaining power" (Stephens 1971: 481). As another well-informed observer put it, "none of Nasser's decisions makes sense unless he thought his armed forces were ready to take on Israel's" (Parker 1993: 76; Gawrych 1987: 12).

Perhaps the most intriguing evidence comes from Nasser himself. In August 1967 he told Abdel Majid Farid, his longtime secretary, that "he was a good chess player; had he known the truth [about his armed forces], he would have played a different game" (Parker 1993: 89). What sort of strategy might that have been? "If I knew the level of the army," Nasser is reported to have said, "I would play politically and not reach the level of the battlefield."[74]

---

is that Nasser saw the risk he was running and was prepared for Egypt to take the first blow and then move on to a political settlement" (1991: 132).

[72] The Israelis apparently shared a similar expectation about superpower intervention (Stein and Tanter 1980: 177).

[73] Parker (1993: 57) details several accounts of this meeting.

[74] Interview with Abdel Majid Farid, London, November 1997. Farid told me that Nasser had related these things to him in informal discussions in his office in the months subsequent to the war.

The Israeli Reaction and War

The last, and arguably most provocative, question is whether, if Nasser had adopted a different, less intransigent strategy, would it have altered Israel's strategic calculations and changed the outcome in 1967?

Analysis of the forces driving Israeli strategy suggests that the crisis could have ended differently had Nasser acted differently in the final days of the crisis. Two considerations were critical to Israel's strategic calculus. First, convinced Nasser would never unilaterally back down, Israeli leaders were concerned about their shipping rights and, increasingly, about the challenge to their deterrent capability represented by Nasser's provocations. At no point did they consider deferring to Nasser's provocations.[75] Second, the Israelis were extremely concerned about the potential American reaction should Israel attack Egypt first and start a war as defense against loss of its shipping prerogatives and deterrent threat.[76] Military action was in fact delayed twice, on May 22 and May 28, while high-level officials traveled to Washington, in large part to test the waters for American support for an Israeli military attack (Quandt 1993: 25–48; Gawrych 2000: 10–12; Oren 2002). Once Israel's political leaders perceived U.S. complicity in an attack, the path was cleared for the June 5 strike.[77]

These considerations suggest that despite the seeming inevitability of war after June 1, had Nasser indeed pursued an alternative strategy in the final days of the crisis, war might have been averted. Had, for example, the president unilaterally rescinded his order to close the straits or recalled his forces from the Sinai—which likely would have gone far to reassure Israel that its deterrent against Arab attack was intact—Israel's leaders likely would have been prompted to rethink their strategy. Alternatively, a major warning by the United States not to proceed with an attack might have prevented the Israeli strike, *even in the face of considerably less substantial concessions* by Nasser.[78] The ramifications for U.S.-Soviet and U.S.-Arab rela-

---

[75] In fact, by May 28 Israel's generals were pressing their political leaders to approve a preemptive strike against Egyptian forces (Stein and Tanter 1980: 180, 236; Oren 2002: 97–98; Segev 2007: 292, 256, 297).

[76] See Stein and Tanter (1980: 214–26) and Yost (1968: 316).

[77] Analysts debate whether the United States supported or was complicit in the attack. Regardless, Israeli leaders believed that the Americans would acquiesce in it. See Quandt (1993: 25–48), Parker (1996: 136–41; 1993:99–124; 1992b: 18), Oren (2002: 122), Hinnebusch (1985: 11), Segev (2007: 245, 276, 334).

[78] Specifically, there was a substantial division between dovish and hawkish elements in the Israeli political leadership (see Segev 2007 for a comprehensive account). A stronger warning by the United States could have strengthened the hand of the dovish contingent in these internal debates. After all, it was concerns voiced by the prime minister and others about American support that had effectively forestalled earlier military action.

tions of an Israeli attack after Nasser had signaled his willingness to backtrack, even modestly, would have raised the costs to the United States of appearing complicit in a first strike and perhaps elicited a clearer warning to the Israelis against proceeding.[79] Given Israel's preoccupation with the American position in the weeks before its attack, a decisive expression of opposition by the Johnson administration would likely have given Israeli officials significant cause for concern.[80]

In sum, although we can never be sure that war would have been avoided, had Nasser indicated a change in Egypt's position on closing the straits, slowed or stopped the deployment to Sinai, or otherwise signaled unilateral retreat between June 1 and June 4—after he was convinced of Israel's intentions, but before Israel attacked—Israel would have had good reason to pause, reconsider, and perhaps permanently delay its strike. Ultimately, the Israelis resigned themselves to war because they saw no hope for such a conciliatory initiative. Nasser's intransigent strategy—a strategy heavily influenced by poor strategic assessment and inflated estimates of Egypt's military capabilities—foreclosed such a peaceful outcome.

Conclusion

In the 1960s Egypt's civil-military relations significantly undermined the quality of strategic assessment. Competition between political and military leaders sparked by shared power and high preference divergence introduced devastating pathologies into institutional processes: information sharing was poor, strategic coordination lacking, the military's competencies in internal monitoring and intelligence compromised, and the authorization process contested. As a result, Egypt was poorly prepared to manage its international relations in the 1960s, let alone the dangerous crisis it faced in the spring of 1967. It was ultimately to pay a heavy price for its internal deficiencies—a humiliating rout on the battlefield, a tremendous blow to its regional stature, and the loss of its territory to Israel. The Egyp-

---

[79] Note also that in the 1967 crisis President Johnson exhibited little willingness to expend political capital on assisting Israel and hence likely would have balked at action that provoked further controversy within the American population and Congress (such as backing an Israeli attack after Nasser had made initial concessions). He was already mired in debate about Vietnam. See Yost (1968: 316), Quandt (1993: 25, 33, 37), Hinnebusch (1985: 9).

[80] Early in the crisis, the Johnson administration did express its desire that Israel exercise self-restraint and sought to promote a diplomatic solution by forging an international armada that would break the blockade of the Straits of Tiran. Johnson sent several letters asking Israel not to begin hostilities (Parker 1992b: 18). Yet, by early June, if the United States was seeking to keep Israel from attacking, it did not signal its preferences very clearly. As noted above, by the time Israel attacked, it perceived that the United States supported an attack.

tian case, in fact, illustrates how a state's internal evaluative structure—the product of domestic civil-military dynamics—can have a profound effect on a leader's strategic calculations in an interstate conflict.

In the next chapter I explore Egypt's civil-military relations and strategic assessment in the 1970s. There I show how significant shifts in the configuration of political-military power and preference divergence yielded a very different institutional environment, with different implications for the country's political-military strategies.

Four

EGYPT IN THE 1970s

WHEN ANWAR SADAT came to power in October 1970 after Gamal Abdel Nasser's death, he was considered a weak choice to fill Nasser's shoes, chosen by the elite because they believed he would be easy to manipulate.[1] Domestically, Sadat's career as speaker of the National Assembly left him without an independent support base (Baker 1978: 123–24; Haykal 1975, 1983; McDermott 1988: 41). Internationally, he was widely dismissed, as Henry Kissinger put it, as "an interim figure who would not last more than a few weeks" (Kissinger 1979: 1276–77; Handel 1981: 290, n. 13; Quandt 1993; Parker 2001: 109; Stein 1999: 2). In effect, while Nasser had risen to power as first among equals in the Revolutionary Command Council in the 1950s, Sadat became president of Egypt by default.

Sadat, nevertheless, went on to achieve an ambitious slate of international goals. In October 1973 he oversaw the launch of a formidable military operation against Israel—a campaign, Sadat gambled, that would ignite negotiations and allow Egypt to win back territories lost to Israel in the 1967 war. After the war he achieved two disengagement agreements and in September 1978 negotiated the Camp David Accords with Israel. Six months later he signed a controversial peace treaty securing the return of the Sinai Peninsula. In the process, Sadat delivered Egypt solidly into the Western camp, abandoning Nasser's positive neutralism for American military and economic support.

How was a man chosen to be president because of, rather than despite, his political weaknesses able to accomplish such a dramatic revision of Egyptian grand strategy? Many observers have commented on the profound international impact of Sadat's ambitious strategies in the 1970s, yet we still have little systematic understanding of what was occurring domesti-

---

[1] After the purge of Abdel Hakim Amer's faction on the right in 1967, the "Left," and Ali Sabri and his cohort, became very influential in Egyptian politics (see note 44 of this chapter). The Left consequently chose Sadat because they thought they could exercise power through him. See Heikal (1996: 160–61; 1975; 1983), Baker (1978: 123–24), Beattie (2000: 34, 40). As one observer put it, "there is nothing in what Sadat said or did in the eighteen years from the revolution to the time of Nasser's death—and certainly nothing in the three years succeeding the June war in 1967—that would qualify him to be Nasser's heir" (Kimche 1974: 12; Handel 1981: 243, also 290, n. 9).

cally that allowed Sadat such latitude and creativity in formulating and implementing these strategies—especially given that so many were controversial and required the support and involvement of Egypt's formidable military establishment.

In this chapter I evaluate a second central hypothesis of this study, analyzing how civil-military relations affected strategic assessment in Egypt in the 1970s. Civil-military relations in Egypt differed dramatically under Sadat from those under Nasser in the mid -1960s, largely as a result of changes in Egypt's domestic politics after the 1967 war. As I describe below, no longer were political and military leaders sharing power as in the earlier period. Rather, by the early 1970s the military's position in the coalition had shifted, and Sadat now dominated its leadership. Despite wielding the upper hand, the president nonetheless clashed with his military chiefs over military strategy and corporate issues.

In states with this configuration of civil-military relations—characterized by political dominance and high preference divergence—I expect strategic assessment to exhibit a "mixed" quality, demonstrating strengths in information sharing, structural competence, and the authorization process, but also weaknesses in strategic coordination. In these settings political leaders can impose safeguards to promote military compliance and thus alleviate problems in information sharing. In addition they retain decision-making prerogatives, ensuring a clearly defined authorization process. Improvements in the military's structural competence in intelligence and internal monitoring are also possible. Problems arise, however, because the oversight mechanisms political leaders employ to promote compliance with their goals can also truncate debate within advisory processes, compromising strategic coordination.

The analysis below suggests that this pattern generally holds in Egypt in the 1970s. There were demonstrable strengths in strategic assessment, which manifest themselves in the deliberative and decision-making processes Sadat employed in developing his political-military strategies. These strengths are vital to understanding Sadat's tremendous international successes in the 1970s. However, there were also some more subtle weaknesses in the methods through which Sadat evaluated some of his strategies. Thus, while the scales tip to the positive in evaluating the quality of strategic assessment in the 1970s, especially when it is viewed through the lens of its international outcomes, there were also procedural weaknesses, consistent with the expectations of the theory outlined in chapter 2.

This chapter begins with some background and then situates the analysis in the extant literature on Egypt and Sadat relevant to the case. It then analyzes civil-military relations in Egypt, beginning with the final years of Nasser's rule, which laid the groundwork for the Sadat period. In turn it examines strategic assessment in Egypt in the 1970s, focusing on the periods prior to and during the 1973 war, postwar disengagement agreements, and the 1979 peace treaty between Egypt and Israel. A final section examines the international implications of Sadat's political-military strategies.

Background to Sadat's Grand Strategy

When Sadat assumed the reigns of power after Nasser's death in September 1970, Israel remained in firm grasp of the territory it had captured from Egypt in 1967. It controlled the Sinai Peninsula and Gaza strip, while the Suez Canal remained closed, with Israeli forces camped out in a long defensive fortification on its east bank. Among the formidable tasks facing Sadat was getting Egypt's land back.

To this end, the Egyptian president initially sought to negotiate the return of the territories peacefully through a series of diplomatic initiatives (for an overview, see Quandt 1993, Aronson 1978). However, an agreement proved elusive because Israel's military success in 1967 left it few reasons to make concessions. "Militarily prostrate and deprived of any of the bargaining power associated with armed strength," Sadat faced the prospect of convincing the Israelis that they had something to gain from a negotiated settlement with Egypt (Cleveland 1994: 319). Eventually Sadat and his advisers concluded that only a major military campaign "would jar both Israel and the two superpowers out of their general lethargy toward Egypt and the Arab-Israeli conflict" (Gawrych 1996: 10; Hinnebusch 1985: 46). A military operation would support Egypt's claims at the bargaining table by demonstrating that Egypt had the wherewithal, if not to win a war, to take large numbers of Israeli lives and jeopardize its security. It would also draw attention to the potentially destabilizing effects of the conflict for American and Soviet relations and therefore engage the United States and the Soviet Union in mediating and resolving the dispute. It was in this context that in 1972 Sadat started planning for war.

From the beginning, Sadat envisaged that war as a prelude to a political settlement of the conflict—as a means of reinvigorating the negotiation process with Israel. To this end, Operation Spark, as Sadat referred to it, sought only a limited victory. It involved crossing the Suez Canal, overrunning Israeli fortifications, and seizing a narrow strip of land on the east bank of the canal, approximately ten to fifteen kilometers wide. It did not aim to retake the Sinai by force.[2]

---

[2] There is some debate about whether Sadat originally intended to continue the offensive to the mountain passes, rather than restrict operations to the canal zone. Most sources agree that Sadat initially instructed his military chiefs to pursue the more limited objectives, and that Commander-in-Chief Ahmed Ismail had no plans to proceed to the passes (for a nice discussion, see Pollack 2002: 101, 603–4; also Parker 2001: 81, 334; el-Gamasy 1993: 267; Aker 1985: 87–98; Dupuy 1978: 482; Insight Team 1974: 296). Gawrych views the major goal

On the afternoon of October 6, 1973, in the midst of Ramadan and Yom Kippur, Egypt launched its offensive across the Suez Canal.[3] The subsequent crossing operation proved remarkably successful. Thousands of men and supporting equipment were transported across the canal. Innovative anti-armor tactics by infantrymen and a dense zone of missile defenses in the canal zone proved substantial advantages in the attack (el-Shazly 1980: 19; Pollack 2002: 104; Amos 1979: 176; Aker 1985: 54; Cordesman and Wagner 1990: 74, 94; Gawrych 2000: 83). The Egyptians had also succeeded in taking the Israelis by surprise, which conferred important operational advantages.[4] Consequently, in the first three days of the war, the Egyptians were able to overcome Israel's defensive fortifications (the Bar Lev line) and establish a bridgehead of Egyptian forces on the east bank of the canal.

However, shortly thereafter, on the night of October 15/16, Israel managed to breach Egyptian lines and from the west bank of the canal circle behind Egypt's forces in the canal zone. By the end of the war, when a UN-sponsored ceasefire took hold on October 25, Egypt retained its bridgehead, but the southerly section held by the Third Army had been cut off from the rest of the military.[5]

The war thus ended under mixed circumstances. Militarily, most analysts focus on the ill-fated position of the Third Army.[6] But equally important,

---

as inflicting casualties; holding territory had been a secondary objective initially (2000: 224). Regardless, that it was to be a limited operation to serve clearly defined political goals is not in question. Tellingly, for example, as soon as the war started, Sadat sent a secret communiqué to the United States in an effort to begin the diplomatic process (comments by Gawrych in Parker 2001: 112).

[3] The war is referred to by Egyptians as the October or Ramadan War, but is better known by Israelis as the Yom Kippur War.

[4] The Israelis got decisive word of the attack only in the early morning hours of October 6; even then they anticipated an attack at 6 p.m. on October 6, not at 2 p.m. when the offensive was actually scheduled. See Handel (1976: 28–39) for a detailed outline of Israeli decisions and intelligence in the days leading up to the war. Also see Segev (2007) and Oren (2002).

[5] On October 22nd the United Nations passed the first of three resolutions calling for a cease-fire. When the first resolution, No. 338, was passed, the Egyptian Third Army was under siege by the Israelis and the Israelis decided to continue their offensive. On the afternoon of the 23rd a second resolution was passed; the Israelis, again, eager to consolidate their gains continued to fight. On the evening of the 24th the Soviets threatened to unilaterally intervene in the conflict if the Israelis did not respect the cease-fire. A day later resolution No. 340 was passed, calling for a return to the October 22nd lines. The cease-fire finally took hold on the 25th. See Bar-Simon-Tov (1991:352-353).

[6] Judged solely on military terms, the latter half of the war had indeed gone poorly for the Egyptians. Yet the picture is not quite as bleak as some observers would suggest. For example, it took the Israeli offensive on the east bank seven days to reach Suez City, much longer than Israel's generals had originally anticipated. In addition, the Israeli offensive was heavy in casualties, especially in the battle at Chinese Farm. Egypt's military also succeeded in preventing Israel from capturing the Egyptian city of Ismailia, which would have cut off logistical support for the Second Army and its positions on the west and east banks (on these points,

from a political standpoint, Egypt still retained its grip on the east bank of the canal when the ceasefire took hold. It had also surpassed all expectations in the vastly improved quality of its military effort and the number of Israeli soldiers killed.[7] As one Israeli general lamented as he battled Arab forces in 1973: "It's not the Egyptian Army of 1967" (quoted in Gawrych 2000: 190). And as General Ariel Sharon put it: "I have been fighting [Arab forces] for 25 years, and all the rest were just battles. This was a real war."[8] Sadat had succeeded in demonstrating to Israel that it would be costly to hold Egypt's territory.

Two comprehensive settlements on the disengagement of military forces followed the war, negotiated under the guidance of U.S. Secretary of State Henry Kissinger.[9] Sinai I (1974) provided for the withdrawal of Israeli forces from the canal zone, limits on Egyptian forces allowed in the area, and the establishment of a UN buffer zone between Egyptian and Israeli forces. Sinai II (1975) secured the withdrawal of Israeli forces beyond the mountain passes in the Sinai. In the end, Sinai I and Sinai II were far more than military agreements. Not only did they reduce Egypt's military options against Israel by limiting the forces the country could station in the Sinai, the agreements signaled Sadat's desire to win the patronage of the United States, and his willingness to make significant compromises in Egypt's relations with Israel to do so. They marked a significant shift in Egyptian foreign policy (Hinnebusch 1985: 54; Meital 1997: 150–51; Safty 1991: 288).[10]

Accordingly, the disengagement agreements laid the foundation for even more ambitious steps in the transformation of Egypt's grand strategy. On November 20, 1977, Sadat took his now famous trip to Jerusalem to address Israel's Knesset in a signal of his commitment to a peaceful settlement. In September 1978 Israeli Prime Minister Menachem Begin and Sadat met at President Jimmy Carter's invitation, which culminated in the Camp David Accords. In March 1979, Sadat and Begin signed the first treaty between Israel and an Arab state. The treaty thus represented the culmination of Sadat's plans laid years earlier with the 1973 war—his efforts to alter Israel's and the superpowers' strategic calculations, catalyze

---

see Gawrych 1996: 74). On Israel underestimating Egypt's capabilities before the war, see Handel (1976: 45–46; Parker 2001: 334). On improvements in Egypt's military effectiveness, see Brooks (2006).

[7] Casualty figures vary for the two-and-a-half-week war but range from 2,500 to 2,800 Israelis killed (and between 5,500 and 8,000 wounded). These were huge numbers for the casualty-sensitive Israelis (Parker 2001: 9).

[8] Quoted in Keegan (1979: 167).

[9] These were preceded by "Kilometer 101" talks, which were convened two days after the ceasefire went into effect. See Parker (2001: 361–74).

[10] For texts of the 1974 and 1975 agreements, see Parker (2001: 352–58).

negotiations, win Egypt's territory back through a political settlement, and secure the country's position in the Western camp (Hagan 1993: 28; Mahmood 1985: 68; Dessouki 1991: 167; Stein 1999: 10–11).

Context of the Sadat Case

In short, despite his unremarkable accession to office, as president Sadat achieved a truly stunning set of political-military objectives. Several themes emerge in the extant scholarship to explain how he accomplished this feat.

One major strand of scholarship focuses on the October 1973 war and Sadat's motives in launching it. Scholars, for example, argue that the president sought to divert attention from the country's economic woes and to vindicate its population after Egypt's humiliating loss in the 1967 war. Alternatively, they highlight Egypt's international situation and the necessity of breaking the strategic deadlock with Israel through military action.[11]

As an explanation for the war and Sadat's grand strategy more broadly, however, focusing alone on his motives to fight is insufficient. Although domestic and international factors may explain Sadat's rationale for engaging in a general military campaign, they tell us little about how the leader arrived at the specific form that action would take: a limited war with explicit political aims. Nor do they explain how he implemented that strategy, ultimately winning the support of his military chiefs when initially his minister of war, service chiefs, and most of the military command ardently opposed it (see below). After all, Sadat's war concept, which was premised on the fact that Egypt's inadequate military could not prevail against its superior adversary, was far from conventional in its military objectives and their relationship to political goals (comments by Gawrych in Parker 2001: 112; Pollack 1998: 60).

Beyond focusing on Sadat's rationale for launching the war, to explain how he executed it scholars sometimes point to changes in Egypt's armed forces in the 1970s, their "professionalization" and improvements in military effectiveness (see Gawrych 2000: 72).[12] Certainly Egypt's military ef-

---

[11] On these themes, see, for example, Stork (1978), Amos (1979), McDermott (1988: 44–45), Gawrych (2000: 131), Hinnebusch (1985: 51). By 1972–73, for example, there were demonstrations by students and workers calling for a return to battle to regain the territories (Beattie 2000: 133).

[12] Professionalization is a common theme. See Hinnebusch (1985: 125), Friedlander (1983: 81), Gawrych (2000: 75). Beattie (1988: 214), Dessouki (1991: 165), Karawan (1994), el-Gamasy (1993). On improvements in military effectiveness as facilitating Egypt's success in war, see Gawrych (2000: 72), Brooks (2007c). More broadly on improvements in Egypt's capabilities, see Dupuy (1978); Pollack (2002), Gawrych (1987, 1996, 2000), Cordesman and Wagner (1990).

fectiveness improved as a result of reforms instigated by Nasser after the 1967 war, which continued under Sadat.[13] Yet, capabilities improvements, once again, cannot explain the character of Sadat's strategy, and especially how the president was able to overrule opposition and promote his *particular* vision for military operations. The military's "professionalization" may go somewhat further as an explanation, in the sense that more officers were promoted who were "mission-oriented" and willing to defer to the president. Yet, attributing Sadat's latitude of action to military deference to political authority obscures as much as it reveals. It tells us little about the conditions that allowed Sadat to promote these professionals and sustain their commitment to his controversial strategies, while sidelining those inclined to oppose them.[14]

Arguments that emphasize learning or rational updating as an explanation for Sadat's strategic choices are similarly inadequate. According to this line of argument, after the debacle of the 1967 war it was natural that Sadat would learn the limits of Egypt's capabilities and therefore employ a more nuanced military strategy in pursuit of his goals (Lieberman 1994: 413; Stein 1996: 145; Leng 2000: 189).[15] Yet Egypt's failure to learn from its prior military experiences belies that updating was such a politically inevitable process in the regime. In the mid-1960s, for example, all data about Egypt's poor military performance in the 1956 Suez conflict were suppressed by the military command. They were released and studied only after the 1967 war (see el-Gamasy 1993: chap. 3). Therefore, why Egypt

---

[13] Although this chapter focuses on the Sadat period, many of the changes in social context occurred after the 1967 war (see below) and are reflected in Egypt's institutions for assessment in the final three years of Nasser's rule. Nasser, for example, claimed control of appointments and was able to veto and approve military policy, which helped clarify the authorization process. He also imposed monitoring devices on his military, improving information sharing. The military's structural competence and strategic coordination also improved. See, for example, el-Gamasy (1993: 72), Gawrych (1987: 546, 554; 2000: 74, 78, 83), el-Sherif (1995: 146–47, 156, 158); Heikal (1975: 50; 1983: 37); Farid (1994: 128, 152); Riad (1981: 50), Dekmejian (1975: 252). To allow space to examine the Sadat period in detail, given its historical importance, I forgo analysis here of these final years of Nasser's life. However, for extensive details on this period, see Brooks (2000: chap. 5).

[14] One could point to the "threat" Egypt faced as a reason why Sadat and his military chiefs cooperated and why they appeared to defer to him—that is, the international situation promoted a convergence of views within the political and military leadership. Yet, beyond a broad and diffuse agreement that Egypt should regain its territory, the "threat" actually created as much conflict over strategic and operational matters as it alleviated. The question remains how Sadat was able to intervene in military affairs to promote his vision of military strategy. (I return to this theme in the discussion of preference divergence below).

[15] For an explication of this argument and a critique of its application to Egyptian-Israeli relations, see Stein (1996). On Sadat, in particular, see p. 141. For a rejoinder to Stein's critique, see Lieberman (1995: 878, 882).

learned in the late 1960s and early 1970s and not before is a puzzle that requires explanation.

An alternative theme on the origins of the 1973 war focuses on Israel's failure to anticipate the attack, rather than on Sadat's rationale for undertaking hostilities.[16] Here scholars blame intelligence officials' adherence to the "concept," which suggested that Egypt would not attempt offensive action against Israel until its capabilities had improved.[17] Alternatively they emphasize Egypt's efforts to obscure its intentions to fight through an elaborate deception plan (Shlaim 1976; Insight Team 1974: 66; Dupuy 1978: 391; Cordesman and Wagner 1990: 23; Amos 1979: 167, 171–72). Certainly Israel's intelligence failed in 1973, and its officials did not foresee Egypt's military offensive. Yet these arguments still do not explain how Sadat was able to conceptualize his limited war, or how he implemented the deception plan to distract Israel as Egypt prepared for it.

Beyond the scholarship on the October 1973 war, a second, smaller literature explores Sadat's peace initiatives, including his pathbreaking trip to Jerusalem and speech before the Knesset, the Camp David Accords, and the 1979 peace treaty (see, for example, Quandt 1993; Famhy 1983; Friedlander 1983; Stein 1999; Meital 1997). This consists primarily of detailed narratives that often emphasize Sadat's personality and life experiences as the source of his policies (Meital 1997: xi). Thus, in the West, Sadat's initiatives are often attributed to his farsighted and risk-acceptant character. One biographer's title captures the view: *Anwar Sadat: Visionary Who Dared*.[18] As Henry Kissinger put it, Sadat's actions "demonstrated the transcendence of the visionary" (1982: 647; see also Karawan 1994: 249; Alterman 1998). More frequently, in the Arab world Sadat's initiatives are attributed to his personal desire for approval ("hero" complex) and self-aggrandizing tendencies (see, for example, Haykal 1983; Fahmy 1983: 283–90; Mahmood 1985: 69; Shoukri 1981).[19]

One limitation of these treatments is that they are often veiled political judgments about the merits of Sadat's objectives far more than analytical

---

[16] On Israel's intelligence failure, see Bar-Joseph (2005), Handel (1976, 1989); Shlaim (1976); Stein (1980, 1982).

[17] This was the finding of the Agranat Commission, convened after the war to evaluate the sources of Israel's intelligence failure. In particular, Israel thought Egypt considered it critical to have an improved air force. Sadat, for example, had gone to the Soviet Union multiple times to try to persuade its leaders to supply him with more and better aircraft but had been unsuccessful. Interview with Aryeh Shalev, former head of the Estimate and Evaluation Department of Israeli Military Intelligence, Jaffee Center for Strategic Studies, Tel Aviv University, Israel, June 1998. A translation of the Agranat report appears in Reich (1995: 120–24).

[18] See Finkelstone (1996).

[19] On this tension in the literature, see Hinnebusch (1985: vii).

accounts. Equally problematic, however, is that they tend to rely on psychological factors—especially his early life experiences and personality—to explain the source of Sadat's vision (or betrayal) without adequately explaining how he was able to translate that vision into reality.[20] Of course, as with all political leaders, Sadat's life experiences shaped his political preferences. But it is difficult to translate Sadat's general disposition or world view into an explanation of his policies—neither the specific form they took nor his ability to execute them. In short, while many in the West have heralded Sadat as a visionary in promoting peace with Israel, few have focused on the underlying domestic factors that permitted him to do so.[21]

Moreover, when analysts do touch on Egypt's domestic environment, they tend to point to the autocratic nature of the state, arguing that it afforded Sadat substantial latitude in crafting policies that reflected his personal preferences (Handel 1981; Karawan 1994; Dawisha 1976). Yet Egypt's regime type is also inadequate as an explanation for Sadat's successes. After all, Nasser, who was arguably far better positioned in the authoritarian state to achieve his goals, was extremely constrained in exercising control over Egypt's political-military strategies prior to the 1967 war.[22] This raises the question, once again, of why Sadat *was able* to project his views into the policymaking process.

In this chapter I explain how and why Sadat had such latitude. My explanation emphasizes the domestic context of Egypt's civil-military relations—what some have referred to as "the process of transition by which the political centre of gravity ha[d] shifted from the armed forces to the civilian technocracy" (Ya'ari 1980: 112–13; also see Dessouki 1991: 157). Specifically, I show how changes in the balance of civil-military power allowed Sadat to formulate his political goals and then translate them into supportive military strategies. In this regard, one of the chapter's central contributions is in explaining a nonevent, the proverbial dog that did not

---

[20] Explanations that emphasize Sadat's personality and character, with references to the effects of his upbringing and life experiences as policy influences, are dominant in the literature. See, for example, Hirst and Beeson (1981: 51), Karawan (1994: 158), Heikal (1975, 1983), Ayubi (1994), Parker (2001: 113), Mahmood (1985: 69), Finkelstone (1996), Fernandez-Arnesto (1982: 66), Hinnebusch (1985: 80), Stein (1999: 3), Beattie (2000: 14–26). Especially pervasive in this literature is an emphasis on Sadat's "peasant background," which is how the president himself, in his autobiography, *In Search of Identity*, explains his policy choices. Ironically, when one look's closely at Sadat's record and life experiences, they do not suggest that Sadat would achieve such great things. As Gawrych put it, "Nothing in Sadat's background suggested he would become one of the most prominent Middle East statesmen of the twentieth century" (2000: 128). For a critique of the personality-based approach as it applies to Sadat, see Karawan (1994); on the "peasant" view, in particular see Alterman (1998: xvii).

[21] The closest study is Friedlander (1983), which provides a general narrative of negotiations, highlighting the impact of individuals and domestic considerations.

[22] On the view of Nasser as a charismatic leader, see Podeh and Winckler (2004: 2).

bark, or in this case, the military that did not balk: Despite the fact that his policies threatened the military's corporate and strategic interests, Sadat was able to win his chiefs' support in conceptualizing and executing Egypt's political-military strategies.

The chapter also makes a second contribution by highlighting less favorable features of strategic assessment. It is common among Arab commentators to complain that Sadat was a unilateralist in decision making, and that he too easily ignored conventions of consultation (Karawan 1994: 253; Haykal 1986: 186; Fahmy 1983). Most scholars blame Sadat's personality—his alleged arrogance and opportunism—for this decision-making style. This chapter suggests, however, that the origins of his consultative tactics were more complex. Sadat's tactics originated in part in his incentives to impose safeguards in order to circumvent resistance to his goals from his military men (and many diplomats as well).[23] The chapter therefore provides an analytical explanation for Sadat's apparent "unilateralism," situating his experiences in strategic assessment in a unified framework that explains both its strengths and its weaknesses.

Civil-Military Relations under Sadat

The Political-Military Balance of Power

To understand fully civil-military relations under Sadat, one must begin with the final years of Nasser's rule. This period laid the groundwork for some of the changes observed in the 1970s and, in particular, shifts in the balance of civil-military power.

Especially important were the events immediately following the 1967 war and the resolution of the power struggle between Nasser and his military chief, Abdel Hakim Amer. As described in chapter 3, the war had gone disastrously for Egypt after Israel's airstrikes on the morning of June 5. Subsequently, on June 9, Nasser offered his resignation in a public speech to the Egyptian masses. Not wanting to be upstaged, Amer followed suit. The speech was greeted with a spontaneous eruption of support for Nasser (although notably not for Amer, about whom the demonstrators remained remarkably silent).[24] Egypt's masses literally poured into the streets. Sixteen hours after his resignation speech was broadcast, Nasser publicly reinstated himself as political leader of the country. As such, "the demonstrators constituted a massive plebiscite compelling Nasser to remain in

---

[23] On opposition to the peace initiatives from diplomats and those within the elite, see Beattie (2000: 234).

[24] "Nasser Decides to Keep His Post," *New York Times*, June 11, 1967.

power" (Beattie 1994: 211).[25] These events revealed that the loyalties of the masses lay with Nasser, as political head of the country, and not with the army. They showed him to be "unrivaled master of his citizenry" (Walz 1967c). Mostly importantly, "At this moment [Nasser] discovered that he was more powerful than the army."[26]

Amer subsequently tried to reassert himself by plotting to secure his and his officers' return to office.[27] Emboldened by the show of mass support, Nasser confronted his military chief. Amer was arrested and later reportedly committed suicide.[28] Nasser then moved to eliminate Amer's clique in the military.[29] Just days after Amer's death, on September 19, *al-Ahram* reported that 181 officers and civilians had been arrested.[30] Ultimately, over a thousand officers were retired (Beattie 1994: 212; Gawrych 2000: 73; Dawisha 1976: 117). This, as I explain below, is key to understanding the lack of political unity of the military observed under Sadat in the 1970s.

Important changes in the civilian arena were also initiated in Nasser's final years. The end of the 1967 war ushered in a period of debate within Egypt's elite about the future of the one-party socialist state and the sources of Egypt's failure in 1967.[31] It also inspired a period of deep anxiety among students and workers about the war, which culminated in large-scale demonstrations in February 1968 against the lenient sentences given to several top officers tried for their incompetence in the conflict. Nasser responded with a promise of mild political and economic liberalization of the regime. He proposed elections to the peak organizations of the Arab Socialist Union, Egypt's sole political party. As a "show of confidence," Nasser also released more than a thousand prisoners arrested in connection with a 1965

---

[25] For popular reaction to Nasser's resignation speech and his reinstatement, see Pace (1967b), Reston (1967). Although the leadership of the Arab Socialist Union may have orchestrated part of the demonstrations, the magnitude of the display was far beyond the organization's capacity and was truly spontaneous (Beattie 1994: 230).

[26] Interview with Dr. Rifaat Said, Cairo, June 1996.

[27] For an intriguing account of the conspiracy, see the press reports by the *New York Times* (Walz 1967a, 1967c, 1967d).

[28] Conceptually the demonstrations were important because they helped reveal the actual balance of political-military power. See chapter 2.

[29] On August 25, Nasser lured Amer to his home and placed him under house arrest. According to Amin Huweidy, then minister of war, three individuals were instrumental in the action: Huweidy himself, Sami Sharaf (the secretary of the presidency), and Sharawy Goma, minister of the interior. Forces were then sent to Amer's home to detain his cohort; a total of fifty men were arrested that evening. The power struggle ended with Amer's suicide nearly three weeks later, on September 14, 1967. Interview with Amin Huweidy, Cairo, May 1996. Whether Amer actually committed suicide or was murdered is unclear (see Beattie 1994: 231).

[30] Reported in Walz (1967b).

[31] See Beattie (1994: 213–29) for a discussion of the postwar debates, the March 30 declaration, and the political economy of Egypt in this period.

plot by the outlawed Muslim Brotherhood to assassinate him (Pace 1967a). In a departure from the socialist-style trends of the mid-1960s, he encouraged relaxation of the restriction of private and foreign capital, and liberalization of import policies with his Declaration of March 30, 1968—policies aimed at winning support from the middle classes. Although limited, these reforms signaled an important shift in the regime (for details, see Ajami, 1982: 477; also see Dekmejian 1971: 259–61; Cooper 1979: 486–87, 490; Hinnebusch 1985: 37; Sadowski 1991: 53). As one observer put it, "in absolute economic terms [the policy] may have been 'timid,' but in political terms it was anything but" (Cooper 1979: 484). Nasser was shifting the center of gravity of his coalition, seeking to buttress its middle-class base (Baker 1978; Cooper 1979).

Despite these overtures to the middle class, however, Nasser was not seeking to abandon the long-standing statist tendencies of the regime. Rather, "in 1968 and 1969, the wind was blowing from all directions" (Ajami 1982: 466). Thus, Nasser also sought to shore up support from workers, peasants, and leftists by, for example, passing a third land reform in July 1969 (Beattie 1994: 224; see also Baker 1978: 212–14). In short, in the late 1960s Nasser sought to bolster his political coalition by appealing to established constituencies and courting new ones.

During this time, the military's own social support also declined significantly. The armed forces were the object of open contempt, as Egypt's citizens blamed its officers for the country's miserable showing in the June 1967 war (Abdel-Malek 1968: 168, xxxi; Be'eri 1976: 325; Dekmejian 1982: 34; Gawrych 2000: 87). "People spit at them, taxi drivers refuse to carry them," one American journalist reported.[32] On June 22, 1967, a prominent Egyptian newspaper, *al-Goumhouria*, published an article openly critical of the military, something that would have been unthinkable just weeks before.[33]

In sum, Nasser's final three years witnessed dramatic changes in civil-military politics: in the expansiveness of the political coalition, in the final showdown with Amer, in the purge of his allies, and in the decline of the military's popular esteem. These changes laid the foundation for Sadat's efforts to configure a coalition to support his rule and for the influence of the military within it.

SADAT'S COALITION

Lacking an independent power base of his own, when Sadat came to power in October 1970 he moved quickly to establish one. As Raymond Hinne-

---

[32] "Double-think, Egyptian Style," *New York Times Magazine*, August 20, 1967, 85.
[33] See "Leftist Cairo Paper Scores Army Chiefs," *New York Times*, June 22, 1967.

busch describes the motivation, "Sadat needed to build his own constituency which would lend him strong and consistent support" (1985: 50; also see Beattie 2000: 45). While he could have turned toward the left, adopting a radical socialist economic agenda, Sadat instead seized upon Nasser's efforts to appeal to middle-class interests (Cooper 1979). According to Hinnebusch (1985: 50), "his choice of the bourgeoisie was a natural one—both its state and private wings," given it was "the most strategic social force in Egypt," had a large role in the state, and would support Sadat's conservative ideological predisposition; many of Sadat's subsequent economic and political initiatives were geared toward strengthening this constituency.[34]

To appeal to commercial interests, for example, Sadat launched a series of liberalization initiatives, including easing controls on Egyptian and foreign capital. Although Law 43 in 1974 would provide for the most significant and far-reaching changes in what has come to be known as the "opening" or *infitah*, from early in his tenure in office Sadat courted the middle classes.[35] In September 1971, for example, he passed new legislation to encourage private investment in the economy. Tax benefits afforded to foreign capital were extended to local Egyptian investors. At the same time, major changes in labor legislation were adopted, including the abolition in 1971 of all trade union branches at factories employing less than two hundred people. Sadat also began to rethink the regime's long-standing policy of sequestration of capital from the landed classes—a concern from the early days of his presidency (Waterbury 1978: 249).[36]

According to analysts of the political economy of the period, these measures won the president support from private-sector commercial interests, including contractors, real-estate speculators, importers, agents of foreign firms, tourist operators, and lawyers. However, one group that benefited in particular, especially after 1974, was the new class of "middlemen" that acted as liaisons between Egypt's unwieldy bureaucracy and foreign firms (el-Sherif 1995: 186). Because the state remained a major actor in the economy as customer, supplier, and regulator, *infitah* created a niche for these middlemen: "These new elements [made] the interstices between the pub-

---

[34] Economic liberalization was also consistent with Sadat's broader grand strategy of positioning Egypt in the Western camp (Hinnebusch 1985: 58–60).

[35] Among the provisions of Law 43 were tax exemptions for profits for newly established companies, for firms operating in free enterprise zones, as well as for income taxes for foreign employees. Wholly foreign owned concerns were now allowed, while Egyptian labor laws were eased or removed (Baker 1978: 144–45: Hinnebusch 1985: 57). In practice, despite their ambitions, there were many problems with the conceptualization and implementation of the policies (Brumberg 1992: 83; Baker 1978: 144–45).

[36] On these pre-1974 measures, see Kamal (1982: 190–91); Waterbury (1978: 222); Hinnebusch (1985: 50).

lic and private sectors the domain of their operations, notably in subcontracting and the black market" (Baker 1978: 150; Hinnebusch 1985: 59, 261). Moreover, as "expediters for the bewildered foreigner," they often engaged in corrupt practices (Baker 1978: 148; el-Sherif 1995: 21).

Sadat also courted other groups. For example, he continued to guarantee university graduates and professionals employment in the state bureaucracy. Consequently, despite his avowed interest in privatization, employment in the bureaucracy skyrocketed throughout the 1970s, growing by 70 percent from 1971 to 1980. By 1978 employment in the civil service and public sector exceeded 3.2 million.[37] Sadat used this state employment to tie the middle classes to the regime (Baker 1978: 150; Hinnebusch 1985: 261). In addition, Sadat strengthened his ties to the rural middle class and rural elites, which by the late 1960s had emerged as the predominant political group in the countryside (Waterbury 1983: 304; Hinnebusch 1985: 252; Beattie 2000: 49; Binder 1978; Sadowski 1991; el-Sherif 1995: 162, 173–74). Old established families, suppressed under Nasser, also reemerged, through business ties to the public sector, and through the redress of Nasser's sequestration policies (el-Sherif 1995: 186).[38]

As a complement to his economic measures, Sadat initiated a modest liberalization of the political system as a way of winning support from liberal elements in the middle class and satisfying participatory pressures (Hinnebusch 1985: 159).[39] Sadat also freed leaders of the Muslim Brotherhood imprisoned under Nasser and encouraged the rise of Islamic politics (Hinnebusch 1985: 50).[40] Generally Sadat's measures permitted greater freedom of movement for Egypt's citizens, while the press was allowed greater latitude to report on major issues: "One could for a while read (rather than decipher) the press" (Baker 1978: 152, 156). Consumer goods

---

[37] The approximately 100,000 university graduates petitioning annually for positions in the bureaucracy practically guaranteed its growth (Palmer et al. 1988: 8). The years 1977 to 1981 saw growth in employment in the civil service by 29.6 percent, or nearly 10 percent annually. This was the equivalent of approximately four times Egypt's population growth during the period, and it surpassed the growth even at the height of Nasser's socialist revolution in the early 1960s, when employment in the state bureaucracy grew by approximately 8.5 percent annually (Ayubi 1995: 300).

[38] Under Nasser, more than six hundred families had suffered state confiscation of their resources. In December 1970 Sadat ordered a review of all past sequestrations and seized property, with the goal of redressing past "injustices" in this area; his desequestration measures and initiatives toward private capital revived the fortunes of Egypt's aristocratic families considerably (Baker 1978: 149; Beattie 2000: 49).

[39] Sadat established a new party system, in which there were three officially sanctioned pillars, later termed political parties—one for the Right, one for the Left, and one for the Center—under the auspices of the Arab Socialist Union.

[40] On "the return of the Muslim Brothers," see Beattie (2000: 114–15).

became more readily available to the middle class as a result of the relaxation of import controls.[41]

Overall, in the years following the 1973 war and *infitah*, an influx of resources and a rise in investment helped generate prosperity, which "widened and solidified the regime's support among those who got the lion's share of the benefits, the bourgeoisie. Revitalization of the private sector created powerful interests with a stake in the regime" (Hinnebusch 1985: 69–70). Yet, not everyone benefited from Sadat's liberalizing agenda. In 1975–76 there were protests by workers against the policies, although these were limited in scale (Hinnebusch 1985: 63). In 1977 Sadat withdrew subsidies on basic foodstuffs and commodities, such as cooking oil and bread, in an effort to meet austerity conditions set by the International Monetary Fund (IMF).[42] In January massive demonstrations by workers erupted on city streets calling for Sadat to rescind the cuts (see Baker 1978: 165–69; Karawan 1994: 255). Although the demonstrations were never a serious threat to the regime, Sadat restored the subsidies, while vowing to cut them incrementally over time (Hinnebusch 1985: 71; Baker 1978: 165–69). In fact, Sadat ultimately maintained much of Nasser's statist economic edifice, including the commodity subsidies for the lower and middle classes (Beattie 2000: 139–43).

In sum, in the early 1970s Sadat was able to solidify his political base with middle-class land holders, employees of the state sector and bureaucracy, professionals and commercial interests, and the new group of "middlemen" (Hinnebusch 1985: 70).[43] Through his medley of policies and concessions, Sadat both strengthened the middle classes and appealed to their interests. They became more powerful in their own right and assumed a more central position in his coalition (Galvani et al. 1973: 4). In sum, Sadat benefited from "the solid base given to his rule by his alliance with the bourgeoisie, both its state and private wings" (Hinnebusch 1985: 50, 89). Cumulatively, the effect of these dynamics was to enhance the civilian base of the coalition.

---

[41] The share of total imports represented by consumer goods rose from 10 percent in 1969 to 28 percent in 1973, and to 34 percent by 1977 (Brumberg 1992: 83).

[42] The inflow of investment in speculative activities had inflated the economy significantly, producing a 30 percent inflation rate by the mid-1970s. To compensate state employees, Sadat had increased subsidies to 30 percent of central government expenditure in 1976. This created balance of payments problems; in exchange for loans, the IMF pressed for austerity measures (Brumberg 1992: 83). This required reform of the economy, consistent with IMF requirements. Sadat thus had to cut Egypt's substantial budget deficit (equivalent to two billion U.S. dollars), which required cutting the military, investment, debt service, or subsidies. He chose the latter.

[43] Sadat also built constituencies within key institutions of the state and strengthened his ties to the elite, especially anti-Nasserites and antileftists (Beattie 2000: 49).

MILITARY COHESION

By the 1970s, the military leadership was much less unified than it had been in the mid-1960s. It lacked cohesive groupings that could present a unified front to Sadat. The change was due in significant part to the purging of Amer's clique in the late 1960s and the failure of a successor cohort to fill the vacuum. The neutralization of Amer's grouping had left the military leadership without a dominant core (Ya'ari 1980: 114; Beattie 1994: 212).

Evidence of the low level of cohesion within the military leadership can be seen in events that occurred shortly after Sadat assumed office. Just six months after taking power, in May 1971, Sadat faced a major challenge from a powerful group of civilian leftists in the Arab Socialist Union.[44] Given their stature in the regime and influence in bringing Sadat to power, this group expected Sadat to defer to them and allow them to dictate policy initiatives (Baker 1978: 125; Haykal 1975:128; 1983:39). On April 25, 1971, one of the leaders of the leftist group, Ali Sabri, challenged Sadat's authority to make foreign policy decisions (Hofstadter 1973: 267). A week after the meeting, Sadat fired Sabri from his post in the ASU.

Significantly, in response, General Mohammed Fawzi, Egypt's minister of war, who sympathized with the Sabri cohort, tried to organize military action against Sadat. He was ultimately unsuccessful because of the lack of unity within the military leadership. Thus, late on May 10, Sadat was supplied with information from his intelligence services of plans for an imminent coup by General Fawzi.[45] Two days later, during a meeting with Egyptian troops at a military base near Suez, the chief of staff of the army, General Mohammed Ahmed Sadiq, told Sadat he knew of the plot and would support the president. Prior to these events, Sadat had cultivated relations with Sadiq, meeting with him and other officers in March and April 1971; through this he "developed an understanding with Sadiq that the latter would do his utmost to guarantee the military's backing" in the event of a confrontation with the Ali Sabri group (Beattie 2000: 66; Perlmutter 1974: 1893). The chief of the presidential guard also refused to

---

[44] In chapter 3 I described how Nasser used the ASU, its youth organization, and its vanguard group to counterbalance the influence of the right-leaning constituency under Abdel Hakim Amer. With the purge of Amer's faction in 1967 there was no longer an effective counter to Sabri's "power center" as it was called. Despite Nasser's efforts to contain the leftists' influence, the constituency became increasingly powerful in the final years of his regime.

[45] Although Sadat publicly stated that a coup plot was uncovered, many questioned whether events had ever reached this point (Baker 1978: 125; Heikal 1983: 40; Beattie 2000: 65). Whether there were actual plans for a coup or not, as Beattie put it, the activities of the Ali Sabri group were "coup-oriented." For overviews of these events, see Handel (1981: 246); Beattie (2000: 62–76); Hinnebusch (1985: 43–44).

follow Fawzi and subsequently implemented a detailed plan to maintain control over Cairo and protect the president from any moves against him (el-Sherif 1995: 50; Haykal 1975: 135–36; Beattie 2000: 68). Fawzi was later forced to admit to his fellow conspirators that he was unable to move a single tank in support of their takeover (el-Sherif 1995: 49). On May 14 Sadat arrested the entire group of conspirators (Baker 1978: 126). The small number of officers who had sided with Fawzi and Sabri were purged (Perlmutter 1974: 191).

The events of May 1971 are often cited as a major turning point in Sadat's subordination of the "left" in his "corrective revolution." However, equally important is what they reveal about the lack of cohesion among Egypt's military chiefs. The military chiefs were divided in their allegiances, and General Fawzi overestimated the loyalty he would command (Haykal 1975: 136; also see Beattie 1988: 216–17).[46] Thus, whereas Amer could rely on the support of his service chiefs and military officials, Fawzi lacked such support. Sadat faced no unified opposition from his military chiefs (Haykal 1983: 41; Hofstadter 1973: 267).

Summary: The Balance of Power in the 1970s

A variety of forces thus interacted to produce a change in the balance of civil-military power in the 1970s: Sadat expanded the social base of his regime, his military lacked cohesive groupings, and its social prestige declined. All of this shifted the regime's center of gravity to the civilian side. One commonly cited indicator of this is the composition of executive cabinets in Egypt during the 1970s (see table 4.1).[47] In June 1967, for example, military personnel held nearly two-thirds of the posts in the cabinet. By March 1968 this figure had fallen to 39 percent, while Sadat's cabinet of January 1972 contained less than a quarter active-duty military officers. Moreover, among the "officer-technocrats" in Sadat's coalition, fewer were concentrated in the humanities, suggesting that the "extraneous military presence was being weeded out" (Cooper 1979: 209). By October 1977, ministerial posts held by the military consisted of the maritime, transport, and communications portfolios under one officer, and the war and war production portfolios under another, positions that could be justified by the military's expertise and responsibilities (Cooper 1982).

[46] On other factors affecting officer attitudes and Sadat's attempts to establish ties with them, see Beattie (2000: 46).

[47] The executive cabinet was not a central locus of decision making on military policy or strategic matters in Sadat's regime; therefore, in this case, it makes sense to use it as an indicator of the overall representation of the military in the coalition.

Table 4.1
Military Representation in Executive Cabinets, 1961–1977

Cabinet	Military (no. in cabinet)	Military (%)
October 19,1961	15	51.6
September 29,1962	16	36.4
March 24,1964	16	36.4
(1965–June 1967, Amer increasingly powerful in regime)		
October 2,1965	19	46.3
September 10,1966	21	55.3
June 19,1967	19	65.5
(September 1967, Amer's faction purged, modest political and economic liberalization)		
March 20,1968	13	39.4
October 28,1968	13	41.9
(September 1970, Nasser dies, Sadat comes to power, greater liberalization)		
October 21,1970	11	33.3
May 14,1971	11	30.7
September 20,1971	15	41.7
January 19,1972	8	23.5
March 27,1973	11	30.5
(October 1973 war)		
April 25,1974	7	20.0
(October 1974, Sadat issues October Paper in which he outlines his outward-looking economic policy; Law 43 passed)		
March 20,1976	4	12.5
November 10,1976	3	9.4
February 2,1977	3	9.1
October 25,1977	3	9.7

Sources: Cooper (1982), Dekmejian (1971). Annotations are my own.
Note: Cabinets range from 20 to 35 ministers.

In sum, under Sadat the military's position in the regime changed, as one analyst puts it, from a situation of significant influence in the mid-1960s to one of "civilian control/military partnership" in the late 1960s and 1970s (Dekmejian 1982: 36; Dessouki 1991: 165). The military was transformed from a powerful political constituency to "a much smaller, weaker component of the elite" (Hinnebusch 1985: 131). It was now "a professional force subordinate to legal authority, its role in policymaking, even in defense matters, radically curtailed" (Hinnebusch 1985: 125; Dawisha 1976: 117). The balance of political-military power clearly advantaged Sadat.

Preference Divergence

Although the balance of power had shifted in Sadat's favor, he nevertheless faced military leaders consistently at odds with his policy priorities. Existing research on civil-military relations provides some insight into the sources of these cleavages.

Some scholarship suggests that the regional "threat" Egypt faced—specifically the occupation of its territory by Israel—could have facilitated a convergence of preferences over strategic, corporate, and professional issues.[48] In actuality, however, tensions with Israel had more mixed effects on the preferences of political and military leaders in the 1970s.

"Threat" did harmonize civil-military preferences in one way: It encouraged the military to focus on improving its capabilities and effectiveness (Gawrych 2000: 75). After the devastation of the 1967 war, Egypt's officers demonstrated greater awareness of the need for discipline and attention to duty in military activity. While not all officers were professionally minded, there was a general sense that the armed forces' involvement in political activities and the civilian apparatus of the state had harmed the military's competence in 1967: Involvement in "civilian affairs" proved detrimental to the officer corps' preparation for war (el-Gamasy 1993; Hinnebusch 1985: 109). The regional environment thus helped to promote a greater conviction that the military had to emphasize its war-fighting capabilities within organizational processes—a view that coincided with Sadat's desire (after 1972) to prepare for war against Israel.

However, the threat environment also exacerbated conflict between the political and military leadership over military strategy. No doubt, a chief concern of both the political and military leadership from 1967 was securing the return of Egypt's land. Nevertheless beyond a general and diffuse agreement on the need to regain lost territory, there were major clashes about how to achieve that goal. Accounts by observers and analysts of this period suggest that these differences were rooted in the organizational interests and socialization of military leaders. In particular, Sadat's commitment to a limited war strategy in 1973, as a catalyst for a negotiated settlement, was contrary to the military's desire to secure the return of the

---

[48] Desch (1999) suggests that when states face external threats, civil-military preferences are harmonized. Although in cases where the state also faces an internal threat (as, for example, in Egypt, where the political leadership faced a challenge from the military), the effect on civil-military relations is more uncertain and depends on preexisting doctrine.

territory by force, through a "total war" of attrition (Riad 1981: 211). For many officers, and especially Sadat's minister of war at the time, Mohammed Sadiq, the uncertainty and risk associated with a political strategy that used military power for diplomatic ends, were anathema.[49] These officers favored a conventional offensive and victory through the application of force.[50]

After the 1973 war, Sadat and his military chiefs continued to clash over military strategy and activity, while disputes over corporate issues also flared. Many officers, for example, disagreed with Sadat's efforts to pursue a ceasefire in the final days of the war, wanting instead to exploit Egypt's early successes and expand the war's aims. Subsequently, disputes manifested in military apprehensions about Sadat's willingness to compromise in agreements with Israel over the numbers of soldiers and equipment that could be deployed in the Sinai. The issue was to emerge in both the 1974 and 1975 military disengagement agreements and the 1978 Camp David Accords (el-Gamasy 1993; Riad 1981; Friedlander 1983; Kissinger 1982). In March 1974, for example, a rebellion by soldiers from Egypt's Third Army broke out in central Cairo over decisions to reduce the troop presence in the Sinai, with the men calling for an end to the ceasefire and preparation for a resumption of hostilities (Indyk 1984: 54; Dekmejian,1982: 37; Haykal 1996: 234). From his officers' perspective, Sadat was single-handedly giving away the military's hard-won gains in the October 1973 war through his concessions.

Finally, the general thrust of Sadat's grand strategy was a source of conflict. Sadat's desire to ally Egypt with the West and the United States, rather than jockey between the superpowers, had enormous implications for the military's strategic orientation and corporate interests. It forced a complete reorientation of its doctrinal focus, away from Israel. Many consequently feared that "peace might jeopardize the security, good pay and perquisites the military enjoyed as long as war with Israel remained a

---

[49] So pronounced were these differences that in November 1972 rumors surfaced of a conspiracy by a group of officers involved in an organization called "Save Egypt," which was opposed to going to war before Egypt gained more offensive weapons. Among those arrested in relation to the plot were the chief of military intelligence, commander of the central district (Cairo), commander of a ranger group, and two division commanders (el-Shazly 1980: 192; el-Sherif 1995; Hirst 1981: 144; Kimche 1974: 27). In fact, the view that Egypt should not wage war until it was ready for total war (rather than a limited war of finite objectives) was widespread in the officer corps (el-Shazly 1980: 189–90). Ironically although they resisted the limited war concept and wanted to delay fighting, many also were opposed to pursuing a negotiated settlement with Israel in order to get the land back. Heikal (1983: 41) reports, for example, that General Mohammed Fawzi told Sadat that the army found proposals by William Rogers, U.S. secretary of state, for a settlement with Israel unacceptable (Rogers visited Egypt on May 4); Fawzi apparently felt that Sadat was selling out to the United States.

[50] See chapter 2 for a discussion of measuring preference divergence.

possibility" (Friedlander 1983: 239). Alignment with the West also forced a change in the military's ideological role in the region. The military went from a "vanguard of [Nasser's socialist] revolution to a regional *gendarmerie*, sent to fight on the side of rightist elements in Zaire, Oman and Libya" (Hinnebusch 1985: 129; see also Karawan 1984; Dekmejian 1982: 39; Alterman 1998: 47). In the latter 1970s, the military would also experience a loss of reserve forces and cuts in its budget by an annual real rate of greater than 20 percent (Ya'ari 1980: 115).

The potential loss of the Soviet Union as a supplier of arms and spare parts also heightened the military's suspicions of Sadat's effort to align with the West. As Sadat pursued his overtures to the West, the loss of Soviet weapons "meant rapid amortization, difficulties in maintenance and a technological lag" (Ya'ari 1980: 115; also Alterman 1998: 46). As early as 1974, during negotiations over the disengagement agreements with Israel, Sadat sought and received assurances from Henry Kissinger that American military aid would be forthcoming. However, substantial American military assistance would materialize only after the Egyptian-Israeli treaty was signed, five years later. Consequently, "among Egyptian military planners, the years 1974 to 1977 saw growing disenchantment with American reliability in both the political and military spheres. They urged Sadat to resume relations with the Soviet Union so that spare parts and perhaps equipment might again be obtained from that source" (Karawan 1984: 175). By 1977 Israel had achieved 160 percent of its pre-1973 war military strength, while Egypt's capabilities had declined by 90 percent (Indyk 1984: 8). So concerned was Sadat about military apprehensions about weapons supply that weeks before the peace treaty was signed negotiations nearly broke down over U.S. reticence to supply Egypt with sophisticated equipment for its air force (Friedlander 1983: 286). In sum, Sadat's "foreign policy forced radical changes in [the military's] traditional role and had a negative effect on its professional interests" (Hinnebusch 1985: 129).

Egypt's military and political leadership may have had a mutual interest in securing the return of the Sinai and developing the capabilities to do so, but from there their interests rapidly diverged. Preference divergence was high.[51]

---

[51] One area that also caused friction over corporate issues, but was ultimately not a major issue, was Soviet training. After the 1967 war the Soviets sent large numbers of personnel to help Egypt rebuild its military. The actual number was never absolutely clear; Western analysts apparently estimated the figure to be about 6,000 (Baker 1978: 129), although figures as low as 850 to as high as 20,000 are cited (el-Gamasy 1993; Hirst and Beeson 1981: 132). Regardless, there were Soviet personnel attached to the major air and naval bases, training facilities, and maintenance depots. They actively participated in training and field exercises (McDermott 1988: 161). The Egyptian military resented the Soviet role, its reticence to supply Egypt with offensive arms, and also the perceived arrogance of the Soviet officers (Hinnebusch 1985: 52; el-Gamasy 1993: 141; el-Shazly 1980: 145). Ultimately, however, the dispute over Soviet military assistance would not prove to be a major axis of conflict between

Strategic Assessment

In short, in the 1970s civil-military relations were characterized by high preference divergence and political dominance. Sadat faced an uncohesive military leadership—a military without strong popular support or ties to civilian constituencies—while he expanded the social base of his regime. The balance of power was in Sadat's favor. However, despite his power position, the military leadership clashed with Sadat over corporate and strategic issues.

Below I analyze how these civil-military relations affected strategic assessment in Egypt under Sadat. I review the quality of the four institutional attributes of strategic assessment—information sharing, strategic coordination, structural competence, and strategic coordination. I also emphasize how those attributes manifested and influenced the specific political and military strategies Sadat pursued: the planning and execution of the 1973 war, the subsequent disengagement agreements, and ensuing peace initiatives. Much of the text that follows is oriented around these events. In the concluding section of this chapter, I show how these four attributes combined to affect the integration of Sadat's political goals and Egypt's military activity in the 1970s.

Information Sharing

Unlike Nasser in the mid-1960s, as president Sadat had considerable access to information about military affairs: Information sharing was relatively unproblematic. The president, for example, was able to meet with his military chiefs freely and had considerable interactions with key officials. Sadat also retained the ability to get data from intelligence officials in his three security services, the National Intelligence Service, Military Intelligence, and the Secret Investigations Department, all of which remained under his direct control or indirect influence (Hinnebusch 1985: 88, 42–44; el-Shazly 1980: 119–20).

Sadat's access to information was also assured through his capacity to impose monitoring mechanisms on the military. One of his more creative tactics in this regard included co-opting the military's top internal consultative body for use as his own advisory body. Sadat used the Supreme Coun-

---

the military and political leadership, for two reasons. First, Sadat defused the issue by ordering the evacuation of Soviet trainers in July 1972 (Hinnebusch 1985: 52). Second, Sadat himself shared the view that Egypt needed to distance itself from Soviet influence (Hinnebusch 1985: 127). Many analysts have focused on the international significance of the expulsion (Lippman 1989; Quandt 1993). However, in ordering the Soviets out, Sadat also neutralized a major dispute with his military.

cil of the Armed Forces (SCAF), which was formally run by the minister of war with the participation of the chief of the General Staff, top army commanders, service chiefs, and head of military intelligence, "to sound out the military elite on the various issues and to inform them of his views," causing the resentment of at least some of the high command (el-Sherif 1995: 30, 374; Gawrych 2000: 78). In addition, Sadat established a permanent office at the Ministry of War (el-Shazly 1980: 115), which allowed him access to military officials at the time and place of his choosing; he was also able to observe internal military activity, as well as to discuss issues and concerns with his military leaders.

The president also engaged officers at different levels of command in order to solicit their insights. Unlike in the 1960s, the military hierarchy remained relatively permeable to the political leader, allowing Sadat ready access to its officers (el-Gamasy 1993; Perlmutter 1974: 193; Beattie 2000: 66). Organizationally, Sadat structured his intelligence agencies to ensure that he would get the "best" information possible about internal military happenings. By inducing competition between the agencies, and guaranteeing some overlap in their responsibilities, he helped ensure that information and conflicting views would be forced to the top (el-Shazly 1980: 120).

One can see these strengths in information sharing in how Sadat planned the 1973 war. In that process, Sadat was able to use his contacts with his military leaders and ability to direct their reporting activities to gain detailed information about a variety of issues, including Egypt's capabilities and military situation (Karawan 1984: 153; Insight Team 1974: 66; el-Badri et al. 1978: 15). During the war he was able to observe events and was fully apprised of debates within the High Command, including sensitive command decisions (see below). Contrast this with Nasser in the 1967 war, who waited six hours after Israel's preemptive attack before he was informed of his air force's destruction (Dupuy 1978: 267; Hammel 1992: 244).

These advantages in information sharing, in particular, would prove especially important for Sadat's capacity to implement his deception plan before the war. From the start, the military realized that successfully crossing the Suez Canal and confronting the Bar Lev line required keeping the Israelis off guard about the likelihood of attack and, if one was to occur, when it would take place (el-Badri et al. 1978: 45; Insight Team 1974: 64). This would preclude a preemptive strike by Israel and allow crucial time for Egyptian forces to cross the canal and entrench themselves before Israel mobilized its reserves for a counterattack (Amos 1979: 167). Consequently, Egypt designed an elaborate deception plan to obscure Egypt's intentions. A program for planting false press reports was developed, including stories that Egypt could not operate its technologically sophisticated equipment in the wake of the 1972 withdrawal of the Soviet advisers. This fed directly into Israel's conception that the Arabs were not able, and hence would not be ready, to mount a significant military operation in the near future. Alarmist stories warning of imminent Israeli attack, alongside reports of accelerated military training and preparations, appeared in Egyptian papers (Amos 1979: 172). These stories resonated with Israeli preconceptions that such exhortations were intended to rally a restless domestic populace.[52] As one analyst observes, these "efforts were part of an imaginative, intensive and well orchestrated strategy of deception which brought rich rewards" (Shlaim 1976: 355–56).

As creative as were many of these measures, however, they would have failed had Sadat not been able to keep word of his real plans from the Israelis. Here is where the capacity to control the dissemination of information at the political-military apex and below—a key dimension of information sharing—was crucial. Thus, under Sadat's guidance, strict restrictions were placed on who had access to what information about the war plans; notes were sometimes taken by hand and conveyed personally (Amos 1979: 171; Haykal 1975: 12). Information about the day and time of the attack had to be handled with particular care. A detailed timetable was developed, stipulating when each layer in the command structure was to be informed of the time of attack (el-Gamasy 1993: 196; Amos 1979: 171). "Senior officers were briefed on October 1; some naval commanders were issued sealed orders to open only when told to; some local army and air force commanders were informed only 48 hours in advance; the troops themselves were told just 10–15 minutes in advance" (Amos 1979: 171). As a result, "most Egyptian officers and troops had no idea war was imminent until the very last moment" (Cordesman and Wagner 1990: 23). When Israelis interviewed prisoners of war, they found that 95 percent of Egyptians captured had learned of the attack only on the morning of October 6 (Amos 1979: 330).

Without this control over the exchange and dissemination of information, it is doubtful whether Egypt could have executed its deception plan and, in turn, given the importance of strategic and tactical surprise to Egypt's military strategy, achieved its successful crossing of the Suez Canal. At issue was not simply the technical aptitude to gather information about the Israelis, but the political capacity of the regime to structure the entire process of information exchange in support of its strategy. Information sharing in Egypt had vastly improved in the 1970s.

---

[52] On the variety of measures taken, see Badri et al. (1978: 46–47), Amos (1979: 171–72), Bar-Joseph (2005: 25–32), Shlaim (1976). Also see Heikal's (1974) interview of Ahmed Ismail. In contrast to Shlaim and others, Bar-Joseph (2005: 31) argues that the deception plan was not as elaborate as it might have been and tends instead to blame the intelligence failure on organizational deficiencies in Israel. Still, most analysts agree that Egypt did manage to obscure a substantial amount of information about its war plans.

Strategic Coordination

Taken as a whole, strategic coordination was mixed in Egypt under Sadat. It was positive in one respect: Unlike Nasser, Sadat could require cooperation from his military leaders and retained latitude to decide the structure of military consultation and advice; this, in some cases, facilitated review of his policies. Take, for example, how the original concept for the war plan in 1973 was developed.

When Sadat assumed office from Nasser in September 1970, there existed no fully developed offensive war plan, only a defensive plan, termed Defense Plan 200 (el-Shazly 1980: 18); over the next two years various war plans would be developed, although none would be fully implemented. In early 1972, increasingly convinced that only military action would break the diplomatic deadlock, Sadat commissioned a report from General Ahmed Ismail, who was then in charge of military intelligence, about the possibility of conducting a war against Israel (Karawan 1984: 153; el-Badri et al. 1978: 15). Among the study's findings were that Egypt lacked the military capabilities relative to its more powerful adversary, Israel, to pursue a total war against the Israelis aimed at retaking the occupied territories by force; nor was restarting the low-intensity firing across the canal, which had been characteristic of the 1969–70 War of Attrition, likely to secure the return of the Sinai (el-Shazly 1980: 30, 94, 116; Haykal 1975: 167–68). Instead the reports underscored the potential value of "design[ing] around the defender's superiority" by launching a limited operation with the goal of retaking a slice of territory on the Israeli-occupied Sinai Peninsula (as described above, in order to spark American involvement in the regional dispute and reinvigorate negotiations with Israel) (Lieberman 1994: 413).[53] As such, the war plan emerged from a systematic evaluative process in which military plans were considered in concert with international constraints, resource limits, and Sadat's political goals (el-Shazly 1980: 17–39; el-Gamasy 1993: chap. 3).[54]

Despite these strengths, as the theory outlined in chapter 2 suggests, there were also notable weaknesses in strategic coordination. These stemmed from underlying divergences in political-military preferences and the oversight methods Sadat consequently employed to protect his goals

---

[53] For Ahmed Ismail's own description of his reasoning process and the calculations that entered the study, see his interview with Heikal reported in *Journal of Palestine Studies* (1974: 216).

[54] As Lieberman (1995: 883) notes, this strategy was not necessarily inevitable, although it may seem so in retrospect. After all, the Israelis never conceived that Egypt might find within its options a limited war; instead they focused on the country's intentions to wage a general attack to regain the Sinai by force or to revisit their strategy in the War of Attrition.

from opposition from his military chiefs; although they safeguarded his interests, these tactics at times also undermined consultation between the political and military leadership.

One method Sadat commonly employed was to limit consultation with officers who opposed his plans and discount their advice in key advisory forums. Sadat often would discuss issues with his generals only after he already had made a decision about the course of action he intended to pursue (Karawan 1984: 152; Hinnebusch 1985: 86; Handel 1981: 249; Stein 1999: 4–6, 11). For example, in July 1972 when Sadat decided to expel the large numbers of Soviet military advisers in charge of training Egyptian forces, he issued the order without first consulting his military chiefs, despite the fact that removal of these advisers and their equipment was not an "insignificant decision as far as Egypt's defense policy was concerned" (Karawan 1984: 152; el-Gamasy 1993: 145–46; el-Sherif 1995: 32; Handel 1981: 272). Similarly, during negotiations with Israel over the post-1973 war disengagement agreements, Sadat purposely evaded consulting with his military chiefs. Thus, in August 1975, when Egypt and Israel were negotiating Sinai II, Chief of Staff Gamasy and members of his military staff were shown the proposed lines for Egyptian and Israeli forces in the Sinai, but they were "given little time to study them or comment on them" (Eilts 1991: 171). Sadat used similar tactics when he was negotiating the military components of the Camp David Accords (Safty 1991; Haykal 1996; el-Gamasy 1993). During the critical months preceding and during meetings at Camp David, then Minister of War Gamasy was rarely consulted (Ya'ari 1980: 116). In short, to evade opposition from his military chiefs, Sadat often neglected to seek their informed opinions about peace proposals, in the process preserving his latitude for action (Haykal 1996: 186; Ya'ari 1980: 121).

Sadat's methods also harmed another dimension of strategic coordination: Joint diplomatic and military advisory forums were inadequate. As described above, Sadat coopted the SCAF as his principal consultative body, which helped facilitate information sharing. This insulated Sadat's initiatives from coordinated military opposition. However, using the SCAF also substituted for routinized coordination between the broader political apparatus of the state and the military (Karawan 1984; el-Gamasy 1993). Arguably the National Defense Council, established by Nasser in 1969 and formally a civilian-based organization, composed of the ministers of foreign affairs, war, planning, economy, and interior and the chief of national intelligence, would have been a more inclusive structure for strategic analysis than the SCAF (el-Sherif 1995: 27; Dessouki 1991: 170; Gawrych 2000: 78). However, in practice, Sadat "set the National Defense Council aside" and throughout his decade in office convened it only twice (during his first months in office) (el-Sherif 1995: 27).

In sum, by restricting the military's role in consultation, maintaining a circumspect attitude toward military advice, and otherwise failing to engage his military leaders and diplomats in joint advisory bodies, Sadat protected himself from criticism and efforts to challenge his policies (Haykal 1996: 186).[55] However, in doing so, he also curtailed debate and consultation about political-military issues. While his ability to enjoin his military chiefs in consultation was an advantage in planning the 1973 war, as I explain later, these weaknesses in strategic coordination would at times undermine his bargaining position as he negotiated peace with Israel.

Structural Competence

The structural competence of the Egyptian military in external intelligence gathering and internal monitoring also improved under Sadat. Critical once again in understanding these changes was the nature of civil-military relations in the regime. With the easing of the fierce rivalry between Nasser and Amer after the 1967 war (culminating in Amer's alleged suicide in September 1967), which had absorbed intelligence resources, the assets of Military Intelligence could be reoriented toward external adversaries and Israel, in particular (el-Gamasy 1993: 43). The task of internal security was transferred in full to the Ministry of Interior (Gawrych 2000: 90). Military Intelligence was also subsequently reformed (Amos 1979: 141; el-Gamasy 1993: 47; el-Badri et al. 1978: 45; Gawrych 2000: 91).

These improvements, in turn, are integral to understanding the process of strategic assessment in Egypt in the months prior to the 1973 war. For example, preparatory to developing the operational plans for the war, Military Intelligence undertook a series of six studies on the current military situation. The studies included (1) analysis of Israeli strategic theory; (2) analysis of the "temperament and thinking" of the Israeli General Staff (i.e., of Israeli beliefs about Egypt's capabilities and perceptions of the regional and strategic environment); (3) the collection of intelligence available on Israeli doctrine and force structure, and on the Bar Lev line; (4) evaluation of the reorganization of Egyptian forces that would be required to address the findings of these studies; (5) analysis of the military and political considerations essential to choosing a date for an attack across the Suez Canal; and (6) the problems of achieving strategic and tactical surprise in such an attack (Insight Team 1974: 66).[56] These analyses folded assessment of tactical issues into a larger survey of strategic factors pertinent to both Egypt's and Israel's military capabilities and plans.

---

[55] Sadat used similar tactics with his diplomats when he anticipated opposition (Stein, 1999: 13; Karawan 1984: 153).

[56] These studies are also recounted in Haykal's interview with Ahmad Ismail (1974: 216).

While enhancing the Egyptian military's intelligence capabilities, civil-military relations also facilitated improvements in its capacity for internal monitoring. Political dominance, brought about by the military's loss of social standing and lack of internal unity in the early 1970s, sustained and reinforced organizational norms that emphasized self-critical analysis by affording greater emphasis on professional qualifications in appointments and promotions. Sadat had greater latitude than Nasser had had prior to the 1967 war to appoint individuals who were skilled officers, valued organizational efficiency, and were concerned about the deleterious effects of political activity on the military.[57] After the 1967 war there was a "conscious effort to promote the most competent officers regardless of political sentiments [which] resulted in very capable leadership at the senior levels of the Egyptian military" (Pollack 2002: 127).[58] "Considerations of merit now weighed in promotions much more heavily than those of loyalty" (Gawrych 2000: 77, also 73, 80; Hinnebusch 1985: 38). Among the pivotal appointments was Mohammed Abdel Gamasy, chief of operations in the October War and later minister of war. Gamasy represented "the very model of the respected non-political professional" military officer (Hinnebusch 1985: 129; "Sadat's Power Base," 160). General Ahmed Ismail, another key appointment, also forswore open politicking and emphasized attention to duty in military activity (el-Gamasy 1993: 155; Haykal 1975: 182). These values, in turn, "were diffused throughout the officer corps" by the top military leadership (el-Gamasy 1993: 157; also see Ya'ari 1980: 113, 115).[59]

This emphasis on merit versus partisanship in appointments had a big payoff. It facilitated the emergence of a more self-aware organizational

---

[57] On the idea that particular configurations of power support particular preferences and attitudes among military officers, see Sechser (2004). In many cases, Sadat promoted officers who placed intrinsic value on their normative roles as "professional" military officers, and he removed or punished those who did not, thereby increasing the costs officers assigned to defying political authority. Note that Nasser in his final years had initiated the change in appointment criteria (Gawrych 1987: 546). In effect the balance of civil-militry power contributed to what many term the "professionalization" of the Egyptian military in this period (Beattie 1988: 214). On professionalism, see earlier in this chapter.

[58] Many of these were officers who had been marginalized by Amer in the 1960s (Ya'ari 1980: 115).

[59] Ya'ari (1980: 113–14) argues that access to sophisticated weaponry and recruitment of officers from a broader strata of society reinforced these trends. However, it is important not to overstate the degree to which prominent officers had forsworn political activity. For example, Mohammed Fawzi, who had been appointed by Nasser in the aftermath of the 1967 war as an "apolitical" disciplinarian in charge of reforming the military, was the same general that sided with the leftist coup faction in May 1971 (discussed above). Also, his replacement, General Sadiq, was supposedly an apolitical leader but often courted military support (Heikal 1983: 40). Hence there were obvious limits to efforts to promote conventions of political supremacy through military appointments.

ethos, willingness to think critically about the country's capabilities, and a capacity for learning. For example, the military review from 1956 that detailed Egypt's failings in the Suez conflict was released and evaluated (it had been buried by Amer in the 1960s). Egypt's war effort in 1967 was also closely scrutinized.[60] The army's chief historian, Major General Hasan el-Badri, undertook a formal study of the causes of the 1967 defeat. A more focused study of the Egyptian air force, which "analyzed the mistakes made by the Egyptians in the air force and air defense since the 1956 war," was also undertaken (Gawrych 2000: 90). The lessons gleaned from these inquiries, in turn, formed the basis for planning in 1973. As one analyst describes it, "what the Arabs did after 1967 was a much more serious and practical examination of their record. Actually, the Arab strategy in 1973 can be described as a system of remedies for the problems which had caused the Arab defeat in 1967; a set of lessons derived from their 1967 experience" (Williams 1975: 173). Learning was therefore key to war planning in 1973. But a necessary precondition was the establishment of a military command willing and able to learn from the past—something afforded by the prior change in appointment criteria and the civil-military relations that facilitated it.

These changes in the military leadership's organizational ethos in turn are critical to understanding how the war plan in 1973 emerged. Most importantly, they promoted self-restraint in how officers conceptualized Egypt's operations and tactics. For example, early on military leaders recognized that the Israeli Air Force was far superior to Egypt's. Consequently, "Egyptian air strategy for the October War was built around this central assumption" (Pollack 2002: 123). Deciding to forgo extensive counterair operations and limit their activities in the air to discrete, well-defined tactical strikes, Egypt's aircraft spent much of the war safeguarded in hardened aircraft hangars built for the purpose; at the same time, as noted above, Egypt focused on building a battery of anti-aircraft guns in the canal zone to protect ground operations from air attack (el-Shazly 1980: 19, 20; Pollack 2002: 104; Amos 1979: 176; Aker 1985: 54; Cordesman and Wagner 1990: 74, 94; Whetten 1974: 275).

A similar approach governed operations on the ground. As one observer put it, "From the outset, Egyptian planners recognized that overall military strategy and tactics would have to be tailored to the character of the manpower available, i.e., small cadres of highly trained individuals (senior officers with extensive backgrounds, academy graduates and some pilots), but also large numbers of Egyptian peasants" (Amos 1979: 195).

[60] See, for example, el-Gamasy's first chapter (1993), where he reviews these lessons; his memoirs from the 1973 war begin with several chapters on 1967 outlining the specific lessons drawn from it.

Egypt's military leaders realized, for example, that the army was poor at executing operations that relied on offensive maneuver, despite its inherent advantages on the battlefield (Pollack 2002: 100). Consequently, the planning staff developed plans for a massive, attrition-style onslaught along the length of the canal, which was better suited to its manpower and tactical limitations. Similarly, in military training leaders often relied on rote memorization because of the low literacy levels of many Egyptian soldiers; every detail of the operation was highly scripted (see Rabinovich 2004: 28; Tsouras 1994: 193–94; Insight Team 1974: 224; Amos 1979: 196; Pollack 2002: 102).[61] Drills ranged in scope from daily firings to hundreds of full-scale water crossings (Amos 1979: 196; Tsouras 1994: 194). In short, this was a military able and willing to understand its weaknesses, as well as strengths, and to make the compromises necessary in order to tailor military policy to its capabilities. Its structural competence had improved considerably.

The Authorization Process

Finally, Egypt benefited from an unambiguous process for making decisions about military and political strategy, in which the political leadership clearly dominated. Thus, in the 1970s Sadat "retained all critical decision-making prerogatives for himself" (Stein 1999: 67; Hinnebusch 1985: 131). Especially important, Sadat controlled officer appointments and promotions (el-Sherif 1995: 229–32). In November 1971, for example, Sadat reconfigured the formal institutional machinery for military personnel decisions to his advantage, first by issuing a presidential decree increasing the sphere of responsibility in promotions of the service branches' Armed Forces Officers' Committees, and then by increasing his control over the composition and regulation of those committees. These measures "helped Sadat make sure that the major posts in the armed forces were staffed by loyal officers; and that there was a high risk involved in not remaining loyal" (el-Sherif 1995: 230).

In short, unlike Nasser in the mid-1960s Sadat retained administrative control of the principal levers of decision making over his military organization. Consequently, Egypt benefited from a clear authorization process, which proved vital to the formulation and execution of the 1973 war and the subsequent peace initiatives. Below I discuss several areas in which decision-making processes were manifested in the war and after.

---

[61] For other examples of the responsiveness of Egyptian military activity and planning efforts, see Cordesman and Wagner (1990: 57), Whetten (1974: 283), Finklestone (1996: 83), Amos (1979: 147–48), Insight Team (1974: 66–67).

Prewar Planning: Limited War Concept

From the start, the clarity of the authorization process, and Sadat's control of appointments in particular, was vital to planning the 1973 war.[62] Although he eventually forged a command supportive of the plan, as detailed above, Sadat initially faced opposition to the concept of a war with limited aims from his minister of war and commander in chief Mohammed Sadiq, as well as other service chiefs. As Gawrych describes it:

> For [Sadiq] it was inconceivable that limited war could bring Egypt political gains. The army's own internal studies estimated that the Egyptian Armed Forces would suffer 17,000 casualties crossing the Suez Canal. . . . Egypt would gain nothing from such a bloody conflict, even if it could hold onto a bit of territory in the Sinai. Therefore, before embarking on any hostilities, Sadiq wanted to have a much better trained and equipped military force. . . . the prevailing military position was quite clear. Only a major war to liberate most, if not all, the Sinai in a single campaign made any sense, and for this kind of struggle, the Egyptian Armed Forces were far from ready (Gawrych 1996: 10).

In sum, Sadiq and most of the high command opposed Sadat's limited war strategy (Neff 1988: 100–101; Hinnebusch 1985: 128; Gawrych 1996: 10; Riad 1981: 211).[63]

Nor were the generals willing to keep their reservations to themselves. In a heated three-hour meeting of the SCAF at Sadat's residence in January 1972, Sadiq, speaking on behalf of the high command, stated his opposition to going to war. Sadat pressed the general to proceed nevertheless, ordering him to have Egypt's military forces ready for war by mid-November 1972. Subsequently, at a meeting of the SCAF on October 24, he learned that Sadiq and most of the senior officers present, including the commanders of the First, Second, and Third armies and head of the navy, continued to oppose the plan, and that Sadiq had resorted to "delaying tactics in carrying out [Sadat's] orders to prepare the Egyptian forces" (Handel 1981: 248; Amos 1979: 104; Rabinovich 2004: 25; Gawrych 2000: 133; Bar-Joseph 2005: 2). The following day, fed up with Sadiq's recalcitrance, Sadat fired him, as well as the deputy war minister and the chiefs of the navy and

---

[62] On the importance of control of personnel decisions as a decision-making prerogative in the military context (which is therefore central to the authorization process), see chapter 2.

[63] Interestingly, these officers' preferences appear to have been the basis of the Israeli "concept" that Egypt lacked the forces to engage in a full-scale attack and therefore would not fight; Israel failed to comprehend the significance in the change of leadership and how that affected Egypt's war plans. See remarks by Aryeh Shalev in Parker (2001: 108–9).

the Central Military District in Cairo (Gawrych 1996: 11; 2000: 128; Haykal 1975: 181). Over a hundred senior officers were removed from their posts (Amos 1979: 106; Tsouras 1974: 67).

The corollary to removing opponents to his war plan was appointing a skilled and competent leadership willing to see through his initiatives. Sadat made a number of important appointments, including the disciplined and charismatic Lt. Gen. Saad Shazly as chief of staff. Major General Gamasy, director of operations, would prove to be another key appointment.[64] However, by far the most important appointment was General Ahmed Ismail Ali, who became minister of war on October 26, 1972. As Sadat himself put it, "The first actual decision on the October 6 war was taken when I removed former War Minister Sadiq and appointed Marshall Ahmed Ismail in his place" (quoted in Amos 1979: 118). Ahmed Ismail was a skilled, experienced, and willing military officer (Amos 1979: 141; Insight Team 1974: 221–22; Karawan 1984: 153; Gawrych 2000: 136). Best from Sadat's point of view, however, was that Ahmed Ismail exhibited a "keen understanding of the subtle relationship between war and politics" (Neff 1988: 101–2). The general understood both the limitations of Egyptian capabilities that made war difficult and the political context that made it essential.[65]

From the beginning, Sadat relied extensively on Ahmed Ismail in refining the concept of the limited war (Amos 1979: 139–40). Serious planning was begun in November 1972; by January 1973 the operational plan, Plan Badr, had been formulated and military leaders had begun translating it into concrete tactical objectives (Amos 1979: 313; el-Shazly 1980: 31–39; Heikal interview with Ahmed Ismail, 1974: 220). In short, a clear authorization process—manifested in the president's control of rights of appointment and dismissal—allowed Sadat to remove officers opposed to his war plan and establish a command willing and able to implement it. This was essential in planning the 1973 war.

Command Decisions during the War

Not only was the clarity of the authorization process central to planning the war, it would prove critical to maintaining the military's adherence to the limited war concept once it began. This is readily apparent when one examines several key decisions during the October War.

The first incident, on October 10, occurred four days after Egypt's crossing of the Suez Canal, and after Egypt had established its bridgehead on

[64] On these and other appointments, see Gawrych (2000: 136–37; 1996:10).
[65] On the general's role in refining plans for the limited war, see Amos (1979: 139–40), Rabinovich (2004: 27).

the east bank. At this point the euphoria of the military's initial achievements began to degrade into controversy. Chief of Staff Shazly and Egypt's other top military commanders began to push to expand the offensive to the mountain passes in the Sinai that were inland from the canal zone.[66] There were, however, serious risks involved in advancing the offensive. Egypt's capabilities were still inferior to Israel's, especially in air power and offensive maneuver; as such, aggressive exploitation of the early successes "might have risked losing everything they won on those days" (Dupuy 1978: 490). Under Sadat's guidance, Minister of War General Ahmed Ismail vetoed Shazly's plan (Insight Team 1974: 229; el-Gamasy 1993: 270).

Four days later, Egypt ended up resuming the offensive anyway. This time Sadat made the decision in favor of pursuing the attack for political reasons. Syria (Egypt's ally, which had cooperated in the war effort) had begun to pressure Egypt to resume the offensive to the mountain passes. If he failed to act, Sadat feared, the Syrians would agree to a unilateral ceasefire, and although in a week's time he would agree to one himself, at this point he was apparently holding out for a commitment by Israel to withdraw from the occupied territories. "[I]n context, the decision appeared unavoidable."[67] For his part, Ahmed Ismail worried about the risks of expanding the offensive, but the chain of command was once again firmly intact: "[Ahmed Ismail] had no choice but to obey his supreme commander" (Gawrych 1996: 56). Hence, "just as the tactical halt on October

---

[66] Many sources cite Shazly as favoring the continuation of the offensive, although in his memoirs he vigorously denies that he favored an advance. Regardless, there were several prominent military leaders pressing for the advance (el-Gamasy 1993: 264; Gawrych 1996: 22, 54; Aker 1985: 97–98; Dupuy 1978: 481). Maj. Gen. Talaat Ahmed Mosallam (ret.), Egyptian Army, confirms that many of Egypt's officers supported the initiative to move to the passes. Remarks by Maj. Gen. Mosallam at conference on "The October War: 25 Years of Lessons," October 9, 1998, National Defense University, Washington DC.

[67] On Sadat's concerns about Syria, see Dupuy (1978: 485), Heikal (1996), Gawrych (2000: 205), Stein (1999: 80), Heikal interview with Ahmed Ismail (1974: 223), Neff (1988: 214). There is some debate about Sadat's exact motivations in coming to Syria's aid. Certainly there were several political advantages to not having Syria sue for an early, unilateral ceasefire and to renewing the offensive, including maximizing Egypt's territorial gains and increasing Israeli casualties and therefore enhancing its postwar bargaining power. Sadat, moreover, could afford to take the gamble, as long as the military offensive did not compromise the bridgehead. Hence it is significant that Sadat used forces from the west bank and not forces deployed on the east bank for the offensive. Military critics are justified in criticizing Sadat for compromising Egypt's strategic reserve and for the poor execution of the attack. As Egypt demonstrated, it still had severe tactical limitations, and it performed poorly once it went beyond the SAM umbrella; it also failed to respond to a gap between the Second and Third armies in the canal zone, which Israel was able to exploit. Nevertheless, the key point is that military leaders recognized Egypt's tactical weaknesses and sought to design around them—which is one indication of the strength of assessment. Also crucial, military strategy, and more specific operational objectives, remained consistent with the broader political aims of the war.

10–13 occurred on Sadat's directive, the decision to resume the offensive following the halt was a political decision" (el-Gamasy 1997: 270).

The chain of command was tested one additional time. After Israel breached Egypt's defensive line on the night of October 15–16, exploiting a gap between the Second and Third armies, many of Egypt's commanders argued that forces should be withdrawn from the east bank of the Suez to support a counteroffensive. Ahmed Ismail, however, refused to redeploy any significant forces for the initial counterattack from the canal's east bank on October 17, fearing it would jeopardize Egypt's positions there. A major rift in the high command ensued. By October 20 Shazly was pushing hard for the removal of four armored brigades from the east to the west bank of the canal to aid the fight. To resolve the dispute, Ahmed Ismail summoned Sadat by telephone to Egypt's command center, Center Ten. That evening, after first consulting with his minister of war for more than an hour, Sadat discussed the issue with the chief of military operations and the heads of the air force, air defense forces, artillery, and military intelligence (Gawrych 2000: 224). Ultimately Sadat decided against removing Egyptian forces for a counterattack (Gawrych 2000: 224; 1996: 69; Dupuy 1978: 519). The president himself noted that the conflict "ended only when I personally went to the operations room and made the decision that the armies would stay where they were."[68]

Two things are notable about these decisions. First, the chain of command remained intact throughout the war despite being tested by significant dissent—the authorization process remained clear, with Sadat enjoying all final rights of approval and veto over military activity. Second, although they may not have been the best tactical choices in each single instance, taken overall, Sadat's decisions were consistent with Egypt's military plan and the broader grand strategy in which it was embedded. Sadat believed that any political leverage Egypt would have after the war depended on it holding the strip of recaptured territory on the east bank of the canal when the superpowers imposed a ceasefire. He therefore vetoed pressures from Chief of Staff Shazly and other military commanders to expand the offensive on October 10.[69] When he later agreed to strike out beyond the canal zone it was for political reasons—because he feared the Syrians would pursue an early ceasefire and compromise his broader political strategy. Finally, seeking to protect Egypt's hold on the territory it had

---

[68] Interview of Sadat in *Al-Ahram*, quoted in Amos (1979: 184). Shazly was fired by Sadat after the war over the disagreements about the conduct of the war (Hinnebusch 1985: 60–61; Aker 1985: 116–17; McDermott 1988: 49).

[69] As one analyst put it, "tactically, Shazly was right, but strategically he was wrong." Remarks by Brig. Gen. Tamari (ret.), Israeli Defense Force, at conference on "The October War: 25 Years of Lessons," October 9, 1998, National Defense University, Washington DC.

seized from Israel along the canal, he refused to allow any major forces to be withdrawn from the east bank to the west to respond to the Israeli breach of its defensive line (Shamir 1998: 82; Rabinovich 2004: 400; Meital 1997: 123). The integrity of the authorization process helped ensure that military activity would remain integrated with Sadat's political objectives. It was essential to executing the 1973 war.

DISENGAGEMENT AND PEACE

Finally, the clarity of the authorization process was essential in Sadat's negotiation of the postwar disengagement agreements and subsequent peace initiatives with Israel. His control of appointments, in particular, would once again prove essential—here as a powerful device for containing opposition to the agreements. Sadat, for example, often appointed rivals to key positions in order to neutralize opposition and increase his latitude for action (Ya'ari 1980: 114; Gawrych 2000: 136). Thus, after the 1973 war Sadat fueled clashes between Hosni Mubarak, chief of the air force, and General Gamasy, chief of staff and later minister of war (Friedlander 1983: 118; Hinnebusch 1985: 88). Consequently, "the rivalry between Mubarak and Gamasy permitted Sadat to make new peace overtures more freely, as neither official possessed the independence or following to unify the military" (Friedlander 1983: 82; Ya'ari 1980: 116). More broadly, by "shifting coalitions and isolating opponents," Sadat preempted dissent and neutralized obstacles to the implementation of his policies (Amos 1979: 246; el-Sherif 1995: 42, 230; Ya'ari 1980: 114–15).[70]

Even more ambitious was Sadat's use of his powers of appointment and dismissal to build positive support for his strategy (Hinnebusch 1985: 74; Beattie 2000: 238). How Sadat prepared the ground for the Egyptian-Israeli peace treaty is instructive. Just two weeks after signing the Camp David Accords on September 17, 1978, Sadat removed Gamasy as minister of war and appointed him special presidential adviser (Stein 1999: 99; Beattie 2000: 238).[71] As Gamasy's replacement, Sadat chose Kamal Hassan Ali, who was unquestioningly in favor of the peace process. It was a shrewd appointment. By appointing Ali to be the new minister of war, he attained greater status in relations with the head of the air force, Hosni Mubarak,

---

[70] On divisions in attitudes within the officer corps toward the peace initiatives, see remarks by General Fahkr in Alterman (1998: 69); "Sadat's Power Base," 160. Also see the discussion of preference divergence above. As noted there, soldiers of the Third Army rebelled against the troop dispositions in the March 1974 agreement.

[71] Gamasy generally supported the president's positions but at times had doubts about some of his specific policy decisions (Fahmy 1983: 266; Friedlander 1983: 82; Hinnebusch 1985: 74; Stein 1999: 99, 225).

who was then opposed to Sadat's peace initiatives (Friedlander 1983: 118).[72] Moreover, Ali was also an ally of Mubarak's. The appointment thus aimed at reconciling the latter to the peace process, while keeping him at arm's distance (Friedlander 1983: 83, 139). At the same time, Sadat appointed a new chief of staff of the army, Major General Ahmed Badawi. Badawi, a war hero, supported the peace agenda and also was popular within the army officer corps and rank-and-file (Friedlander 1983: 240).[73]

• • •

As these events reveal, throughout the 1970s Egypt enjoyed a clear authorization process that conferred final decision-making power on Sadat. This clarity represented a dramatic departure from the mid-1960s, when Amer consistently challenged Nasser's ability to exercise decision-making prerogatives. Under Sadat, lines of accountability and responsibility were clearly drawn in how strategy was chosen and implemented. The country could pursue its goals decisively, avoiding the incoherent and contradictory policies endemic to Egypt in the mid-1960s.

International Implications

So how did these institutions for strategic assessment affect Egypt's political-military strategies, and ultimately its international relations in the 1970s? By far their most profound effects on Sadat's strategies were positive. Egypt's internal strengths in assessment allowed the president to translate his political goals into supportive military strategies and activities. Egypt, in fact, achieved a remarkable degree of political-military integration in the 1970s. As I discussed in chapter 1, the ability to integrate a state's political objectives with its military strategy and capabilities can be a tremendous advantage to leaders as they pursue their goals in the international arena. It maximizes their chances of achieving those objectives.

In particular, the pivot of Sadat's entire strategy, the 1973 war, both reflected and promoted Sadat's international ambitions. The epitome of politics by other means, the limited war served Sadat's goal of reenergizing negotiations with Israel in order to regain Egypt's lost territory. Yet it also acknowledged the shortcomings of Egypt's capabilities by providing for a

[72] Both Mubarak and Gamasy, for example, had been excluded from the delegation to Jerusalem in 1977; Kamal Hassan Ali, then in his position as intelligence chief, represented the military (Friedlander 1983: 82).

[73] Also on Sadat's use of appointments to maximize his latitude for action, see Dekmejian (1982: 39–40).

campaign with narrowly defined objectives, not a total reconquest of the Sinai Peninsula. In addition, the strategy reflected the constraints and opportunities afforded by the regional and international environment. Sadat explicitly planned that an Arab-Israeli war would spur superpower involvement in settling disputes between Israel and Egypt.

In turn, after the war, Egypt's disengagement agreements with Israel helped assure the U.S. role in mediating negotiations between Israel and Egypt. In so doing, they also laid the groundwork for the Camp David talks in 1978 and subsequent negotiations with Israel, which culminated in the 1979 peace treaty and the return of the Sinai Peninsula to Egypt's control.

Moreover, when it was signed, that treaty was not just an end in itself but a means to a broader political goal. It represented more than the settlement of a territorial dispute and relaxation of tensions with Israel. Sadat's peace with Israel furthered a broader sea change in grand strategy. Whereas Nasser had pursued a policy of nonalignment—jockeying between the superpowers in an effort to boost his influence with both—Sadat chose to align Egypt securely in the Western camp. By making peace with Israel and thereby demonstrating his pro-Western credentials, he was able to secure American financial and military aid and invite foreign investment. Sadat had conceived and implemented a new concept of how to secure Egypt at home and abroad (Hagan 1993: 28; Mahmood 1985: 68; Dessouki 1991: 167; Stein 1999: 10–11).

All four attributes of strategic assessment contributed to Sadat's ability to achieve this remarkable degree of political-military integration. Perhaps most importantly, they helped Sadat carry out the October 1973 war. Improvements in information sharing were key in the formulation and execution of the war strategy. Sadat's ability to gain unchecked access to information and to monitor military activity assured that he would have accurate data about the strengths and weaknesses of Egypt's capabilities, relative to Israel's, and how this would bear on his military options. In turn, once the strategy and its supportive operational concept were developed, clear lines defining how and to whom information was to be conveyed helped ensure the success of the deception plan.

The structural competence of the military would also prove critical in planning and executing the 1973 war. Improved military leadership, brought about by a greater emphasis on skill and talent in appointments, which was sustained by a structural situation in which Sadat dominated his chiefs politically, resulted in extensive reflection in war planning about Egypt's capabilities. The result was a carefully conceived, detailed, and comprehensive operational plan tailored to Egypt's resources (Gawrych 2000; Pollack 2002; Dupuy 1978; Cordesman and Wagner 1990; Brooks 2006).

Finally the clarity of the authorization process—in which Sadat retained control of decision-making prerogatives—helped ensure the implementation of the limited war, as well as his subsequent peace initiatives. Throughout the 1970s, Sadat relied on his powers of appointment, in particular, to ensure the implementation of his policies. Recall, for example, that when Minister of War Mohammed Sadiq opposed the concept of launching a limited war in 1972, Sadat was able to fire him and large numbers of his supporters. Sadat then put General Ahmed Ismail, who supported the strategy, in charge of war planning. During the war, Sadat was able to overrule opponents and ensure that Egypt's tactical decisions remained consistent with his political objectives. Sadat would similarly face-down opponents after the war and contain powerful officers, like Hosni Mubarak, who opposed his peace initiatives with Israel.

Posing a series of counterfactual questions highlights the importance of the integrity of the authorization process: would, for example, the president have been able to implement the limited war plan if he had been unable to remove Sadiq, who opposed it, and replace him with General Ahmed Ismail? What would have happened if Sadat had been unable to overrule officers pushing to expand the offensive on October 10 and Egypt's forces in the canal zone had been overrun as a result? And finally, what if the military command had resisted redeploying its forces as called for by Egypt's postwar disengagement agreements with Israel, or balked at the demilitarization stipulations in the 1979 peace treaty?

Failure at any of these critical junctures would have compromised Sadat's political objectives. Without a war in October 1973, Israel would have remained reluctant to restart negotiations with Egypt. In turn, had Egypt compromised its foothold on the east bank during hostilities, it would have squandered any bargaining leverage Sadat could get from the war, undercutting Israel's incentives to make concessions in those negotiations. After the war, had the Egyptian military refused to pull back its forces, or had Sadat been unable to offer promises of nonbelligerency implicit in the disengagement agreements, those negotiations also would have sputtered, jeopardizing any future peace deal. Without demilitarization of the Sinai as agreed in the 1979 treaty, Israel would never have agreed to the peace initiative.

In short, Egypt's internal institutions for strategic assessment—and the opportunities for careful planning and leverage they afforded the president—underlay Sadat's remarkably integrated political-military strategy.

The Consequences of Poor Strategic Coordination

Nevertheless, despite Sadat's many advantages, the internal decision-making environment was not always helpful to the president. Recall that, in an effort to neutralize potential opposition to his policies and strategies, Sadat employed two oversight tactics in managing his military subordinates—he tended to bypass in advisory processes those from whom he anticipated opposition and to appoint likeminded officials to key positions. Although Sadat was able to convene his military leaders and review proposed policies upon his discretion, his use of these tactics at critical moments undermined the joint military and political consultation essential to strategic coordination.

These weaknesses, in turn, had two negative consequences. As I explain below, first, they hurt Sadat at the international bargaining table with Israel. He made tactical concessions that many of his "advisers found unnecessary or too forthcoming" and that may not have been required from Israel's perspective (Stein 1999: 7). Second, poor strategic coordination harmed Sadat's reputation as a serious negotiator, which also cost him crucial support within the elite.

Sadat's decisions during negotiations over the disengagement agreements underscore these weaknesses in his bargaining tactics. In talks with Israel, Sadat offered concessions on the disposition of forces that some argue were unwarranted (Haykal 1996; el-Gamasy 1993). Thus, for example, in discussions with the American delegation involved in negotiations in January 1974 over Sinai I, Sadat's minister of war General Gamasy insisted that Egyptian missiles not be withdrawn any further than twenty-five kilometers from Egypt's front lines at the Suez Canal. He argued that Egypt's anti-aircraft missiles, which had proven so useful during the war, would be useless to protect its forces from Israeli aerial attacks otherwise. To his great dismay, Gamasy later learned that Sadat had agreed to a withdrawal of thirty kilometers (Haykal 1996: 199, 232–33). Ultimately, Sadat agreed to reduce Egypt's forces on the eastern bank of the canal to seven thousand men, thirty tanks, and a limited number of artillery pieces (el-Gamasy 1993: 335–36). To preserve future military options, military leaders at the time considered it essential to have at least thirty-five thousand men and maintain three hundred tanks on the east bank under missile protection.[74]

Had Sadat consulted with his military leaders, Gamasy (1993: 336) argues, he might not have agreed so readily to the concessions on military deployments. As the general describes his experiences in the negotiations, "I had expected Sadat to consult General Ahmed Ismail, or me, when I arrived in Aswan to sound out the opinions on the military aspects of the agreement, including the size of forces that should be kept in Sinai in order effectively to defend the military gains there. There was no need—politically or militarily—to accept this reduction in troops and weapons." Sadat even surprised Henry Kissinger with the magnitude of his concessions, and in particular with his willingness to limit his forces to 30 tanks in the canal

---

[74] Note that this was before the peace treaty was signed, and Israel still held the Sinai and Gaza; military options to try to regain the lost territory were not yet foreclosed.

zone; Kissinger had reportedly told Israel that he did not think Sadat would settle for any less than 250. Accounts of Israel's side suggest they were prepared to accede to 200 (Quandt 1993: 198–200; Haykal 1996).

A similar pattern of concession making is apparent in talks between Israeli and Egyptian officials in December 1977, following Sadat's trip to Jerusalem. Prior to the Camp David meetings, General Gamasy reports that he was shocked to learn that Sadat had already agreed to demilitarize the area 150 kilometers east of the strategically important mountain passes in the Sinai Peninsula. The general brought his concerns to Sadat's attention, arguing that the proposed demilitarization "put [Egyptian] forces in a weaker defensive and offensive position, which was unacceptable from a military perspective" (1993: 381). Fifteen months later, when the peace treaty was signed, Gamasy's worst fears were realized. The agreement called for these and other limits on Egyptian forces in Sinai.[75] As Safty put it, reflecting a general theme in insiders' accounts of the decision-making process: "Sadat had single handedly given away all that the Egyptian army had won with great sacrifice. Without consulting anybody, he had caved in to the Israeli request that the Egyptian military presence east of the canal be reduced to nothing" (1991: 288).

Similarly, analysts suggest that Sadat also failed to make the most of American support for a settlement for the Palestinians during and after Camp David (Hinnebusch 1985: 67–68; Stein 1999: 7). Despite his own interests in a comprehensive settlement, Sadat undercut his own negotiators, unnecessarily signaling his willingness to abandon the Palestinian issue. In turn, absent concerted pressure from Sadat and therefore "relieved of the need to do so," as Hinnebusch describes it, "the US proved unwilling to extract concessions from Israel" (1985: 68).[76]

Ultimately it is impossible to know whether Israel would have given more on any of these issues had Sadat bargained harder. Perhaps he could have won some concessions on the disposition or number of forces in the

---

[75] Immediately adjacent to the canal zone (Zone A), the Egyptian military was allowed to deploy one mechanized infantry division, not to exceed 230 tanks, 480 armored personnel carriers, and 22,000 personnel. However, in the rest of Sinai (Zones B and C), few military forces, besides police installations, were allowed. On specific terms, see the annexes to the Egyptian-Israeli peace treaty reprinted in Reich (1995: 158–59). Among the limitations, the Egyptians were forbidden to use airfields in the Sinai to deploy military aircraft, except for limited military transport; hence, another of the military's worst fears—the potential loss of vital airfields for defense of Egypt—was realized. On concern about airports and Egypt's military strategy and operational concerns, see el-Gamasy 1993: 374–81.

[76] Although Sadat was widely perceived as abandoning the Palestinians with his bilateral agreement with Israel, it is not clear that he intended to at the start; see, for example, the discussion of Sadat's preferences and rationale for his ultimate concessions in Mahmood (1985). Also see Parker (2001: 333).

Sinai; progress on the Palestinian issue seems less likely given Menachem Begin's opposition to a comprehensive territorial settlement. But, arguably equally important, had strategic coordination between the political-military leadership been better, Sadat might have influenced the perception that he was too willing to sacrifice on key national security issues. In the eyes of many, by "ignoring" his advisers he failed even to bring some issues to the table that warranted rigorous negotiation. Ultimately, skepticism about the disengagement agreements and peace treaty was worsened by the perception that Sadat was a weak and ineffectual negotiator (Safty 1991).[77]

In much of the history of this era, especially in accounts from outside the region, these criticisms of Sadat are buried beneath assessments of the president's remarkable international achievements. The West, in particular, views Sadat as a great visionary in promoting peace with Israel.[78] But from an analytical perspective, careful scrutiny of the effects of civil-military relations on strategic assessment, and in turn on Egypt's political-military strategies, suggests that a more nuanced story is appropriate. Both Sadat's concessions and the perception that he was marginalizing advisers and therefore offering Israel unnecessary concessions were real downsides to the decision-making environment. Other strengths in the authorization process, information sharing, and structural competence overshadow weaknesses in strategic coordination, but the pathology was present. This is why, despite Sadat's remarkable achievements, Egypt in the 1970s is still a "mixed" case of strategic assessment.

---

[77] For example, his foreign minister, Ismail Fahmy, was so disillusioned with Sadat's "political tactics" that he resigned over the issue, despite his general support for Sadat's policies (Karawan 1994: 259–60; Fahmy 1983; Hinnebusch 1985: 73).

[78] See, for example, the essays and central themes of the edited volume by Alterman (1998).

Five

BRITAIN AND GERMANY AND THE FIRST WORLD WAR

THE FIRST WORLD WAR has been one of the most significant and studied events of modern times. In this chapter I begin the focused cases that complement the comprehensive Egypt studies by examining the strategic assessment process in two of the war's principal protagonists: Britain and Germany. I analyze the institutions in which these countries' leaders evaluated their political-military strategies in the fateful years leading up to the war.

Despite similarities in region and historical era, I expect to observe very different competencies in strategic assessment in the two states. Britain (1902–1914) was far better positioned to develop functional processes for analyzing strategy. Some might be surprised to learn that I expect—and find—that Britain actually had relatively good assessment in the decade before the First World War, at least between political and military leaders, despite its devastating experiences in the war.

In Germany (1888–1914), where preference divergence was also low but civil-military power was shared, I anticipate that strategic assessment should have been more problematic. Given Wilhelmine Germany's well-observed tendencies toward self-defeating political-military strategies, this expectation might be unsurprising. Yet less understood are the underlying reasons why at the time Germany's leaders were so incapable of recognizing, let alone addressing, their counterproductive policies—that is, why they were prone to such poor strategic assessment. In this chapter I examine how the state's civil-military relations contributed to these deficiencies.

The chapter also extends the analysis of Britain into the wartime period (1914–1918), in which civil-military relations were best characterized by shared power and high preference divergence, allowing me to explore variation in strategic assessment over time within the democratic state.[1] Especially after 1915, a powerful partnership between army chiefs emerged in Britain, while political leaders ruled with divided and weak coalition governments. Military and political leaders also increasingly clashed over how to fight the war, yielding competition for control of military strategy. Un-

---

[1] For more on detail on case selection, see chapter 1.

like the prewar decade—but for different reasons from those in Wilhelmine Germany—I expect wartime Britain to have been very poor at strategic assessment.

Britain, 1902–1914

In the first British case, which covers the years between the end of the Boer War and the First World War (1902–1914), I expect that low civil-military preference divergence and political dominance should have produced relatively good strategic assessment. Information sharing, strategic coordination, the military's structural competence, and the authorization process should have encouraged rigorous analysis of Britain's political-military strategies.

Below I evaluate the historical record to see how it matches the predictions of the theory. First, however, I situate my analysis in context of the extant literature on Britain prior to the war.

The Context of the Prewar British Case

For many observers, any effort to analyze strategic assessment in Britain in the first decade of the twentieth century might be easily overshadowed by the wars that followed and preceded the era: the Boer War and First World War. In fact, for those familiar with these wars, it may seem odd to hypothesize, as I do here, that strategic assessment would have been anything better than horrible in the interim period. Like many wars before it, and although it ultimately recovered, Britain initially misjudged its adversary and the forces required to address it in the Boer War. In the First World War the British found themselves similarly ill-prepared for the nature of the conflict and the deadly trench warfare that would ensue on the western front. Given these unremarkable performances, we might expect Britain to have been woefully ill-equipped for strategic assessment in the decade between these two wars.

Yet, as I argue below, the process of strategic assessment in fact exhibited many strengths in the first decade of the twentieth century. Britain innovated and developed new institutional mechanisms for analyzing strategy, which facilitated improvements in assessment. Consequently, it underwent a remarkable strategic reorientation from its focus on colonial issues to developing a specific strategy and operational plan for war against Germany on the continent. In many critical areas it was better prepared for war in 1914 than at any time prior in its history.

One body of scholarly literature would not be surprised by this argument. For these scholars, this decade was a period of coherent, rational response to a rising German threat.[2] In particular, Britain's efforts to reconfigure its foreign relations with its competitors—manifested in the ententes with France and Russia—are viewed as an efficient response to its strategic situation (see Kupchan 1994: 125; Howard 1972: 29–30; Kennedy 1983). Other scholars adopt a somewhat more measured view of Britain's strategic shift in the decade. Friedberg (1988) notes, for example, that the adjustment was more contingent and varied across economic, diplomatic, naval, and military policy arenas. Yet he also observes positive changes in Britain's structure for military planning and strategic assessment, viewing them as among the more successful areas of change.[3] This theme of change in Britain's military planning institutions is echoed within the historical literature (Gooch 1974, 1994, 1996; Philpott 2002; Hamer 1970; Jackson and Bramall 1992; Johnson 1960). In this chapter I demonstrate how civil-military relations—by alleviating the incentive and propensity for competition over these assessment institutions and thereby allowing functional concerns to rise to the top—facilitated these significant reforms.

The British case also underscores another central point of this book: There is not a deterministic relationship among the quality of assessment, a state's ultimate strategies, and outcomes in international relations. Exogenous forces can override functional civil-military strategic assessment. Despite the activities of the Committee of Imperial Defense and General Staff described below, and the strengths in strategic assessment they represented, the domestic political situation greatly constrained Britain's ability openly to debate its strategy in the decade before the First World War. In particular, it precluded discussion within the public sphere and government as a whole about a "continental commitment" (i.e., a commitment to participate in a European war in the event of German aggression) and the development of the mass army needed to meet such an obligation. These domestic obstacles originated in divisions in the Liberal party and cabinet, which governed Britain at the time, between radicals and more moderate factions. The radicals were ardently opposed to increasing ties with France, let alone committing to fight on its behalf in the event of war (Weinroth 1970; Kupchan 1994: 127). They fiercely opposed conscription, which the prospect of intervention on the continent raised, given the challenge it represented to domestic norms and traditions (Friedberg 1988: 222, 276;

---

[2] See Friedberg (1988: 293–94) for a summary of this perspective.

[3] Also see Kupchan (1994: 115–21) for a similar view. Friedberg evaluates strategic adjustment from 1899 to 1905 in four areas. He describes adjustment as most positive in naval matters, followed by military (i.e., army) affairs. He regards adjustment in the economic sphere as worst. He attributes Britain's problems to elites who were wary of the restructuring of domestic society in ways that economic change and military adjustment would have entailed. Note that the study stops at 1905, when Britain had just begun to reorient toward the German threat, and merely touches on the period after that.

Kier 1997). They also tended to be ideologically suspicious of the concept of a large standing army and were against increases in the budget to maintain one (Bond 1996: xv; Jackson and Bramall 1992: 7). All three of these issues exercised the radical wing considerably, and the Liberal party prime ministers Henry Campbell-Bannerman (1906–1908) and Herbert Asquith (1908–1916) were extremely reluctant to raise them and jeopardize support for their leadership (Williamson 1969: 303–4; Steiner and Neilson 2003: 221). In short, this case illustrates how other factors—in this case intracivilian dissent—can constrain assessment and therefore influence strategy and international outcomes. Yet what remains striking is how effective assessment was within the civil-military sphere, and how much analysis of Britain's strategic situation and planning took place between political and military leaders, *despite* this constraint.

Civil-Military Relations

In general the first decade of the twentieth century in Britain was a time in which there were few systematic cleavages over strategic, corporate, or professional issues observed between political and military leaders. Many of the causes of conflict that the extant literature on civil-military relations might highlight were absent.[4] The level of international threat was not the impetus for significant political-military hostilities. Nor were religious or social issues, like class, a major source of tension. The officer corps exhibited a relatively high degree of homogeneity; throughout the nineteenth and early twentieth centuries, the officers corps continued to be recruited from the same classes of society that ruled the country, even after the abolition of purchase in 1871 (Hamer 1970: 16; Feuchtwanger and Philpott 1996: 1; Corrigan 2003: 306). There were some tensions over corporate issues; however, there were not systematic axes of conflict between political and military leaders over these issues.[5] Within the army itself there was not a unified view of corporate issues, professional standards, or strategic matters (Hamer 1970; Jackson and Bramall 1992: 14; Feuchtwanger and Philpott 1996: 1). In sum, while differences in viewpoints and clashes between individual personalities were common, there were no deep-seated, recurrent conflicts between political and military leaders in the period

---

[4] See chapter 2 for a review of this literature.

[5] By the conclusion of the nineteenth century, generational changes within the officer corps had also alleviated many of the broad historical tensions between army and parliament, as new groups of officers socialized in the post-Cardwell era assumed key positions. On these tensions, see Hamer (1970: 6, 14, 172), Jackson and Bramall (1992: 8–9); on generational changes, see Hamer (1970).

(Gooch 1996, 53; Feuchtwanger and Philpott 1996: 19). Preference divergence, in the terms of this study, was low.[6]

Political leaders were also clearly dominant (Feuchtwanger and Philpott 1996). Power was concentrated in a succession of Conservative and Liberal governments at the turn of the century, with the Liberals taking the helm in 1906 under Henry Campbell-Bannerman, followed by Herbert Asquith in 1908.[7] Governments relied on coalitions of mass and more focused civilian constituencies; the army played no direct or indirect role in the coalition. Nor was it politically unified around a leader or movement. In fact, after 1871 internal differences in the officer corps, fed by the Cardwell reforms at that time, helped political leaders leverage tensions and divergences of opinion within the service. As one scholar put it, "the history of army administration in the last quarter of the 19th century is one in which civilians exploit this division of the soldiers, and the inner history of the war office is the story of civilian domination with the soldiers left divided and weak" (Hamer 1970: 13, 29). This is not to say that military leaders did not at times try to influence policy, and even resort to political intrigue in their efforts to promote particular positions.[8] In fact there were many opportunities for doing so because of the class alignment between the officer class and senior politicians; these individuals were wont to meet socially, if not professionally, and generals were known to raise issues with their political counterparts (Corrigan 2003: 306). Yet, critically, during this decade, military officers did not operate as a unified bloc and represent the kind of political force that would emerge, for example, during the First World War with the Haig and Robertson partnership. In sum, civil-military relations in Britain before the war were characterized by low preference divergence and political dominance, which should have produced relatively functional routines and structures for strategic assessment at the political-military apex.

---

[6] There was one exception to the generally low level of systematic conflict. It involved the Home Rule Bill for Ireland (i.e., granting a united Ireland its own parliament with control over internal affairs), a major goal of Liberals since 1886. In March 1914, disputes between British soldiers and politicians over enforcement of home rule resulted in the famous "mutiny" by British officers, known as the Curragh mutiny. British military officers refused to participate in the violent repression of opponents to home rule and threatened to resign. Hence there were tensions between the political and military leadership in this area. However, these events did not have a substantial impact on civil-military relations in the longer term because they were overshadowed by the July 1914 crisis; the start of the war shifted the attention and focus of the government away from these issues (Sweetman 1986: 13, 16; Jalland and Stubbs 1981: 780).

[7] Note that throughout I use the term "government" in its technical sense, to refer to the prime minister and his cabinet.

[8] See the discussion of Sir General Henry Wilson (Strachan 1997: 132–33).

Strategic Assessment

Two things are notable right from the start about strategic assessment in Britain from 1902 to 1914. First, in the absence of systematic cleavages between military and political leaders, neither information sharing nor the authorization process appears to have been especially problematic, while improvements in structural competence were observed. For example, within the sizable historical literature on this era, with its detailed analyses of events and debates, accounts of concerted efforts by military and political leaders to withhold private information from each other are remarkably absent. This does not mean that efforts to conceal information did not occur, but it does suggest that these happenings were not significant enough to draw the attention of historians. Similarly, there is little evidence of efforts to challenge or subvert the decision-making powers of the prime minister and his cabinet (like those observed during the war, which are heavily commented on in the literature). This suggests that competition over decision-making prerogatives was indeed relatively rare; historians have little reason to report on these "nonevents." In addition, improvements in the military's structural competence in intelligence and internal structures for self-evaluation do appear to have been realized, especially within the general staff (Philpott 2002).[9]

Second, and conversely, what *is* clear in the literature is the emphasis placed on improvements in strategic coordination—in the advisory processes for analyzing strategy and military activity between political and military leaders—throughout the historical scholarship. Much of this chapter focuses on these improvements, given their considerable importance in understanding strategic assessment in Britain at the time.

In the decade prior to the First World War, Britain undertook some major innovations in strategic coordination. The impetus for these reforms was Britain's failings in the Boer War. Although poor performance in the early phases of war was nothing new in the history of Britain's imperial conflicts (Howard 1972: 12), the army's widely publicized problems in the Boer War, as well as its expense and manpower demands, had been especially disturbing to politicians and the mass public (Hamer 1970: 174–201; Gooch 1996: 54–55; Jackson and Bramall 1992: 27–28). As the official inquiries into the war framed it at the time, these difficulties demonstrated

---

[9] Recall that, as outlined in the research design, in these shorter cases I emphasize some attributes of strategic assessment and for reasons of space do not treat all equally. Hence, while I see evidence for the claim in the historical literature that structural competence in internal monitoring and intelligence improved (witness Haldane's and other reforms), much of this chapter emphasizes the vital changes in strategic coordination that occurred at this time.

the inadequacy of the ad hoc approach to planning to which Britain was accustomed and weaknesses in the "machinery" of civil-military relations (Gooch 1996: 54; Kochanski 2002: 25). In short, Britain needed improved infrastructure for bringing the services together with politicians in broader consultative processes.

Of course, many states, as a result of wartime failures, have had incentives to enhance their machinery for strategic assessment. Striking is the degree to which Britain was able to satisfy its functional needs. These improvements emerged from a reform process spearheaded by civilians.[10] In particular the final report in 1904 of an investigatory committee led by Lord Esher would form the basis for major restructuring of the defense establishment. Lord Haldane, as secretary of state for war, would also play a seminal role in implementing the recommendations and in organizational reform of the army (Johnson 1960: 11, 26–29; Bourne 1989: 16; Sweetman 2002: 33–34).[11] Civilian politicians sometimes disagreed about the details of institutional reform during this process, but the effort remained grounded in a recognition that better security planning was essential (Sweetman 1986: 17; Hamer 1970: 13, 29, 243–45).[12]

As a result of these reforms, Britain exhibited significant improvements in assessment, especially in the quality of strategic coordination. One major innovation was the establishment of the Committee of Imperial Defense (CID) in 1902 and the creation of its secretariat to establish agendas and keep records (and therefore enhance its institutional independence) two years later, as a result of the Esher Report's recommendations.[13] The CID represented an unprecedented development in British military organization on several levels (Johnson 1960; Jackson and Bramall 1992: 36–37; Hamer 1970; Gooch 1996: 63). First, it was an independent consultative entity, separate from the cabinet as a whole. Although cabinet ministers often sat on it, including the foreign minister and secretary of state for war, the only statutory member was the prime minister; its members served at his pleasure. Thus the CID was an entity for the prime minister and his

---

[10] Military leaders did participate in the debate, although civilians ran the show. For example, prominent army officers, such as Lord Wolseley and the Duke of Cambridge, were quite active in the discussion (see Hamer 1970: 160–62; Feuchtwanger and Philpott 1996: 1).

[11] On Haldane's seminal role, also see Barnett (1970: 362–63), Strachan (1997: 122), Coogan and Coogan (1985). An army council, similar to the Board of the Admiralty, was also established as a collective body to analyze policy for the navy.

[12] This was the continuation of a long-standing trend. Between the late 1860s and 1880 alone there were no fewer than eighty-nine official entities charged with analyzing one or another aspect of military affairs (Barnett 1970: 334).

[13] This gave the CID its own bureaucracies to control the agenda and communications and provide technical information and ideas. Much of the work of the CID was to devolve into subcommittees, and the CID as a whole met much less frequently.

top political and military advisers to review and analyze strategy at least somewhat removed from the politics of the cabinet at large. As one historian frames it, "for the first time in British history a special body, including both cabinet members and the prime minister on the one hand and service officers on the other, convened regularly and kept minutes of their deliberations" (McDermott 1979: 103). This was especially significant at the time, as I elaborate below, given the preoccupation of the Liberal party with domestic reform, suspicion of any continental commitment in its military strategy, and general reluctance to engage defense matters in the government as a whole (Johnson 1960: 84–85, 96).

Second, because the CID was a coordinating body for strategy and military policy, both military and civilian representatives had equal standing in terms of speaking and calling for papers. The CID itself had important agenda-setting power in terms of identifying issues that warranted study. It developed an elaborate system of standing and ad hoc subcommittees to oversee inquiries on a variety of issues.[14] Overall, its goal was to promote coordination and to encourage civilian officials and the services in the area of defense "to face more directly than they need do now, the question of what it is which they undertake to do, and what are their resources for doing it" (Gooch 1994: 284). It sought, as the Esher Report outlined, " 'continuous study of (relevant) questions' " in defense analysis and to address the need " 'for coordinating defense problems or for dealing with them as a whole' " (cited in Sweetman 2002: 33; McDermott 1979: 102–3).

The establishment of the General Staff in 1904 was a second key institutional innovation. Its creation was "part of the same grand design of Lord Esher to improve the government's facilities for strategic planning and war preparation" (McDermott 1979/1985: 105). The CID and General Staff in fact were tightly linked with each other and with the War Office. For example, the General Staff constituted the War Office's department for strategic planning, and its chief became the sole adviser to the secretary of state for war on strategy and military operations. At the same time the chief of the general staff and director of military operations sat on the CID and advised its secretariat; in fact, all military advice supplied to the CID after 1904 came from the General Staff (McDermott 1979/1985: 104).

In short, Britain created several new institutions for strategic assessment during the decade following the Boer War. Nevertheless, as I argue throughout this book, one has to look beyond these formal institutions to see how they operated in practice. In this regard, both the CID and the General Staff emerged as important forums for the analysis and review of

[14] On these aspects of the CID, see Johnson (1960: 91–93, 105).

British strategy and military activity. I review the activities of these entities in detail below to illustrate the strengths in strategic coordination observed in Britain at the time.

From the start the CID took on meaty issues. For example, in its early years it focused on Britain's relations with Russia (until the entente of 1907); the committee in one instance studied the land forces required to defend India against war after a Russian invasion (Howard 1972: 15–20; Johnson 1960: 95). After 1905, while Russia remained a central concern, the CID also began to narrow in on Germany, recognizing it as Britain's most likely and most dangerous new threat (Gooch 1996: 62–63). For example, in August 1905 the secretary of the CID recommended to then prime minister Arthur Balfour that the General Staff study the military problem posed by German violation of Belgian neutrality in the event of war (Howard 1972: 41–42; Philpott 2002: 97).[15] Talks between the British and French military staffs to coordinate their activities were also initiated in 1906 by the General Staff and overseen by the CID.[16] Also in 1906 the British Expeditionary Force (BEF) was created.[17] These early initiatives were the start of a long process, in which the CID and General Staff would play a central role, of surveying and redefining British strategy in the decade before the First World War and reorienting it toward a potential war on the continent.

Take, for example, the CID's actions in a 1908–1909 inquiry by one of its subcommittees into the "Military Needs of the Empire" (Williamson 1969: 100; Howard 1972). Interpreting its mandate broadly, the committee solicited presentations from the General Staff and the Admiralty about the requirements of continental defense (Williamson 1969:108). When the General Staff made a recommendation calling for deployment of the BEF to the left flank of French forces to support the French (versus Belgians) in the event of war with Germany, the committee endorsed the plan (quoted in Williamson 1969: 110). Its final report, while affirming the right of the cabinet of the day to decide the merits of sending a force abroad, concluded that "in the initial stages of a war between France and Germany,

---

[15] In fact, the General Staff had already gotten a good start dealing with these issues (McDermott 1979/1985: 108). In January 1905 the director of military operations ordered a war game based on the concept of Germany violating Belgian neutrality in pursuit of an attack on France, which had been played in April and May, in the midst of the first Morocco crisis. As such the war game identified issues and principles for military planning that would endure until the outbreak of the 1914 war (Howard 1972: 42; Philpott 2002: 96; Gooch 1996: 62; Strachan 2002: 80).

[16] Although informal until 1910, the talks continued until the war, with "political sanction at the highest level" including that of Foreign Secretary Sir Edward Grey and Secretary of State Lord Haldane, both members of the CID (Philpott 2002: 97, 101; Strachan 2002: 84).

[17] The BEF was not intended for the continent when it was established (defending India was the prevailing scenario), but its role after 1908 would clearly emerge as such.

in which the British Government decided to support France, the plan to which preference is given by the General Staff is a valuable one and the General Staff should accordingly work out all the necessary details."[18] As such, the "subcommittee's report, which the CID adopted, conferred respectability on the strategy of intervention" in a continental war (Williamson 1969: 111; see also Steiner and Neilson 2003: 209).

If the 1909 report affirmed the general direction for strategic planning, the CID meeting of August 23, 1911, in the turmoil of the Agadir crisis, is often cited as the major milestone in defining British military strategy. As in earlier deliberations, but this time with greater portent, the country's political and military leaders sought to settle the essentials of Britain's strategy to deal with Germany and its European neighbors. In a packed all-day meeting, the committee heard formal presentations by the army and navy chiefs about British military strategy and plans for war against Germany (the meeting was well attended with the exception of the radical ministers who were out of London and not summoned; Steiner and Neilson 2003: 213).

Events at the 1911 meeting illustrate the evaluative process at the time. The navy's proposal for war on the continent included launching an amphibious attack, a landing of the army on the northern German coast, and a blockade of German shipping. However, "when subjected to searching analysis" by the committee, this strategy was found lacking in clear principles and convincing logic (Gooch 1994: 291; 1996: 73). Members of the committee observed that Germany could easily transport via railway five to ten times the number of troops as the British could hope to land, and that the amphibious force would easily be destroyed; a blockade would work too slowly (Johnson 1960: 115–16; Gooch 1996: 63, 69). Instead, after a lengthy presentation by General Wilson, director of military operations, the committee concluded that the best way to confront the German threat was to deploy the British Expeditionary Force to the continent in the event of hostilities (Gooch 1996: 63; Johnson 1960: 116–17).

As one analyst describes the upshot of this deliberative process: "Tested by agnostic ministerial critics, the army's proposals conformed far more closely than the navy's to politicians' conception of British interests in Europe and how best to defend them" (Gooch 1994: 296). Some have criticized this process as an example of politicians simply favoring the army over the navy (D'Ombrain 1973: ix–xi, 22–23), but accounts of the discussion suggest that committee members engaged in a rigorous analysis and

---

[18] Excerpt from the report appears in Howard (1972: 46); also see Williamson (1969: 111). In conceptualizing the nature of Britain's potential involvement on the continent, the committee at this point did not rule out the military option of independent action in Belgium, although it did lean in the direction of supporting France (Strachan 1997: 94).

debate about the proposals.[19] Ultimately "civilian politicians played the role of referee in a series of hard-fought bouts in which the Army proved the stronger contestant" (Gooch 1996: 74). Most importantly, the meeting represented the first time that the services would be bound to a single strategic conception by the prime minister (Williamson 1969: 112).[20]

The CID thus played an important role in facilitating strategic coordination and in helping frame analysis of Britain's strategic options, including military involvement in a war against Germany. Especially striking is that it did so despite the domestic opposition by radicals in the party and cabinet even to contemplating, let alone committing to, fighting on the continent. This was no small feat given the intensity of opposition. Take, for example, the political fallout from the 1911 meeting. Although the radicals in the cabinet were not invited, the word of the meeting was subsequently leaked to them; they were infuriated at being left out and, especially, at news of ongoing staff talks between the British and French militaries (information about which heretofore had been closely held by the CID's principal members). The ensuing uproar precipitated a major cabinet crisis with one of the chief radicals, Lord Morely, charging Prime Minister Asquith, Foreign Minister Grey, and Lord Haldane with undermining British foreign policy. Asquith appeased his opponents when he issued a carefully worded declaration stating that staff talks would not take place if they bound the country to intervention, and that if a promise to aid France was undertaken, the cabinet would be allowed to consent upon it (Williamson 1969: 200–204; Johnson 1960: 119).

The vagueness of the statement ensured that the talks could continue, but the incident nonetheless illustrated the political perils of raising the issue of continental involvement (Williamson 1969: 200, 203–4). In particular, the cabinet uproar sent a clear warning to soldiers and politicians in the CID about the danger of engaging in broad discussions of grand strategy; they were much more careful in how they addressed issues afterward, framing them in terms of smaller, less ambitious themes. As one historian put it, "the political repercussions of the [1911] meeting" helped inspire "the Committee's circumspection" in discussing strategic matters afterwards (Williamson, 1969: 191).

---

[19] See the analysis reviewed in Gooch (1994: 292–93). Previously in the decade, the CID had tended to favor the navy's plans for defending the United Kingdom (Gooch 1994: 287, 294). Others do, however, critique the CID for not doing more to stem interservice rivalry (Strachan 1997: 125; Johnson 1961: 236; Gooch 1994: 306; D'Ombrain 1973).

[20] The prime minister required the navy to accept the strategy coming from the War Office and to develop plans for deploying the BEF to the continent; he appointed Winston Churchill First Lord of the Admiralty to ensure interservice cooperation in implementing the continental strategy (Williamson 1969: 194–96, 312; Johnson 1960: 117).

In fact, because of the political sensitivity of the issues, aside from the 1911 meeting, Liberal party prime ministers Campbell-Bannerman and Asquith were generally disinclined to use the CID for broad strategic debate.[21] Asquith, in particular, feared "exacerbating existing divisions" in the cabinet (Steiner and Neilson 2003: 221); public comment on issues such as the role of the expeditionary force "would have antagonized the radicals within the Cabinet and Liberal party" (Williamson 1969: 303). In short, "the reluctance of the Prime Minister to face the Cabinet to say nothing of Parliament, with the consequences of a switch to a continental strategy discouraged any possibility of open debate" (Steiner and Neilson 2003: 221; Williamson 1969: 304). Consequently, as Kupchan (1994: 127) characterizes it, members of the CID were forced to work quietly behind the scenes, "outside the purview of many politicians."

The dissent within the Liberal party and cabinet and the constraints on debate it generated renders all the more significant the CID's and General Staff's efforts to address strategic issues—and the strengths in strategic coordination those activities at the time represented. A great deal was done in practice within the entities, if not in theory in the government as a whole, to analyze and refine British strategy. After the 1911 meeting in which the continental strategy was affirmed, for example, preparations accelerated in the CID and General Staff for a war on the continent. The CID, engaged in what one scholar refers to as the "phase of preparations," undertaking a range of studies, including those on control of railways, ports, and local waters in a war, the control of cables and radio, and provisions for importation of food in the event of a naval blockade of the British Isles (Johnson 1960: 94, 98). These investigations would be compiled in the War Book of 1911–1914, which included a detailed chapter of the actions to be taken by each government department in the event of war (Johnson 1960: 97; Bourne 1989: 16).

More specific planning for military operations was overseen by the War Office and General Staff. After 1911 three areas received special attention: (1) mobilization plans for the BEF; (2) transportation of the force across the Channel; and (3) movement and location and provisioning of the force once in France (Williamson 1969: 311). These all involved detailed planning. Mobilization, for example, required coordination with all the major post offices and railways so that forces could be drawn from across Britain and Ireland to the principal port of embarkation at Southampton as quickly as possible. Planning for transportation required making detailed arrangements to charter merchant ships to carry forces to the French ports at Boulogne and Le Havre in coordination with the navy, which would pro-

---

[21] Their Unionist predecessor Balfour (prime minister 1902–1905) had been more willing to do so.

tect them in transit (see Bourne 1989: 16–17). These preparations supplemented more long-standing efforts by the director of military operations (DMO), Henry Wilson, to prepare the army for conflict on the continent, including refocusing the curriculum at the staff college to focus on a European war and attending to mundane details such as ensuring that large maps of the Franco-German frontier appeared on classroom walls (Philpott 2002: 100).

Arguably most important, however, was the progress made in coordinating military activity with the French in the years prior to the war. In 1906, as noted above, under the watch of General Grierson as the first DMO, the Anglo-French military staff talks were initiated on an informal basis, providing for meetings and exchanges between the French and British militaries. These were continued under Sir John French in his various roles in the British army and accelerated under Wilson as DMO (Philpott 2002: 101–2). Even in the absence of a formal policy statement from the Liberal government committing Britain to aid France, these activities went far to consolidate British strategy. As one historian characterized their significance: the "talks committed Britain, in case of intervention, to a particular military strategy of such magnitude as to constitute a policy decision" (Williamson 1969: 199). As Lord Esher, who opposed involvement on the continent, complained in a discussion with Asquith in October 1911 following the August CID meeting, "I reminded him [Asquith] that the mere fact of the War Office plan having been worked out in detail with the French General Staff (which is the case) had certainly committed us to fight, whether the Cabinet likes it or not and that the combined plan of the two General Staffs holds the field. It is certainly an extraordinary thing that our officers should have been permitted to arrange all the details, trains, landings and concentrations, etc, when the Cabinet have never been consulted" (cited in Williamson 1969: 197).

In short, the CID and the General Staff provided for the coordination of political and military leaders and the analysis of strategic issues. They helped facilitate strategic coordination in Britain in the decade before the war. These entities, of course, were not perfect. Some have criticized the CID, for example, for not doing more to stem interservice rivalry and for not engaging in more broadly framed discussions of grand strategy (in large part for the reasons discussed above).[22] Nonetheless, historians agree that

---

[22] See note 19 above. Some historians also question the importance of the CID's activities, and in particular the significance of the 1911 meeting, on the grounds that, despite developments in military strategy in the "inner cabinet" of the CID, the cabinet as a whole had not signed onto the "continental commitment," and as a result the CID did not more frequently sponsor broad ranging debates of strategy (Strachan 1997: 79; Steiner and Neilson 2003: 213–14). Most historians, however, emphasize the importance of the CID despite these constraints. See Howard (1972: 42–45), Kennedy (1988), Johnson (1960: 160), Williamson

these bodies provided an invaluable organizational forum for surveying the country's strategic and military options. "Although it could not resolve all issues to everyone's satisfaction, [the CID] did reach consensus on many important questions facing Britain as it reoriented its strategy from the wider world toward Europe and the growing German threat" (Gooch 1994: 284). Along with the General Staff and Army Council, the system allowed for communication between military and civilian branches of government at different levels (Kennedy 1988: 40). Through the CID in particular, the "services were being drawn into the joint consideration of strategic planning in a way which, while not perfect, had been completely impossible only a decade before. Although not always agreeing, the experts were able to place their views before each other and before the politicians as freely as they were willing to do" (Johnson 1960: 95). In Strachan's (1997) terminology, these institutions allowed for "integrated control" of political and military issues. As such, the "politico-military system prior to 1914 was, compared to most other powers, an excellent one" (Kennedy 1988: 40; Johnson 1961: 238; Hamer 1970: 260).

International Implications

How did these assessment institutions influence Britain's international relations in the first decade of the twentieth century? First and most importantly, as I describe below, they facilitated a dramatic reorientation of British strategy. The strategy that emerged from the debate and discussion in the CID and General Staff identified likely German actions in the event of hostilities, addressed the potentiality of the violation of Belgian neutrality, affirmed the necessity of aligning with France, foresaw the deployment of the BEF to the continent, and developed operational plans consistent with the objective. Second, they facilitated a significant improvement in Britain's preparation for war. As I also elaborate below, although far from perfect, in part because of domestic political constraints, they enabled Britain to be substantially better prepared for war on the continent in 1914 than for many prior wars in its history.

Strategic Reorientation

This reorientation represented a major transition in strategic thinking—a "revolution" as one historian refers to it (McDermott 1989: 99). To appreciate fully its magnitude, one has to reflect on the strategic context Britain found itself in at the turn of the century. At the time Britain had two

---

(1969), Pugh (1993: 141), Gooch (1996: 66–67, 74), and the citations in the text above. For key texts, see Gooch (1994: 284–85, n. 23).

main preoccupations. The first was safeguarding its empire, and in particular protecting India against a possible invasion by Russia, as well as securing the route to the South Asian colony through the Mediterranean. As one historian put it, India was "what the British Empire was all about," and securing it was a major priority. Competition with Russia in the "Great Game" in the Middle East and Asia had "shaped the political consciousness of a generation." Thus when the CID was formed in 1902, the expansion of the Russian Empire was its major concern. Of the eighty meetings of the CID from 1902 to 1905, defending India was the primary if not only topic at more than fifty of them (Howard, 1972: 14–20). Moreover, when the first set of inquiries into the purposes of the BEF was undertaken in January 1907 (after its establishment in 1906), the emphasis was on the requirements of an Indian campaign (Williamson 1969: 94). The name of the CID—Committee of *Imperial* Defense—is revealing in itself. That the entity would ultimately spend so much time preparing Britain for a European war is more than a little revealing.

A second preoccupation of politicians of the day was territorial defense: ensuring the defense of the island in the event of an invasion by France (until the 1905 entente) and later by Germany (Howard 1972: 13, 20).[23] Territorial defense would remain a concern for much of the decade before the war, with regular inquires affirming the navy's role in territorial defense and the army's latitude to be deployed abroad.

Fighting a war on the continent was a distant third proposition at the turn of the century. By 1905, as noted above, Germany had begun to gain the attention of the CID, and the emphasis in strategic planning was secured after the 1908/1909 CID inquiry. Yet even then the focus on the continent was by no means inevitable. As natural as the conclusion that Germany was a growing threat and that Britain should prepare itself to meet it may seem in retrospect, Britain's strategic priorities were not nearly so uncomplicated at the time; Britain had a diverse array of security interests with which it had to contend, including (not least) protecting its vast empire (Kochanski 2002: 24). Unlike Germany, whose primary strategic problem was simpler—defending its western and eastern frontiers—Britain faced a more complex set of contingencies (Strachan 2002: 86).

Despite the magnitude of this shift in strategy, some observers might nevertheless view the impact of civil-military relations and strategic assessment as trivial: Realists might expect that Britain would have responded to the looming German threat regardless of the state's internal processes of

---

[23] Formal inquiries by the CID ultimately put this concern to rest. For example, a 1905 study concluded that the British navy was capable of defending against an amphibious invasion, and that any forces that did get through could be handled by militia and volunteers (Howard 1972: 22, 37; Williamson 1969: 97).

strategic assessment. Yet two things suggest the Realist view is at best incomplete. First, there is little evidence that such a strategic orientation was indeed a foregone conclusion, given the divisions within the civilian elite, without the forums of the CID and General Staff. Certainly the internally divided Liberal party and government as a whole were doing little on this front. They were reluctant even to talk about the issues given their ideological distaste for them.

Second, that Britain would respond in the way it did is not self-evident given the findings in the other cases of this book. Those cases suggest that in many instances states do not respond productively to external threats; their assessment institutions complicate, rather than facilitate, the formulation of strategy. This raises the question of what is distinctive about the nature of civil-military relations that eased the reorientation of British strategy. One possibility is that an environment of low preference divergence and political dominance is most consistent with a Realist view: In these environments, civil-military strategic assessment evolves such that external stimuli are more readily registered internally. In other settings the domestic politics of civil-military relations obstruct assessment processes and the evaluation and response to developments in the international arena.

War Preparation

The second major effect of Britain's strategic assessment institutions was on the level of British military war preparation. As Lord Hankey, then secretary of the CID, put it when the British cabinet finally did make the decision to go to war in August 1914, "they knew that the arrangements which had taken so long to prepare were set in motion . . . every detail had been worked out for the Mobilization of the Regular Army and its transport to a place of concentration in France . . . everyone knew what he had to do" (quoted in Hamer 1970: 260–61; Johnson 1961: 131–32, 144, 238; Barnett 1970: 372). Prior reforms in army organization, in particular, had made considerable difference. They turned the army into "the best equipped and trained land force that Britain has ever sent into the field at the outbreak of war" (Jackson and Bramall 1992: 43; Williamson 1969: 90). "As a result, Britain was better prepared for the First World War than for almost any war in her modern history" (Pugh 1993: 141–42). "The CID's work through its secretariat and its subcommittees . . . had carried the state of British preparedness far beyond that of [the Boer war]. . . . this was completely unlike the unorganized state in which Britain had faced and fought for two and a half years the Boers in South Africa only a decade before" (Johnson 1960: 118). As one historian of the era nicely summarizes it, the role of the CID in preparing for war "has generally been acknowledged as an invaluable asset to the war's opening phases especially" (Johnson 1960: 141, 161). The quality of prewar strategic assessment thus reaped important rewards.

Nevertheless, there were limits to Britain's preparedness. Not least was that Britain did not have the mass army—or plans for developing it—that it would ultimately need to battle the Germans on the western front. In part this was due to failure to foresee and plan for the magnitude, duration, and nature of the ensuing world war (Gooch 1994: 278–83; French 1996: 76). Most officers assumed that a war would be short, lasting a few months, and would be decided in a series of short two- to three-day battles (Steiner 2003: 205; Johnson 1961: 238).). They did not appreciate the advantages that technological innovations like machine guns and barbed wire would provide to the defense and how this would change the nature of warfare (Snyder 1991a; Van Evera 1991). Nor did they develop before the war new tactics that would prepare them to fight given these technological realities.[24] To put these failings in context, however, Britain was not alone in facing these problems. Not one of its continental counterparts fully foresaw the nature or duration of war.[25] This was a transitional time in which the modern battle system was emerging. It was objectively difficult to master and even took the tactically proficient Germans four years to do so (Biddle 2004).

Beyond these failures of imagination, the Liberal party radically opposed increasing the size of the army for ideological and fiscal reasons. "The question [of the size of the army] could not be discussed openly in a Cabinet of men opposed to standing armies and conscription and backed by an articulate public whose votes were needed" (Steiner 2003: 224). As a result of these political constraints, before the war Britain did not have either the men or materiel to fight a lengthy European conflict. As one historian describes the consequence, in retrospect, "There was a glaring contradiction, never fully debated, between Britain's new land strategy and her resources" (Steiner 2003: 221).

It is nonetheless important to note, however, that this was not due to lack of trying by the General Staff and some of its political counterparts. Although they did not foresee trench warfare, they did recognize the merits

---

[24] They did develop doctrine for training, and the General Staff developed the Field Staff manuals in 1908 and 1909 to provide guidance to commanders in the field (Steiner 2003: 204–5). Yet these outlined general principles for action and still contained a great deal about colonial conflicts. In general, commanders were left to define the specifics of their tactics given the nature of the conflict situation they faced. Strachan critiques Britain's war preparations for this and points to several other areas where more could have been done to prepare the British army for a continental war (2002: 90–91).

[25] This was generally the case, although some scholarship suggests the German chief of staff, Helmuth von Moltke, did anticipate the true nature of the war. On the Förster thesis, see, in English, Herwig (1997: 36, 49), Mombauer (2001: 211).

of having a large army to fight on the continent. As Strachan (2002: 92–93) describes it:

> The General Staff advocates of continentalism were fully aware of [the needs for a large, conscripted force]. In January 1906, [then DMO] Grierson, in sketching out the pattern of possible support for France in a war against Germany, spoke of sending "troops to an unlimited extent." Robertson, writing at around the same time, was more specific. Britain needed to put in the field "a contingent of at least the same proportionate strength as those we supplied when fighting in alliance with other Powers in a similar cause a hundred years ago."

Specifically General Robertson, then head of Foreign Military Intelligence at the War Office, wanted be able to send 100,000 men to the continent in two weeks and have at least half a million others ready for immediate deployment. There were others who expressed similar concerns. General Henry Wilson was an especially forceful advocate for increasing the size of the expeditionary force (Philpott 2002: 103). He lobbied hard for conscription in peacetime, aligning himself with the conservative Lord Roberts, head of the National Service League, who pushed compulsory service both for home defense and for the contingency of a continental war (Strachan 1997: 93; Williamson 1969: 304). Ultimately, however, the members of the General Staff were "obliged to contemplate continental war with what they considered an inadequate force . . . . the rational alternative was to make the best of what was available" (Philpott 2002: 104). The plan they developed called for deploying British forces to the left flank of French forces in the area of Maubeuge, near the Belgian border (Bourne 1989: 13). The idea was that Britain's six divisions would extend the French line and help make the difference between defeat and victory in the first battle with the Germans (Steiner 2003: 223; Bourne 1989: 13). In short, the General Staff developed a strategy within the constraints of the army available. As the official historian of the war, Sir James Edmonds later captured it: "Britain never yet entered upon any war with anything approaching such forwardness and forethought in the preparation of the scanty military resources at the disposal of the War Office" (quoted in Bourne 1989: 15).

In summary, while many of the civilian and military members of the CID and General Staff developed and communicated the need for a continental strategy, a clear commitment from Britain's government as a whole was lacking (Strachan 2002: 93; Philpott 2002: 110; Kennedy 1988: 40; Coogan and Coogan 1985: 116, 118; French 1996: 31–32, 81). Nonetheless, "Considering the limitations of the parliamentary system, just about everything that could be done by way of military and political preparations in the circumstances was done" (Ritter 1970: 50). As Philpott (2002: 11) describes the position of Britain's military leaders: "They advised the government should reconcile policy and strategy; they advised that the British army should be large enough and equipped to play a decisive military role on the continent; they advised on where and how to use the BEF once it reached the continent. If politicians had been willing to act on this advice, then Britain's and Europe's military history might have been very different."

Britain during the War, 1914–1918

In contrast to the prewar period, I expect very poor routines for assessment to have emerged in Britain during the First World War. As I elaborate below, civil-military relations in Britain during the war contrast starkly with the preceding decade as a result of several factors: First, a powerful partnership emerges between army leaders, and they draw political support from the public, conservatives, and much of the press; second, the Liberal party prime ministers Asquith and Lloyd George depend on coalition governments and rely on a highly fractured political base; and finally, systematic conflicts over military strategy in the war emerge, especially between Lloyd George and his army chiefs (on which this chapter focuses).[26] In these civil-military settings—characterized by high preference divergence and shared power—I anticipate competition over information and decision-making prerogatives to generate weaknesses in all four attributes of assessment. Wartime Britain should have been seriously deficient at strategic assessment.

Below I evaluate this hypothesis. However, once again, I begin with some analytical background on the wartime case.

The Context of the Wartime Case

Surprisingly few scholarly studies in political science have been completed on the period in British history during the First World War.[27] Much more has been written by historians, especially about relations between Lloyd George and his generals. Within the historical literature two themes resonate. The first is a debate about the quality of generalship on the western

---

[26] I focus on Lloyd George's relations with the army, especially in the final two years of the war when he was prime minister, for reasons of space and because of the significance of those relations for military strategy during the war (see chapter 2 for my research design). But his clashes were not the only run-ins politicians had with the military leadership during this period. In May 1915 the army leadership helped discredit Secretary of State for War Kitchener, thereby threatening the tenure of the Asquith government. See, for example, the discussion of the tactics used by the army leadership against Kitchener (Strachan 1997: 126–27; 130–31; French 1996: 99).

[27] Scholars have been more interested in the events leading up to 1914. One exception is Goemans (2000), but his focus is quite narrow and emphasizes shifts in Britain's war aims and the factors that affected its terms of potential settlement.

front; that is, how much are the generals to blame for failures of operational planning and tactics versus the objective challenges of fighting a modern industrialized war, with new technologies and without an established mass army. In the scholarly lexicon, how much were the generals myopic "donkeys" or victims of difficult circumstances? While some completely absolve Douglas Haig, commander of the British Expeditionary Force in France, for Britain's failings on the western front, most lay at least some blame for poor operational planning and tactical stagnation on his shoulders, and many are extremely critical of his leadership.[28]

The second theme emphasizes conflict between army leaders and politicians over military strategy; once again in the scholarly lexicon, between "westerners/brass hats" who wanted to focus Britain's energies nearly exclusively on the western front and "easterners/frock coats" who emphasized operations in eastern Europe and northern Africa and the Middle East.[29] Commentary on the poor state of civil-military relations and on the political intrigue to which both Lloyd George and military leaders resorted as each sought to promote its vision of military strategy is also commonplace.[30]

This book suggests we should not be surprised that these themes coincide in the historical literature. The analysis below demonstrates how, in fact, they are linked: Conflicts over strategy and the political leverage of the military complicated coordination between political and military leaders in debating strategy and military activity. Specifically, poor strategic assessment impaired analysis of the military offensives on the western front, especially those like Passchendaele in the fall of 1917, whether they should be undertaken and how many resources should be devoted to them versus other strategic options. They also contributed to tactical stagnation by rendering virtually impossible a debate about the quality of "generalship" on the western front.

The First World War case is thus a stark contrast to the prewar situation: In a relatively short period of time, as a result of developments in the army leadership, domestic environment and debates over military strategy, the intensity of conflict and balance of power in civil-military relations shifted.

---

[28] On the "donkeys" theme, see Terraine (1963), Hart (1930), Winter (1991); for a review of the historiography, see Simpson (1991). Also see the bibliographic references in French (1995: 1–2). Authors such as Terraine (1963) and Corrigan (2003) defend Haig; most sources, however, are very critical.

[29] On the brass hats, see, for example, the discussion of the historiography of the period and the cites listed by Beckett (1991: 89–112). Also see Corrigan (2003), Woodward (1983).

[30] On political intrigue, see Bourne (1989: 150); Suttie (2005: 153–55), French (1996: 78–79), Strachan (1997: 132–33), Pugh (1988: 111–13), Spears (1972: 7), Woodward (1983), Bond (1968), Corrigan (2003: 306). Many of these scholars also comment on the poor state of civil-military relations.

The quality of strategic assessment between political and military leaders consequently degraded considerably.

Civil-Military Relations

It is arguably an understatement to observe that civil-military relations in wartime Britain, especially between the Lloyd George government and army leaders, were conflictual. At the root of the political-military dispute were divergent priorities in military strategy, and specifically debates over where Britain should concentrate the bulk of its military effort during the war. The army leadership became wedded to a western strategy, one that favored concentrating resources against the German Army on the western front (i.e., in France and Belgium). According to observers, these preferences originated in the socialization of military officers, and military precepts that dictated concentrating force against the "decisive point" (Jackson and Bramall 1992; Barnett 1970: 386–87).

Especially as prime minister after December 1916, David Lloyd George favored a different, "eastern" strategy—one that while supporting the defensive effort in the west, put greater emphasis on challenging the German allies in the Balkans and Middle East as a way of diverting resources and pealing them away from German influence.[31] By the time Lloyd George became prime minister, he had become disillusioned by the failure of the army's large-scale offensive battles (Pugh 1988: 110). He was also concerned with securing Britain's empire and world position after the war, which in part motivated his focus on operations in the Balkans and elsewhere. Army leaders consistently derided this strategy, which in their view absorbed resources that otherwise might be committed to the western front.[32]

In addition to the conflict over strategy, a confluence of events altered the balance of power between political and military leaders during the First World War. The wartime prime ministers, Herbert Asquith and David Lloyd George, who were both from the Liberal party, governed with a divided support base, which rendered their positions insecure. The Liberal

---

[31] Lloyd George became prime minister after the deadly Battle of the Somme, which in part explains his growing suspicion of the generals' attrition battles on the western front. Prior to 1916, when Asquith was prime minister, Lloyd George had been more inclined to support them (Turner 1988: 124). On the intensification of conflict between Lloyd George and the generals, see Bond (1968), Corrigan (2003: 306). See Kennedy (1988) for discussion of the alternative strategies.

[32] Douglas Haig (see below) was especially intolerant of any discussion of operations beyond the western front. Chief of Staff Robertson exhibited greater recognition of the need to consider alternative theaters but still believed these were by far secondary to the western front (see, for example, Winter 1991: 2).

party at this time was in a period of decline and was riven by internal factions. The war, in turn, put enormous stress on the party, proving in one historian's estimation to be a grievous "disaster" for its internal unity (Douglas 2005: 323; see also Pugh 1995: 11–12). In August 1914 Asquith won support for entry into the war, but as it progressed the Liberal party remained extremely conflicted (Pugh 1993: 152; Douglas 2005: 178). In turn, to avoid a wartime election, which the party could not hope to win, in May 1915 Asquith formed a coalition government with the Conservative and Labor parties (Pugh 1995: 11–19; 1993: 152; Douglas 2005: 168). Subsequently, when Lloyd George replaced Asquith as prime minister, after the latter resigned under criticism for his management of the war, he inherited an extremely weak political base (Turner 1988: 125). Not only did Lloyd George have to contend with a government in which he shared power with the conservatives, the Liberal party itself was internally divided in its support for him and Asquith, who remained party leader (Strachan 1997: 133; Pugh 1995: 9; David 1970; Fry 1988; French 1996: 77). Lloyd George struggled to form a government and ultimately none of the cabinet ministers in the Asquith government were included. In fact, most of Lloyd George's parliamentary support came from conservatives and many of the jobs in his government were held by them (Turner 1988: 124).[33]

Concomitantly, one of the most powerful partnerships in British military history emerged at this time: Field Marshal William Robertson and General Douglas Haig were appointed, respectively, chief of the Imperial General Staff (CIGS) and commander in chief of the British Expeditionary Force in December 1915, forming a tight alliance at the apex of the army leadership (Woodward 1983: 74; Corrigan 2003). The chiefs were popular with the public at large; in the late nineteenth century, the army had begun to gain a following, despite the public's traditional aversion to it (Townshend 1989). The chiefs also had the ear of the conservative press, which was eager to criticize the government when it violated military opinion in operational and strategic matters (French 1996: 78–79; Woodward 1983: 51). Two papers in particular, *The Times* and the *Morning Post*, were unerringly supportive of the generals (Strachan 1997: 132). Thus, "Robertson and Haig were not above inciting [the press] to render Lloyd George a public rebuke if he threatened to interfere in their business" (French 1996:

---

[33] When Asquith's government fell, the cabinet included thirteen members of the Liberal party; nine Unionists (conservatives), and one from Labour; those numbers under Lloyd George were, respectively, eight, twelve, and two (hence more conservatives than Liberals) (Douglas 2005: 175–76). So bad were the divisions that by the spring of 1918 large numbers of Liberal MPs were voting regularly against the government on wartime matters (Douglas 2005: 179).

79).³⁴ This is not to say that Robertson or Haig sought political influence for its own sake and to challenge civilian control directly and in principle, but that their strong professional convictions dictated protecting the army from "affronts" by politicians (Strachan 1997: 133).³⁵

The cumulative effect of divided and weak political coalitions, combined with an environment in which the military enjoyed important ties to the press and popular support, was to shift the balance of power in wartime Britain from the political establishment toward its military chiefs.³⁶ For Britain's political leaders, open opposition and public appeals by the military establishment were to be avoided because they could jeopardize the government. Hence while the military occupied no direct position in the coalition, its ability to threaten the government's tenure in office indirectly meant it was a vital constituency nonetheless. In practice, if not in theory, political leaders (Asquith and Lloyd George) were sharing power with their military leaders. Each side had political resources it could marshal against the other. In turn, I expect this political-military competition to have undermined severely strategic assessment.

Strategic Assessment

Contrary to what the theory predicts, one might, on first glance, assume that the process of evaluating and deciding strategy was actually relatively straightforward and coherent in Britain's wartime governments. A subset of the cabinet was convened under Prime Minister Asquith, in a War Committee, and later under Lloyd George in a War Cabinet with its own secretariat. These entities provided the principal forums for strategic assess-

---

³⁴ See, for example, the numerous instances of the press forcing Lloyd George to balk at asserting his prerogatives over the military cited in Woodward (1983: 106–8, 110–11, 133, 139, 141, 269). Also see French (1996: 98–100). Also important were ties to the king, who heavily supported the military chiefs (Strachan 1997: 132).

³⁵ While it may seem odd to think of the military as capable of wielding so much political power in a democratic state like Britain, military chiefs were using this power to defend prerogatives they believed were essential to safeguarding the military and not for an overt takeover of the state. Hence, although the military abided the British constitutional tradition, this did not necessarily mean it was opposed to using its influence against a government it disagreed with as leverage over institutional prerogatives. As one observer puts it: "widespread respect for the general framework of the political system did not inevitably translate itself into acceptance of the legitimacy of the government in power" (Gooch 1996: 76). On different realms of military contestation, see Colton (1979), Ben Meir (1995); also see the discussion of these issues in chapter 2.

³⁶ Note also that although the king retained no formal command responsibilities over the army, during the war he often backed Haig and the generals against the politicians (Gooch 1996: 60; French 1996: 90, 91).

ment[37] and met regularly to survey political issues and military strategy.[38] Within them military leaders formally presented issues and political leaders decided strategic matters (Gooch 1994: 198–99). The army was subordinate to the government, which controlled it through the secretary of state of war, who chaired the Army Council, which in turn gave instructions to chief of the Imperial General Staff (CIGS), while the War Cabinet and politicians retained final "unequivocal" authority over British strategy (Strachan 1997: 135; Corrigan 2003: 307).[39]

The reality of strategic assessment at the time, however, was far more complicated than those formal processes suggest and was heavily shaped by the politics of civil-military relations. Shared power and high preference divergence created both the incentives and the capacity for political and military leaders to compete over institutional prerogatives, in the process undermining the routines and structures essential to strategic assessment.

Competition was manifested, to start, in the authorization process.[40] While military leaders never overtly challenged political leaders' formal decision-making powers, the political implications of acting against military opinion often served as a practical brake on executive powers. In particular, the Liberal party prime ministers faced serious constraints in exercising their executive prerogatives because of divisions in their coalition governments. For Lloyd George, for example, any conflict with army leaders raised the prospect that his conservative secretary of war, Lord Derby,

---

[37] As prime minister, Asquith relied initially on the entire cabinet to make decisions. In late 1914 he established a cabinet committee of at first six, and later twelve, members to oversee decision making. In the autumn of 1915, this war council was reorganized into a War Committee, which would report to the cabinet as a whole. After Lloyd George became prime minister, he established a War Cabinet of five to seven ministers with a secretariat; he relied on it as the principal forum for analysis and decision making. In June 1917 he also convened a special War Policy Committee charged with investigating Britain's wartime situation. See French (1995: 40, 94, 101); Suttie (2005: 129), Turner (1988: 125), Ritter (1970: 53, 57).

[38] The War Cabinet met almost daily.

[39] Once war began politicians reverted to the cabinet as the primary executive decision-making body, viewing the CID as an advisory body operable in peacetime. Arguably this put Britain at a disadvantage because the cabinet, and even the subset of the War Cabinet, had so many issues to deal with (French 1995; 1996: 76; Johnson 1960: 136, 139–40, 159; Strachan 1997: 126). Civil-military relations worsened the situation, rendering a less than ideal situation even more dysfunctional.

[40] In the text I focus on the authorization process, information sharing, and strategic coordination; this is consistent with my effort, discussed in the research design, to focus on the most salient attributes in the briefer cases. While the discussion of the failure of tactical innovation in the First World War below and evidence that hierarchical norms suppressed critical thought within the chain of command are suggestive of weaknesses in the military's structural competence, I did not find clear linkages between civil-military dynamics at the apex and conventions of foreign intelligence gathering or internal monitoring and therefore prefer to withhold a conclusion on these issues.

would resign and the Tories would withdraw support for his leadership. As one historian describes the constraint posed by Derby's opposition, "As a result of this dilemma the story of the next two years [of his wartime leadership] was the story of Lloyd George's devious and debilitating efforts to influence military strategy by roundabout means" (Pugh 1988: 111). The machinations that ensued in Lloyd George's competition with his generals to assert control over strategy seriously convoluted the authorization process for military strategy at the apex of the state.

Robertson's initial appointment as CIGS in December 1915, before Lloyd George became prime minister, foreshadows this intense competition. Seeking to elevate the position of chief of the General Staff, before he agreed to take the position under the Asquith government, Robertson demanded that he be given several prerogatives, including rights of appointment for military officers (a privilege previously held by civilians). Haig and Robertson subsequently lobbied the king, and George V, sympathetic to his generals, supported the enhancement of the CIGS' powers (Strachan 1997: 132). Prime Minister Asquith consented and "the result was to confer on [Robertson] powers enjoyed by no other holder of the office [of CIGS] before or since" (Bourne 1989: 146; Woodward 1983: 102). It also represented a "severe truncation" of the duties of the secretary of state for war (Corrigan 2003: 314). When Lloyd George assumed that position six months later, in June 1916, the stage was therefore set for a serious confrontation.

Predictably, Lloyd George "chafed at the powerlessness of his position" and insisted upon the return of his appointment prerogatives as secretary of state for war (Strachan 1997: 134). His demands presented Asquith with a dilemma: "if he supported Lloyd George on his terms, the 'soldiers' party' [the Conservatives] would be inflamed and Robertson might resign [as CIGS]. With public trust in the army high, this would endanger his government" (Woodward 1983: 100). Asquith was unwilling to confront Robertson. Lloyd George retreated and acquiesced in the status quo.

After Lloyd George became prime minister in early December 1916, these battles over process, fueled by divergent preferences over military strategy, intensified. Take, for example, Lloyd George's efforts soon after taking office, in December/January 1916/17, to promote a surprise attack against Austria-Hungary along the Italian front. His plan, consistent with his preferences over military strategy, called for transferring heavy guns from the western front to Italy for the offensive. Robertson and Haig were dead set against the initiative. They were especially alarmed at the prospect of removing forces from the western front to support it. The intrigue that followed "in both camps belongs on the pages of a cheap spy novel" (Woodward 1983: 139).[41]

---

[41] See Woodward (1983: 138–40) for a review of these events.

Hoping to win support for the campaign from the Italians, in early January 1917 Lloyd George set off for a conference of the allies in Rome, which Robertson was also set to attend. When the train on which both leaders traveled arrived in Rome on January 5, "a comical race to get the ear of the Italian commander in chief took place" (Woodward 1983: 140). Robertson got to him first and succeeded in sowing doubts about the merits of Lloyd George's initiative. Nevertheless, during the meetings on January 6, Lloyd George circulated his proposal to his fellow political leaders and lobbied for their support. Then the Italian commander of the army, Field Marshal Luigi Cadorna, who had been sitting with Robertson in another chamber, was brought in. Cadorna proceeded to echo all the negative arguments Robertson had made against Lloyd George's proposal. As Robertson later referred to the latter in a communiqué to Buckingham Palace, "Not much will come of it."[42] He was right: Lloyd George's plan was not pursued.

Unable to directly overrule his army leaders in deciding British military strategy, Lloyd George resorted to more wily methods to claim the upper hand in decision making. Among his more innovative tactics was endeavoring to place British forces—and most importantly Haig—under a unified military command, headed by French generals. There were good reasons for trying to assure coordinated action with the allies. However, the unified command also had more practical utility as a pretext for wresting decision-making prerogatives from his military leaders (French 1996: 103; Strachan 1997a: 137; Bond 1968: 69; Corrigan 2003; Woodward 1983). As one observer framed it, "Lloyd George had thought out this device [of a unified command] in order to supersede Haig and Robertson because he did not feel politically strong enough to dismiss them" (Spears 1972: 7; Corrigan 2003: 322).

Lloyd George's first attempt to subordinate his generals occurred in February 1917 when he successfully encouraged the French commander Nivelle to propose the establishment of a unified command at a conference in Calais.[43] Robertson signed the Calais agreement. However, he then returned to Britain to marshal political opposition to the initiative and defend Haig's position as commander of British forces in France. Lloyd George was forced into a corner. He considered firing Haig or "goading him into resigning" (Woodward 1983: 151). However, he feared that Robertson and Secretary of War Derby would then resign. One of Lloyd George's advisers, Lord Hankey, warned against the action arguing that if "Haig resigned,

---

[42] Quoted in Woodward (1983: 141). Ultimately, the plan was circulated to the general staffs without any endorsement from the politicians.

[43] For an account of these events, see Woodward (1983: 146–53). Also see Corrigan (2003: 321).

the government would very likely be defeated" (cited in Woodward 1983: 151). Lloyd George retreated.

Eventually, Lloyd George succeeded in establishing a unified command and sidelining Robertson (although Haig would retain his position throughout the war). In November 1917 he supported the establishment of an interallied war council, the Supreme War Council, which would thereafter control allied military operations and effectively subordinate the British army to its authority (Jackson and Bramall 1992: 102–3).[44] Although initially unperturbed by the proposal, when Robertson heard that Lloyd George had chosen another general, Sir Henry Wilson, over Robertson to represent Britain on the council (which differed from the rest of the allied militaries, which were represented by chiefs of staffs), he was greatly alarmed and demanded to be appointed instead (Corrigan 2003: 324; French 1996: 102–3; Strachan 1997a: 137). Lloyd George's subsequent maneuverings afforded Robertson two unpalatable options: sitting on the council and giving up his position as CIGS to Wilson, or remaining as CIGS with reduced powers (French 1995: 219). Unwilling to accept the compromise, Robertson was effectively fired in February 1918. Even then, "having screwed his courage to sticking point to dismiss Robertson in February 1918, [Lloyd George] told one of his aides that, 'we [i.e., his government] may be out next week' " (cited in French 1996: 76–77; Woodward 1983: 120). Lloyd George ultimately survived the confrontation through various creative political manipulations (Pugh 1988: 115; French 1996: 77).[45]

In sum, as these examples illustrate, the authorization process was highly contested, as Lloyd George, stymied in his efforts to exercise his decision-making prerogatives by the military's political power and his government's weaknesses, was forced to resort to indirect means to control military activity.

The authorization process, however, was not the only casualty of political-military competition. Information sharing and strategic coordination suffered as well. These flaws are evident in debate over one of the major battles in the war, the third battle of Ypres in 1917 (Passchendaele). In the summer of 1917 Haig had begun to lobby hard for a new offensive on the western front in Flanders in order to clear the Belgian coast and eliminate

---

[44] For accounts, see Bourne (1989: 151), Corrigan (2003: 324–25), French (1995: 218–19).

[45] Key also was that there was significant opposition to the prospect that Asquith might become prime minister if Lloyd George was removed (French 1995: 219). It also helped that after the devastating losses of Passchendaele (see below), the conservatives and press were more critical of Robertson and the generals, which strengthened Lloyd George's hand (Strachan 1997a: 137; Bond 1968: 63). Wilson subsequently replaced Robertson as CIGS. Lloyd George initially found him more agreeable but would eventually become frustrated with Wilson's commitment to the western front (Strachan 1997: 139; French 1995: 220–21).

threats to allied shipping posed by German submarine bases. In a series of meetings in June 1917, the War Policy Committee (an offshoot of Lloyd George's War Cabinet) met to review the proposal. The ensuing review process was extremely flawed, in large part because of problems in information sharing.

Most importantly, Haig misrepresented the magnitude of the campaign he planned to the politicians on the council. At the time, given the devastation experienced at the Battle of the Somme and other battles, British politicians had begun to grow wary of supporting large-scale offensives on the western front. Haig, however, had great ambitions for his Flanders campaign. In private he planned for a "great strategic victory" in which British forces would achieve breakthrough, thereby turning the tide of the war for good, even potentially prompting the Germans "to accept terms" (Suttie 2005: 127, 129). However, in his representations to the committee, Haig greatly underplayed his real ambitions: "Mindful of the politicians' anxiety regarding great offensives and high casualties . . . Haig's language was cautious" in his memoranda about the offensive (Suttie 2005: 127). He proposed to the committee that he would undertake a series of small, phased thrusts aimed at limited strategic objectives, along the lines of those achieved recently by the allies at Vimy Ridge, which could be stopped at any time (Suttie 2005: 127; French 1995: 112). In short, as one historian (himself a critic of Lloyd George) subtly frames it, "Haig and Robertson were not in fact being entirely straightforward with the Committee" (Suttie 2005: 130).

Haig was less than forthcoming about other issues relevant to the offensive as well. He concealed information about the extent of mutinies that had been occurring in the French military, and which might compromise the military's support for the plan (Suttie 2005: 136; French 1995:113). And although Haig did not deliberately withhold any specific information about the weather and the terrain in Flanders, he did fail to raise the issue for discussion, despite the fact that "the soil was not, to be sure, ideal for a major campaign in which artillery was dominant" (Suttie 2005: 137). With heavy rains, Flanders would turn into a deadly swamp in the main phase of the offensive in October/November.[46] More broadly, the commander was wont to resist sharing information: "Haig himself was never very keen to explain things to the War Cabinet" (Kennedy 1988: 42).

Problems in strategic coordination compounded these weaknesses in information sharing. When called to give evidence in the War Cabinet about

---

[46] In his own three-volume set of memoirs, Lloyd George is scathing in his criticism of his generals and in his claims of being the victim of deception. Leaving aside his claims, even a highly skeptical historian reviewing his claims (Suttie 2005) agrees that on the points above the prime minister was correct—Haig did misrepresent his views on several issues in the debate about the Flanders campaign. On other misrepresentations, see French (1995: 114).

the Passchendaele campaign, Haig stubbornly refused to acknowledge any of the "dubious assumptions and likely dangers inherent in the plan" (Bond 1968: 67). Even more telling was Robertson's failure to convey his concerns about the plan. At the time Robertson's strategic views had begun to diverge from Haig's, and his faith in large-scale offensives on the western front had begun to falter (French 1995: 218–19). As one historian describes it, while "Haig believed that it was possible to achieve a breakthrough on the western front, Robertson argued, with increasing conviction, that the battle was one of resources, that only limited objectives could be gained, and that strategy should reflect these operational constraints" (Strachan 1997: 136).

Notwithstanding his doubts, the political situation and apprehension about Lloyd George's pro-eastern agenda prevented Robertson from expressing his opposition in meetings of the War Cabinet. The CIGS was wary of putting the ball in Lloyd George's court and therefore resisted participating in a rigorous debate about the proposal (Bond 1968: 66): "when confronting Lloyd George, Robertson covered over these internal divisions and presented a common military front" (Strachan 1997: 136; Corrigan 2003: 320; Bourne 1989: 148). He "stifled his doubts" due in part to his allegiance to Haig and to his "overwhelming mistrust of Lloyd George" (Bond 1968: 63, 66). As it was, had Robertson voiced any of his reservations about the offensive, "there can be little doubt that Lloyd George would have been emboldened to force a showdown with Haig" (Bond 1968: 69).[47] In sum, suspicion between army leaders and Lloyd George, born from their deeply divergent views of strategy, hindered the quality of debate and coordination between them (French 1996: 106–7).

Ultimately, the plan for the offensive advanced with the War Cabinet's approval, in part because politicians felt that Britain needed a victory to shore up French morale and ensure its continuation in the war, and because alternative plans were viewed as infeasible (French 1995: 122). However, even then they placed severe restrictions on Haig, requiring that the offensive "on no account be allowed to drift into a protracted, costly and indecisive operation" and should be called off if success was in question (in neither case was this guidance heeded) (Suttie 2005: 134–35; French 1995: 122). Lloyd George, for his part, remained skeptical of the plan but did not veto it. Once again, fear that opposition to the military might jeopardize his political future intervened. At the time he faced a series of serious political crises and wanted to reduce the chance of a united campaign by the Tories and Asquithian Liberals against his government (Pugh 1988: 113).[48]

---

[47] This was not the only incident of its kind: Robertson's "refusal to argue at the War Cabinet" was quite frequent (French 1996: 106).

[48] Suttie, a fierce critic of Lloyd George, argues that these political constraints were overstated, pointing principally to the fact that the prime minister survived Robertson's ouster eight months later. He goes on to argue that even if Lloyd George was politically constrained,

Debate in Britain about the spring 1918 German offensives, a major turning point in the war, provides a second example of these weaknesses in information sharing and strategic coordination. Although the allies would eventually turn the tide against strategically exhausted Germany, in the spring of 1918 the Germans achieved their elusive breakthrough on the western front, winning major territorial gains and raising the specter of an allied defeat in the war. Prior to the offensives, in January 1918, the director of military operations under Robertson, Sir Frederick Maurice, began to warn the political leadership that the Germans were planning a spring offensive (Gooch 1968: 213; Spears 1972: 20). At the time he cautioned that British forces were insufficient to counter the attacks and asked that reinforcements be sent to the western front (Gooch 1968: 214). Lloyd George, however, was skeptical of the call for additional forces and instead had his own plans for how Britain should focus its resources; he was then pushing for an offensive against Aleppo by General Allenby in Palestine, once again consistent with an "eastern" strategy.

Despite the seriousness of the issues, instead of encouraging the kind of forthcoming debate about the prospect of a German attack that was arguably warranted, Lloyd George simply evaded the issue by calling for another in a series of general reviews of the war (Gooch 1968: 215). The War Cabinet in turn discounted Haig's and Maurice's views about the offensive without much systematic consideration (Gooch 1968: 215), deciding that because there was little talk of the attack that the chiefs must be misguided. As one of Britain's generals later criticized the politicians for failing to engage the issues: "It was much as if people sitting in a chalet in the Alps had asked for the solution to a crossword puzzle, deaf to the rumble of the avalanche of which their experienced guide had warned them" (Spears 1972: 20). Requests for reinforcements from Britain were declined while forces were retained in Palestine that might have been transferred to the western front (Gooch 1968: 218; Spears 1972: 8–9). When the German attack came on March 21, Britain was completely unprepared and overwhelmed.

The ensuing "Maurice Debate," as historians refer to it, further underscores the poverty of dialogue and coordination between political and military leaders. On April 9, 1918, Lloyd George made a speech to the House of Commons in an effort to answer critics who accused him of depriving Haig of the troops needed to defend again the German offensives (French 1995: 234).[49] Lloyd George proceeded to distort the facts about Britain's

---

the prime minister should have resigned himself or vetoed the offensive regardless of the consequences. This, however, neglects the powerful effect the domestic political situation had on Lloyd George (Suttie 2005: 153–55).

[49] For accounts of the Maurice Debate, see French (1995: 234), Strachan (1997: 139, 142), Gooch (1968), Maurice (1972).

troop strength and to lay blame for Britain's failures on the generals. He stated first that the British army had been stronger in January 1918 than in January 1917 on the western front, and that forces in Palestine were largely not "white" troops (implying the prime minister had not diverted forces from the western front for his Palestine initiative). Both statements were suspect on various grounds.[50] Bonar Law, in response to questions in the House of Commons on April 23, did little to clarify the situation (Gooch 1968: 217).

General Maurice, in turn, was infuriated by what he viewed as the politicians' dissembling about the causes of Britain's lack of preparation. He corresponded with Robertson about what actions he should take.[51] On April 30 Maurice sent a letter to the current CIGS, Sir Henry Wilson, alerting him to the problems in the figures cited by Lloyd George in his April 9 speech (Maurice 1972: 96–97; Gooch 1968: 219).[52] When Wilson did not reply, on May 6 Maurice wrote a letter to the editors of five major newspapers outlining the alleged misstatements. The letter provoked a major uproar in Parliament. In response, Lloyd George, the consummate politician, gave a highly technical but ultimately dazzling speech in the House of Commons countering the accusations of deception. Subsequently, the House divided on a motion to set up a select committee to investigate the issue; Lloyd George managed to win the vote 293 votes to 106 (Pugh 1988: 116; Gooch 1968: 224).[53] The issue was thereafter put to rest.

Interestingly, in explaining his decision to go the press, Maurice later argued that he was hoping to spark a debate about how military issues were being evaluated and decided in the war. He advocated several changes in observed practices, including establishing a system whereby the checking of information about military affairs would be devised and the conventions associated with soliciting military advice improved (Maurice 1972: 114–15; Gooch 1968: 228). Others saw more pernicious motives at play, viewing

---

[50] In particular, the increases were due to the inclusion of figures for supporting arms in the combatant numbers (Strachan 1997: 139; Gooch 1968: 215, 226). The figures on Palestine forces were also incorrect (Gooch 1968: 226, also 218, 220). Also see Pugh (1988: 117).

[51] Recall that on February 18 Robertson had been replaced as CIGS by Sir Henry Wilson. For copies of the letters, see Maurice (1972: 117–19).

[52] Maurice was informed of the speech before it was given on April 9 but was not asked to give any figures (Gooch 1968: 225; Maurice 1972: 92).

[53] Once again opposition to Asquith, who was the obvious alternative to serve as PM but was widely distrusted by the conservatives, was a central reason the latter supported Lloyd George (Strachan 1997: 138, 141; French 1995: 234–35). The Liberals also divided 98 in support of the prime minister to 71 for Asquith's motion for a Select Committee to investigate the matter (Douglas 2005: 179).

Maurice's campaign as the outcome of a conspiracy by army generals to undermine Lloyd George (Turner 1988: 130).[54]

In fact, as Gooch (1968: 211) argues, the events associated with the Maurice debate are most revealing in what they demonstrate, as he puts it, about "the relationship of politicians to their professional military advisers"—a relationship that was far from healthy. In reflecting on Maurice's recommendations, he notes that "How far such a system as that advocated by Maurice would have succeeded remains a matter for speculation. Certainly Lloyd George gave it no chance to do so. His conduct in the debate effectively precluded the discussion of such questions" (228). In effect, the battles between political and military leaders over strategy prohibited the critical analysis of German war intentions in spring 1918 and requirements on the western front, as well as the process involved in deciding them. Instead, strategic assessment amounted to intrigue and tactics by both sides to win over the public and opposition to their positions.

International Implications

What effect did Britain's assessment institutions have on its strategy and military activity during the war? First, they meant that British strategy, and its relationship to political objectives, remained ambiguous throughout the war. There were no clearly defined goals, beyond the elusive concept of retaining the "balance of power in Europe," let alone an effort to clearly define and generate a military strategy that followed from those objectives. Instead Lloyd George and his generals maintained different conceptions of Britain's political goals and military strategies. Military generals saw as their principal goal annihilating the German army in order to deter future attempts at military adventurism. Militarily this translated into concentrating Britain's energies on the western front on the premise that "The German Army's destruction could only be accomplished on the Western Front where its main forces were deployed" (Bourne 1989: 148).

Lloyd George saw things differently. He sought to prevent German domination on the continent and therefore believed war could ultimately be won only on the western front, but he also had other goals: to ensure that at the end of the war Britain's control of its empire and global position was assured (French 1995: 4, 9, 10). He supported operations in the Balkans and in the Middle East not simply in order to defeat Germany's allies and to "knock the props out" from under Germany. Rather, he sought "imperial influence and control" and to "preserve Britain's freedom of action" (Bourne 1989: 150, 149; French 1995: 2, 8, 10).[55]

[54] On this view, also see Gooch (1968: 211).

[55] Lloyd George was also concerned about sustaining popular support for the war and efforts to minimize casualties on the western front (French 1995: 6, 7). Of course, this is not

Throughout the war there was no effort to reconcile these competing visions of what the war was about and how it should be fought. Lloyd George sought to push his conception of the war and its goals under the constraint of a domestic political situation that rendered his government vulnerable, while the generals pushed to preserve their latitude of action. Ultimately the generals succeeded in winning support for many of their proposed offensives and stymieing Lloyd George's initiatives largely through their adroit political maneuverings, through allies in the Unionist party and within the pro-Asquith faction of the Liberal party, and because of the prior failures of eastern campaigns that had been pursued, such as the landing in October 1915 at Salonika and the ill-fated Gallipoli/Dardanelles campaign in April 1915 (Bourne 1989: 149). In the end, British strategy amounted to a series of large and deadly offensives on the western front intermingled with a smattering of campaigns in Italy, Central Europe, North Africa, and the Middle East. Some might argue that this was the appropriate outcome—Britain did need to concentrate resources on the western front—and that as a result British political-military strategy did show an integration of ends and means (Kennedy 1988). Regardless, it was a *default* outcome, rather than the product of forthcoming debate between political and military leaders. The strengths and weaknesses in both strategies and how they related to political objectives were never clearly defined.

Nor did discussion of operational methods receive the kind of forthcoming and rigorous debate that was arguably warranted. Take, for example, Haig's ill-fated offensive in Flanders in 1917 (Passchendaele). As noted above, Lloyd George was skeptical of the planned offensive from the start. However, rather than overrule his generals and risk his government, the prime minister approved the campaign (Bond 1968: 68, 69). Lloyd George's initial reservations were largely justified. Between 260,000 and 300,000 soldiers perished, with little strategic gain (Woodward 1983: 186).[56] As it was, "Passchendaele [came] to symbolize all that was wrong and wasteful about the way the war was fought on the Western Front" (Suttie 2005: 5).

Civil-military relations also adversely affected tactical activity by undermining serious debate about Haig's leadership of British forces in France. Lloyd George, as secretary of war and later as prime minister, was often skeptical of the army's tactics in its mass attrition battles on the west-

---

to say that an eastern strategy was superior, but that the entire conversation about strategy was truncated. From the "westerner's" perspective, missing from the strategic concept was a clear idea of how successes in the periphery would translate into German defeat on the western front. Failures in Gallipoli, Salonika, and elsewhere also raised questions about the approach (see Kennedy 1988: 48). For critiques of Lloyd George's perspective, see Corrigan (2003), Bourne (1989: 148). Others, like French (1995) are more sympathetic to the prime minister's strategic views.

[56] On debate about numbers of war dead, see Suttie (2005: 144–45).

ern front. There were good reasons to be concerned. When in September 1916, for example, Lloyd George traveled to France to observe operations, he was alarmed to find substantial deployments of British cavalry at the front.[57] It does not take much to imagine the questionable utility of cavalry facing artillery in trench warfare. While in France, Lloyd George raised the issue in the presence of French commander General Joffe; he also queried General Ferdinand Foch about the differences in French and British artillery tactics. When the British generals learned of Lloyd George's criticism and conversation with Foch, they set the press against him. Subsequently, "Lloyd George, although infuriated by this press campaign, was all too aware that it was political suicide to be linked with criticism of Haig, who was the embodiment of the army in the public mind. His response, published in the [newspaper] the *Morning Post*, was full of praise for the army and its leaders" (Woodward 1983: 108). In short, Lloyd George faced serious obstacles to raising questions about Haig's leadership.

As noted above, Haig remains a controversial figure, with historians assigning more and less blame to him versus the inherent challenges of fighting the war (Kennedy 1988: 52; Keegan 1999: 31).[58] Even among his defenders, however, Haig is rarely portrayed as a great innovator (Woodward 1983: 76; Kennedy 1988: 52, 55). Under his leadership the army was slow to recognize weaknesses in its tactics and operational approach (Gooch 1995: 191; Kennedy 1988: 50–51; Gooch 1996: 191).[59] As a result, "the same operational concept which had shown itself infeasible on the Somme in 1916 was still being used by Haig under similar operational conditions in 1917 (and probably would have been used again in early 1918 had he possessed enough troops). Even the most devout Haig followers find that difficult to justify" (Kennedy 1988: 59–60). Thus, while there is no guarantee that had Lloyd George succeeded in wresting powers of appointment

---

[57] Haig and his generals were fiercely attached to the cavalry. For example, when in May 1915, in an effort to address the shipping crisis brought about by German submarine warfare, the War Committee turned to the issue of cavalry and its necessity in battle, the generals balked and refused to discuss the issue (according to A.J.P. Taylor, feeding horses on the western front "used more shipping space than was lost to German submarines"; cited in Woodward 1983: 90).

[58] Haig's defenders often point to the formidable obstacles facing the army, which included shortages of men and materiel and the "unprecedented nature of industrialized warfare" (Kennedy 1988: 52). Certainly, as noted above, some of Britain's problems stemmed from a failure to anticipate the length of the war (a problem shared by all the belligerents), shortages of men and munitions (and the lack of industrial capacity to supply the latter), and the fact that the initial forces of the well-trained British Expeditionary Force had been decimated in the Battle of the Marne (see Kennedy 1988). However, many others point to deficiencies in Haig's leadership in exacerbating whatever persisting constraints Britain faced.

[59] For similar arguments about the inadequacies of Haig's organizational skills and oversight of training and staff work (as well as command in battle), see Winter (1991: 150–51).

and dismissal from his generals and that Haig's subsequent ouster would have spurred tactical innovation,[60] the commander's long tenure certainly did nothing to facilitate it. In sum, in the heavily politicized environment it was difficult to force the kind of disciplined and forthcoming dialogue that could have exposed the poverty of Britain's operational methods and doctrine in the war, and the necessity of rethinking its commitment to at least some of the ill-fated offensives on the western front.

Wilhelmine Germany

Civil-military relations in Wilhelmine Germany contrast with both British cases and provide an opportunity to evaluate a third central hypothesis of this study: States in which political and military leaders share power but preference divergence over corporate and strategic issues is relatively low exhibit special weaknesses in strategic coordination and the authorization process. Although Kaiser Wilhelm II tended to sympathize with his generals' and admirals' preferred corporate policies and strategic concepts, he also depended on military support, as well as that of other conservative social forces, in his coalition. Strategic assessment should generally have been poor as a result.

Key to understanding these situations is the way that low preference divergence and shared power interact and affect assessment institutions. In principle, because preference divergence is low, there are few obstacles to functional concerns overriding particularistic interests in shaping assessment institutions: Routines for information sharing and authorization process are relatively uncontroversial, as neither the political nor military leadership has incentive to invest in arguing over institutional processes. The problem resides in how the military's structural power in the regime affects strategic coordination. The military operates outside the boundaries of the political state, and opportunities for systematic review of military policy are idiosyncratic and not well established. In addition, although the autho-

---

[60] Could at least some tactical innovation have been spurred by removing Haig from command? Many of Britain's generals were lacking in creativity and independent initiative, due to the social traditions and conventions associated with the historical development of the British army (Kennedy 1988: 53). There is little evidence within the many historical texts surveyed here that there was a coherent split within the army and alternative competing visions for how to win the war. However, analysts point to some British and Australian officers who might have proven more responsive to innovation, notably Generals Sir Herbert Plumer, Sir Henry Rawlinson, Sir Ivor Maxse, and Sir Jon Monash (Barnett 1970: 404; Kennedy 1988: 51; Suttie 2005: 154). Some of these men were responsible for the innovations that finally did occur near the end of the war, when Germany itself ran out of steam and was forced to concede (Gooch 1995: 192). Even then, tactical change remained a bottom-up affair and had to be lobbied for by Haig's subordinates (Kennedy 1988: 51, 70).

rization process may appear to be relatively defined, it is in reality fundamentally ambiguous; ultimate rights of veto and approval, even if they appear formally settled, are ill-defined in the structural situation.

Before evaluating this hypothesis I begin with some analytical and historical context on the Wilhelmine case.

Context of the Wilhelmine Case

Wilhelmine Germany is often cited as the epitome of a strategically ineffective state—a state that pursued political-military strategies that were at best extremely costly and risky and at worst counterproductive to its own interests. Political scientists have sought to explain the reasons for these strategies in a number of ways. One prominent theory blames the German military's organizational parochialism and captivation with the "cult of the offensive," arguing that these fueled a destabilizing war plan, which in turn helped precipitate the First World War (Van Evera 1991, 2001; Snyder 1991a; for a critique, see Sagan 1986).[61] Jack Snyder, in his seminal book *Myths of Empire* (1991b), focuses on how the military services, as part of a logroll in the cartelized Wilhelmine state, promoted self-defeating political-military strategies. Richard Ned Lebow (1981), in contrast, argues that the Kaiser's cognitive and emotional stresses in decision making caused mismanagement of German foreign policy. Still others see German strategy as less shaped by miscalculation and domestic politics, and more by international imperatives and the necessity of arresting Germany's declining power position in the face of a growing challenge from Russia (Copeland 2000).[62]

Lacking in all these studies, however, is an understanding of the state's internal process of strategic assessment and how it contributed to Germany strategy: It is unclear why, given the heavy predisposition toward pathology implied by much of the literature, political and military leaders were unlikely to recognize the danger signs and at least try to recalibrate their strategies accordingly. Hence, if the "cult of the offensive" argument is correct and the military's organizational biases generated dangerous doctrine, why was there not better oversight of military activity and restraint in its leaders' participation in deciding the country's military strategies? Why within evaluative processes were the counterproductive policies and

---

[61] The "Cult" argument accords with the broader "inadvertent war thesis," which proposes that wars are the result of "military necessities" in the form of rigid war plans, offensive doctrines, and pressure to mobilize first. For a critique, see Trachtenberg (1991: 56).

[62] Specifically, Copeland (2000) attributes German strategy and especially its pursuit of war in 1914 to its power position and efforts to challenge Russia militarily while at the peak of its relative strength.

blatant contradictions between political and military goals highlighted by Snyder (1991b) often not identified, let alone addressed? Alternatively, if the kaiser's emotional and cognitive state was as precarious as Lebow suggests, why were there not greater checks in the policymaking process that might have offset these tendencies? Finally, even if we accept that German strategy was more a deliberate outgrowth of international incentives than the byproduct of internal factors, a rationalized assessment process that might have identified alternatives and perhaps checked the pursuit of risky and costly options to address that situation is strikingly absent.[63] In short, missing in the extant literature is an understanding of what was taking place within the country such that vital checks and balances in strategic assessment were absent. This chapter argues that Wilhelmine civil-military relations help explain the deficiencies.

This scholarship in political science coincides with a much vaster literature by historians on the origins of the First World War. The central dispute within this historical scholarship has long been over Germany's war aims in 1914 and responsibility for the war. Fritz Fischer's thesis that the war was a premeditated outcome of German elites' response to an untenable domestic situation and quest for world power provides the frame of reference for the historical debate (Hewitson 2004; Mombauer 2002; Schollgen 1990; Langdon 1991; Ferguson 1992). Many scholars in this vein analyze the long-term political and social conditions in Germany that inspired its international ambitions and insecurities.[64] As such, this research focuses on "broader issues that led inevitably to armed conflict" and not necessarily on actual decision making in Germany (Wilson 1995: 4).

A more narrowly defined literature emphasizes actual "decisions for war," and specifically those decisions in the July 1914 crisis (Hewitson 2000: 571). Here debate turns on the motives, meanings, and significance of actions of particular individuals—especially Kaiser Wilhelm II, Chancellor Bethmann Hollweg, War Minister Erich von Falkenhayn, Chief of Staff Helmuth von Moltke, as well as their Austrian counterparts—at various points in July and early August (Joll 1984; Geiss 1967; Albertini 1953; Wilson 1995; Schmidt 1990; Tuchman 1962). One conventional view within this scholarship has long been that the war was "inadvertent"—the product of inflexible military plans and mobilization schedules, the "short

---

[63] Striking is the degree to which in Copeland's (2000) fascinating account of the July 1914 crisis, extremely complicated strategies by German leaders to achieve an ambitious set of political and military objectives were little debated and pursued as if self-evident, despite their reliance on a range of contingencies and actions by other states sometimes inconsistent with their self-interests.

[64] Key themes include the role of social Darwinism (Kaiser 1983), the economy and constraints on military spending (Ferguson 1992), popular opinion (Mommsen 1973), and the international situation (Schollgen 1990).

war allusion," and militarism. Scholars in this tradition also almost universally emphasize the confused and idiosyncratic nature of assessment in Germany during the July crisis.

Two themes emerge within the historical literature that might account for these weaknesses in Germany's evaluative processes. The first is that Germany's constitutional structure and political institutions predisposed it to poor strategic assessment by supplying so many decision-making prerogatives to the kaiser; the system was prone to break down because it vested so much responsibility in one person who could not possibly manage a task of such magnitude (Herwig 1988: 81–82; Mombauer 2001: 14–34; Deist 1982). Yet what this explanation neglects is that the same constitutional structure operated quite differently under Wilhelm II than it had under his predecessor, Wilhelm I, when Bismarck was the kaiser's chancellor (Craig 1955: 213–15, 226–29; Ritter 1970: 120).

A second theme in the literature suggests one reason why the deficiencies may have been more pronounced under Wilhelm II: the kaiser's personality and psychological state (Mommsen, 1990). Wilhelm II in fact has been the subject of considerable psychological profiling.[65] Hence Kohut (1982) argues that the kaiser's relationship with his parents promoted a distorted view of foreign policy issues, such as relations with Britain. Hull (1982) contends that Wilhelm II's military and civilian "entourage" shaped his policy preferences and encouraged his promilitary affectations. However, as historian Richard Evans notes, while intriguing, links between these psychological portraits and the policymaking process are underspecified and do not adequately account for the country's strategic choices (1983: 488).[66]

More broadly, individual psychology is at best an incomplete explanation for the Wilhelmine case. As Rosen (2005) has argued, political systems often evolve in ways that can both alleviate and intensify the effects of individual idiosyncrasies on strategic choices. The task is to explain why the system lacked essential checks and balances in Germany at this time. Here we can look to its civil-military relations and, in particular, the structural situation in which the military occupied such a central role in the political coalition. In other words, the kaiser's personality and psychology may have fueled his militaristic inclinations, as the psychobiographical literature cited above contends, contributing to low political-military preference divergence. Yet we also need to examine how those preferences interacted with the balance of power in civil-military relations to grasp fully why strategic assessment was so deficient.

[65] On psychobiographical accounts in general, see McDermott (2004: 189–214).
[66] Another set of critiques argues that Wilhelm was too inconsistent in his preferences to create what is sometimes referred to as a "personal regime" and that he tended to use his latitude mostly for symbolic activities (Hewitson 2004: 199; Deist 1982; Evans 1983).

Below I analyze how this configuration of power and preferences shaped strategic assessment within Germany during this time period. My goal is not to review or explain the origins of the country's strategies in the Wilhelmine era in their entirety—an obvious impossibility given the complexity of the case and necessary brevity of my treatment. Rather, my objective is narrower: to show that whatever the international, social structural, psychological, domestic political, or other forces that might have motivated German strategies in the era, the latter were unlikely to benefit from a careful assessment of their costs, risks, feasible alternatives, or inherent contradictions. In other words, poor assessment did not "cause" Germany's domestic and international situation and the incentives it engendered but ensured that any pathologies in the strategies leaders pursued to address the country's circumstances were unlikely to be addressed.

Civil-Military Relations

As noted above, Wilhelmine Germany was characterized by a relatively low level of political-military preference divergence. In large part this was due to Kaiser Wilhelm II's identification with the military's corporate, professional, and strategic interests, which was fueled both by personal and domestic political factors. Thus, on the one hand, shared preferences were perpetuated by class issues, and specifically by the overlap of interests between the army's officers and Germany's agrarian aristocrats, which figured prominently in the kaiser's coalition (see below).[67] On the other hand, shared preferences were reinforced by the kaiser's personal predilection for all things military. As the psychological studies cited above suggest, his youthful exposure to the military had made a substantial impression on him (Rohl and Sombart 1982). Kaiser Wilhelm II consequently "preferred military companions, military manners and military advice to any other" (Craig 1955: 239). The kaiser was strongly supportive of the military's organizational interests, and his views of military strategy tended to align with its leaders' perspectives on critical issues.

In addition, the military was a powerful force in Wilhelmine Germany, both for historical reasons and because of the popular esteem it enjoyed. This was a time in Germany in which militaristic, nationalistic, and social Darwinian ideas were pervasive. In the years before the First World War, public opinion had taken on a life of its own, and this set of ideas had intense popular appeal (Mommsen 1973; Snyder 1991b: 104; Schollgen

---

[67] The officer corps retained its aristocratic character throughout this period, despite increases in officers from middle-class backgrounds (see Craig 1955: 235, 237–38). See chapter 2 on social structural factors (such as class) as an influence on the intensity of civil-military preference divergence.

1990: 105–19); the rise of organizations like the Pan-German League, the Army League, and the Navy League helped mobilize the sentiments and embed them in society. These trends, as well as the historical position of the German army, helped elevate the stature of the military; it had substantial latent power and constituted a major force within the kaiser's coalition.

The kaiser, however, also had a broader base of support within conservative societal groups. The prominence of the state of Prussia within Germany and the influence of the agrarian aristocracy as well as other farmers within it rendered these groups important allies for the kaiser; in fact, much of the army's officer corps had traditionally been drawn from the Prussian Junkers, helping to reinforce his relationship with both groups. In addition, the Junkers had coalesced with industrialists in the famous coalition of "iron and rye" in which the Junkers supported a naval buildup in exchange for grain tariffs (Kehr 1977; Berghahn 1973; Fischer 1975; Wehler 1985).[68] It was this coalition of groups on which the kaiser relied as his political base. Moreover, he relied on them at a time when the country was undergoing tremendous domestic political change. The Social Democratic party, which advocated franchise reform and other progressive changes in the government and constitution, was becoming increasingly powerful; in the elections of 1912 it emerged as the largest party in the Reichstag. The conservatives, the officer corps, and the kaiser all rallied against this common "threat" to their respective prerogatives. To a large extent, then, the kaiser, the military, and conservative social forces operated in symbiotic coexistence.

In sum, Wilhelmine Germany can be characterized as a case of shared power and low preference divergence. The kaiser's position and influence depended on the ongoing support of the military, yet he also drew support from the conservative social groups with which he allied. The kaiser's close ties with his military leaders and shared preferences mitigated conflict between them. The period was marked by a remarkable coincidence of interests between the military and political leadership.

Strategic Assessment

These civil-military relations shaped strategic assessment in several ways. In some areas they were beneficial. They paved the way for relatively easy

---

[63] The strongest case for existence of this coalition of iron and rye is made in Eckart Kehr's (1977) classic work, as well as in the works cited above. More recent historical work has challenged the basis of this scholarship, arguing, for example, that the inherent conflicts in economic interests in the groups militated against any enduring and established coalition of industrialists and landowners (see, for example, the essays in Eley and Blackbourn 1984; Evans 1987). For an overview, see Hewitson (2004: 10, 33). A middle ground accepts the core thesis of the marriage of iron and rye but recognizes it as a less secure and more troubled relationship characterized by conflicting as well as compatible interests (see Snyder 1991b).

sharing of information across the political-military divide. As in the historical literature on Britain, there is very little evidence that military leaders deliberately or consistently sought to deceive Wilhelm II and conceal information from him. The kaiser had frequent access to his military leaders, and they seemed forthcoming, when requested, with information he sought.[69]

In contrast, as the theory predicts, weaknesses in strategic coordination and the authorization process generated profound problems in assessment. To start, structures for strategic coordination were underinvested, reflecting the underlying structural relationship between the military and political leadership in which the military enjoyed substantial autonomy in the state. This is not to say there was not a lot of interaction between the political leader and his military counterparts. There was plenty. The kaiser was surrounded by military officials in a variety of forums. For example, the kaiser maintained close relations with members of the Military Cabinet (Herwig 1988: 81; Mombauer 2001:32). Wilhelm II also brought together all his military aides and assistants into a "royal headquarters," which included generals assigned to Wilhelm as advisers, military aides, and the chiefs of the Military and Marine cabinets (Ritter 1970: 127). The kaiser, in turn, granted the right of immediate, direct audience (*Immediatrecht*) to no less than forty army and a similar number of naval officers (Herwig 1988: 82; Mombauer 2001:22). Given the kaiser's affinity for all things military, the fact that he sought to surround himself with generals and admirals is relatively unsurprising.

The problem was that these frequent meetings did not translate into a systematic set of routines for evaluating military strategy and its integration with political objectives. Entities such as the kaiser's royal headquarters, for example, facilitated meetings but tended to be governed by poorly defined processes; as such the headquarters had "no clear-cut functions whatsoever" (Herwig 1988:82). The Military Cabinet and other entities operated to the almost complete exclusion of representatives of the diplomatic and political arena. As such they were symptomatic of the dislocation of professional diplomats from military and foreign policy (Craig 1955: 240–41; Ritter 1970: 127).[70] Among the *Immediatstellen*, rivalries and power struggles were frequent as they vied for the kaiser's attention; the meetings did not amount to routinized debate among an established set of advisers (Mombauer 2001: 22–23).

Moreover, while the kaiser met regularly with no less than eighty naval or military officers, only two audiences with the civilian side would take

---

[69] Even in accounts that are critical of the military's influence and provide detailed accounts of how it manifested, as in Craig (1957), Ritter (1970), or Mombauer (2001), poor information sharing does not emerge as a major theme. Recall that the theory does not have a clear prediction for structural competence, so I do not address it here.

[70] On the eclipse of the role of diplomats, see Craig (1955: xvii, 241, 295–98).

place—with the Civil Cabinet and Reich chancellor—and then much less frequently (Deist 1982: 177; Ritter 1970: 127). More broadly, during this time period the prerogatives of the General Staff increased significantly,[71] while the War Ministry's influence over the military diminished (Craig 1955: 226–33; Goerlitz, 1953:132; Herwig, 1994:245). In short, in a consultative system in which diplomats were increasingly marginalized, the autonomy of the military from political offices grew considerably (Huntington 1957: 103). This undermined the quality of strategic coordination within the German state at this time.

Evidence of these dynamics can be seen in what has come to be called the kaiser's "war council" meeting in December 1912. The meeting occurred during the Balkan wars (1912–1913) between the Balkan League and Turkey; these wars mattered for Germany because they raised the prospect that a broader conflict would break out, involving its ally, Austria-Hungary, against Russia (Russia supported the Balkan League). Against this backdrop, on December 2, 1912, Germany's prime minister Bethmann Hollweg gave a speech to the Reichstag pledging German support to Austria in the event of a war with Russia. Subsequently, the British, in communications with the German ambassador in London, Prince Lichnowsky, warned that they would not remain neutral in the event of a continental war involving Germany, especially if in the course of the conflict it attacked France (Rohl 1969: 660). As I elaborate below, the kaiser was extremely alarmed by the message, especially this apparent confirmation of British involvement in a continental war, which was a major concern of Germany at the time (Stevenson 1997: 29). The events that followed are revealing.

On December 8 the kaiser called a meeting to discuss with his military leaders Germany's position. He proceeded to lay out a case for going to war. Chief of the General Staff Moltke, who was concerned about Germany's declining relative military status, responded that he thought war on the continent was unavoidable, and the sooner it occurred, the better (Trumpener 1976: 83; Mombauer 2001: 210).[72] Admiral Tirpitz, chief of the Reich Navy Office, however, warned that the navy needed the delay of at least a year until its preparations for a conflict would be complete. The kaiser then agreed to postpone any decision for war. In the end Moltke too declined to advocate a European war, arguing that the public needed to be prepared first (Rohl 1969: 663).

---

[71] One indication was the growth in the size of its staff, which increased from 239 officers in 1888 to 625 on the eve of the outbreak of the war (Goerlitz 1953: 96; Mombauer 2001: 35; Herwig 1988: 82).

[72] Moltke worried about the growing military capabilities of the entente powers (and especially Russia) and thought a war should come before Germany's position declined relative to its adversaries'.

This meeting has been central to an unresolved debate about Germany's war aims, with Fritz Fischer pointing to it as evidence that Germany's aggressive actions in July 1914 were premeditated and planned eighteen months prior, and other scholars discounting Fischer's interpretation (Stevenson 1997: 16–17; Hewitson 2004: 4; Turner 1974; Rohl 1969; 1994: 162–65; Mombauer 2001: 135–45; Fischer 1975: 160–64). Perhaps most telling, however, is what the war council reveals about the state of strategic assessment in Germany at the time: as Annika Mombauer puts it, "in highlighting military decision-making in Imperial Germany with all its particularities" (2001: 142).[73] First, the meeting included three admirals—Alfred von Tirpitz, August von Heeringen (chief of the Admiralty Staff), and Georg Alexander von Muller (chief of the Naval Cabinet)—as well as the chief of the General Staff, Helmuth von Moltke (Mombauer 2001: 139).[74] It did not include the diplomats: "Characteristically the War Council included neither Bethmann nor the Foreign Minister, and not even the War Minister" (Stevenson 1997: 17). In fact, the chancellor, Bethmann Hollweg, was told of the meeting's discussion only afterwards, by Admiral Muller (Fischer 1975: 163). Bethmann was understandably exasperated by his exclusion. It was he who coined the term "war council" when referring to the meeting (Rohl 1994: 165).

Equally significant was how the meeting dealt with the foremost diplomatic issue in Germany at the time: relations with Britain. The meeting was in fact ostensibly called because of Britain's statements about its prospective intervention in a continental war. At the time, the diplomats, and especially Bethmann, had been working steadily to improve relations with Britain, in the hope that the island nation could help stabilize Germany's position on the continent and ease its expansion overseas (Mommsen 1968: 38). In addition, and especially critical, both the kaiser and Bethmann hoped Britain might stay neutral in any future European war involving Russia or France (Jarausch 1973: 140). Yet, during the war council there was no systematic study or analysis of British policy and how Germany's actions might influence it. Even had the political leadership been convinced that British intervention in a future war was unavoidable, as some contend, they might have at least more fully considered and debated the ramifications of such a potentiality.

The poverty of strategic analysis in Wilhelmine Germany is also apparent in the failure to consider the political ramifications of the country's war

---

[73] For transcripts of accounts of the meeting by three officials, see Rohl (1994: 162–65). Some, like Mommsen (1968: 12–13), dispute the significance of the war council meeting. But a lot of his claims have now been challenged based on new historical evidence (Mombauer 2002: 151).

[74] There is some uncertainty about whether the chief of Military Cabinet was present as well.

plan, the Schlieffen Plan. The plan called for fighting both France and Russia, first by defeating France in a massive strike in the west in the window of opportunity provided by Russian mobilization, and then shifting forces to a campaign against Russia in the east. Critical to the plan, given the need for speed and the obstacles of French defenses, was that it called for marching through Belgium at the war's start despite the latter's neutral status. Although considered a military necessity, violating Belgian neutrality also considerably heightened the odds that Britain would immediately enter the war—something, once again, Germany wanted to avoid, especially its political leaders like Bethmann Hollweg as well as the kaiser (Jarauch 1973; Levy 1991: 77). In short, the Schlieffen Plan greatly complicated the attainment of one of Germany's major diplomatic goals: keeping Britain out of a continental war.

To understand why Germany maintained the plan with little serious consideration of its diplomatic implications, one must look to the inadequacies of strategic coordination in the country at the time. As Ritter, an early and ardent critic of civil-military relations in the era, describes the problem, the failures stemmed from a divorce of political and military planning, which originated in turn from the military's autonomy from the political apparatus of the state (1970: 193–206; also see Herwig 1988: 87; 1955: 257; Levy 1991: 85). The army, in fact, had long before unilaterally dismissed the importance of violating Belgium's neutrality and the prospect of British intervention. "That Britain would not remain neutral was a mere hiccough for the General Staff" (Mombauer 2001: 209–10). Hence even while the diplomatic apparatus pushed in one direction in relations with Britain, the military's war plans pushed in another. The contradiction was not addressed (Herwig 2003: 181).[75] In fact, it was scarcely discussed (Ritter 1970: 205). With the exception of one superficial inquiry in 1913 (years after the plan's original conception and long after Anglo-German relations had begun to degrade), the General Staff never seriously considered other operational plans and alternatives to the Schlieffen two-front concept (Ritter 1970: 205; Deutsch 1984: 12).[76]

---

[75] The problem was not that the German chancellor was unacquainted with the plan. He had known the plan's basic outline since December 1912 (Turner 1988: 207; Herwig 1988: 87), although he did not know of one critical element: The plan called for taking of the Belgian city of Liege immediately, which would accelerate the pace of war preparations and reduce the time for diplomatic maneuvering (Ritter 1970: 266; Taylor 1965: 88–90).

[76] A similar argument could be made for weaknesses in the war plan, the origins of which historians have traditionally debated: whether they were inherent in Schlieffen's concept (see Addington 1966) or introduced by his successor, Moltke (see Craig 1955: 279–80; Turner 1985: 212; Goerlitz 1953: 135). For an overview of the debate, see Mombauer (2005), Turner (1985). In highlighting these flaws, observers point to logistical problems in the plan. See, for example, Keegan (1999: 36), Addington (1966: 9), Kennedy (1988), Herwig (1988), Stevenson (1997: 16–17). Even more far reaching is Zuber's (2002) controversial thesis that the Schlieffen Plan did not even exist. This would certainly explain why there was no debate about it!

Scholars today continue to dispute what exactly German political leaders believed about the prospects of British involvement in a continental war. Some accounts suggest that Germany's political leaders fully anticipated Britain's intervention in a potential war and were even relatively unperturbed by it (Deutsch 1984: 8; Trachtenberg 1991: 85; Copeland 2000).[77] Others suggest that Germany was convinced Britain would not intervene and fight (Levy 1991: 72). The traditional view is that Germany's perceptions varied over time, but securing British neutrality was a major objective throughout the decade, including in the final days of the July crisis.[78] Regardless of where one falls in this debate, however, no account suggests that Germany's evaluations rested on a reasoned analysis of the probability of British intervention. Nor were the *consequences* of British intervention debated, despite, for example their potentially major implications for how Germany's allies, like Italy, might react in the event of war (Mombauer 2001: 210). As one analyst observes about the British issue, "It is noteworthy and leaves one somewhat staggered that no one then or later seems to have urged the convocation of a crown council or lesser gathering of civil and military leaders to deal with a problem of such moment to the German fate" (Deutsch 1984: 9). And as Bethmann Hollweg later lamented (perhaps self-servingly), "there never took place during my entire period in office a sort of war council at which politics were brought into the military for and against 'consideration' " (quoted in Herwig 1988: 99).

These weaknesses in strategic coordination would prove especially glaring during the July 1914 crisis that preceded the outbreak of the First World War. Recall that the crisis was catalyzed by the assassination of Austrian Archduke Ferdinand in late June by Serbian nationals. Initially, Germany encouraged Austria to take an assertive stance against Serbia, many historians now agree, because it wanted to precipitate (at least) a localized war, which would reconfigure the balance of power in the Balkans (see the discussion in Mombauer 2002: 15; Stevenson 1997: 18; Langdon 1991). On July 5th the kaiser met with the Austrian envoy, Count von Hoyos, and offered full assurances of German support in the event of war over the issue. He did so, however, without first meeting with his political and military officials; it was only later, "in a series of dispersed meetings," that the kaiser, his generals, and Chancellor Bethmann Hollweg discussed the

---

But the larger point holds in that systematic inquiry into operational plans (whatever their content) and political goals was not pursued.

[77] The strongest claim about Germany's view of British intentions strikes me as difficult to support. It is belied, for example, by the striking reaction the kaiser and Bethmann had in the final days of the crisis when they got news that Britain might stay neutral if Germany refrained from attacking France. The kaiser put military operations on hold until he realized he had misunderstood the offer. See the discussion in Mombauer (2001: 219–26).

[78] For a recent reiteration of this view, see Mombauer (2001).

kaiser's "blank check" to Austria (quoted in Stevenson 1997: 17; Mombauer 2001: 191; 2002).[79]

Subsequently, on July 23, Austria issued a list of demands to Serbia about how the situation would be investigated and handled. These were intended to be deliberately unacceptable. Yet, to Austria and Germany's surprise, Serbia complied with nearly all the demands. The kaiser initially reacted that the cause for war might be eliminated and recommended this view be communicated to the Austrians (Geiss 1967: 223; Mombauer 2001: 199). He subsequently changed his view and supported Austria's assertive policy.

Both the kaiser and Bethmann would change course again after they received word, via a telegram from the German ambassador in London, Prince Lichnowsky, on July 29th that Britain had offered an "unequivocal warning" of its involvement in any continental war (Stevenson 1997: 29). They then began to push Serbia to accept a so-called Halt in Belgrade and stop escalating the crisis (Mombauer 2002: 17; Geiss 1967: 268; Albertini 1953: 520). The reasons given for the Halt vary. The traditional view is that it was precipitated by Lichnowsky's telegram about British intentions, which chastened Bethmann and the kaiser into retreat. Others suggest that news of a partial mobilization by Russia was the cause because this meant that localization of the war was unlikely (Trachtenberg 1991: 85–86). Alternatively Copeland (2000) argues that it was part of a complex strategy in which Germany was hoping to spur Russia to declare general mobilization, while keeping Austria on board for war involving Russia: Essentially, Germany was seeking a continental war, but it wanted to be able to blame Russia for precipitating it. Regardless of the rationale for the retreat at the end of July, diplomatic and political considerations required slowing events.

Up to this point the military did not play a significant role in the crisis. However, by the end of July the chief of staff, Helmuth von Moltke, was becoming increasingly worried about the fate of the Schlieffen Plan. Concerned that Germany would lose its opportunity to strike France before turning east, he started pushing for German mobilization; Bethmann, in contrast, still wanted to delay, either (or both) because he feared British involvement or because he wanted to wait until Russia mobilized first and could be blamed as the aggressor in the conflict (Mombauer 2001: 199).[80] To satisfy Moltke, on the evening of July 30, after an intense and sometimes heated meeting, Bethmann finally agreed that on the following day at noon he would support German mobilization regardless of Russia's actions.

---

[79] To be fair, the kaiser did convey that he intended to speak with his chancellor about the issue (Trumpener 1976: 62; Hewitson 2004: 199).

[80] For different characterizations of Bethmann's preferences and debate about them, see Trumpener (1976: 76), Langdon (1991), Ritter (1970), Trachtenberg (1991: 85–86).

However, just before the deadline on July 31 news of Russian mobilization was received. The kaiser signed the order authorizing mobilization on August 1 (Stevenson 1997: 30).

Notable about these events is what they reveal about the poor quality of strategic coordination in Germany at the time. As one historian summarizes the evaluative process during the July crisis, Berlin "was a house without direction. Orders were issued, countermanded, then reactivated. Wilhelm II and Moltke undertook radical, sometimes daily shifts in their war policies. Each telegram from London and each piece of intelligence from East Prussia occasioned acrimonious debate and fundamental shifts in policy" (Herwig 2003: 183; Stevenson 1997: 31). Joint political-military review was decidedly confused and ad hoc. There were few, if any, efforts to analyze German strategy systematically. "In July 1914 there never took place a grand council of state to decide the critical issue of war or peace in a rational, coordinated manner" (Herwig 2003: 186).

This was especially critical because political and military leaders were guided by different concerns throughout the crisis. Whatever his underlying preferences for war, Bethmann focused on diplomatic issues in late July, keeping Britain neutral if possible, and ensuring Russia mobilized first, before Germany (Mombauer 2001: 208). The military under Moltke was concerned about preserving its capacity to implement the Schlieffen Plan. As Trachtenberg characterizes it, while one side needed to slow events, the other hoped to accelerate them. The two sides were "working at cross purposes." This was due in no small measure "to the astonishing lack of coordination between the political and military authorities" (Trachtenberg 1991: 90). In short, strategic coordination was extremely poor.

Unfortunately, this was not the only problem afflicting strategic assessment in Wilhelmine Germany in the years leading up to the war or during the July crisis itself. The authorization process for deciding strategy was also poorly defined. On a day-to-day basis the kaiser exercised daily control of military affairs. But the military's substantial influence, its autonomy from political processes, and its relationship with the kaiser, meant that ultimate lines of accountability and domains of responsibility were poorly defined.

Take, for example, an exchange between military leaders in Germany and its ally, Austria-Hungary, in 1909. In January Germany's chief of staff, Helmuth von Moltke, received a letter from Conrad von Hotzendorff, chief of the Austrian General Staff.[81] The letter inquired into where Ger-

[81] On these events, see Craig's account (1955: 286); also see Ritter (1970: 241–45). Ritter does not attach the same level of importance to the January letter, arguing that it did not represent a clear-cut assurance of support. Interestingly, however, he does point to a letter written by Moltke in March about where a German attack would come in the event of an Austrian offensive, which he characterizes as "crucial to [Austrian Chief of Staff] Conrad's planning and the whole relationship between the two allies on the outbreak of war" (Ritter 1970: 245).

many would concentrate its forces in the event Austria went to war with Serbia and Russia. Although superficially about military matters, implicit in the missive was an assumption, first, that Austria "might find it necessary to invade Serbia," and, second, that Germany would come to its aid in the event of such an offensive (Craig 1955: 289). In other words, the letter presumed that Germany would support Austria in a war against Serbia.

In his reply, Moltke did nothing to address the implicit assumption about Germany's commitments. Instead the military chief simply stated that Germany was prepared to mobilize against Russia (Serbia's ally) if Russia intervened in an Austro-Serbian conflict. Ostensibly about military matters, the letter therefore also contained an implicit and powerful political message. As Craig concludes, "It is difficult to over-estimate the importance of this statement for in the plainest terms it amounted to an admission that Austria had a right to expect German support even in a war caused by her own provocation" (1955: 289). Before sending the letter, Moltke apparently informed the kaiser and chancellor of its contents. However, in Wilhelmine Germany's dysfunctional assessment institutions, where the ultimate accountability of the political and military leadership for security issues was ill-defined, the broader strategic ramifications of what was purportedly a military-to-military communiqué were not addressed.

During the July crisis these ambiguities in German decision making would prove even more conspicuous. Here is it instructive to consider once again the events leading up to the kaiser's mobilization order for German forces on July 31. Recall that just prior, on July 29 and 30, the political leadership had been trying to slow the crisis. Moltke was pushing in the opposite direction, concerned that military necessity dictated rapid mobilization of Germany's forces. For example, on July 28th he went so far as to draft a memorandum in which he commented on Germany's political and military situation, entitled, appropriately enough, "Assessment of the Political Situation." In it he made the case for German mobilization even upon news of partial mobilization by Russia (Mombauer 2001: 201–2; Turner 1965: 314). By July 29 Moltke had become "adamant" that Germany mobilize (Mombauer 2001: 203). However, Bethmann still declined to support the measure. Moltke acquiesced (Herwig 2003: 180; Mombauer 2001: 203; Hewitson 2004: 202).[82] Subsequently, after " 'endless negotiations' " he and Bethmann arrived at a "time and face-saving compromise," finally deciding on the July 31 mobilization deadline (Mombauer 2001: 204; Geiss 1967: 271; Herwig 2003: 180). Moltke himself then proceeded to have his adjutant draft the Kaiser's declaration to the country's citizens

---

[82] This was possibly because the information available to him at that point suggested that Russian mobilization preparations were not as advanced as he feared (Turner 1985: 215; Mombauer 2001: 200; Trumpener 1976: 77).

and armed forces announcing Germany's mobilization (Geiss 1967: 270; Herwig 2003: 181).

Telling about these events is what they reveal about the authorization process—in what they reveal about how decisions were being made and who had the informal power to exercise key prerogatives such as agenda setting and rights of approval. The dynamics are subtle: Contrary to conventional views, this is not the case of a German leader simply losing control or being dictated to by his military: "civilian decision-makers were [not] innocent victims of a military conspiracy, . . . Rather, the evidence suggests that at different times in the crisis, decisions were predominantly made either by the civilians or the military" (Mombauer 2001: 185; Stevenson 1997: 31). Both military and civilian leaders were playing a role in deciding German strategy—although what role, when, is less clear.

Finally, and especially revealing of these ambiguities in the authorization process, is one particular set of events that occurred on July 30 (*before* Moltke got Bethmann to agree to the deadline for German mobilization the following day) (Mombauer 2001: 205). At 5:30 p.m. on that day, Moltke informed the Austrian attaché in Germany that he desired its immediate mobilization against Russia so that Germany could follow suit. Later that evening he telegraphed the Austrian chief of staff, Conrad von Hoetzendorf himself, commanding Austria to "stand firm against Russian mobilization. Austria-Hungary must be preserved, mobilize at once against Russia. Germany will mobilize" (Geiss 1967: 270). In sending this message, Moltke effectively "took action to nullify Bethmann's change of policy"—that is, to "nullify," what in the conventional view was, Bethmann's then standing policy of slowing the crisis (Turner 1965: 315).

The reaction of Count Berchtold, the Austrian foreign minister, upon receiving the message is striking. "How odd!" he reportedly exclaimed, "Who runs the government: Moltke or Bethmann" (quoted in Keegan 1999: 64; see also Craig 1955: xvii; Turner 1985: 215: Geiss 1967: 270-71; Turner 1965: 315). Berchtold's reaction captures it perfectly: It was indeed unclear exactly who was making decisions in Germany.[83]

International Implications

How did these weaknesses in strategic coordination and ambiguities in the authorization process influence Germany's international relations? Most important, they predisposed the country to pursuing disintegrated and often dangerous political-military strategies. Whatever the structural, do-

---

[83] For a similar example of these ambiguities in decision making, see the discussion of the kaiser's efforts on August 1 to cancel the mobilization of German forces; see Hewitson (2004: 200), Mombauer (2001: 208–26).

mestic political or other factors driving the state to pathology, its inadequate assessment institutions assured that these internal contradictions were unlikely to be analyzed, let alone reconciled.

This is strikingly evident in the failure to weigh and measure several key aspects of German foreign policy and strategy at the time. Most notable was the clash between political and military objectives inherent in the Schlieffen Plan. The war plan encouraged Britain's potential involvement in a continental war by requiring a march through neutral Belgium at the war's start, even while the political leadership saw as one of its most desired goals keeping Britain out of a major European conflagration (or at least delaying its entry); after all, even if political leaders believed British intervention was likely, throughout the decade before the war they continued to hope, and concertedly work for a different outcome. Therefore they should have been deeply concerned about a military strategy that basically guaranteed British intervention.

Yet the contradiction inherent in Germany's political goals and military strategy was never addressed. Instead, as noted above, the military developed its offensive war plan in virtual isolation from political oversight. As I recount earlier in this chapter, across the English Channel, the British General Staff was at the same time developing war plans with profound and equally controversial political implications. Yet, they were overseen by the civilian advisory body, the Committee of Imperial Defense. In Germany, however, "The point of total planning for war was never reached. Unlike the defense councils in other western countries, Germany's top military and political agencies never got together. Diplomats and generals, economic and military agencies—indeed even the army and navy themselves—had no opportunity to adjust and harmonize their plans" (Ritter 1970: 125).

Other issues beyond the implications of British intervention in a continental war also received scant attention.[84] Among them was the state of German military capabilities and whether its armed forces, population, and economy could prevail in a total war. Historians now suggest that Moltke was aware and sometimes quite anxious about the prospect of a long and protracted conflict on the continent and was not captivated by the "short war illusion," as some have previously argued.[85] Yet, whatever doubts Moltke may have held in private about Germany's prospects in war, these issues were little reviewed and analyzed jointly by the political and military leadership. There was no forum providing for, or requiring, such analysis of the limits of German capabilities and its capacity to mobilize for war.

[84] On these points, see the discussion in Mombauer (2001: 209–16).
[85] This argument is associated with the historian Stig Förster. In English, see Herwig (1997: 36, 49); Mombauer (2001: 211).

Indeed, as a result, many political figures "completely overestimated Germany's military strengths." Little attention was also given to Austrian capabilities, about which the German military harbored even more doubts (Mombauer 2001: 213–14). Perhaps most alarming, however, is if indeed Moltke did anticipate that Germany could become mired in a drawn-out and deadly war, neither he nor his political counterparts were encouraged to rethink the adoption of what were, even by the most generous standards, risky and often counterproductive political-military strategies in Germany's foreign relations and international crises in the decade before the war.

Beyond these implications for Germany's capacity to integrate its political goals and military activities, a more subtle effect of strategic assessment on the country's international relations also warrants mention. Recall that in chapter 1 I noted that one effect of a state's ill-defined authorization process is to complicate other states' efforts to read its preferences. Germany under Kaiser Willem II is suggestive in this regard. Ambiguities in spheres of responsibility and authority over security and military issues may have complicated the efforts of its ally Austria-Hungary to interpret its role in a future conflict in the Balkans. Take, for example, the January 1909 exchange of letters between Moltke and the Austrian chief of the General Staff in which Moltke implicitly offered support to Austria in the event of war with Serbia. At least according to one historian, the letter affected Austria's expectations of German assistance. According to Craig, "Conrad [the chief of the General Staff] regarded Moltke's promises as 'binding written agreements,' and he and those who thought as he did were encouraged to pursue their fateful course in the Balkans" (1955: 289). By conveying a more belligerent view of German preferences than its treaty commitments implied, Moltke's ill-considered message may have bolstered the convictions of "adventurers in Vienna" in an assertive Balkans policy.

Ambiguity in the authorization process may have had even more serious consequences in July 1914. Moltke's telegram on July 30 to Austria to convey German support for its mobilization is critical in this regard. According to the account by Count Berchtold, the message had a substantial impact on Austria's beliefs about German preferences in the crisis. The foreign minister reportedly told his Imperial War Council the morning after receiving Moltke's message, " 'I have sent for you because I had the impression that Germany was beating a retreat but I now have the most reassuring pronouncement from responsible military quarters.' The council then decided to submit the order for general mobilization to the [Austrian] emperor Francis Joseph for signature" (Turner 1985: 215; see also Craig 1955: 293; Geiss 1967: 272). On July 31 Austria mobilized for war against Russia. If indeed Germany was trying to counsel restraint on Austria's part at this point in the crisis, as one prominent strand of historical literature contends, Moltke's intervention apparently did little to advance that cause. As it was,

Germany's efforts to temporize "failed in part because of the violation in principle that top-level decision-makers maintain centralized political control of diplomatic and military actions and ensure that their diplomatic signals to allies as well as adversaries are not subverted by subordinates" (Levy 1991: 81).

• • •

In sum, in the years leading up to the First World War, Germany's processes for strategic assessment were extremely problematic. As Craig describes the implications: "In no previous period of German history had there been so obvious a need for careful coordination of planning and action between the political leadership, the diplomatic representatives, and the armed services of the nation. No such coordination was ever achieved, a fact which is not the least important of the reasons for the failures of German foreign policy in this period" (1955: 255; also see Keegan 1999: 46). Put simply, poor strategic assessment in Wilhelmine Germany helped ensure that "there was precious little consistency between strategic means and national political goals" (Herwig 1988: 88; 1994: 245).

Six

PAKISTAN AND TURKEY IN THE LATE 1990s

AN ESTABLISHED NUCLEAR STATE, Pakistan engages in a fierce rivalry with India over the disputed territory of Kashmir and is a pivotal player in South Asia. Similarly, Turkey, with its simmering dispute over Cyprus, restive Kurdish population, and role in the future stability of Iraq, also occupies a central position at the nexus of the Middle East and Europe. These states' regional salience makes it vital to understand when and why they might be prone to better and worse strategic assessment.

Much like Egypt, Pakistan and Turkey are also countries in which the military has historically occupied a prominent position in civilian society and politics. In both, analysts have long commented on the military's role in domestic politics and in foreign policy. As I described in the research design in chapter 2, this shared feature provides an opportunity to test how more subtle variations in these states' civil-military relations affect strategic assessment—to show how, even in states where military involvement in political life is a relative constant, differences in their processes for assessment depend on more contingent variation in the balance of political-military power and preference divergence.

In short, there are good practical and theoretical reasons for analyzing assessment in contemporary Pakistan and Turkey. In this chapter I investigate these two cases, continuing the short case studies begun in chapter 5. I anticipate very different outcomes in the two studies. Both states should exhibit weaknesses in how they engage in strategic assessment, but the origins of the flaws should differ, and their intensity and scope should be much worse in Pakistan.

Specifically, in Pakistan I explore the case of a political leader, Nawaz Sharif (1997–1999), who came to power with a sizable civilian mandate but faced military leaders with whom he was increasingly at odds over corporate and security issues—a situation consistent with civil-military relations characterized by shared power and high preference divergence. In chapter 2 I hypothesized that in states like these, evaluative and decision-making processes are undermined by competition between political and military leaders as they seek to advance structures that protect their interests in security policymaking. These states are very poor at strategic assessment.

In the Turkish study (1996–1999) I investigate a case in which the military dominates in relations with the political leader, but with whom its preferences over strategic and corporate issues diverge—a situation of high preference divergence and military dominance. One advantage of having power concentrated in one side (in this case, the military) is that the authorization process in security matters should remain clearly defined. As a result, these states are capable of choosing and implementing internally consistent political-military strategies. Also notable is that much of the deliberative process about security issues should be internalized within the military organization. Consequently, strategic coordination is apt to suffer as advisory processes marginalize, or operate outside the boundaries of, the political and diplomatic apparatus of the state. In short, states like Turkey in the late 1990s are prone to some strengths in strategic assessment, as well as specific weaknesses. Nevertheless they are still better positioned than those in which mutually empowered political and military leaders are engaged in unmitigated power struggles for control of security policymaking. Hence Turkey should exhibit some shortcomings, but Pakistan in the late 1990s should be fully deficient at strategic assessment.

Pakistan, 1997–1999

The Pakistani Case in Context

To say the military is an important theme in the scholarship on Pakistan is an understatement. As one analyst captures it, "one cannot understand Pakistan's politics without studying the role of the military" (Rizvi 2003: 97). Most of this literature focuses on issues related to internal governance. Accordingly, scholars study the reasons for the military's coups, the origins of its disengagements from office, and the social crises and weaknesses in civilian democratic institutions that accompany them; often folded in is discussion about the military's normative beliefs about its guardianship role and its permeation of the state apparatus (see Rizvi 2000: 1–16; Hoyt 2001: 974; Haqqani 2005: 263; Kukreja 1985; Shafqat 1997; Cohen 1984; Cloughley 2000; Cheema 2002; Ganguly 2000).

The Pakistani military's influence in security policy is also an important theme (see, for example, Cohen 1984: 105–33; Rizvi 2000: 190; Cheema 2000). This is evident in a central debate about nuclear stability in South Asia in which the preferences and influence of the military and how they affect security decision-making emerge as vital issues. For example, Hoyt (2001) points to the strategic myopia of the Pakistani military, and Sagan (2000) to its organizational parochialism as reasons why nuclear deterrence and stability may be in jeopardy in the region (also see Sagan and Waltz 2003: 96–97).[1]

Themes of military influence and poor strategic assessment also appear in empirical studies about the many conflicts between India and Pakistan, as, for example, in analyses of Pakistan's most recent armed confrontation with India, the 1999 Kargil war. In explaining Pakistan's questionable actions in provoking that war, scholars often observe that the internal civil-military analytical process seemed to be flawed with critical issues left unexamined (Ganguly 2001: 115; Ganguly and Hagerty 2005: 158; Singh 1999: 124). They also observe poor coordination between the political and military leadership in the crisis and debate the prime minister's versus military leaders' roles in authorizing the plan for invading Kargil (for different views, see Rizvi 2000: xvi; Ganguly 2001: 115; Ganguly and Hagerty 2005: 151; Haqqani 2005: 250; Dixit 2002: 43; Singh 1999: 134). In short, scholars often point to the military's influence over security policy.

Nonetheless, many of these treatments incorporate the military's influence in a tangential or idiosyncratic matnner. Even those that tend to be more systematic do not focus specifically on the issue of strategic assessment.[2] In the text that follows I apply this book's general theory to the Pakistani case, focusing on one pivotal period in the country's recent history. I analyze strategic assessment during the tenure of Nawaz Sharif when the 1999 Kargil campaign took place. My aim is not to explain the causes of the conflict and Pakistan's motivation in launching the Kargil operation in their entirety (these are often attributed to Pakistan's incentives to focus international attention on the Kashmir dispute, the state of Indian politics, reduced surveillance near the Line of Control, and other factors), but to show how poor assessment predisposed Pakistan toward a destabilizing crisis in spring 1999 by rendering it unlikely that key assumptions about the international reaction to the operation would be questioned and whether or not political goals would be served by the tactical military action.[3] While

---

[1] The military in particular emerges as a theme in debates about the possibility that limited conflicts will become more or less likely between Pakistan and India given their nuclear status (the stability/instability paradox). See Ganguly and Hagerty (2005: 152, 159), Kapur (2006). For an overview, see Krepon (2005).

[2] Schofield (2000) provides the most analytically developed approach in the literature on Pakistan, arguing that its "military regimes" are prone to destabilizing policies. Tremblay and Schofield (2005) add that hybrid military-civilian regimes in Pakistan are even more prone to dangerous strategies because of their nationalist appeals. Note that the intuition of this book's theory is generally consistent with these scholars' views in that there is an important distinction between situations of military dominance and those of shared political-military power. Yet, unlike the present work, these others do not seek to develop a more general theory for how civil-military relations affect strategic assessment.

[3] See Ganguly and Hagerty (2005: 152), Dixit (2002: 37, 41).

various exogenous factors laid the groundwork for the Kargil war, civil-military relations under the Sharif government help explain why the country was ripe for crisis that spring.

Civil-Military Relations

When Nawaz Sharif became prime minister in February 1997, he was elected with an overwhelming majority in Parliament. His party, the Pakistan Muslim League (PML), took an unprecedented 134 of 217 seats in the National Assembly and performed well in provincial elections (Rizvi 2000: 226). Although turnout was low, the election results were widely considered "unprecedented and astounding," rendering Sharif "the most powerful prime minister in Pakistan's history" (quotes appear, respectively, in Kukreja 2003: 251; Rashid 1999: 410; also see Haqqani 2005: 243; Syed 1998: 117). Sharif came to power with a sizable civilian following.

The new prime minister, however, was still forced to contend with Pakistan's "premier institution": the military (Kukreja 2003: xvii). Like his predecessors, Sharif faced a military establishment that was highly esteemed among Pakistan's citizens and enjoyed a singular position in the country's society and politics, in large part because of its important role in the country's history (Rizvi 2000: 1; Cloughley 2000; Cheema 2002). Many then (and now) considered the military to be the most meritocractic and capable organization within Pakistan. In addition, it exhibited a highly cohesive leadership such that military leaders consistently operated as a "corporate entity" (see Rizvi 2000: 5). Strict organizational norms and rigid internal conventions for promotion and appointment ensured that military leaders spoke with a unified voice; those who betrayed the norm were punished by the organization.[4]

As a result of the military's generally powerful position, the relationship between Pakistan's political leaders and its military chiefs, including that of Sharif and his generals, is often described as one of shared power, bargaining, or mutual coexistence (Rizvi 2000: 2–3). When Sharif first entered office with such a strong mandate he was advantaged in his relations with his military leaders. They nonetheless represented a powerful influence in his coalition with which he had to contend.

To start, Sharif had relatively amicable relations with his military chiefs: "the new government started with popular support and the goodwill of the military" (Rizvi 2000: 226). Sharif had been prime minister before, and although he had left office under pressure, the military was largely comfortable with him. He had originally risen in the government's ranks under the

---

[4] See, for example, the discussion of the replacement of the corps commanders for violating "army discipline" (Rizvi 2000: xvi).

regime of General Zia-ul-Haq and was a protégé of the military establishment (Shafqat 1997: 236).[5]

In addition, the military had strong reason to hope that Sharif could succeed in stabilizing Pakistan's economy and political arena, which were rent with corruption and instability. The Pakistani military retains a strong corporate interest in maintaining the country's economic viability. "The top brass expect the civilian government to ensure effective and transparent governance and socio-political stability," in part because of the necessity of maintaining high levels of defense spending and in part "from the assumption that a polity in turmoil cannot sustain a professional military."[6] As retired Lt. Gen. Talat Massod, formerly in charge of Pakistan's defense production industries, put it, "the military understands the importance of a strong economy and industrial base capable of sustaining its Armed Forces." The military's own track record for dealing with economic issues was poor.[7] Moreover, had the military opposed Sharif, it would have been costly to Pakistan's relationship with international financial institutions vital to its economic recovery.[8]

Sharif's rosy position would not last.[9] The prime minister proved incapable of dealing with the country's myriad economic problems and the endemic corruption of the political establishment. His failure to produce promised reform turned many of Pakistan's citizens against him, undermining his support base. It also threatened the professional interests of the army, who became increasingly alarmed about the state of the national economy and its implications for internal stability (Rizvi 2000: xiv, xv, 191, 231; Faruqui 2003: 34; Dugger 1998). Compounding these difficulties were Sharif's growing conflicts with the political establishment. When he first came to power, Sharif had used his position in Parliament to amend the

---

[5] When Sharif first became prime minister following the 1990 election he was supported by the military (there were, for example, allegations that the elections had been illegally influenced by the army's intelligence wing, which funded Sharif and his allies). The relationship between Sharif and the military soured somewhat in 1993 when Sharif went to battle against the then president. See Hasan Iqbal Jafri, "Sharif versus the Military," *Business Times* (Singapore), December 9, 1997, 10.

[6] Rizvi (2000: 13, 14). The military's involvement in the domestic economy has also magnified its interests in economic policy (Risvi 2000: 14).

[7] See comments by military leaders in Jose Manuel Tensoro and Shahid Ur-Rehman, "The Watchers," *Asiaweek*, August 8, 1997, 41. See also comments by General Aslam Beg, former chief of the army, in John Kifner, "Pakistan Army at Ease, Even in Nuclear Choice," *New York Times*, June 23, 1998, 83.

[8] See "Pakistan: Nawaz the Bold," *Economist*, April 5, 1997, 35.

[9] By the fall of 1998, both the population at large and the army were becoming increasingly restless under Sharif's rule. In September 1999, one month before the coup that removed him from office, there were large demonstrations against the government. Zahid Hussein, "Pakistan: Ambushing the Army," *India Today*, October 19, 1998, 73.

constitution by withdrawing the power of the president to remove the prime minister. The military initially sat on the sidelines of the controversy that ensued, "out of respect for the electoral mandate of Nawaz Sharif" and to give him a chance to prove himself (Rizvi 2000: 228). However, the military's patience began to wear thin in the fall of 1997 when Sharif undercut the powers of the judiciary and presidency,[10] revealing his desire to enhance his control over the state apparatus at the expense of more rationalized governance (Haqqani 2005: 244; Syed 1997: 119).

In sum, Pakistan under Nawaz Sharif fits the parameters of an environment characterized by "shared power" and "high preference divergence": Conditions were ripe for competition for control of security policymaking. Sharif had a civilian social base from which he could draw support but faced an influential military with its own support within civilian society and cohesive leadership. During his tenure in office the exact balance of power fluctuated, with Sharif arguably in his strongest position when he came to office with a large civilian mandate and weakest when he was forced from office in 1999.[11] In addition, preferences increasingly diverged, with the military becoming more and more frustrated with Sharif's mismanagement of the country's economic and political affairs.

Strategic Assessment

These civil-military relations adversely influenced strategic assessment in Pakistan under Nawaz Sharif. Their effects on the authorization process and strategic coordination were especially pronounced.[12] To start, competition undermined strategic coordination by reducing the incentives for both Sharif and his military chiefs to participate in joint advisory and decision-

---

[10] The 13th Amendment, passed by the Senate and National Assembly on April 1, 1997, removed the president's power to dismiss the prime minister. *Economist*, April 5, 1997, 35. See the report by Jason Burke, "Pakistan: Marching to the Brink," *India Today*, October 25, 1999.

[11] As one sign of how far his fortunes had fallen, the coup was largely supported by the population at large (Rashid 1999: 409; Rizvi 2000: xvii).

[12] As I explained in chapter 1, I focus my analysis on those assessment attributes that emerge as most salient in these shorter cases. In the Pakistan case I anticipate that poor information sharing should have been very significant. However, there is a dearth of public information available about dialogue between Sharif and his chiefs, as a formalized process by which it would have been recorded was for the most part lacking (which in part reflects the idiosyncrasies of civil-military assessment in Pakistan at the time); even those who have interviewed the principals have a difficult time deducing precisely what was said in conversations between Sharif and the chiefs. Structural competence is also difficult to assess within the confines of a short, supplementary case based on secondary literature since the kinds of data required are not easily accessible. Hence I focus on strategic coordination and the authorization process.

making forums. In this instance, the conflict was expressed in disagreement over the establishment of a National Security Council, which I examine below as a way of illustrating these weaknesses in strategic coordination.

The issue of the National Security Council was raised before Sharif came to power. Just one month prior to the February 1997 elections, Pakistan's president Leghari established the Council for Defense and National Security (CDNS).[13] At the time it was presented as a routinized entity for coordinating between the civilian and military leadership that would "advise the government on everything from national security to economic issues" (see Xu and Yang 1997). Although Sharif at least superficially welcomed the entity "to curry favor with the military," he also had reservations about it (Haqqani 2005: 242). During the election season he was pointedly ambiguous about whether he would allow such an entity to continue to function were he to become prime minister. After his victory he was more definitive. In April 1997 Sharif distanced himself from the CDNS, and it was never convened.

Sharif's decision to abandon the CDNS was not the last he would hear about the issue during his tenure in office, however. With growing apprehension about Sharif's capacity to govern the country, the chief of the army staff and chairman of the Joint Council, General Karamat, began to talk publicly about "the injurious implications of the economic drift and political dissention on internal stability and external security" (Rizvi 2000: 231; Kukreja, 2003: 256). In turn, on October 5, 1998, in a speech to naval officers, Karamat raised the issue of establishing a National Security Council, which would "create an institutional arrangement at the highest level for devising effective policies for coping with the ongoing problems" (Rizvi 2000: 231; also see Haqqani 2005: 248).[14] Arguing that "internal security" was the major threat facing the country and that more needed to be done to coordinate policy, Karamat proposed that the council be widely representative and backed by "a team of credible advisors and a think-tank of experts" (quoted in Baurah 1998). Implicit in Karamat's proposal was also that the council "would give the military a formal role in the political-decision-making process" (Jones 2002: 36). The general's remarks were

---

[13] The ten-member body was set up on January 6, 1997. Its members included the president; prime minister; chairman of the Joint Chiefs of Staff; army, navy, and air force chiefs; and ministers of defense, foreign affairs, and interior.

[14] Also see Farhan Bokhari, "Pakistan Army Chief Seeks Policy Role," *Financial Times*, October 7, 1998, 4. The idea of an NSC was first introduced by General Zia-ul-Haq when he ruled Pakistan. According to the general at the time, the model for establishing such a council was Turkey, where the military had an institutionalized mechanism for participating in politics. See "Army and Governance—Not Always in Step," *Business Line*, October 16, 1998. Interestingly, after Sharif's ouster, General Musharraf established a NSC-style entity under his leadership (Haqqani 2005: 259; Cheema 2000: 153).

believed to reflect those of the entire army leadership[15] and caused a major commotion in the Pakistani press, which was split in its views of the merits of the council.[16] Sharif, for his part, was far from enthusiastic about the concept. After a tense meeting between Karamat and Sharif in which Sharif reportedly accused the general of trying to destabilize the government and undermine democracy, Karamat resigned his post. It was a major moment in Pakistani civil-military relations. Karamat's resignation represented the first time an army chief of staff left office in Pakistan under pressure from political authorities (Rashid 1999: 410).[17]

Why had Sharif chosen to abandon the CDNS and to block the establishment of a follow-on entity? A National Security Council represented a formalization and routinization of the military's influence in decision making, which Sharif was unwilling to abide. The military already claimed oversight of the activities of the Sharif government. As the retired General Beg, former chief of the army, characterized the military's role, "we [the military] have to keep watch so things do not go wrong" (quoted in Tensoro and Ur-Rehman 1997: 41). Sharif apparently was unwilling to endure the advancement of the military's efforts to claim what he perceived to be veto power over political initiatives.

This debate about the council is significant for two reasons. First, it underscores the forces influencing Pakistan's institutions for strategic assessment at the time. Far from debate about how best to promote better decisions, underlying conflicts and concerns by both the military and political leaders about preserving and advancing their prerogatives upstaged discussion of the functional requirements of policymaking. Second, although motivated by disputes over domestic political issues (which were often framed in security terms), these events illustrate the obstacles to developing advisory processes for systematic analysis of the country's security strategies and policies as well. At the time the country lacked a functioning

---

[15] Former chief of the army staff Aslam Beg reported that Karamat's comments reflected the views of the corps commanders and senior officers from the other services. See Hussein, "Pakistan: Ambushing the Army." Karamat argued that the reforms necessary to implement International Monetary Fund conditions, including tax reform, spending cuts, currency realignment, and associated restructuring would be politically difficult, and that institutionalizing the military's role in decision making was necessary to support the parliamentary majority in its efforts to accomplish these controversial reforms.

[16] On debate about the NSC, see Dugger, "Pakistani Premier Prevails in Clash with General"; Muhammad Akram Sheikh, "Constitutional Legitimacy of National Security Council," *Business Recorder*, October 13, 1998. On the idea that Pakistan could benefit from an NSC, see Faruqui (2003: 131).

[17] It was widely presented in the press as an illustration of the prime minister's powerful position. See, for example, "Sharif Emerges as Most Powerful Prime Minister for Decades," *Independent*, November 23, 1998; Dugger, "Pakistani Premier Prevails in Clash with General"; Hussain, "Pakistan: Ambushing the Army."

entity for coordinating political-military activity. Consultation would occur on an ad hoc basis. The Defense Committee of the cabinet, which was formally charged with coordinating diplomatic and military activity, was rarely convened; when it was called to order in July 1999, on the eve of Sharif's visit to the United States to resolve Pakistan's Kargil crisis (discussed below), it was the first meeting that had taken place in nearly a year (Lodhi 1999: 6).[18] Similarly, the Defense Council, a policy-advisory body whose members formally include the ministers of defense, finance, and foreign affairs as well as the chief of the joint staff and service branches, failed to function. The military did retain internal processes for consultation, such as the Joint Chiefs of Staff committee. But in practice these functioned poorly (Faruqui 2003: 203).[19] Moreover, they did not substitute for a body that would bring together the political and military apparatus of the state to evaluate key national security issues. To the extent there was routinized political-military consultation, it consisted of periodic three-way meetings among the prime minister, army chief, and president, sometimes referred to as the Troika.[20] In sum, one important component of strategic assessment—strategic coordination—fell prey to civil-military competition.

Similar weaknesses can be observed in Pakistan's authorization processes. The state lacked clear procedures for authorizing military and security strategy. Instead, political and military leaders clashed over control of decision-making prerogatives.

One area in which competition manifested itself was over control of appointments and promotions. As I described in chapter 2, appointments are important indirect instruments for controlling the military organization (they allow a leader to shape the internal activities of the military) and as such often become implicated in disputes over who enjoys final rights of approval and veto over military policy. Initially Sharif was quite successful in enhancing his control of appointment prerogatives. Less than three months after coming to office, he oversaw the passage of legislation that granted him, as prime minister, unprecedented powers of appointment and dismissal of military leaders. Sharif also succeeded in having his own preferred candidates appointed to top positions, even when it violated norms of seniority in the Pakistani military (Rizvi 2000: xvi).[21]

---

[18] Also see "Who Really Runs Pakistan," *The Economist*, June 26, 1999.

[19] On the structures of these entities, see Cheema (in Lavoy et al. 2000: 173). Also important is the corps commanders meeting (Rizvi 2000: 2).

[20] Rizvi describes the general practice in Pakistan of meetings between the prime minister, army chief, and president. There is, however, little public information available about how these meetings operated under Sharif and how extensive they were (Rizvi 2000: 2, 190). Regardless, however, they did not constitute a joint forum for comprehensive analysis and evaluation of policy. Also see Kukreja (2003: xv).

[21] On April 26, 1997, less than a month after the passage of legislation that granted him powers of appointment and dismissal, Sharif ordered the country's top naval officer to retire.

The military, however, was not content to let Sharif have his way. The selection of the successor to General Karamat (who, as discussed above, had resigned over the dispute about the National Security Council) is instructive in this regard. When Karamat resigned, Sharif tried to choose a close ally, General Ziauddin, for the post. Ziauddin was the chief of the Directorate of the powerful Inter-Services Intelligence (ISI) and was distrusted by military leaders. One observer describes what happened:

> The army brass was livid and felt it had been humiliated [over Karamat's removal]. Sharif's first choice for Karamat's replacement, [General] Ziauddin, was rejected. The corps commanders were clearly unwilling to allow a man known for his close connections to the Sharif family and his [Pakistan Muslim League] loyalties to lead them. But neither was the prime minister prepared to accept General Ali Quli Khan, the senior-most candidate.[22]

Ultimately the military and Sharif decided on a compromise candidate: Lt. Gen. Pervez Musharraf, who was chosen over two more senior generals, both of whom resigned in protest (Haqqani 2005: 248; Jones 2002: 37). Sharif anticipated (ultimately wrongly) that Musharraf would prove compliant because of his ethnic background; he was an Urdu-speaking refugee from India without an ethnic base in Pakistan, whereas most of the prominent officers in the army were from Pakistan's dominant Punjab province (Haqqani 2005: 248).[23]

Still, Sharif was not satisfied. He attempted to create a more compliant command by appointing allies to the key posts of corps commander in the Pakistani army. This created further dissension in the ranks, and by the end of September 1999 military leaders were fed up with Sharif's machinations and confronted the prime minister. From the dispute emerged yet another compromise: Musharraf's probationary one-year term would be extended, while the military would support Sharif's recent appointments among the army corps commanders.[24]

It did not take long for the truce to fall apart. In early October the army removed one of Sharif's newly appointed generals (Cloughley 2000: 405).

Only once before had a civilian prime minister removed such a senior military officer. See Farhan Bokhari, "Pakistan Navy Head Fired after Bribery Claims," April 26, 1997, *Financial Times* (London), 1.

[22] Cited in Jason Burke, "Pakistan: Marching to the Brink," *India Today*, October 25, 1999, 48. In fact, after the October coup observers expressed surprise that the army had rallied behind a non-Punjabi officer. In late January 2000 reports surfaced of power struggles between Musharraf and other generals with a Punjabi base. See "Power Struggle on in Pak. Army?" *The Hindu*, January 31, 2000.

[23] Musharraf proved to be quite independent. See " 'Sharif Must Be Repenting for Making Me Army Chief'," *The Hindu*, November 2, 1999.

[24] See "Pakistani Naval Chief Resigns," Agence France Presse, October 2, 1999.

In retaliation, on October 12, Sharif dismissed Musharraf altogether (conveniently, the general was out of the country at the time). Sharif then appointed his original choice for army chief, General Ziauddin, to the post. This was the proximate cause of the coup that removed Sharif from power (Cloughley 2000: 406; Rizvi 2000: xiv.).[25]

These events once again demonstrate how conflicts over substantive issues between the political and military leadership are manifested in disputes over institutional matters. Efforts to control decision-making prerogatives over security policy and military activity were expressed in disputes about how officers would be appointed and how consultation would take place. Domestic political competition between military and political leaders eclipsed functional concerns about how best to regulate political-military activity.

Further evidence of these weaknesses in both strategic coordination and authorization processes can be seen in how Pakistan made critical strategic decisions during the Kargil war in the summer of 1999. In May of that year Pakistani troops, in collaboration with fundamentalist militants, launched incursions into mountainous zones regularly held by the Indians, across the Line of Control (LOC) in the disputed state of Jammu and Kashmir. Two months later, Pakistan was forced to withdraw from the area under international pressure.

In the current context, striking is both the poor evaluation of the military's plans for Kargil and ambiguity about how the decision to launch the invasion in spring 1999 was made in the first place. For example, accounts diverge considerably about how much Nawaz Sharif knew about the operation before it was undertaken. While it appears that military plans for such an invasion had been around for some time (Singh 1999: 133), considerable uncertainty remains about who was behind the decision to launch the offensive that spring, and how and why the decision was made. Some accounts suggest that Sharif was briefed about plans for the invasion, but there was little analysis of the operational details and potential strategic implications of what may have been presented as a limited operation.[26] Some conclude, based on their tracking of events, that even if Sharif had

---

[25] Also see Burke, "Pakistan: Marching to the Brink"; " 'Sharif Must Be Repenting for Making Me Army Chief '."

[26] Ganguly suggests that the action was probably initiated as a narrow operation ("a limited probe"), but that the military subsequently expanded it (2001: 121). It may be that the military said they were going to send a small contingent across the Line of Control, but not that they were going to launch a large operation (for such a conclusion, also see Jones 2002: 103; Qadir 2002; also see Haqqani 2005: 250). Jones notes that the evidence suggests that the operation was begun as early as October 1998, at which time Sharif may have been told that there would be limited probes. The full-scale operation was not discovered by the Indians, and Sharif says he was not informed about it until May 1999 (Jones 2002: 92).

been briefed about the broad parameters of the plan, the military must have held back significant information (Jones 2002: 101). Conversely, other accounts assert that he knew of the planned operation in its entirely from the start.[27] Sharif himself later protested that he was informed of the operation only after it had started (Ali 2000).

During the crisis, audiotapes surfaced of telephone conversations between Pakistan's generals discussing the invasion and outlining what to advise the politicians to do in upcoming talks with India over the hostilities.[28] The tapes implied that Sharif and his staff had been left out of the loop in decision making. For example, the comments of one of the generals conversing on the tapes imply that Sharif had been told about the operation only after it was launched (Jones 2002: 101). Pakistan's generals nonetheless rejected efforts to place the responsibility for the offensive on their shoulders. They publicly stated that Sharif had participated in key decisions during the entire campaign (Singh 1999: 134).

This confusing series of claims and counterclaims underscores the very ambiguity and incoherence in authorization processes in Pakistan at the time—processes that make it difficult to discern from where decisions were originating, and to judge the rationale behind them. To this day it is unclear whether Sharif authorized the action in Kargil or whether the military acted on its own (Husain 2000).

What is nearly universally agreed on, however, is that even if Sharif was told of the plan before it was launched, it was not subjected to searching analysis, and its full implications were not analyzed (Bhushan 1999; Lodhi 1999; Ganguly 2001; Faruqui 2003; Jones 2002). There was no rigorous examination of the plan, and strategic coordination was woefully inadequate. As Jones notes, even if the army informed Sharif of the intended invasion, the absence of any record, analysis, or ongoing consultation about the matter "indicates at the very least, there was no thoroughgoing debate about the implications of the Kargil operation" (2002: 103–4). Instead, the military made several critical assumptions about how the international

---

[27] For different interpretations, see Lewis Dunn et al. (2000: 248), Ganguly (2001: 115), Kapur (2004: 10), Rashid (1999: 412), Jones (2002: 103), Qadir (2002), Rizvi (2000: xvi), Haqqani (2005: 250), Singh (1999: 134).

[28] The tapes of two conversations, from May 26 and May 29, between Chief of the Army Pervez Musharraf and Chief of the General Staff Lt. Gen. Mohammed Aziz, were obtained by India under mysterious circumstances. If authentic, as most believe, the tapes also suggest that the Pakistani military was dictating political moves to the government; this included the options available to Pakistan's foreign minister in then imminent consultations with Indian officials in New Delhi. In the tapes, the military leaders say that they intend to direct the foreign minister, Sartaj Aziz, not to offer any concessions, or agree to a ceasefire of any kind. For an outline of what the tapes suggested Sharif knew, see Dinesh Kumar, "Secret Tapes Bare the Strategy of a State within a State," *Times of India*, June 12, 1999.

community would react to the operation and how India would respond militarily, which largely went unexamined.[29] As one analyst described it, "little attention was paid in the plan" to these vital concerns (Haqqani 2005: 251; also see Ganguly 2001: 115; Singh 1999: 122–24; Kapur 2006: 46, n. 45).

In sum, the Kargil Heights invasion illustrates the poor state of strategic assessment in Pakistan at the time. The country lacked a functioning entity to coordinate political and military activity. It also lacked a clear authorization process that delineated rights and responsibilities in making critical decisions about the country's international activities. As I explain below, the episode in turn illustrates the devastating international consequences that can follow from poor strategic assessment.

International Implications

The Kargil Heights invasion is just the sort of disjointed and poorly considered action endemic to states with competitive civil-military relations. Political goals and military activity were completely disintegrated in the country at the time.

Initially, the Kargil plan may have made sense tactically. The Indians vacated the positions in the Heights every winter and resumed them in the spring; in 1999 they had been slow in resuming them, providing Pakistani forces a window of opportunity to occupy the posts themselves. However, most analysts agree that strategically the Kargil plan lacked a clear rationale and was poorly integrated with political objectives (Lodhi 1999: 2; Ganguly 2001). As one analyst describes it:

> The problem with the Kargil operation was that for all its tactical brilliance in conception and execution, it was flawed in that no attention was paid to the inevitable diplomatic fallout. When considering grand strategy, all relevant factors—ranging from the economic to the diplomatic—are carefully studied. The military equation is placed in the larger international context before taking a decision. This was clearly not done, with the result that the Kargil adventure has backfired with serious consequences (Husain 2000).

As another put it, in planning for Kargil, "There was a lack of synergy between the political and military elements in the sense that the likely political consequences were not fully debated" (Bhushan 1999: 101).

In fact, the invasion ran counter to the prevailing temperate trend in Indo-Pakistani relations. Ironically, observers had initially heralded Sharif's victory as a turning point in relations between the South Asian rivals

---

[29] On these assumptions, see Kapur (2006: chap. 6, pp. 11–15).

(Ganguly 2001: 115, 123; Jones 2002: 95; Ganguly and Hagerty 2005: 149, 151; Haqqani 2005: 249). During and following Sharif's assumption to office, outsiders had been optimistic about closer relations with India and Sharif's promise to resume bilateral talks, which had stalled since 1994. The Indian foreign secretary and high commissioner (ambassador) to Islamabad had commented, "I think Nawaz Sharif, compared to most in Pakistan, is less jingoistic and a practical politician" (quoted in Lawrence 1997). These initial prognostications proved correct when in February 1999 the countries' respective prime ministers signed the Lahore agreement, which pledged new cooperation between the rival states. However, three months later the implementation of the plan for the Kargil invasion killed this burgeoning spirit of cooperation, creating questions even among Pakistan's elite about why the country pursued the Kargil plan when it did (Bhushan 1999: 103).

More broadly, most analysts agree that Pakistan damaged its own reputation as well as its ongoing efforts to internationalize the conflict in Kashmir. "On the international scene the Pakistanis were viewed as the aggressors, and the decade-long turmoil in Kashmir in which more than 50,000 lives had been lost was forgotten" (Faruqui 2003: 15). The ill-fated Kargil invasion had set back the Pakistanis' overarching goal of resolving the conflict in Kashmir.[30] Both the Group of Eight countries and the European Union were swift in condemning the country's provocations.

The strategically questionable decision to launch the invasion is underscored by Sharif's efforts to end it. As one observer put it, "The panicked and undignified manner of Islamabad's climbdown in the face of unprecedented international pressure was just as ill-thought as the backing for the Mujahideen incursion that mistook tactics for strategy and predictably backfired" (Lodhi 1999: 2; also see Amir 1999). Rather than negotiate some face-saving concession in exchange for a pullout, Sharif made the hasty decision to travel to the United States and meet with President Clinton, surprising not only Pakistani officials but Americans as well (Lodhi 1999: 4; Mazari 2000). The declaration Pakistan won from the United States in exchange for its decision to retreat represented a shallow victory: it was largely sympathetic to India and reflected the international consensus that Pakistan had engaged in unjustified aggression in launching the Kargil invasion. For example, rather than secure a promise for an immediate cease-fire, it accepted the premise that Pakistan would need to withdraw to its preinvasion position before hostilities would be formally ended (Lodhi 1999: 3). In addition, despite President Clinton's assertions that he would focus greater attention on the Kashmir conflict, the declaration offered no real commitment to international mediation (which Pakistan favored and

---

[30] On flaws in the strategic logic of the invasion, see Ganguly (2001: 121–22).

India opposed) and reiterated the necessity of bilateral negotiations to resolve the conflict. Militarily and diplomatically, the country had been isolated, while its principal adversary gained substantial international sympathy from the crisis. As a Pakistani newspaper columnist put it, "So at the end of the day, India came out smelling of roses, while we had egg all over our face."[31]

Ultimately, the Pakistani case is significant because it illustrates the way in which poor strategic assessment contributed to the disintegration of the country's political goals and military activity. Put bluntly, it shows the risks these civil-military relations generate for strategic failure, or, as one former Pakistani diplomat more delicately put it, "a poorly thought out and ad hoc attempt" to manage a state's international relations (Bhushan 1999: 100). Take, for example, the characterization of the lessons of the Kargil debacle by Pakistan's former ambassador to the United States:

> The most important lesson of the two month crisis ensues from the disastrous consequences of unstructured governance. The Kargil affair has exposed systematic flaws in a decision-making process that is impulsive, chaotic, and overly secretive. . . . Instead of putting collective, institutionalized decision making in place that makes considered, deliberate and rational choices in grave matters of war and peace, capricious behavior characterized by policy extremes is engendered by the present arrangement, at much cost to the country. . . . The failure to objectively assess national strengths and vulnerabilities during the Kargil crisis was, in large part, a consequence of such unstructured, personalized decision making, and led to the avoidable diplomatic debacle (Lodhi 1999: 6).

Like Pakistan in the summer of 1999, states with poor strategic assessment are often dangers to themselves and to others in the international arena.

Turkey, June 1996—April 1999

Below I analyze Turkey in the late 1990s. I examine a case where the military has gained substantial domestic leverage over the political leader, and where processes for strategic assessment become de facto internalized within its organizational control. I find that these civil-military relations yield both strengths and weaknesses in assessment's four institutional attributes. Before elaborating on these, I begin with some context for the Turkish case.

---

[31] Quoted in Husain (2000). On the "empty" nature of the declaration, see Ayaz Amir, "For This Submission What Gain," *Dawn*, July 23, 1999. In response to the weaknesses revealed in its tactical forces, India also increased its defense expenditure by 28 percent in the aftermath of Kargil, an amount equivalent to Pakistan's entire defense budget at the time (Husain 2000).

The Turkish Case in Context

In many ways the scholarly literature on Turkey parallels that on Pakistan, emphasizing the military's role in the modern state. Since the birth of the republic in the 1920s, the military has engaged in two coups in which it ruled directly for short periods (1960–61 and 1980–83) and two interventions in which it orchestrated civilian politics indirectly (1971, 1997) (Robins 2003: 75–76; Karabelias 2000: 130; Heper and Guney 2000: 636; Hale 1994). Much of the literature seeks to explain this pattern of intervention.

Analysts, for example, emphasize the origins of the military's guardianship role and how the legacy of Kemal Ataturk shaped the doctrine of the Turkish armed forces (Muftuler-Bac 1999: 247; Robins 2003: 163; Jenkins 2001: 33; Birand 1991: 68; Rouleau 2000; Larrabee and Lesser 2003: 27). Such reflections are sometimes embedded in narrative accounts of the Turkish military and its internal institutions in order to explain how it reproduces its "ideology" and socializes its officers (Birand 1991; Karabelias 2000: 139; Jenkins 2001: 30–33; Hale 1994: 319). Alternatively, scholars debate the causes of the military's "moderating" versus "ruler" role in internal politics (Jenkins 2001: 6; Muftuler-Bac 1999: 247; Hale 1994: 309–17; Birand 1991: 68; Heper and Guney 2000: 647). Central issues include weaknesses in political institutions and the military's esteemed position in Turkish society (Jenkins 2001: 16–17); these themes also are manifested in debates about whether Turkey's citizens are "ready" and/or "willing" to engage in unmitigated democracy (Robins 2003: 31; Kinzer 2001: 11–12, 18; Larrabee and Lesser 2003: 29). In short, scholars tend to emphasize the military's role in internal governance, reflecting the fact that, as Karabelias (2000: 130) puts it, "If there is one element on which all researchers . . . agree, this is the assumption that the military institution has been the most important force behind the social, economic and political structure of the Turkish state."

Also, as in scholarly research on Pakistan, the military's role in foreign and security issues is a pervasive, if less systematic, theme (see Robins 2003: 69). The military's preferences are noted in discussions of Turkey's relations with its Kurdish population, Greece, Israel, Syria, Iran, and the European Union (Yavuz 1997: 29; Jenkins 2001: 67–82; Ozcan 2001: 22; Muftuler-Bac 1999: 250; Bengio 2004: 86). Analysts also observe the military's influence in the country's National Security Council (see below) (Kinzer 2001: 15; Robins 2003: 76; Jenkins 2001: 50–51; Ozcan 2001; Muftuler-Bac 1999: 248; Heper and Guney 2000: 637; Larrabee and Lesser 2003: 28). Yet, as Ozcan notes, very few detailed, systematic treatments of security policymaking exist: "Literature on Turkish foreign policy appears to have overlooked the military's role" (Ozcan, 2001: 13; for a similar point, see Hale 1999: 90). In fact, surprisingly often, the military is not even mentioned in accounts of Turkish foreign policy or is referred to only obliquely as the "Kemalist establishment" (see, for example, Eralp 2004, Celik 1999, Radu 2003).

The dearth of theoretical analysis is especially striking during periods in which the military is widely recognized as the dominant actor in security policymaking, such as during the Islamist government of Necmettin Erbakan in the late 1990s, which I analyze in this section. Scholars do note the military's increased activism under the Erbakan government (Ozcan 2001: 13; Muftuler-Bac 1999: 246; Bengio 2004: 85), but often in context of the February 28 proclamations through which the military sought to circumscribe Islamist influence in the state and the "displacement" coup that precipitated Erbakan's ouster in 1997 (Yavuz 1997: 30; Altunisik and Tur 2005: 60; Heper and Guney 2000; Ayata, 2004). Some also attribute to the military's influence key security policy decisions at the time, such as the strengthening of the Turkish-Israeli alliance and the failure of Erbakan's overtures to the Muslim world (Jenkins 2001: 76; Yavuz 1997; Ozcan 2001: 23; Bengio 2004: 86).

During the Erbakan period, to explain the military's growing profile, analysts sometimes refer to the nature of the security issues facing Turkey in the 1990s (Ozcan 2001: 13; Jenkins 2001: 39). Alternatively, Jenkins observes that the military's role increased because political-military preferences over security issues diverged (2001: 7, 57). In a different vein, Robins (2003: 64, 77) refers to the fragmentation of politics and Erbakan's political weaknesses as precipitating causes of military influence. Missing, however, are more theoretically grounded efforts to account for the military's role in security policy-making, let alone its impact on strategic assessment.

Below I analyze the Erbakan case.[32] In the process I integrate several themes within the extant literature and explain how they produced important patterns in strategic assessment in Turkey in the late 1990s.

---

[32] This case focuses on the period in which Necemettin Erbakan was prime minister (June 1996–June 1997). However, it also includes the subsequent tenure of Mesut Yilmaz. Yilmaz succeeded Erbakan after the military forced Erbakan from office. Both the Islamist leader and his successor relied on a fragmented coalition; for Yilmaz this consisted of his conservative Motherland party and two leftist parties (Robins 2003: 67). Preference divergence was most pronounced under the Islamist Erbakan. However, although firmly part of the secular establishment, because of the weakness of his coalition Yilmaz also had to take care not to alienate interests sympathetic to the Welfare agenda (Hale 2000: 198). On tensions between the Yilmaz government and the military, see Stephen Kinzer, "Turkey Turns Away from Europe toward New Strategic Relationships," *International Herald Tribune*, December 29, 1997. Also see Jenkins (2001: 63–65).

I end the case study with the appointment of Bulent Ecevit as prime minister after the elections of April 1999, in which Ecevit's leftist Democratic Left party made substantial strides. As the "reborn darling of the pro-secular establishment," he did not represent a threat to military interests. Ecevit had in fact been in power since January 1999, when he formed a minority government after Yilmaz lost a no-confidence vote over corruption charges. Ecevit had a much stronger base than his predecessors and fewer conflicts of principle with the military. "Turkey's Hawkish Generals Seen Courting Disaster," *Mideast Mirror* 11, no. 153 (August 8, 1997).

Civil-Military Relations

The accession of Necmettin Erbakan to the position of prime minister in the summer of 1996 marked an important moment in contemporary Turkish history. It was the first time a candidate from an Islamist party was chosen to lead the Turkish Parliament. Support for the Islamist Right, with its platform of clean government and free bread, had been steadily increasing in the 1990s.[33] Consequently, in the December 1995 elections Erbakan's Welfare party (WP) won 21 percent of the popular vote, surpassing the mainstream center parties, the Motherland party and True Path party, which each won slightly over 19 percent of the vote. It was a big moment for Turkey and for Erbakan.

Erbakan's status was nonetheless deceiving. Despite his electoral successes, the prime minister was weak politically. He ruled over a fractious and divided coalition. Twenty-one percent of the vote was far from a popular mandate, and his party won less than one-third of the seats in Parliament. In fact, Erbakan's party was at first looked over in the process of forming a government.[34] In addition, much of the population remained wary of the Islamist party and its challenge to the country's secular traditions. Nearly 80 percent of Turkish voters had cast their ballots for secular parties, and "many feared and detested [Erbakan]" (Kinzer 2001: 70, 76). "The majority of the population remained vigorously opposed to the Islamist's agenda" (Jenkins 2001: 18).[35] In sum, the political arena was sharply fragmented at the time, leading one prominent periodical to conclude that "the Turkish political scene has never experienced the degree of weakness and fragmentation it is witnessing now"[36] (Robins 2003: 64; on fragmentation also see Muftuler-Bac 1999: 246, 253; Hale 2000: 196; Jenkins 2001: 15; Altunisik and Tur 2005: 54). Although Erbakan was prime

---

[33] Local elections in 1994, in which the Welfare party received 18.6 percent of the vote, gave some indication of its growing influence (Muftuler-Bac 1999: 249). Also see Celestine Bohlen, "Turkey's Islamist Party Knocks on Door in Sunday Vote," *New York Times*, December 22, 1995, A10.

[34] Eventually, in June 1996, Erbakan did form a coalition government with the True Path party, but only after considerable haggling and after a three-month-long coalition government between the True Path and the Motherland parties had fallen apart. On tensions between the Welfare and True Path parties, see Kinzer (2001: 69). Also see Hale (2000: 197).

[35] At the middle of the Welfare party's term in office, in December 1996, as the military began to warn about the threat to secularism posed by the Islamists, confidence in the military rose to 81.3 percent while only 16.3 percent reported trusting politicians (Jenkins 2001: 18). On public confidence in the military and opinion polls, also see Heper and Guney (2000: 646), Kubicek (2001: 36).

[36] Quoted in "Turkey's Generals Rule Supreme as Its Politicians Totter," *Mideast Mirror* 12, no. 82 (April 30, 1998).

minister, he governed over an internally factionalized coalition and lacked a strong, unified civilian support base.

At the same time, Erbakan also faced a very powerful military establishment. Like the Pakistani military, the Turkish military's prominent position in society is rooted in the particular history of the country and a domestic political environment in which it is highly esteemed (Robins 2003: 75). It is the most respected institution in the country. Cultural norms and practices reinforce the preeminent position of the military.[37] As one analyst describes it:

> The political role of the military in Turkey has grown out of a specifically Turkish historical, social and cultural context. But the military's pre-eminent role in Turkish life is not merely a historical hangover. Not only is Turkish society still dominated by the values, attitudes and traditions which underpin the role of the military but, to the vast majority of Turks, the military and military values still lie at the heart of any definition of what it means to be Turkish (Jenkins, 2001: 9; also see Heper and Guney 2000: 636; Birand 1991: 97).

The military regularly trumps all other institutions in polls of Turkey's most trusted institutions, with nearly 80 percent of the population ranking it first during the 1990s, and only 15 percent of the population reporting they found politicians trustworthy (Jenkins 2001:16). As Jenkins puts it, the military has its own "popular mandate" (2001: 18; Robins 2003: 31). High cohesion within the officer corps, observed under Erbakan's tenure, is also encouraged by rigorous socialization processes that promote adherence to Kemalist ideology (see below) and strict military discipline (Karabelias 2000: 139, 140; Jenkins 2001: 30–31; Rouleau 2000).

Combined, these dynamics put Erbakan in a precarious situation. The internal divisions in his coalition government and the narrowness of his support base meant his position relative to his military chiefs was weak. The balance of power clearly favored the military. Even worse, Erbakan's preferences over a range of issues diverged from those of his military chiefs. Scholarship by Legro (1995) and Kier (1997), which focuses on the particular cultural history of militaries in assessing their preferences, helps illuminate the sources of this conflict.[38] The Turkish military has strong organizational identification with secularist values and with the legacy of Kemal

---

[37] For example, tenth-grade students in Turkey must take a year-long class taught by a current or retired officer that discusses the military's perspective on history and security issues. Douglas Frantz, "Military Bestrides Turkey's Path to the European Union," *New York Times*, January 14, 2001.

[38] See also chapter 2, where I discussed how insights from the extant literature on civil-military relations can help in identifying the origins of preference divergence.

Ataturk, who in the early twentieth century helped shaped the Turkish military's corporate ethos by promoting "modern" pro-Western values.[39] Hence, the military largely perceives Islamic fundamentalism, if not religious piety, as a threat to its own corporate interests and to society, which it perceives itself as protecting. As the self-professed guardians of Kemal Ataturk's legacy, the military establishment fiercely distrusted Erbakan and the ideologically motivated Welfare party. Air Force Commander Ahmet Corekci nicely captured the military's position: "those who threaten the independence of the secular and democratic Turkish Republic will find the Turkish nation and the armed forces against them" (Fraser 1996). Divergent preferences also manifested themselves in strategic matters. Erbakan sought to promote Turkey's "Muslim identity" and advance its relations with its Arab neighbors, Iran, and other Muslim states while the military sought to deepen its ties to the West and to Israel (Hale 1999: 97; 2000: 314–15; Bengio 2004: 86; Ayata 2004: 269).

In sum, in the late 1990s Turkey's politically powerful and cohesive military leadership faced a weak and fractured political coalition headed by a prime minister sharply at odds with military preferences. Civil-military relations were characterized by military dominance and high preference divergence.

Strategic Assessment

Strategic assessment in Turkey in the late 1990s was heavily influenced by these civil-military relations. Military dominance resulted in the internalization in the military of much of the state's deliberative processes and decision making for security matters.[40] The authorization process also remained clearly defined with decision-making prerogatives in the military's hands, despite efforts by the political leadership to claim those privileges.

One manifestation of this military-dominated authorization process was in military appointments. During his tenure in office, Erbakan tried to increase his control over these prerogatives, but the military continued to define both the method and criteria for senior officer promotions, appointments, and dismissals.[41] In Turkey at the time, for example, it was common

---

[39] Specific values espoused by Kemalism include a commitment to secularism, maintaining Turkey's territorial integrity, and cultural homogeneity (see Jenkins 2001: 7).

[40] As described in chapter 2, the power of the military affects the default institutional arrangements that emerge in these settings. Where preference divergence is high, as in the Erbakan case, the political leader will try to subvert those structures but will meet with limited success in altering institutional patterns in his or her favor.

[41] Decisions regarding new appointments in the command structure, officer promotions (admirals and generals), and retirements were taken at an annual meeting of the Supreme Military Council (SMC) held in August of each year. Composed of fifteen top army generals and chaired by the Turkish prime minister, the council allowed the military a dominant hand in these processes. On these general practices, see Jenkins (2001: 25–26).

practice for the military to fire officers suspected of harboring sympathies for Islamist causes. Unhappy with this state of affairs, Erbakan often resisted such dismissals.[42] At one meeting of the Supreme Military Council (SMC) on May 26, 1997, he was "asked" to sign a decree announcing the dismissals of 141 officers for "fundamentalist activities." Erbakan tried to delay signing the decree.[43] He also tried to avoid subsequent meetings in which officers would be cashiered. Despite these efforts, the military repeatedly and successfully "demanded" government approval for the expulsion of pro-Islamist officers.[44] In all, during 1997 and 1998 the military leadership dismissed 541 officers on suspicion of "Islamic activities."[45] This important lever of control over military activity—appointments and promotions—remained firmly in the military's hands.

The military's role in the late 1990s in Turkey's National Security Council, ostensibly an advisory body, also underscores the clarity of the authorization process in which prerogatives were concentrated in the hands of military chiefs (see, e.g., Ozcan 2001: 17–20). In general during this period the NSC would operate in the following fashion.[46] The entity had ten members, which included the president, four ministers (prime minister and ministers of defense, interior, and foreign affairs), and five top military leaders (chief of staff and commanders of the army, navy, air force, and gendarmerie), as well as a general secretary, who was a military officer. Prior to the (usually) monthly meetings, the General Secretariat, largely staffed with military personnel, created the agenda and worked closely with the Turkish General Staff in developing supporting documents on issues for discussion, including written materials and briefings. In effect this granted the General Secretariat, and by extension the military, agenda-setting power, a key decision-making prerogative (Ozcan 2001: 17–19). Moreover, the apparent balance in civilian and military membership was

---

[42] For example, in August 1996 eighteen officers and thirty-two soldiers were dismissed; the following December, sixty-nine officers were cashiered. See Seva Ulman, "Turkish Troops Discharged over Religion," United Press International, December 10, 1996.

[43] Although the military retained substantial control over appointments by tradition, other governments, such as that of Turgut Ozal in the early 1990s, had exercised greater influence in these processes. Ozal's power was due in large part to the enormous popular support he enjoyed. See Jenkins (2001), Rouleau (2000), Robins (2003: 31), Karabelias (2000: 137–38, 141), "Turkey's Hawkish Generals Seen Courting Disaster." Ozal was even able to make controversial decisions in regard to the Kurdish issue and Turkey's participation in the 1991 Gulf War (Ozcan 2001: 15).

[44] On the expulsions, see "The Increasing Loneliness of Being Turkey," *Economist*, July 19, 1997, 21. Also see Stephen Kinzer, "The Islamist Who Runs Turkey," *New York Times*, February 23, 1997, sec. 6, 28.

[45] "Turkish Army Expels 86 Officers on Disciplinary Grounds," Deutsche Presse Agentur, December 4, 1998. Also see Altunisik and Tur (2005: 58).

[46] This discussion of the NSC is based on Jenkins's and Ozcan's analyses of the entity. See Jenkins (2001: 50–55), Ozcan (2001: 17–19).

deceiving in its implication that the former had substantial influence in the NSC; as one analyst puts it, "as no voting ever takes place, the numerical composition of the NSC is virtually irrelevant" (Jenkins 2001: 51; Hale 2003: 121). Instead, "recommendations" would be decided by consensus; as a former chief of the General Staff once put it, "We do not count fingers; we just convince each other" (Ozcan 2001: 18).[47] In practice, military leaders tended to be the chief "convincers."

Although long an important component of the state's security infrastructure, under Erbakan the military-dominated NSC became especially influential in national security policymaking: "The Turkish military's active role in foreign policy became much more pronounced during the [Erbakan] government" (Aykan 1999: 181; Ozcan 2001: 19; Rouleau 2000). The National Security Council became even more active in defining the agenda for discussion, and in openly pressing for adoption of its policies. The most vivid illustration of this activist role occurred in a pivotal meeting of the council on February 28, 1997. At that meeting the military presented the government with a list of far-reaching measures designed to curb the influence of religion in Turkish society and politics on the grounds that Islamist fundamentalist sentiment represented a major threat to the security of the secular state. Although he resisted, after nine hours Erbakan finally signed the measure.[48]

In fact, despite the influence of the NSC, Erbakan often tried to resist its recommendations and, more broadly, to claim the military's decision-making prerogatives.[49] When, for example, the military issued the February 28 recommendations, Erbakan questioned its right to do so, insisting that they were not binding on the government; in an interview two weeks later, he skirted the issue of adopting the measures, arguing that "the council is a consultative council. Therefore it is not a matter of rejecting or accepting these decisions."[50] Military leaders clearly did not share this view. They turned up the heat. Through contacts with members of the legislature, public expressions of opposition, and statements of dissatisfaction with the prime minister's inaction on the anti-religious measures, the military forced defections from Erbakan's coalition and ultimately precipitated his resignation (see Kinzer 2001: 76).

---

[47] This discussion raises questions about subsequent changes in the nature of the NSC, which the Islamist-led government under Prime Minister Erdogan, elected in 2002, succeeded in passing. One reason (consistent with the theory) cited for Erdogan's success is the support he had in society—he was in a considerably stronger position than was Erbakan. Some suggest that the preferences of Erdogan's party are also different, and that he is far more conciliatory toward the secularist position (Altunisik and Tur 2005: 65; Hale 2003; Ayata 2004).

[48] "Turkey Still Teetering on Brink of the Secular-Islamist Showdown," *Mideast Mirror* 11, no. 54 (March 18, 1997); Jenkins (2001: 62).

[49] "The Lessons of Erbakan's Premiership," *Mideast Mirror* 11, no. 164 (August 26, 1997).

[50] "Turkey Still Teetering on Brink of the Secular-Islamist Showdown."

As one analyst captures the NSC's role at the time, "Erbakan's tug-of-war with the military ... show[ed] the government and parliament as little more than facades whose sole function is to rubber stamp and implement the policies decided by the military command through the National Security Council."[51] A London-based periodical on the Middle East characterized the enhanced role of the NSC in the following terms:

> [The military] thus turned the National Security Council—half of whose members are military men—into the real forum for debating national issues (not just security-related ones, but everything from economics and education to sport) and the final arbiter of state decision-making, although the decisions are supposed to be mere "recommendations." ... Turks and foreigners alike now look to the monthly meetings of the National Security Council [for major decisions], while parliament has been reduced to near irrelevance.[52]

Despite Erbakan's efforts to enhance his prerogatives, which might have complicated decision making, the authorization process in security matters remained clearly defined with the military at the helm.

Finally, civil-military relations also influenced strategic coordination—in this case, negatively. The state lacked a rigorous forum for joint consultation between the military and political apparatus of the state.[53] The NSC might have played this role, but in practice norms within the entity worked against informed and open debate both between political and military leaders and among the service chiefs appointed to the body. As noted above, briefings and documents for the NSC were developed by the General Secretariat, which was essentially an adjunct body of the military. Civilian ministers had no equivalent entity to gather information and analyze issues (sometimes the ministers would not even get materials before the meetings). Within the body, it was "virtually unheard of" for the NSC's civilian members, or outside it, for members of the cabinet or Parliament, to question the military's views (Robins 2003: 76). Nor in meetings of the NSC would the force commanders ever contradict the chief of staff (Jenkins 2001: 51). In effect, the critical analysis of policy options and scope of debate were truncated, with the NSC operating more as a means for communicating military preferences than a truly rigorous consultative entity (for other examples, see Jenkins 2001: 50).

---

[51] "The Lessons of Erbakan's Premiership."

[52] "Turkish Operation from First to Last," *Mideast Mirror* 11, no. 93 (May 15, 1997). Also see "Turkey's Generals Rule Supreme as Its Politicians Totter."

[53] By convention the military retained ties with the civil servants staffing the Ministry of Foreign Affairs, and therefore its members did have regular contact with that apparatus of the state; however, traditionally the bureaucracy tended to operate autonomously from the Parliament and from the government, and therefore contact with civil servants did not equate to contact with political leaders and the broader diplomatic arena (Jenkins 2001: 72).

All of this was compounded by weaknesses in information sharing, which are evident in how Turkey managed its growing relationship with Israel and in other areas of its foreign relations. For example, in late February 1997, the chief of the General Staff visited Israel to promote ties with the latter without even informing Erbakan's government beforehand (Yavuz 1997: 30). Erbakan also protested that he was not told the content of key agreements with Israel (Yavuz 1997: 32). Even more significantly, the military failed to inform the political leadership before launching its May 1997 invasion of northern Iraq.[54] Erbakan was reportedly infuriated about not being consulted (the military justified this on the grounds that it was necessary to ensure strategic surprise). In fact, the media was told about the campaign before the prime minister; he learned about it from the press (Jenkins 2001: 63).[55] In sum, political dominance and high preference divergence heavily influenced how Turkey engaged in strategic assessment at the time. They promoted clarity in authorization processes but also undermined strategic coordination and information sharing.

International Implications

How did this mix of institutional attributes affect Turkey's strategies and international relations in the late 1990s? First, similar to the Pakistani case, it affected Turkey's ability to integrate security goals and military activity. In stark contrast to its South Asian neighbor, however, Turkey was able to maintain consistency in its political-military activities. Although Erbakan sought to reorient Turkish foreign policy, in many substantive areas Turkey's security goals remained consistent with longstanding trends and with the country's military strategies and activities in the period.

In the mid-1990s Turkey's grand strategy and security goals reflected several trends and priorities; among them was a generally pro-Western orientation, including a strong commitment to NATO and interest in potential membership in the European Union, a burgeoning alliance with Israel, and aggressive confrontation of Kurdish rebels and acrimonious relations with neighboring states that allowed rebel forces to operate on their territory. When he came to power, Erbakan had very different ideas about the direction of Turkey's military and security policies. In his "campaign for Muslim solidarity," the Islamist leader sought to reorient security

---

[54] Operation Poised Hammer, launched on May 14, aimed at rooting out allies of the rebel PKK operating from Iraq. It involved between 25,000 and 50,000 Turkish troops.

[55] In addition, as another sign of the internalization of the policy process within the military, the Turkish General Staff initiated working groups on a range of political issues at the time, beyond its traditional realm of operational and tactical subjects (Jenkins 2001: 50).

priorities away from a preoccupation with the West and the security alliance with Israel (Kinzer 2001: 70; Altunisik and Tur 2005: 58; Hale 1999: 97). He had campaigned, in particular, on promises to sever ties with Israel (Yavuz 1997: 29). Erbakan instead sought to promote stronger relations with Iran, Libya, and the Muslim Middle East at large. To this end, within weeks of becoming prime minister he first visited Iran, rather than the customary Western capital, where he forged a $20 billion natural gas deal (Yavuz 1997: 29).[56] He also visited Libya and Nigeria, where he sought to establish a Development-Eight (D-8) group of Islamic countries in imitation of the G-8 (Robins 2003: 66).

Despite Erbakan's flirtation with a pro-Islam foreign policy, the authorization process remained clearly defined. The military retained a solid say over definitions of who and what constituted a threat to or an ally of the Turkish state. This in turn ensured that its security goals and military activities would remain consistent in their pro-West orientation.[57]

Turkey's relations with Israel and its forging of a series of agreements in 1996 underscore this continuity.[58] In February 1996, after long negotiations, the Turkish military signed a then secret agreement with Israel providing for joint training between their respective militaries. Subsequently, in April 1996, while negotiations over who would assume the premiership in Turkey were ongoing, the military leaked word of the agreement, in the process "making clear to all political parties, and especially the Islamist RP, that they were sufficiently powerful to control the strategic direction of foreign policy, regardless of who formed the government or occupied the premiership" (Robins 2003: 260). Later that summer the military concluded negotiations on a second agreement on defense cooperation with Israel. By this point Erbakan had become prime minister and, predictably, given his preferences to reduce ties with Israel, tried to stall signing the agreement, but ultimately the military prevailed (Robins 2003: 262).

Erbakan was later forced to sign a third agreement granting Israel contracts to upgrade Turkey's military aircraft. Although he once again tried

---

[56] Erbakan subsequently signed an agreement for joint cooperation in military aviation development with Iran. See Dilop Hiro, "Iran: Demirel and Erbakan Embrace Tehran," Interpress Service, December 22, 1996. The initiative was later abandoned.

[57] For example, during Erbakan's tenure as the country's first prime minister from an Islamic-based party, the NSC went so far as to redefine the major threat facing the country as *Islamic orthodoxy*. The council forced Erbakan to sign a decree asserting that religious fundamentalism had surpassed the Kurdish rebellion as the major threat facing the secular Turkish public. See "Islamist Prime Minister Accepts Army's Demand on Fundamentalism," Deutsche Presse-Agentur, May 26, 1997. Also see Yavuz (1997: 30–31).

[58] On the motivations driving the Turkish military in its deals with Israel, see Bengio (2004: 87).

to kill the initiative, after being told by the Turkish chief of staff "that you are acting emotionally. This project is so important for the Turkish armed forces and has to be vitalized as soon as possible," Erbakan acquiesced and the deal was made.[59] Subsequently, when the prime minister tried to stymie Israeli-Turkish relations by "postponing" scheduled military exercises with Israel set for the summer of 1997, those exercises proceeded as planned.[60] During the spring and summer of 1997 there were several highly visible military exchanges between Turkey and Israel (Yaphe 1997: 2; Robins 2003: 265).[61] In short, the Turkish military regularly vetoed Erbakan's interventions, contributing to the consistency of its foreign policy. As Bengio (2004: 86) concludes, "Evidently, the success of establishing relations with Israel, in the face of continuing opposition, was because the military was the moving force behind the policy, if not its architect."

In addition, even while Turkey's relations with Israel intensified, Erbakan's own pro-Muslim foreign policy initiatives sputtered and died. For example, when he tried to negotiate a defense cooperation agreement with Iran in December 1996, the idea, as William Hale puts it, "was vetoed by the General Staff" (Hale 2000: 315; Ozcan 2001: 23). In fact, far from enhancing relations with Iran, two months later, during a visit to Israel, the Turkish chief of staff made remarks supporting the characterization of Iran as a backer of terrorism, which precipitated a major diplomatic imbroglio (Ozcan 2001: 23).

Similar continuity can be observed in Turkey's relations with Iraq. Despite Erbakan's efforts to improve ties with the regime, during his tenure in office the military planned two major military offensives in northern Iraq in order to root out Kurdish rebels.[62] In fact, so brazen was the military's disregard for the prime minister's initiatives, and so clearly were they in charge of strategic decision making, that military leaders initiated the Iraq campaign just hours after Erbakan finished meeting with the visiting Iraqi trade minister without informing Erbakan ahead of time.[63] Once the invasion began, Erbakan proved equally powerless to end it. In June 1997 he told reporters that the operation had "come to an end."[64] The military

---

[59] Quote appears in "Turkish PM Opposes Jet Upgrade Deal with Israel," *Jerusalem Post*, December 1, 1996, 12.

[60] "Erbakan 'Postpones' Turkey's War Games with Israel and U.S.," *Mideast Mirror* 11, no. 92 (May 14, 1997). Also see "The Lessons of Erbakan's Premiership."

[61] On Erbakan's opposition to the ties to Israel and the military's success in forcing him to acquiesce in the policy, also see Hale (2000: 298), Yavuz (1997: 30).

[62] There have been many incursions into northern Iraq since the 1980s (Gresh 1998).

[63] "Turkey Seen Emerging as Overlord of Northern Iraq," *Mideast Mirror* 11, no. 104 (June 2, 1997).

[64] Quotes in this paragraph appear in "Dispute Grows as Turkish Army Demands Funds for Incursion in Iraq," Deutsche Presse-Agentur, June 7, 1997.

leadership then publicly contradicted him, castigating him for such an announcement when it had no intention of calling off the invasion. Analysts were quick to recognize the dispute, concluding that "divergent statements reflected the growing division between Erbakan, who is trying to put a deeper Muslim stamp on Turkish society, and the military, which sees itself as a guarantor of Turkey's secular tradition."[65]

Beyond vetoing Erbakan's initiatives, the military also set the agenda in Turkey's diplomatic relations with other states. As one analyst characterizes it, "arguably the best evidence of the weak civilian government and the shifting responsibility for policymaking came between late 1997 and autumn 1998" when the chief of staff, Ismail Hakki Karadayu, undertook a broad diplomatic campaign in the region (Robins 2003: 68). He visited Cairo, Georgia, and Azerbaijan to secure relations with these states and attended a Western European Union meeting in Athens to discuss improving relations with Greece. He also traveled to Russia to discuss issues related to arms sales to Cyprus, relations with Iran, and support for the Kurdistan Workers Party (PKK).

Finally, and especially intriguing in the context of Erbakan's inefficacy in altering Turkish grand strategy, was the degree to which outside observers recognized the primacy of military preferences, looking to Turkey's generals to extrapolate trends in the country's international relations. For example, numerous articles were written in the London-based periodical *Mideast Mirror* calling attention to the military's dominance over foreign policy and security issues. As one commentator writing in spring 1998 put it, "events in Turkey over the past year showed that it is the generals rather than party leaders who 'hold the keys to the political game'."[66] The article goes on to discuss the military's strategy toward the Kurds, weighing the "mindset" of the military toward security issues in general. A similar article assessing the prospects for change in the Israeli-Turkish relationship under Erbakan points to the military's dominance in combination with the prime minister's political weaknesses as major reasons to anticipate little change.[67]

---

[65] Erbakan also tried to withhold funding for the Iraqi operation: three weeks after the invasion, the military's requests for $350 million in additional funding were unmet. After an emergency meeting between Erbakan and senior military officials on June 6, the money was allocated. See ibid. In addition, Erbakan tried to end Turkish support for "Operation Provide Comfort" in which the United States was supplying aid to the Kurds in northern Iraq. Erbakan reportedly described it as a sinister Western plot intended to divide Muslim countries. Ultimately Turkey maintained its support, albeit the name was change to "Northern Watch" (Hale 2000: 226).

[66] Comments by Mohammed Noureddin in the pan-Arab weekly *al-Wasat*; these are cited in "Turkey's Generals Rule Supreme as Its Politicians Totter."

[67] "No Chance of Erbakan Burying Turkey's Military Accord with Israel, Arabs Told," *Mideast Mirror* 10, no. 143 (July 24, 1996).

More broadly, observers noted "that these days we no longer hear any voices from Ankara except those generals."[68] Whatever Erbakan's efforts to recast Turkey's military and security goals, observers were clearly focusing on military preferences and activities in assessing its policies. As Robins nicely captures it, there "was increasingly little doubt as to which institution Turkey's friends and adversaries alike were obliged to take most seriously" (2003: 68).

In sum, in nearly every domain, foreign and military policy remained consistent internally and with established trends: military cooperation toward Israel intensified, incursions into northern Iraq continued, and Turkey maintained its diplomatic agenda in relations with Europe and its Arab neighbors. In addition, overtures to the European Union (which Erbakan opposed on "cultural grounds") continued.[69] Hence despite Erbakan's concerted efforts to redefine Turkish security policy, "Scrutiny of the period of [his] government shows that Turkey's traditional foreign policy was not adulterated; indeed, if anything, the secular, pro-Western nature of it was actually strengthened" (Robins 2003: 66). Turkey thus avoided one pathology of poor strategic assessment: disintegrated political-military activity. Clear authorization processes allowed the state to maintain continuity in its security goals and military activities.

Weaknesses in strategic coordination, however, offset these institutional strengths, impairing strategic assessment in other ways. One of the byproducts of poor strategic coordination is that it encourages short-sightedness in considering the political implications of military activity. In Turkey's case, its political-military activity was internally coherent but nonetheless overlooked important political and strategic realities.

One area in which such a weakness seemed to be evident was in the contradiction posed between the military's hard-line approach to the country's Kurdish rebellion, and the suppression of cultural rights and persecution of the Kurdish population it engendered, and Turkey's (and the military's own) interest in joining the European Union and pro-Western orientation.

---

[68] The article cited here refers to comments in two prominent Arab periodicals in its assessment of the prominence of military opinion in strategic matters. See "Why Are Turkey's Generals Striking an Anti-Arab Posture," *Mideast Mirror* 11, no. 113 (June 13, 1997). Similar observations can be found elsewhere: a report from the National Defense University refers to "the [Turkish] military's expanded alliance with Israel, without the apparent consent of the civilian government." See Yaphe (1997). Another report referred to the fact that "despite government denials, it is widely believed that the Turkish military has acted unilaterally in forging ties with the Israeli Defense Forces." This appears in "Turkey Special Report," *Middle East Economic Digest*, August 7, 1998. These reports highlight the degree to which outsiders placed substantial emphasis on the military in analyzing Turkey's security preferences.

[69] For discussion of Erbakan's hostility toward the EU, see Hale (2000: 239), Kinzer (2001: 74); Ayata (2004: 269).

At the time, the military advocated the necessity of a repressive approach toward the Kurds in violation of the European Union's Copenhagen Criteria on Democracy, Freedom and Protections of Minorities, despite the fact that the country was then entering a sensitive period with the European Union, in which the latter was contemplating its prospective candidacy.[70] The NSC secretary general's remarks in a rare on-the-record interview captured the prevailing views of the military in the late 1990s. In the discussion, General Cumhar Asparuk ruled out the possibility of Kurdish-language broadcasting and education despite pressures from the European Union to relax restrictions in these areas.[71] In addition, the military sharply defended constitutional provisions that privileged its influence in decision making in contravention of the norms and conventions of EU member states. As General Cumhar Asparuk told the *Financial Times*: "Turkey was not yet ripe for full civilian control of the armed forces" (see also Duner and Deverall 2001: 3; Hale 2003: 121; Kubicek 2001; Frantz 2001). In sum, Turkish military activity and policy was at odds with its broader political objectives.

Finally, civil-military relations and assessment institutions had an additional, provocative implication for Turkey's international relations. Recall that in chapter 1 I discussed how, through their effects on the information available to others about a state's preferences, the authorization process within a state can influence how others perceive its threats and promises. Intriguingly, the Turkish case suggests that the clarity of the authorization process at the time, with the military at the helm, enhanced the credibility of Turkey's threats in international relations.

In this context the outcome of a little noted crisis between Syria and Turkey in October 1998 is intriguing (see Olson 2001 for an overview). At the time, in an effort to consolidate recent gains against Kurdish rebels, the Turkish military threatened to intervene with force in Syria to remove rebel bases, and to apprehend the leader of the PKK, Abdullah Ocalan, if Syria's president Hafez al-Asad did not take action himself. It was a serious demand. Outside analysts observed that Turkish generals were dead set on armed conflict with Syria if the Arab state did not concede. For example, at the height of the crisis, Turkey's chief of the General Staff, General Huseyin Kivrikoglu, gave a widely noted speech characterizing the conflict

---

[70] On the contradiction posed between the Turkish military's prosecution of its war against Kurdish nationalists and EU membership, see Rouleau (2000). Also see Altunisik and Tur (2005: 121), Muftuler-Bac (1999: 248), Stephen Kinzer, "First Question for Europe: Is Turkey Really European," *New York Times*, December 9, 1999. Also see "Bringing Turkey into Europe," *New York Times*, editorial, December 13, 1999, A32. For the European Union's official view, see European Union, *1999 Regular Report from the Commission on Turkey's Progress toward Accession*, October 1999, 46.

[71] Interview cited in Jenkins (2001: 70; also see 81–82).

as "a situation of undeclared war between Turkey and Syria" (Olson 2001: 105; Gorvett 1998; Jenkins 2001). Observers clearly saw this as an initiative being pursued by the military, which was perceived as eager to press the issue with armed force, if necessary (Robins 2003: 77). Mesut Yilmaz, who became prime minister after Erbakan was ousted, was reported to be "doing the bidding of the Turkish military establishment," whose generals were "itching to fight," believing that surgical strikes against PKK forces in Syria were necessary to win the war against the rebels.[72] Even had the prime minister opposed the initiative, he would have been powerless to stop it; his lack of popularity was "forcing him to seek the army's support. He consequently ha[d] to do whatever the army [told] him to."[73] In other words, the military was firmly and perceptibly behind the threat.

Early in the crisis, Syria was apparently unmoved by the Turkish threats, viewing them with "indifference," despite the fact that Turkey had deployed thousands of forces to its border.[74] In fact, initially Syria simply denied that PKK forces were operating on its territory, while its foreign minister defiantly warned that "Syria would not be cowed by military threats."[75] Syria's leaders, however, would soon change their minds about the wisdom of such an approach. According to Turkish intelligence sources, as the threats to intervene in Syria escalated, Syria's chief of staff and defense minister began to urge acquiescence (Aykan 1999: 177). Syria's president Hafez al-Asad reportedly became highly concerned about the "credible threat of intervention" represented by Turkey's statements and actions (Larrrabee and Lesser 2003: 38; also see Olson 2001: 107, 113–14). He even reshuffled the leadership of key departments in the anticipation of possible war with Turkey (Bikbayev and Palaria 1998).

In the end, however, that war was not to be. Facing the prospect of armed conflict with a powerful adversary that it was militarily unprepared to fight, Syria caved. On October 20 Syria and Turkey signed an agreement in which Syria gave in to nearly all of Turkey's demands. After years of providing haven for the PKK, the Syrians ousted Ocalan and his supporters (for

---

[72] Commentary is from "What Is Turkey Actually Demanding in Its Ultimatum to Syria," *Mideast Mirror* 12, no. 194 (October 8, 1998). On extending the case to include Mesut Yilmaz's tenure, see note 32.

[73] See "Turkey Likely to Launch 'American Style' Air Strikes against Syria and Lebanon's Bekaa," *Mideast Mirror* 12, no. 200 (October 16, 1998).

[74] It is important to note that these deployments and activities alone do not appear to have been sufficient to convince Syria of Turkey's resolve. Syria did not initially appear daunted by the deployments; perhaps this is because forces had been sent before, most recently in 1995, with little consequence. They alone did not necessarily signal Turkey's intent (Olson 2001:102; Aykan 1999: 177–78). Also see "Troops Being Sent to Syrian Border," BBC Summary of World Broadcasts, Part 2: Central Europe, the Balkans; Turkey; EE/D2465/B.

[75] "Turkey's 'Undeclared War' on Syria," *Mideast Mirror*, October 2, 1998.

details, see Olson 2001: 107; Aykan 1999). "The military," as Robins put it, had "created the conditions under which Syria felt obliged to expel the leader of the ... PKK" and accede to Turkey's other demands (Robins 2003: 77). Thus an escalation of the crisis was averted and the dispute was relegated to the minor footnotes of history. This incident is suggestive of one of the strengths of a situation in which the authorization process is clear such that the response of decision-makers is easy to read: These states may have greater credibility in committing to particular courses of action.

Seven

U.S. POSTCONFLICT PLANNING FOR THE 2003 IRAQ WAR

BY NOW MANY PEOPLE ARE familiar with U.S. weaknesses in postconflict planning for its 2003 Iraq War: In the months leading up to the invasion, a failure of those in charge to plan adequately for the stabilization phase of the war contributed to the breakdown in security after the fall of Saddam Hussein, which alienated the Iraqi citizenry and fueled a nascent insurgency against American forces.

To date, several conventional wisdoms have emerged about why planning failed for postconflict Iraq. Many attribute it to then secretary of defense Donald Rumsfeld's combative personality and inability to engage in an open-ended evaluative process in the course of war planning. Others blame the tunnel vision of the Bush administration and its tendency to hold fast to flawed assumptions about the postwar environment and dismiss alternative views. Regardless, most prevailing explanations suggest that poor postconflict planning stemmed from idiosyncratic factors exclusive to Secretary Rumsfeld and the administration he served.

In this chapter I situate the U.S./Iraq case in context of this book's argument about the causes of strategic assessment. Specifically, the case evaluates a central hypothesis of the study about how civil-military relations characterized by high preference divergence and political dominance affect strategic assessment. In the United States, long before the Iraq War was on the Bush administration's radar screen, political and military leaders were up in arms over defense reform; the political leadership, although clearly dominant, faced a military leadership opposed to its "transformational" vision. I anticipate that these civil-military relations will create particular incentives and constraints that shape processes for strategic assessment. Underlying disputes over policy and strategic issues induce political leaders to employ oversight mechanisms to ensure military compliance with their initiatives. As I described in chapter 2, while these tactics mitigate problems in information sharing, allow for improvements in structural competence, and provide for a clear authorization process in security matters, the safeguards are also often counterproductive to strategic coordination. They truncate political-military dialogue and limit the range of perspectives represented in advisory processes. Consequently, I expect this configuration of civil-military relations to generate variable strengths and weaknesses in the four attributes of strategic assessment, overall producing a mixed set of institutions.

In this chapter I find evidence of civil-military relations' "mixed" effects on strategic assessment. However, the most striking result is the profound weaknesses in strategic coordination observed in the United States prior to the Iraq War, especially when those flaws are viewed from the perspective of their international consequences. Any advantages in strategic assessment the United States enjoyed in planning the war have often been eclipsed by these deficiencies and the insurgency they helped to precipitate.

Before developing this argument, I begin with some background on the inadequacies of the American postconflict plans and situate the case in context of existing explanations.

Background to the U.S. Case

When the United States went to war in March 2003, its war plan consisted of four phases. Phase I, "Deterrence and Engagement," included the buildup of forces in the region. It laid the foundation for the future combat effort. Phase II, "Seize the Initiative," involved initial, mostly covert operations by special operations and other forces preparatory to the major ground force invasion. Phase III, "Decisive Operations," consisted of the major combat phase of the war: the drive to Baghdad and the removal of the regime. The final phase, Phase IV, "Postwar Operations," and the one on which I focus here, entailed the transition from a combat situation to a secure, stable, and orderly situation on the ground. As such, Phase IV was part of the war plan and was independent of (although in principle integrated with) ensuing civilian-led efforts to oversee reconstruction and governance in liberated Iraq. In short, military plans called for efforts to ensure a smooth transition from war to peace in the immediate aftermath of hostilities.

Despite its centrality, however, many observers view Phase IV as especially poorly conceived and executed. In so doing they make two central claims.[1] The first is that plans for Phase IV were undeveloped. Planning came late, and many of its components were poorly worked out. Moreover, plans did not foresee potential contingencies, including a massive breakdown in security in the days following Saddam Hussein's ouster. As a result,

---

[1] Numerous studies have emerged recounting these inadequacies. See Gordon and Trainor (2006), Fallows (2006), Packer (2005), Ricks (2006), Woodward (2004). Also see the text below.

forces on the ground after the regime's fall were ill-positioned and had little guidance for managing the degrading security situation.

The second major complaint is that Phase IV was underresourced. There were insufficient forces on the ground to ensure order in the transition from combat to a postcombat environment. Ultimately the ground war plan—COBRA II—called for the involvement of 190,000–200,000 troops. Some 170,000 ultimately participated, which analysts have argued was too few to ensure stability on the ground (Gordon and Trainor 2006: 460). The deployment of follow-on forces that might have aided the transition—such as the First Cavalry Division—was canceled. Moreover, the types of forces available on the ground after the regime's fall were not necessarily ideal. As Tommy Franks, the chief of Central Command, himself later acknowledged, more civil affairs units and military police were needed (Gordon 2004).

In short, in both concept and resources the United States was unprepared to execute the stabilization phase of the war. Herein lies a central puzzle of the Iraq War: Why did the U.S. military, with the know-how, experience, and responsibility for Phase IV fail to formulate and execute fully its own war plan?

Context of the U.S./Iraq case

Among observers of the war, several explanations have emerged to account for the deficiencies of postcombat preparations for the spring 2003 Iraq War. None, as I explain below, completely captures the origins of the weaknesses in planning processes.

The first explanation is that the flaws were due to Secretary of Defense Donald Rumsfeld's combative personality and his agenda to assert civilian control over the military. According to this line of argument, Rumsfeld's management style and abrasive personality alienated the military leadership (Herspring 2005: 380). In addition, rumor held that the secretary had read Eliot Cohen's (2002) influential book, *Supreme Command*, which was widely interpreted as making the case for active civilian involvement in the planning and conduct of war: "It was commonplace among the Bush team that the military needed stronger civilian oversight" (Gordon and Trainor 2006: 3; Stevenson 2006: 180; Herspring 2005: 381). Combined, these dynamics marginalized the military's role in assessment, preventing comprehensive dialogue about the country's war plans (Cordesman 2003: 153). In short, as these observers frame it, one does not have to look to *civil-military* relations to explain postwar Iraq but can simply lay blame on the *civilian* side of the equation.

Indeed, Rumsfeld may have been a difficult personality to work with. And he may have wanted to ensure that the military understood he was in charge. But as an explanation for the postconflict debacle, these observations are left wanting. After all, Rumsfeld was universally abrasive. Yet, as I explain below, he continued to engage those whose views generally aligned with his own. For example, his extensive interactions with Tommy Franks about the plans for major combat operations suggest he could be a serious, albeit challenging, interlocutor.[2] His personality alone does not explain Rumsfeld's pattern of relations with different entities and individuals in the military.

Rumsfeld may also have wanted to assert civilian control. But demonstrating clear civilian control is not the same as marginalizing one's officers. In Eliot Cohen's laudatory account of Abraham Lincoln's wartime leadership, for example, it was not that Lincoln ignored his officers, but that he listened closely to them but then acted in ways he felt was appropriate. In sum, neither of these arguments explains why Rumsfeld's relations with *particular officers* were so poor, and why norms of discussion developed in ways that limited the scope of discussion about critical issues.

A second argument suggests that planning failures were due to the insulated nature of the Bush administration: Independent of the state of civil-military relations, Rumsfeld and his staff were immune to advice about postwar Iraq. The Bush administration had a particular conception for how the war would unfold. The working concept within the Department of Defense and the administration for the aftermath of the combat phase was that once the United States removed Saddam Hussein from power, it could replace the chiefs of Iraq's ministries and bureaucracies, appoint new lead-

---

[2] For details on the extensive interactions, see Woodward (2004), Franks (2004), Gordon and Trainor (2006). Some might argue that while Rumsfeld may have frequently interacted with individuals like Franks, he was not really engaging them. But narrative accounts suggest there was a mutual exchange between the leaders, especially about the combat plan (not about the postwar phase, however, which I discuss below). Moreover, the outcome of the debates about troop numbers reflects this engagement. Most reports cite Rumsfeld originally wanting only 50,000–70,000 forces. Franks's first-cut initial estimates in December 2001 called for 385,000. The first plan Franks presented for Rumsfeld's review, Generated Start, in February 2002 called for 275,000. After multiple interactions in which the number went down and then up again in an "accordion-like" manner, the final plan for ground forces, COBRA II, was closest to Generated Start (Gordon and Trainor 2006: 28–29, 36, 94, quote appears on 88; Hooker 2005: 32–33). As Michael O'Hanlon (2004–05) puts it when describing this engagement over the plans for combat operations: "Rumsfeld also allowed himself to be talked out of some of the bad ideas he or others around him may initially have held about how to win such a war. Notably, the initial hopes among some civilians that a war plan could be executed with only a few tens of thousands of American troops were ultimately dashed by a responsible military planning process." Franks tends to argue that he led the discussion, although most accounts put Rumsfeld in the role of chief instigator. See Bacevich (2004).

ers, and the state would continue to function. As Condoleezza Rice, President Bush's national security adviser, put it, the concept was that after the Iraqi army was defeated "you would be able to bring new leadership but we were going to keep the body [of the government] in place."[3] The ship of state would remain intact with new captains. The U.S. military would be greeted as liberators, and people would rally to the cause of the newly configured Iraqi state. There would be no postwar security breakdown for which to plan (Slevin and Priest 2003; Bensahel 2006: 456–58). In short, from this perspective, no amount of insight from his officers could have swayed the tunnel-visioned secretary from his preexisting beliefs that there would be no postwar disruption for which to plan (Packer 2005: 116).

The principal evidence marshaled for this view is that there was, in fact, significant information available to Rumsfeld from civilian think-tanks and within the State Department that suggested that postwar security would be a major problem, but Rumsfeld failed to heed it. In particular, the State Department funded an extensive initiative, the Future of Iraq Project, which brought together groups of expatriates and regional experts to study postwar issues and was largely ignored by the Pentagon.[4]

That Rumsfeld may have discounted these analyses, however, is not necessarily surprising, especially given his apparent distrust of the underlying motives of the institutions that authored them. He was especially suspicious of the State Department, believing it did not regard democracy as possible in Iraq and was looking to sabotage plans for the war (Rieff 2003).[5] In fact, executive bureaucracies often engage in fierce rivalries and distrust each other's motives. Minimizing outsiders' advice is nothing new in Washington's interagency politics.

In addition, and especially critical, even if Rumsfeld did ignore commentary from the State Department and from civilian think-tanks, it does not explain why postconflict planning was so poor. This is especially true for the problem I am investigating here: the failures by the U.S. military to prepare for the immediate, postcombat stabilization tasks required of the war plan.[6] After all, as described above, postwar stabilization was an essential component of the war, involving "the transition from high intensity

---

[3] Quote appears in Gordon (2004).

[4] For detail on the Future of Iraq studies, see Phillips (2005: 127), Fallows (2004a), Packer (2005: 124).

[5] The administration was similarly suspicious of the motives of think tanks. See, for example, the discussion of Condoleeza Rice's interactions with the Council on Foreign Relations and Center for Strategic and International Studies in Packer (2005: 111–12). On State and Defense rivalries, also see Mendenhall (2005).

[6] In other words, I am largely leaving out the civilian side of reconstruction and postwar governance issues, with the exception of briefly discussing the military's relations with the Office of Reconstruction and Humanitarian Assistance (ORHA) (see below).

combat to the post conflict period, when the security environment was still uncertain and officials had to deal with the immediate aftermath of war" (Hooker 2005: 35).[7] Civilian preexisting beliefs only go so far in explaining why Central Command (CENTCOM), the unified combatant command in charge of planning and executing the war in Iraq, did not invest more resources in developing the war plan's final phase. The broader puzzle is why those beliefs were not more effectively challenged—especially by those within the military with different perspectives and experiences in postcombat stability issues—and why CENTCOM in turn did not prioritize these issues. After all, many civilians enter conflicts with naïve conceptions of how wars will unfold. This alone does not explain why civilians were not disabused of their flawed assumptions, and why assessment was so poor in 2002–2003. Instead, to explain why, I argue, we need to examine how prior disputes and the methods Rumsfeld used to manage them influenced conventions of dialogue in the Pentagon.

There is a third, albeit less frequently articulated, potential explanation for the nature of postwar plans: that there was, in fact, nothing wrong with the process of strategic assessment, and that Rumsfeld simply disagreed with any opposing arguments offered and, unfortunately, given the uncertainty inherent in the postwar situation, was just unlucky in guessing wrong about what would happen. In other words, Rumsfeld engaged in a careful weighing of all contingencies but, based on a reasoned evaluation of the issues, decided that the analysis did not support encouraging the military to invest in planning for potential postwar security problems.

The problem with this argument is that there is no evidence to support it. Beyond Rumsfeld's own assertions that civil-military assessment was healthy, there is no cause for believing it was (Ricks 2001a; Loeb and Ricks 2002). Rather, the facts the secretary marshaled to support his claims often seemed to undermine rather than support them.[8]

Take, for example, the April 2006 "revolt of the generals." In that month several recently retired generals, many of whom had occupied key command positions in Iraq, made a series of public statements and comments criticizing the secretary's management of the prewar planning process.[9] Among the

---

[7] As Tommy Franks described it in August 2002, CENTCOM forces would be in Iraq at least for "an initial two- to three-month 'stabilization' phase and then an eighteen- to twenty-four-month recovery phase during which the bulk of the invasion force would be removed." In a briefing paper in September 2002, he noted that there would be a "posthostilities" phase lasting for a year or more (quotes appear in Gordon and Trainor 2006: 68, 74; see also Franks 2004: 351).

[8] For an example of his assertions along these lines, see Cordesman (2003: 154).

[9] The generals in opposition included Army Major General Paul D. Eaton, who commanded the training of Iraqi security forces until 2004; Marine Lieutenant General Gregory Newbold, director of operations, Joint Chiefs of Staff, 2000–2002; and Army Major General John Batiste, who commanded an army division in Iraq before retiring.

charges leveled were that Rumsfeld stifled advice and intimidated potential dissenters, including the Joint Chiefs of Staff. Rumsfeld's response was to try to portray these outspoken generals as expressing a minority view—as a disgruntled few among a sea of serving and retired officers. The Pentagon also released a "fact sheet" to military retirees and civilian analysts to use in countering the criticisms. It contained a reference to the number of meetings Rumsfeld held with the Joint Chiefs and combat commanders: The figures cited were 139 and 208, respectively (Mazzetti and Rutenberg 2006). However, curiously, these numbers covered the period "from 2005 to the present," that is, from 2005 to April 2006. This was an odd defense to offer to a critique about *prewar* planning (nor, incidentally, was the number of meetings alone evidence of active engagement). In addition to these talking points, the then current chairman of the Joint Chiefs, General Peter Pace, who had been vice chairman during the prewar planning, as well as the former chairman General Richard Myers came to Rumsfeld's defense. In published statements, Myers, for example, asserted that Rumsfeld "allowed 'tremendous' access for presenting arguments."[10] However, we might expect that, given Myers' self-professed "mind meld" with the secretary,[11] and perhaps the fact that criticism of Rumsfeld's treatment of the Joint Chiefs might also reflect poorly on his role as chairman, the general would defend the secretary. Similarly, it is no surprise that Peter Pace would also defend Rumsfeld given his position as chairman in April 2006.[12]

Of course, one might also question the motives of the disgruntled generals, arguing that they had a stake in assigning blame to Rumsfeld given the poor course of a war in which they played central roles. Yet, even if we leave aside the post hoc accusations by these disillusioned generals, detailed studies of the period suggest that the process at the time was indeed flawed, as do contemporaneous press reports (see, for example, Loeb and Ricks 2002, Ricks 2001c, 2001e, Purdum 2003; Hersh 2003). The most prominent and detailed accounts, by Gordon and Trainor (2006), Woodward (2004), and Ricks (2006), all of which are based on extensive interviews and documentary evidence, recount the marginalization of the Joint Chiefs and other weaknesses in the evaluative process. In sum, there is simply no evidence that the process for strategic assessment was healthy. In fact, as I argue below, there are good reasons to expect—based on U.S. civil-military relations—that it should have been extremely unhealthy.[13]

---

[10] "Rumsfeld Did Not Intimidate Joint Chiefs, Ex-Chairman Says," Associated Press, April 17, 2006.

[11] Quoted in Gordon and Trainor (2006: 46).

[12] As one historian put it, the tradition of military deference to civilian authority warranted that he come to his boss's defense: "if he had not spoken out, he would have been making a very strong statement" (quoted in Shane 2006).

[13] One final explanation is that formal institutions at the political-military apex, and especially the 1986 Goldwater-Nichols reforms, caused the problems in assessment (Strachan 2006). These reforms strengthened the role of the chairman of the Joint Chiefs at the expense

Civil-Military Relations

Two things are notable about civil-military relations in general during 2002 and early 2003. First, it was a period of political dominance.[14] This was true despite indications that the military's political influence had been on the upsurge in the 1990s when it faced a political leader, President Clinton, who was perceived as "weak" on defense issues (Kohn 1993; Weigley 1993). There were signs that the officer corps was becoming more politically self-aware during that time, as part of a long-term trend since the end of the Vietnam War. Studies showed that more officers affiliated with a political party, largely the Republicans, than in the past, when higher percentages identified themselves as independents (Feaver and Kohn 2001). During the contested 2000 presidential election, get-out-the-vote drives and related activities were critical in marshalling military votes in support of Bush (Singer and McKerney 2000; Wood 2000). Retired generals and admirals were also increasingly inclined to align in partisan battles, endorsing candidates like Clinton in 1992 and 1996, and George W. Bush in the 2000 election. However, despite gaining influence, the military lacked standout figures who might translate that influence into a challenge to the civilian leadership. It lacked a currently serving military leader, for example, with the stature of Colin Powell, whose influence in the 1990s caused some to warn of a crisis in civil-military relations (Kohn 1993/94; Weigley 1993; Feaver 1995).[15] In sum, while the military was arguably a more politically potent constituency than in the past, its influence over the political coalition was still limited, and it lacked

---

of the service chiefs and promoted a system whereby the latter are outside the operational chain of command and therefore easily bypassed in the planning process (Murdock 2004). Yet, Chairman Myers, far from overshadowing the service chiefs and eclipsing their participation, as the reforms might predict, was actually a *weak* participant in the assessment process (Herspring 2005: 405–6). Moreover, formal institutions do not explain why Rumsfeld was so estranged from the Joint Chiefs and so disinclined to engage the chiefs more openly. After all, Goldwater-Nichols does explicitly allow for "advice on request" from the members of the Joint Chiefs.

[14] This analysis focuses on the secretary of defense, Donald Rumsfeld, as the key political leader, rather than on President Bush himself. It does so because of the role Bush assigned to Rumsfeld in seeing through Bush's vision of military reform. Bush was heavily in favor of transformation, and Rumsfeld was his agent of change at the Pentagon (Stevenson 2006: 180). On the theme of transformation in the 2000 presidential election and in subsequent statements, see Ricks (2001e), Weinraub and Shanker (2003), Fallows (2004a). Although Rumsfeld was largely in charge of military reform, note that once war planning for Iraq began, Bush was briefed a number of times on progress in developing the plan. For accounts see Woodward (2004), Gordon and Trainor (2006).

[15] On the importance of standout figures enhancing military influence, see Feaver (2003: 208–9).

a unifying figure who might mobilize that influence. Politicians, true to constitutional script, remained politically dominant.

The second notable feature of this period was the intensity of preference divergence observed over corporate issues. Relations started out relatively harmoniously.

It is no exaggeration to say that when George Bush was elected to office in November 2000 there was a general sigh of relief within the officer corps and military services. After its disenchantment with the Clinton administration, the American military was finally going to get a leader with whom it could see eye to eye. The "grownups" were back in power.[16] The Bush administration's pledges to stop "nation building," in particular, were well received by many in the uniformed services who questioned Clinton's interventions in Somalia, Bosnia, Kosovo, and Haiti in the 1990s.[17]

Despite this auspicious start, relations soon soured at the Pentagon. At issue was a philosophical difference about how to undertake defense reform. Rumsfeld came to office with a self-professed goal to "transform" the military. "Transformation" was associated with the increasing use of precision weapons, increasing reliance on new technologies, substituting information for mass, and speed and flexibility of action on the battlefield.

The uniformed services disagreed with both the specific tenets of Rumsfeld's proposals and the pace of change the Secretary envisioned (Ricks 2001a; 2001b). They especially feared that his proposals would require jettisoning much loved weapons and equipment. The navy worried that it might lose aircraft carriers. The air force feared procurement of long-range stealth fighters, including the expensive air-to-air combat aircraft the F-22, might be up for reconsideration.[18] Tensions, however, were especially acute within the army. Rumsfeld's vision posed a direct challenge to the army's organizational concept of how war should be fought: with lighter forces more reliant on technology than boots on the ground versus with heavy reliance on ground forces and mass armies. Specifically, the army was concerned it might lose two additional active divisions (it had already been cut to ten during the 1990s). Also worrisome was the fate of systems like the mobile artillery system, the Crusader, the relevance of which Rumsfeld questioned for the future battlefield (it was eventually cut). Moreover, even those systems that the army leadership, including Chief of Staff Eric Shinseki, considered transformational, such as the Stryker wheeled combat vehicle and Future Combat System, were questioned by the civilian leadership.[19] In general, Rumsfeld saw the

---

[16] See, for example, comments by former secretary of the army Thomas White (2004b).

[17] See statements by Ricks (2004a).

[18] On Rumsfeld's efforts to reduce the number of F-22s procured, see Edmonson (2002b), Wayne (2006).

[19] On differences in Rumsfeld's and Shinseki's vision of transformation, see Boyer (2002), Engel (2003), Gibney (2004), Loeb and Ricks (2002), Herspring (2005: 394).

army as hidebound and blindingly conservative in its approach to warfare. He "complained that the army is too resistant to change, while army officers claim the defense secretary does not sufficiently appreciate the value of large, armored conventional ground forces" (Loeb and Ricks 2002).

Relations among the uniformed services were especially charged prior to the September 11 terrorist attacks. So alienated was the civilian and military leadership that it was common speculation within the beltway that Rumsfeld would be the first to leave the Bush administration. September 11 and the Afghanistan War muted these conflicts. But they reemerged. In 2002, prior to the Iraq War, the services and Rumsfeld remained at odds over reform.[20]

In sum, analytically the U.S. case resembles a situation of high preference divergence and political dominance. Although clearly dominant, Rumsfeld faced a military that was disaffected and at odds with his corporate priorities. These civil-military relations, in turn, had several effects on strategic assessment.

Strategic Assessment

One thing these civil-military relations did ensure was that the authorization process was clearly defined. Rumsfeld retained decision-making prerogatives, exercising both agenda setting and rights of approval over military policy and activity. He was heavily involved in decision making and war planning. In fact, so active was Rumsfeld that he reclaimed prerogatives typically delegated to the military. Among the more controversial of these was Rumsfeld's involvement in approving the pace and design of force deployments to Kuwait for use in the Iraq War.[21] Although Rumsfeld has been criticized for the decisions he made with this and other interventions, from the perspective of this study, the fact that there remained a clearly defined authorization process (rather than an ambiguous or contested one) was an advantage. It ensured that clear decisions could be made.

---

[20] These conflicts over transformation that predated the Iraq War laid the foundation for disputes with Rumsfeld. But conflict over strategy toward Iraq may have compounded the differences. Reportedly some top generals and admirals, including some members of the Joint Chiefs, saw the strategy of containment as less risky and more effective than war (see Ricks 2002a, 2002b). This would have magnified Rumsfeld's incentives to keep these officers at arm's length.

[21] Beginning in November 2002, Rumsfeld intervened in deciding how and when forces would be deployed to Iraq in the process referred to as the time-phased force and deployment list (TPFDL). This was a major source of contention with the army, who blamed some of the logistical problems observed in Iraq on Rumsfeld's interventions. See Fallows (2004a), Gordon (2004), Gordon and Trainor (2006: 96–97, 99).

Information sharing also does not seem to have been especially problematic between the military and political leadership. This is due to the fact that the latter retained the capacity to impose monitoring and other oversight mechanisms on the military to mitigate both the incentives and capacity of its leaders to withhold their private information. Rumsfeld was able to structure relations with his chiefs to ensure that he would have information about military activity on demand; he was often selective in choosing with whom he consulted and was persistent in pushing for information from his subordinates. He also invested in several monitoring mechanisms, which were not without controversy but did ensure his access to information. At the beginning of his term he established a series of study groups designed to investigate and report on a range of procedural and policy issues.[22] During planning for the Iraq War, he was regularly briefed in what analysts describe as an "iterative" or "adaptive" planning process, which allowed him both to monitor and to inject guidance and exercise influence in decision making (Hooker 2005: 33–34). In short, political-military assessment does not appear to have suffered from poor information sharing or from ambiguities in how decisions were made.[23]

Despite these strengths, however, strategic assessment as a whole was far from healthy. Although Secretary Rumsfeld clearly had the authority to dictate to his military subordinates and structure relations to ensure access to information, he also faced what he perceived as a recalcitrant bureaucracy motivated to resist his initiatives. The challenge before him involved getting his military organization to comply with his directives, not just formally, but in the day-to-day, mundane processes that are essential to implementing policy. To address this situation he resorted to a variety of oversight methods to manage his military leaders and promote their compliance with his goals.

The problem, as I describe below, is that these tactics also affected the process of evaluating strategy and operational plans at the civil-military apex. They undermined the comprehensiveness of debate and likelihood that alternative perspectives would be brought to bear on prevailing conceptions and assumptions. Put simply, they compromised strategic coordination.

---

[22] See Editorial Desk, "Making Way for Pentagon Reform," *New York Times*, August 20, 2001, A16; Stevenson (2006: 181).

[23] With regard to structural competence, I predicted in chapter 2 that, independent of the military's absolute level of competency, political dominance and high preference divergence allow for improvements in internal monitoring and in intelligence analysis of foreign military capabilities. While there may have been improvement, there is not clear evidence to support or disprove this in the U.S. case as of this writing. Consistent with the parameters for the shorter studies laid out in chapter 2's research design, I emphasize the attributes that seemed most significant in the case—in this one, strategic coordination.

Managing Dissent and Poor Strategic Coordination

The first oversight method Rumsfeld used was to limit the frequency and nature of interactions with those officers he perceived as resistant to his philosophy of military reform. Rumsfeld met and talked with Pentagon officials regularly, including the chairman of the Joint Chiefs of Staff, Richard Myers, the vice chairman, Peter Pace, and especially, when planning the 2003 Iraq War, Tommy Franks, head of Central Command. Yet these officers tended to share his views on issues of transformation. As noted above, Myers, for example, was an air force general and former head of Space Command and therefore more inclined to be sympathetic to Rumsfeld's campaign for transformation; as noted above, he once publicly described his relations with Rumsfeld as sharing a "mind meld."[24] Franks too was generally supportive of Rumsfeld's philosophy.[25]

At the same time, Rumsfeld tended to bypass those officers and entities that he considered overly hidebound and resistant to change;[26] informal dialogue and intense interaction tended to be limited to those military officers with whom Rumsfeld saw eye to eye. Especially significant, Rumsfeld tended to marginalize the Joint Chiefs of Staff (Gordon and Trainor 2006: 140; Slevin and Priest 2003; Stevenson 2006: 184; Herspring 2005: 396). Although not in the operational chain of command in wartime,[27] because of their positions as heads of the military services and the wealth of experience necessary to achieving those positions, the service chiefs are often important actors in consultative processes. Rumsfeld, however, had poor rela-

---

[24] Quoted in Gordon and Trainor (2006: 46).

[25] See, for example, his remarks at a December 2002 press conference describing the significance of war games designed to test preliminary war plans for Iraq (Gordon and Trainor 2006: 521, n. 12).

[26] On those officers with whom Rumsfeld had good relations, see Woodward (2004: 325). On alienation, see Ricks (2001e), Hersh (2003), Loeb and Ricks (2002).

[27] The U.S. military is organized around two primary structures: the services and the unified combatant commands. The services are in charge of training and equipping personnel, but service chiefs are not in the command structure during wartime. Rather, the unified combatant commander for the particular region is in charge of planning and executing the war (there are five regional commands: Southern, Pacific, Northern, Central, and European); the services supply forces to the unified combatant commands for use in war. Central Command is in charge of most of the Middle East. Hence, Tommy Franks, as head of CENTCOM, was the military person in charge of developing the actual war plan for the Iraq War. The Joint Chiefs of Staff includes the army chief of staff, the commandant of the marines, the air force chief of staff, the chief of naval operations, a chairman, and a vice chairman; it also has an extensive staff (the "Joint Staff") to support its activities. The chairman of the Joint Chiefs is designated the principal military adviser to the president.

tions with the Joint Chiefs—and especially the army chief of staff—as a result of prior clashes about transformation.[28]

A second tactic Rumsfeld employed was to appoint people with similar preferences to key positions and to sideline those who did not share his views (Stevenson 2006: 180; Herspring 2005: 381, 383). Take, for example what happened when Lt. Gen. Gregory Newbold resigned his position as director of the Joint Staff, reportedly out of frustration that Rumsfeld was regularly bypassing the entity. By convention the chair of the Joint Chiefs, then Richard Myers, picks subordinates. But when Rumsfeld interviewed Myers's selected successor for Newbold, Lt. Gen. Ronald E. Keys, the secretary found him unsuitable. Rumsfeld told Myers to find a different candidate, and the chairman then came up with an individual more to "Rumsfeld's liking" (Gordon and Trainor 2006: 7; Loeb and Ricks 2002; Herspring 2005: 383). As one observer noted, "Gradually, Rumsfeld succeeded in replacing those officers in senior Joint Staff positions who challenged his view. 'All the Joint Staff people now are handpicked' " (Hersh 2003).

Rumsfeld used similar tactics when he was looking for a replacement for Eric Shinseki, chief of staff of the army. In an unusual move, he pulled Peter Schoomaker from retirement. In so doing, the secretary effectively implied that he believed there were no other three- or four-star generals in the army worthy of the job—an affront to those in the service and an indication of the degree to which he sought to mobilize particular viewpoints (Coryell 2003). Schoomaker was viewed as an aficionado of special forces, which were a key component of Rumsfeld's vision of transformation. He had also formerly headed the Special Operations Command. Also in a break with tradition, Rumsfeld personally interviewed all nominees for three- and four-star positions in the military (Loeb and Ricks 2002; Ricks 2001a).

In retrospect, these tactics might raise red flags for those concerned about strategic assessment in the 2003 Iraq War. However, at the time these methods likely seemed rational from the perspective of a political leader, like Rumsfeld, trying to protect his immediate policy priorities. After all, it makes sense to appoint people who will carry out one's initiatives, rather than foot-drag. Replacing officers in key positions is, in fact, a powerful means for affecting change within a military organization. As the secretary himself characterized his tactics, promoting his chosen candidates was potentially "the single most transformational step" he would take during his tenure in office (Edmonson 2002a). It would help him deal with what he perceived to be "the main threat to a more efficient and innovative

---

[28] On poor relations with the army, see Woodward (2004: 207), Gordon (2004), Gordon and Trainor (2006), Shanker and Schmitt (2003), Hersh (2003). Rumsfeld was often perceived as favoring the navy and air force.

defense structure ... the Pentagon bureaucracy" (Gordon and Trainor 2006: 9). Limiting the participation of officers whose underlying disagreements may stymie exploration of alternative options and prevent debate and momentum building in favored areas also made sense for a political leader seeking to advance his vision.

Nevertheless, while they may have served Rumsfeld's goals, they had a devastating effect on norms of discussion and the scope of debate about military activity more broadly. Restricting serious consultations to a small group and marginalizing "outsiders" limited the range of views represented in consultation at the civil-military apex, squeezing out space for discussion of alternative perspectives on critical issues. At the time observers, for example, questioned whether the military felt free to offer its best advice to its political superiors (Loeb and Ricks 2002). Some noticed that "There is a nearly universal feeling among the officer corps that the inner circle is closed, not tolerant of ideas it does not already share, and determined to impose its ideas, regardless of military doubts."[29] Interviews with numerous officers revealed a strong current of opinion that viewed Rumsfeld as dismissive of contrary advice, "trusting only a tiny circle of close advisers" (cited in Loeb and Ricks 2002; Ricks 2001c). Officers "complain[ed] bitterly that their best advice is being disregarded by someone who has spent most of the last 25 years away from the military" (Loeb and Ricks 2002). Others questioned whether Rumsfeld "supported plain-spoken assessments from his battlefield commanders even if they may not necessarily agree with the perception that the administration has" (quoted in Purdum 2003). As one observer at the time summarized it: "Communications between the civilian and military sides of the Defense Department are catastrophically broken" (Woodward 2004: 322).

In sum, processes for strategic coordination were seriously troubled in the Department of Defense in 2002 and early 2003. With the exception of Tommy Franks and those few individuals with whom Rumsfeld saw eye to eye, the military and civilians were alienated and not fully engaging each other in evaluative processes. The oversight methods to which Rumsfeld resorted in order to protect his corporate interests had compromised the overall quality of strategic assessment at the civil-military apex.

War Planning

Above I described the general state of civil-military strategic assessment. Below I examine more specifically how those flaws in assessment manifested in the war planning process in 2002–2003 in which the military de-

---

[29] Commentary is by Loren B. Thompson, a defense analyst at the Lexington Institute who has close ties to defense contractors and the military. It appears in Loeb and Ricks (2002).

vised and the civilian leadership approved the operational plans guiding the conduct of the war. As I detail below, poor dialogue and the marginalization of dissenters generated a series of interrelated flaws in the planning process. These flaws, in turn, contributed to major weaknesses in postconflict preparation: underdeveloped plans and insufficient forces for the stabilization phase.

Before proceeding with the discussion of postwar issues, however, it is important to note that assessment, as expressed in the war planning process, was not wholly pathological, in the sense that it did serve Rumsfeld's interests in creating opportunities for externally imposed change in military activity. Here the clarity of the authorization process and Rumsfeld's capacity to mitigate problems in information sharing would prove huge advantages to him as he pursued his goals. They facilitated the introduction of new ideas and analysis in war planning—ideas that departed from status quo conceptions within the services about war fighting.

While not everyone agreed with the contours of the war plan that ultimately emerged from this war-planning process (especially the number and composition of forces it called for),[30] it nonetheless yielded an operational approach that departed significantly from that first conceived by military planners. The contingency plan that formed the initial basis of discussions, OPLAN 1003, was strongly evocative of the 1991 Gulf War, in the size and composition of the force, the pace of deployments, and general philosophy. In contrast, Rumsfeld's preliminary war concept called for the deployment of a significantly smaller force; reports put it at 50,000 to 75,000 troops. Through an iterative process, Rumsfeld and Franks developed a plan that called for a force closer to 200,000—a plan that likely reflected neither man's first choice, but an intermediate option (Fallows 2004b). The plan was consistent with a classical breakthrough operation, and, although not radical, it was innovative in some areas, notably in the speed with which the invading force would proceed to Baghdad, the significant use of special operations forces, and the simultaneity of air and ground operations.[31] By being able

---

[30] As I explain below, one of the main concerns was that there would not be enough forces for the postwar environment. But there were also serious concerns that the United States would not have enough troops and armor to prosecute the war and take Baghdad quickly and with low costs. The decision not to leave stronger forces in the rear areas to provide security and support, as traditional planning would have called for, was especially controversial (Cordesman 2003: 151). These views were encapsulated in public debate about the war plan after U.S. forces got bogged down due to attenuated supply lines about a week into the war (Weinraub and Shanker 2003; Atkinson and Ricks 2003).

[31] The use of special operations forces was described by a RAND Corporation study of the war as "the largest and most complex mission for these forces in the nation's history." See "Iraq: Translating Lessons into Future DoD Policies," report and letter dated February 7, 2005, to Donald Rumsfeld by the RAND Corporation. Also Krepinevich (2003).

to focus on those who shared his preferences, Rumsfeld could evade the bureaucratic inertia of the services, which had their own parochial ideas about how to fight the war.[32] He was able to marginalize those who were wedded to convention and resistant to his war-fighting philosophy.

Regardless of the strengths described above, things were far from healthy in war planning in 2002–2003, especially for the postwar phase. Specifically, weaknesses in strategic coordination had three devastating effects on postwar planning.

First, they meant that the full range of opinion about what could occur in the postwar environment was not fully represented in consultative processes. Part of the problem is that the forthright views of individuals with experience in postwar issues, within the Joint Chiefs and the army in particular, would not be solicited or analyzed in a manner conducive to comprehensive search and analysis. Especially poorly engaged in the war-planning processes reportedly were the chiefs of the military services. As Gordon and Trainor put it, "The Joint Chiefs of Staff had been pushed to the margins of the war planning" (2006: 140). The Joint Chiefs "were kept at arm's length from the planning process" (Stevenson 2006: 185–86; Herspring 2005: 399).

In addition, by sending the signal that "obstruction" would not be tolerated, Rumsfeld appears to have encouraged an ethos of self-censorship among senior military leaders. There were personal and organizational costs to offering unpopular opinions or those for which the logic was not fully developed or evidence established. This discouraged, rather than encouraged, open debate.[33] As one officer describes the general effect of the poor communication between political officials and many of their uniformed subordinates, in this sort of environment "you don't get the sort of push back you need to have the dialogue, the understanding, the debate out of which you will synthesize better ideas" (Van Riper 2004; see also Woodward 2004: 322). Individuals withhold their opinions and tread lightly in dialogue with the political leadership.

A second problem in war planning followed from the first: By truncating dialogue with those within the military who were concerned about the postwar environment, Rumsfeld missed an opportunity to influence those within the military who were not. Despite the expertise of some individuals,

---

[32] At the start, the army (and others) very much envisioned the war as a redux of the 1991 Gulf War; they remained fixed to the Powell Doctrine. The air force, for example, argued for a lengthy air campaign preceding ground operations similar to that in the Gulf War (the air campaign was ultimately much more limited in 2003 and coincided with the start of ground operations). See Keegan (2004: 141), Gordon and Trainor (2006: 44).

[33] This, for example, is a central theme in Lt. Gen. Gregory Newbold's (2006) critique of war planning.

the army as a whole—the chief service in charge of stabilization efforts—had long had an organizational culture that minimized the importance of the activities essential to what in military parlance is referred to as stability operations. In the 1990s this organizational culture, in fact, fueled skepticism over interventions in Bosnia, Kosovo, Haiti, and Somalia: The army viewed these "Operations Other than War" as sideshows that distracted from its chief war-fighting mission (Avant 1996–97; Feaver and Gelpi 2004). Given the prevailing culture, the military as a whole was not highly invested in stability operations in general, and in Iraq in particular. Moreover, and especially consequential, Tommy Franks was not highly focused on these issues. As an army officer he reflected army culture and was not naturally inclined to emphasize such activities. In addition, he had not served in any of the campaigns in the 1990s in the Balkans. "Franks had no experience in Bosnia or Kosovo and was inclined to think of nation-consolidating efforts as an afterthought" (Gordon and Trainor 2006: 139). Therefore, to get Franks to prioritize postwar planning and ensure that CENTCOM invested significant resources in thinking about the post-Saddam security environment, pressure would need to be exerted on Franks and the military by those outside the organization—by civilians. But civilians had little reason to ask questions and exert this pressure. Prevailing assumptions—sustained by the failure to engage those who did have alternative perspectives about the stabilization phase of the war—suggested there would be no postwar security problem, so why push Franks to plan for it.

Finally, the structural situation in civil-military relations and the poor consultative environment it fostered had a third effect on planning: The Iraq war plan would become implicated in the underlying bureaucratic battle between the secretary and his generals.

In the absence of constructive dialogue with his subordinates, Rumsfeld had incentives to look to other methods to persuade potential dissenters of the merits of reform as he conceptualized it. Consequently, Rumsfeld's desire to lay bare the logic of transformation meant that Iraq would be used as a proving ground for his concept of warfare. As such, the design of the war plan "was part of his broader goal to prove that the military could be transformed for the twenty-first century into a different kind of fighting force. He really saw Iraq as a great big laboratory" (Purdum 2004). The war plan was not just about defeating the Iraqis but about defeating a particular bureaucratic mindset. It both reflected and promoted Rumsfeld's organizational vision.

This too would have consequences for Rumsfeld's willingness to invest in search and analysis and pressures he would exert in war planning. Using Iraq as a "laboratory" for military transformation meant Rumsfeld had an investment in a particular way of doing things, which foreclosed, or at least greatly limited, alternative ways of conceptualizing how the war could and should be prosecuted (Kagan 2004). As former secretary of the army Thomas White put it, "The type of operation a stability operation is . . . is boots on the ground and it is very untransformational" (Packer 2005: 117). Consequently, Rumsfeld would have disincentives to invest in analysis about the requirements of a large-scale postwar stabilization effort; doing so "went against the whole thrust of Rumsfeld's Defense Department, in which the overriding goal was military transformation" (Packer 2005: 117).

From Planning to Plans

In turn, these three procedural weaknesses had several concrete effects on the U.S. operational plan, 1003V, for the Iraq War. First, the formulation of plans for the postwar phase would be delayed and, as a result, underdeveloped. They would be based on untested assumptions and fail to foresee critical contingencies. Second, the plans would not supply enough troops for the postwar phase. Third, and related, decisions would be made to cut off the supply of forces at the end of the war's combat phase, further exacerbating the troop insufficiency in the postwar phase.

UNDEVELOPED POSTWAR PLANS

In theory CENTCOM should have been carefully planning for Phase IV from the start: It was in charge of developing military plans and designating forces that would be required to maintain order during the transition from combat to a postcombat environment. As Franks himself reports, Phase IV was part of the war plan from its inception.[34] Yet an entire year of intensive planning for the combat phase of the war plan had taken place before the final phase had begun to be addressed in any concerted manner (Gordon and Trainor 2006: 77; Phillips, Lauth, and Schenck 2006: 14). Rather, in progress reports to the Pentagon on war planning, issues pertaining to the postwar phase were often referred to as "open items" (Packer 2005: 119). No real plan was developed (Ricks 2006: 109–10). To the extent CENTCOM did begin developing a detailed plan, OPLAN Iraqi Reconstruction, it did not do so until February 2003. This plan was not completed until the end of April, more than a month after the war had begun; for a war of choice in which there was a long lead-up time, this was remarkably late.[35]

---

[34] See note 45.
[35] Eighteen months—twelve intensely focused—were spent refining the war plan for major combat operations. Planning began in November 2001 and was in full swing by February 2002 (Gordon and Trainor 2006: 75–94).

Similar dynamics were observed in efforts by those in charge of the war's ground campaign to prepare for the postwar phase. In August 2002 Lieutenant General David McKiernan was appointed head of CENTCOM's land component, Coalition Forces Land Component Command (CFLCC), which would oversee all operations for ground forces in the invasion campaign, including those associated with the stabilization phase.[36] McKiernan had been one of Army Chief of Staff Eric Shinseki's "most trusted officers" and had served in Bosnia during NATO's intervention in its civil war (Gordon and Trainor 2006: 75). From the start he recognized the military would play an important postwar part, and CFLCC's supporting plan for the ground campaign, COBRA II, involved planning for all four phases of the war.

The problem, once again, is that CFLCC's serious efforts on Phase IV came too late. It was only during exercises for COBRA II in January and February 2003 that CFLCC's staff became aware of significant problems with the postwar phase. Subsequently, they began to work on a new plan called ECLIPSE II. At first glance, ECLIPSE II sounded reasonable. The plan anticipated that CFLCC might be in control of postwar Iraq for as long as six months, after which it would hand off to a civilian administrator or another military administration working with an interim civilian Iraqi government. As such, ECLIPSE II laid out guiding concepts, as recounted by Gordon and Trainor, such as "control as we go" and the necessity of a "rolling transition" from Phase III to stability operations. The plans in turn called for the military to "secure key infrastructure," to "support the restoration of critical utilities/basic services," and critically to "support the maintenance of public order and safety" (Gordon and Trainor 2006: 145).

ECLIPSE II unfortunately remained underdeveloped. It was only completed on April 12, 2003, more than three weeks after the war's start. As one official disparagingly described it, "the Eclipse plan was 'PowerPoint deep'" (quoted in Gordon and Trainor 2006: 145; Ricks 2006: 79–80). Perhaps even more important, it was based on several unchallenged assumptions. The most significant of these was that it assumed security could be quickly turned over to remnants of the Iraqi police and army, and U.S. forces would not have to play a central role in securing the country. Especially striking about this assumption is that it was in direct conflict with the other provisions of the war plan. The plan called for destroying critical command and control functions of the Iraqi army and government to accelerate the fall of the regime. However, without that command and control infrastructure it would be hard to mobilize Iraqi military and police forces

---

[36] COBRA II was the plan for ground forces; it supported CENTCOM's operational plan, OPLAN 1003V.

after Baghdad fell.[37] The possibility that Iraqi forces would not be available or that the security situation might be more serious was not considered. CFLCC's staff simply did not fully probe the various contingencies involved in securing the country. As one observer put it, "There was no Plan B" if things did not go as initially forecast (Packer 2005: 118). "No planning occurred for scenarios where [prevailing] assumptions might not hold" (Bensahel 2006: 458).

To their credit, CFLCC planners did recognize at least some of the problems in their preparations for the postwar situation. In February 2003 some planners warned General McKiernan that U.S. forces might be poorly positioned for Phase IV activities. An analysis at that time suggested modifications might be warranted to control the borders, identify key infrastructure to be protected, and allocate "adequate resources to quickly reestablish post-war control throughout Iraq" (Peterson 2004: 10; Gordon and Trainor 2006: 146). Crucially, however, it was too late to change the combat plan to ensure its better integration with postcombat activities. McKiernan did not want to move forces around that might compromise the combat phase, and CFLCC's planners did not push their commander to consider the changes (Gordon and Trainor 2006: 146; Peterson 2004: 11). Herein lies the root of the problem with the planning activities: The combat plan and its relationship to postwar stabilization had not been conceptualized together.[38]

Why did the military fail to invest more resources in planning Phase IV from the start? The problem was that, with the civilians uninterested and Tommy Franks himself occupied with "winning" the war against Saddam, the military chief had little incentive to elevate the priority of postwar planning within his staff and its subordinate organizations. Instead, the postwar element was treated as the poor stepchild of the combat phase of the war: "All the A-team guys wanted to be in on Phase III, and the B-team guys were put on Phase IV" (Fallows 2004a: 13). As an officer involved in planning efforts at CENTCOM frames it, "From an operational perspective our main focus was on the first three phases and Phase IV is something we were planning but there were many intangibles and we didn't focus as much time on it as we should have" (Gordon and Trainor 2006: 139). Fi-

---

[37] On this contradiction, see Gordon and Trainor (2006: 145).

[38] Unlike preparations for the postconflict *security* situation in Iraq, efforts were made to plan for humanitarian relief; this included the provision of food and basic needs for Iraqis displaced by the war. These plans followed directives by the White House and Pentagon that this relief be available at the start of combat operations. In other words, the displacement of Iraqis was viewed as a natural consequence of Phase III combat operations. Hence, unlike planning for the security environment in the stabilization phase, preparations for humanitarian relief did not clash with core principles for how the war should be fought. On these planning efforts, see Woodward (2004: 147), Bensahel (2006: 454–55).

nally, as another planner, an air force major, put it: "The amount of pressure we would get from CENTCOM on phase IV wasn't enough, frankly" (Packer 2005: 120). Clearly, Franks did not press his planners to emphasize these issues.[39] In sum, delays and lack of prioritization meant that plans for Phase IV were underdeveloped, untested, and, in the words of one CFLCC planner, Lieutenant Colonel Steven W. Peterson, "ineffective" (Peterson 2004: 10).

Finally, it is worth examining some key events during the war to get a full sense of the scale of the problems in the war plans. Take, for example, the experience of the Third Infantry Division. In the days following the capture of Baghdad, its troops, which had led the attack on the capital, were forced to stand by and watch the security situation degrade.[40] They had no orders to act upon. "Higher headquarters did not provide the Third Infantry Division (Mechanized) with a plan for Phase IV. As a result, Third Infantry Division transitioned into Phase IV in the absence of guidance" (Rieff 2003). Commanders were forced to improvise plans and make decisions on their own. As one administration official described it, "All of the sudden they got there—and there was no intent. There were no rules of engagement. Everything was for the battle" (Packer 2005: 137). The contrast with the combat phase of the war is striking. Take the activities of one unit, the Second Battalion, Seventh Infantry, of the Third Infantry Division. During the war its tasks included taking the Baghdad airport. To prepare, prior to the battle for Baghdad, the battalion "rehearsed their own roles and the contingencies they might face over and over again" (Rieff 2003). In contrast, the Third Infantry Division in its After Action Report stated that a fully articulated plan for the stabilization phase—let alone opportunity to prepare for it—was never supplied to its forces.[41]

The inadequacies of the war plans were also evident in the military's poor coordination with the civilian-led reconstruction side of the postwar effort. As it was conceptualized, the military remained in charge of security and postcombat stability operations for the postwar phase and was sup-

---

[39] In fact, so concerned were the Joint Chiefs about the lack of planning by CENTCOM for the postwar situation that in October 2002 the Joint Staff drafted its own plan for Phase IV. This would lead to the establishment of Joint Task Force IV, one of the more unusual innovations of the war-planning process. For details, see Gordon and Trainor (2006: 141–44).

[40] Arguably, the Third Infantry Division should not have been left with the postwar situation to deal with alone or perhaps at all. Having just fought their way to Baghdad, forces were exhausted and in a combat mindset.

[41] "Third Infantry Division After Action Report; Operation Iraqi Freedom." Accessed on June 15, 2005, at *http://www.globalsecurity.org/military/library/report/2003/3id-aar-jul03.pdf.* See, for example, page 13 of the report. Note that the marines in southern Iraq had similar problems. Gordon (2004).

posed to coordinate its efforts with the civilian reconstruction effort, in the Office of Reconstruction and Humanitarian Assistance (ORHA), which was headed by retired General Jay Garner. In theory, coordination might have been eased because ORHA was established and administered by the Department of Defense.[42] In fact, the entity was supposed to be equal in status and to "plug in" to CENTCOM's war-fighting activities as the latter planned for the deployments of civil-affairs units and military forces needed for the postwar stabilization effort. CFLCC, CENTCOM's land command, was placed in operational command of ORHA.[43]

In reality, however, throughout its short existence, ORHA remained peripheral to the war-planning effort, and CFLCC's coordination with it was minimal (Bensahel 2006: 461). An incident that occurred just three days before the war is particularly telling in this regard. After arriving in Kuwait and while awaiting instructions about ORHA's situation once its members were deployed to Baghdad, some of its officials took it upon themselves to draw up a list of sites that needed to be secured upon the fall of city; this, for example, included the Iraqi Museum because of its symbolic importance. On March 26, 2003, they sent the list to the military war planners stationed at Camp Doha, on the Kuwait-Iraq border. Two weeks after the war, when the museum and other facilities had been looted, those ORHA members went to Camp Doha to find out what had happened to their list. As one participant recalled, they encountered a British soldier who, when queried, replied, "Well you know, I just became aware of this big stack of stuff that you ORHA guys did yesterday." As one observer nicely captures the problem, the "military simply didn't understand ORHA's importance. 'It was as if these guys did not have a clue what Jay Garner was about,' he said. 'There was no priority given to the essential aspects of [ORHA's] mission.'"[44] Clearly ORHA and the uniformed military were not working together.[45] Postwar plans were underdeveloped, to say the least.

---

[42] ORHA was established in January 2003 as a civilian staffed entity after it was decided that the Defense Department (and not the State Department) would take the lead in overseeing reconstruction of the country after the war. ORHA itself suffered from numerous problems due to politicized staffing, lack of resources, and related issues. Details appear in Gordon and Trainor (2006), Phillips (2005), Packer (2005). On its follow-on organization, the Coalition Provisional Authority, see Rathmell (2005: 1013–38).

[43] In fact, Franks had deliberately put ORHA under the control of his local commanders, "rather than taking responsibility for the postwar effort himself, with the higher authority of CENTCOM" (Packer 2005: 134; Phillips 2005: 126).

[44] Quotes in this paragraph appear in Packer (2003; 2005: 135). For other examples of how the military placed little priority on ORHA's activities, see Rieff (2003).

[45] ORHA's isolation from the military had other damaging effects. Garner's team, for example, planned to move into the southern city of Basra to begin reconstruction immediately after the war started in order to refine their operations before proceeding to the Sunni-controlled north. To facilitate his plans, Garner had been anticipating that U.S. and allied forces crossing from Kuwait into Iraq would leave forces in place to provide for rear security as they made their way to Baghdad. But as it turned out, there were not sufficient forces for that task and, as

248 CHAPTER SEVEN

Sending Too Few Troops

Even had U.S. forces had better plans, however, they likely would have had too few forces to support them. The number of troops required for the ground campaign was in fact one of the most debated issues between Rumsfeld and Franks during war planning. Crucially, however, theirs was almost exclusively a debate about the number of forces needed to win the conventional component of the war. The iterative process recounted in careful detail by Bob Woodward, Michael Gordon, and Bernard Trainor, for example, focuses on what would be needed for the victory against Saddam Hussein's military.[46] Questions were raised about the size and mix of forces necessary to accomplish that mission. But Franks and Rumsfeld were not debating how many forces would be needed for all four phases of the war: for prewar initiatives, major combat operations, and the transition to postwar stabilization. Phase IV was not conceptualized on its own terms. As a RAND Corporation report put it, "The possibility that [postwar] activities might require more resources, or a different mix of resources, than the earlier [combat] operations was not contemplated."[47]

Conventions of dialogue between military and political officials played an important role here by reducing opportunities for outsiders to enter the discussion about troop levels that was taking place between Franks and Rumsfeld. As noted above, the army's organizational culture led it to be wary of stability operations in general. However, some within the service and in other branches voiced concerns at the time about the need for troops for the postwar stabilization effort.[48] Moreover, within the senior military

---

McKiernan explained to one of Garner's associates in late February, "he had no intention of sending troops into Basra until Baghdad was taken" (Gordon and Trainor 2006: 157). Without them, Garner's team could not progress to Basra. Garner's initial assumption was a safe one because it is common military practice in war planning to leave forces behind to secure the rear. Garner had not been privy to the war plan, nor did the military consider how to integrate its activities with any civilian reconstruction activities when formulating its operational concept.

[46] In Franks's own memoir (2004), where he recounts the development of OPLAN 1003V (the final war plan), tangential references to Phase IV pepper the narrative. But these references are remarkably strong on generalities and weak on specifics. Most amount to general comments by Franks that assert that he recognized at the time that Phase IV would be long and hard (see, for example, 389, 393, 484). In one reference the general does say that he anticipated Phase IV would require 250,000 troops. But if he was convinced of that, why weren't plans developed to ensure that those forces would be available? After all, after the taking of Baghdad, he agreed to the cancellation of the deployment of the First Cavalry Division (see below). In sum, Franks does little to make the case that CENTCOM was prioritizing planning for the postwar security environment. Also see Bacevich (2004).

[47] See "Iraq: Translating Lessons into Future DoD Policies."

[48] Within the army and other services, including some on the staff of the Coalition Forces Land Component Command (see below for details on CFLCC), were individuals who were concerned about the postconflict environment. Also, Hawkins, the head of the Joint Chiefs'

leadership, the army's chief of staff, Eric Shinseki, was arguably especially capable of providing essential information about what could unfold in the postcombat phase and the force requirements essential to meeting those contingencies (see Gordon 2004; Purdum 2004). After all, he had been in charge of the stabilization force in Bosnia, where postwar disorder had been a major issue.

The army chief clearly had a different perspective about postwar issues from that prevalent within the civilian leadership at the time. Shinseki's widely noted congressional testimony before the war and the reactions it elicited are telling in this regard. On February 25, 2003, in testimony to the Senate Armed Services Committee, the army chief was asked how many forces would be needed to occupy Iraq after it was defeated. He first deflected the question. Then, when pressed, he gave an answer. "I would say that what's been mobilized to this point, something on the order of several thousand soldiers, are probably, you know, a figure that would be required." He went on to explain his reasoning: "We're talking about posthostilities control over a piece of geography that's fairly significant, with the kinds of ethnic tensions that could lead to other problems. And so, it takes a significant ground force presence to maintain a safe and secure environment to ensure that the people are fed, that water is distributed, all the normal responsibilities that go along with administering a situation like this."[49] Shinseki's actual estimate of the forces required was reportedly 400,000.[50]

Two days later Paul Wolfowitz, the deputy secretary of defense, told the House Budget Committee something very different. In a clear allusion to Shinseki's testimony, he asserted that "some of the higher end predictions that we have been hearing lately . . . are wildly off the mark." He continued: "It is hard to conceive that it would take more forces to provide stability in post-Saddam Iraq than it would take to conduct the war itself and to

---

ill-fated effort to push postwar planning along, Task Force IV, estimated that similar numbers would be needed (Gordon and Trainor 2006: 102; Gordon 2004; Purdum 2004; Gibney 2004; Fallows 2004a). Within the broader organization of the army there was also institutional memory about postwar situations, which suggested they were often severely challenging. For example, in October 2002 the Strategic Studies Institute at the Army War College began a study assessing all recent occupations by U.S .forces to help guide the army in preparing for the aftermath of combat operations in Iraq. See Crane and Terrill (2003). Also note that an analysis of the requirements for stabilizing Iraq in the late 1990s by former CENTCOM commander General Anthony Zinni estimated such an operation would require 380,000 forces (Gordon and Trainor 2006: 460).

[49] Eric Shinseki, testimony on "The Fiscal Year 2004 Defense Budget," Hearing of the Senate Armed Services Committee, February 25, 2003.

[50] These figures were consistent with the numbers arrived at by Shinseki's staff (Gordon and Trainor 2006: 102; Fallows 2004b). On the factors that influenced Shinseki's estimates and other forecasts, also see Ricks (2006: 96, 98).

secure the surrender of Saddam's security forces and his army. Hard to imagine."[51] In fact, Wolfowitz's testimony underscores his naiveté about postwar stabilization planning, which is quite different from preparing for major combat. As one analyst characterizes it, "However many forces might be required to defeat the foe, maintaining security afterward [is] determined by an entirely different set of calculations, including the population, the scope of the terrain and the necessary tasks" (quoted in Gordon 2004). It was just these sorts of considerations that seemed to inform Shinseki's estimate.

Wolfowitz's reaction to Shinseki is telling. It reveals much about how discrepant views were being handled and the extent of the alienation and the depravity of dialogue between the army and political leadership at the time. As one analyst concluded, the confrontation "must have reflected the really deep disagreements going on within the Pentagon then, and a sign of the civilian leadership's impatience with what they viewed as the lack of cooperation from the uniformed military" (quoted in Fallows 2004b; also see Ricks 2006: 100). Shinseki's treatment was also a powerful signal of what was at stake to the military officers who held alternative views about the postwar situation if they voiced them. As one observer put it: "[Wolfowitz's] message to Shinseki was a message to everyone in and out of uniform at the Pentagon: The cost of dissent was humiliation and professional suicide" (Packer 2005: 117).

Astounding though it may seem in retrospect, as a result of dynamics like these, serious tensions in the views of political and military officials were never productively addressed. There was little effort to examine, let alone reconcile, the underlying assumptions about the situation in Iraq that produced such dramatically different expectations about the postwar environment (Hooker 2005: 38).

CUTTING OFF THE FLOW OF FORCES

A final problem stemming from poor assessment was the decision to turn the flow of forces off as the combat phase of the war came to an end in April 2003. Recall that Rumsfeld had pushed from the start for a relatively small combat force to be sent to the region. Franks and he had debated the issue considerably, ultimately arriving at a compromise figure in the fall of 2002. However, when General McKiernan became head of CFLCC that

---

[51] Wolfowitz proceeded to pose an analogy between the relief effort in northern Iraq established after the Gulf War, where forces had not been required for twelve years of operations, and postwar Iraq, dismissing in a phrase the recent U.S. experience in the Balkans, which arguably provided a more apt analogy. Testimony in Hearing on Fiscal Year 2004 Defense Budget, House Budget Committee. February 27, 2003.

same fall, he expressed worries about the number of forces called for by the operational concept that prevailed at the time. His primary concern was that there would be sufficient forces for the combat phase, but he also thought additional units could help the effort to secure Iraq once Saddam Hussein was ousted (Gordon and Trainor 2006: 75–94, esp. 98; Ricks 2006: 75). Eventually McKiernan did get Franks, and in turn Rumsfeld, to sign on to more forces for the campaign (Gordon and Trainor 2006: 93). Although this was still far below Shinseki's and others' recommendations, these extra forces could have been helpful to the stabilization effort. Critically, however, part of the compromise was that many of the additional forces would be deployed only after the war had started; deployments were based on a "rolling start" concept, whereby forces would continue to flow to the region after the campaign had begun. In principle this arrangement was workable. In practice, however, it proved to be a huge problem. After the taking of Baghdad proceeded smoothly, Rumsfeld pressed and Franks agreed to cancel the deployment of many of the follow-on forces that could assist with postwar stabilization tasks. Among the forces they agreed to "off-ramp" was the First Calvary Division stationed at Fort Hood, which was on orders to deploy and ready to ship out; its deployment to the region was canceled on April 21.[52]

Why would Rumsfeld push so concertedly for these forces to be off-ramped? Presumably there was little harm in letting their deployment proceed. Even had he discounted their necessity for postconflict stabilization, at the least they could provide extra security and welcome relief to U.S. forces on the ground in Iraq. Weaknesses of strategic assessment brought about by civil-military relations are once again paramount in understanding why Rumsfeld was so eager to turn off the flow of forces. In the absence of constructive dialogue with his service chiefs, and especially the army, Rumsfeld sought to prove the merits of his war fighting philosophy by showing— not just telling—his generals that one did not need a large, heavily armored force to prevail in Iraq. Allowing the reinforcements would have diluted the lesson, while including more troops at the start might have slowed the advance of U.S. forces, undermined flexibility on the ground, and therefore imperiled his war fighting concept (White 2004b). As a West Point military historian put it, "I believe [Rumsfeld's] determination to continue to validate [his] view of the war led him also sharply to constrain the number of ground forces that he sent" (Kagan 2004). As another observer put it, "In many ways the war plan drove the postwar plan" (quoted in Brinkley and Schmitt 2003).

---

[52] They in fact anticipated that there would be a draw down to 30,000 forces by early May; the day before the war started they began planning for removing U.S. forces once Baghdad had been taken (Shanker 2004; Gordon 2004; Packer 2005). On the debate about troop cuts, see Ricks (2006: 121–22).

• • •

In sum, civil-military relations manifest in three interrelated problems in war planning. First, individuals with knowledge of the postwar situation were not rigorously engaged in consultative processes, and those who might have offered alternative perspectives faced significant incentives to engage in self-censorship. This truncated conversation and helped perpetuate existing, optimistic assumptions about the postwar security environment. Second, as a result of unquestioned assumptions and Rumsfeld's efforts to make the war plan conform to his concept of transformation, civilian officials did not press their military subordinates to emphasize the postwar situation. CENTCOM was not getting pressure from above to pay attention to the postwar stabilization phase. Finally, the absence of constructive dialogue generated incentives for Rumsfeld to resort to other methods to persuade his critics of his war-fighting philosophy—the war plan itself became implicated in the philosophical battle over transformation. These problems in turn contributed to three major deficiencies in the U.S. war plans: a poorly developed concept for the final, stabilization phase; too few troops sent for that phase; and exacerbation of the troop insufficiency by decisions to cancel deployments at the end of combat phase.

In short, poor strategic assessment—perpetuated by problematic civil-military relations—had powerfully, and devastatingly, undermined the U.S. strategy for the Iraq War.

International Implications

In spring 2003 U.S. forces were indisputably successful in removing Saddam Hussein from power. Although the forces got bogged down a week into the war with logistical difficulties, they responded flexibly to that and other challenges facing them. It helped of course that the Iraqis were such a weak adversary, which failed to take full advantage of American forces' attenuated supply lines and other vulnerabilities during the war.

The United States nevertheless won the hot war in 2003, only to find itself entangled in its simmering aftermath. Even as Bush declared the end of major combat operations on May 1, it was becoming clear that the war might not be over. A growing insurgency was supplanting the conventional fight.

In turn, the lack of well-conceived postwar plans and troops to support them had two effects on the insurgency in postcombat Iraq. First, they yielded a vacuum of authority in the weeks following the fall of Baghdad, which sent poor signals to Iraqi citizens and would-be insurgents. With the removal of the regime, Iraqis were left without a government to regulate and protect them. The lack of visible forces securing key areas and promoting an assertive image of authority was devastating. Isolated incidents of looting soon escalated into a massive effort as people began to realize there was no one in charge.[53] The looting ultimately touched all the vital sectors of the state and economy. The electrical grid and crucial infrastructure were destroyed. Among the major casualties, in fact, were Iraq's government ministries—the very ministries that, in prevailing assumptions, were supposed to continue to govern in the new Iraq, and that the U.S. military had purposely left intact during its air campaign.[54]

This disorder created a strong sense of uncertainty and insecurity for the newly freed Iraqi population. The damaged infrastructure and inability to get things up and running also raised questions about the competency of American forces. As one analyst describes it,

> There's always looting and chaos in a postwar situation. It just comes with the territory. What was so problematic about it was the image that it left in the minds of ordinary Iraqis—that they had not traded Saddam's fall for something that would be safer and better. In those vital early days and weeks when the Iraqis were looking for signs that their lives were going to improve, in many cases in the immediate aftermath, their lives were worse. They had no power, no security, no water. It was grim and they blamed the Americans for that and that was problematic.[55]

The looting and the failure to manage effectively the postwar environment raised even more critical questions about the motives of the Americans. The management of the Oil Ministry is telling. After Saddam Hussein's fall, the United States sent forces to guard key installations, including the Oil Ministry. Critically, however, they did not have a plan to protect other key sites such as the symbolically important museum (whose significance, ironically, had been noted before by ORHA officials). This fueled speculation about why the United States was in Iraq in the first place. " 'It's not that [the Americans] could not protect everything,' a leader in the Hawza Shiite religious authority told [one journalist], 'it's that they

---

[53] The economic cost of the looting was estimated at twelve billion dollars (Packer 2003).
[54] Garner's ORHA also suffered from the lack of forces. There were not enough troops to secure the offices in which Garner's team was working. Consequently, the team was delayed for nearly two weeks in Kuwait before it was deployed to Baghdad after the city was taken. Once there, they did not have the security escorts necessary to perform their tasks. CENTCOM's land component could not provide this support (Garner 2003; quote appears in Slevin and Priest 2003).
[55] Purdum (2004).

protected nothing else [but the Oil Ministry] . . . so what else do you want us to think except that you want our oil.' "[56]

Debacles such as these won few hearts and minds in this critical transition period. Insurgencies rely on popular support—or at least complicity—to conceal activities and to supply recruits. Conversely, local populations have to be motivated to take risks and report on the activities of aspiring insurgents in their midst. In the tumultuous security environment, they had little reason to trust American authorities and provide critical information that might have identified key instigators and arrested the growth of the insurgency early on.

The security environment also sent a bad signal to would-be rebels. " 'We were incompetent as far as they were concerned,' [one consultant to American officials] said. 'The key to it all was the looting. That was when it was clear there was no order. That also told them they could fight us-that we were not a serious force' " (Packer 2005: 138). "Instead of having this postwar sense that 'a new cop is in town, things are in order now, don't dare challenge the U.S.' there was instead a dawning realization that no one was in control and no one could stop the looting."[57]

Second, with too few troops the United States lost momentum in pursuing rebels and in arresting the nascent insurgency. As the chief intelligence officer for the land war put it, "First we did not have enough troops to conduct combat patrols in sufficient numbers to gain solid intelligence and paint a good picture of the enemy on the ground. Secondly, we needed more troops to act on the intelligence we generated. The [insurgents] took advantage of our limited numbers" (cited in Gordon 2004). Not only were there insufficient numbers of troops, but their equipment and the pattern of their deployments were problematic. As noted above, the Third Infantry Division, which was the first large unit to arrive in Baghdad, was unprepared for securing the city. As a mechanized division (i.e., an armored division), it lacked body armor for its troops to carry out foot patrols. In addition, no troops arrived in the crucial city of Falluja, in the Sunni triangle, until April 24 (Gordon and Trainor 2006: 462). This was two weeks after they entered Baghdad.

Of course, no one can say for sure what might have happened in postwar Iraq had the United States been better prepared for the postcombat transition. But there can be no doubt that the lack of comprehensive planning and forces ruined any opportunity to derail a burgeoning insurgency in the weeks following the fall of the regime. As one observer frames it: "The real question is, did there have to be an insurgency? Did [the United States] help create the insurgency by missing the window of opportunity in the

[56] Quote appears in Rieff (2003).
[57] Fallows (2004b).

period right after Saddam was removed from power."[58] Even if some kind of insurgency or opposition movement to the U.S. presence had been unavoidable, might it have been less intense?[59] Might it have had less popular support from the start and therefore taken a less devastating course?

Ultimately, the insurgency has greatly complicated, if not permanently undermined, efforts to establish a stable government and polity in Iraq (Diamond 2004). Ironically, however, it was not just U.S. strategic interests and Iraq's future that were imperiled by the insurgency, but the very reform program trumpeted by Rumsfeld. Immediately following the declaration of the end of major combat hostilities in May 2003, Rumsfeld was flying high. Numerous press articles talked about him now having the political capital with Congress and the public to force profound and controversial organizational change at the Pentagon (Ricks 2003). With the insurgency still capturing headlines years after the taking of Baghdad, observers began to question whether he had the clout to accomplish his goals (Shanker and Schmitt 2005; Ricks and Loeb 2003). Rumsfeld's ambitious program to transform the military may have been yet another casualty of the strategic failure of Iraq.

The sad part is that at least some of the flames fueling the insurgency could have been dampened had civil-military relations been different: had army leaders, and others skeptical of Rumsfeld's philosophy for change, been better engaged in consultative processes before the war. As it was, the United States had critical flaws in how military and political officials were coordinating with each other.

These risks of poor strategic coordination were recognized by some at the time. Prior to the war, officers questioned whether aspects of a potential war in Iraq "are being sufficiently weighed—or dismissed as typical military risk aversion." Five months before the war a three star general noted: "If there is an atmosphere where contrary views aren't well-received, you may move into an operation that isn't well-advised." And as one troubled Republican senator put it during the 2003 war, "My biggest concern is the confidence of the civilian and military leadership in each other. It's critical to our success."[60] These individuals were right to worry.

---

[58] Quote by senior American officer appears in Gordon (2004).
[59] On this point, see Phillips, Lauth, and Schenck (2006: 22–23).
[60] First two comments appear in Loeb and Ricks (2002); third appears in McManus and Schrader (2003).

Conclusion

FINDINGS AND IMPLICATIONS

INTERNATIONAL LIFE IS inherently complex. Managing it is a difficult endeavor for any political leader, but some are better prepared than others. One reason has to do with their state's civil-military relations. Domestic relations between political and military leaders influence the institutions in which leaders engage in strategic assessment during international conflicts. Sometimes these processes generate relatively sound analysis of a state's capabilities and external environment. At other times they promote miscalculations and misjudgments in a leader's strategic choices. Empirically, as I summarize below, the effects of civil-military relations vary significantly across time and place.

The Pattern of Outcomes

Strategic assessment was extremely poor in Egypt in the mid-1960s. Gamal Abdel Nasser ruled with the support of civilian constituencies but faced a powerful faction in the military led by Abdel Hakim Amer, whose preferences diverged over strategy toward Israel and corporate issues related to the management of the armed forces. Consistent with the theory's expectations, shared power and high civil-military preference divergence bred competition over institutional matters that compromised all four attributes of strategic assessment. Amer undermined Nasser's efforts to monitor military activity, limiting the latter's access to critical information and in the process obstructing information sharing. The chief also contested Nasser's control of decision-making prerogatives, which was manifested in disputes over appointments and, during the 1967 crisis, over rights of approval and veto over key military decisions. Amer and his chiefs also resisted forthcoming participation in advisory processes such that there were no effective forums for joint review and analysis of security issues. In turn, competition indirectly undermined the military's structural competence in intelligence as its resources were redirected toward political targets; incentives to elevate considerations of partisanship in appointments also undermined organizational norms of self-critical evaluation. Consequently, not only did Egypt have poor mechanisms for analyzing its adversaries' resources and the country's external environment, it was incapable of assessing its own military capabilities.

Poor strategic assessment devastated Egypt internationally. Most significantly, it fueled an inflated estimate of Egypt's military capabilities in the May–June 1967 crisis with Israel. Nuanced assessments of the depth of Egypt's own weaknesses in leadership and training and Israel's strengths in these and other areas were sorely lacking. Nasser was consequently forced to rely on quantitative estimates of the military balance, which suggested a moderate basis for optimism in a confrontation against Israel: Egypt could hold its own, if not prevail, in a war of short duration. Consequently, Nasser maintained an intransigent strategy in a crisis that was to end in a devastating rout of Egyptian forces. By his own admission, had he known the magnitude of his military's failings, he would have pursued an alternative strategy that fateful spring.

Better strategic assessment was observed in Egypt in the 1970s when civil-military relations were characterized by political dominance and high preference divergence. When Anwar Sadat came to power he rejuvenated the middle-class base of his regime; he also faced a military whose social standing and internal cohesion had declined significantly. The change in civil-military relations afforded far more access to information than Nasser had in the mid-1960s, and information sharing improved. Sadat also was able to place greater emphasis on skill in appointments and reorient military intelligence resources toward external targets, improving the military's structural competencies in intelligence and internal monitoring. Equally important, the authorization process was clearly defined: Sadat retained final rights of approval and veto in strategic decision making. He was able to appoint individuals willing and able to translate political goals into supportive military activity.

These institutional strengths profoundly affected Sadat's ability to achieve his political goals. He was able to elicit his military leaders' support in formulating the limited war strategy for the October 1973 conflict. When some military leaders, including his minister of war, opposed the limited war concept, he overruled them, thereby removing a significant obstacle to the plan's implementation. Improvements in the military's structural competence facilitated the development of operational plans, as well as supportive tactics and training regimens, tailored to Egypt's resources. Sadat consequently was able to implement his sophisticated war strategy in 1973 aimed at reenergizing negotiations over territories lost to Israel in 1967. Subsequently, despite the profound and adverse implications for the military's strategic orientation and corporate interests, the president neutralized military opposition to his postwar disengagement agreements and controversial peace initiatives with Israel. In 1979 he signed a peace treaty with Israel that called for severe restrictions on military activity in the Sinai Peninsula. Overall, Egypt experienced a remarkable integration of political goals and military means in the 1970s.

Sadat's Egypt, nonetheless, was not without some flaws in strategic assessment. To circumvent opposition from his military, Sadat at times marginalized his chiefs in consultative processes, which truncated dialogue and compromised strategic coordination. Some analysts argue that Sadat subsequently made unnecessary concessions on force deployments in the disengagement agreements with Israel after the 1973 war and in the demilitarization of the Sinai in the 1979 peace treaty. More important, by not more systematically engaging his subordinates he fueled an image of himself as a leader too willing to sacrifice Egypt's security requirements without hard bargaining. This cost him crucial domestic and regional support for Egypt's grand strategy. In retrospect, when viewed through the lens of their international outcomes, the positives of strategic assessment under Sadat outweigh the negatives. Yet, a closer, analytically driven look reveals those institutions to have been mixed in their attributes, consistent with the predictions of the theory in chapter 2.

Like the studies of Egypt, the British cases reveal how variation in civil-military relations affects strategic assessment even while a state's regime type is unchanged. How leaders engaged in strategic assessment in democratic Britain before and during the First World War depended heavily on particular dynamics within its civil-military relations. Prior to the war, political dominance and low preference divergence allowed British politicians to make great strides in improving Britain's processes for assessment. Free from military competition or the need to tailor assessment institutions to reign in military leaders at odds with their priorities, politicians focused on functional reforms. They innovated a new infrastructure for coordination of political objectives with military policy. Improvements in the frequency and intensity of dialogue among military officials and politicians were observed. One indication is the development and activities of new, formal advisory bodies such as the Committee of Imperial Defense (CID).

Britain nevertheless soon found itself bogged down in the long and deadly First World War. Ironically, in 1914 Britain had been strategically and operationally more ready for that war than for any prior conflict in its history. The CID reoriented British strategy from its imperial focus to prepare for a war against Germany at a time when many British politicians were publicly distancing themselves from a continental commitment. Detailed operational plans were developed to deploy the British Expeditionary Force to the continent. But Britain failed to prepare fully by, for example, building the large mass army it would ultimately need to face the German challenge. A major problem was that prior to 1914 the civilian elite disagreed about how much Britain should engage itself in European affairs, and whether they should commit the country to fight in a potential conflict on the continent. The British case thus shows how even where civil-military relations promote relatively functional institutions for assessment, other factors may sometimes override those institutional strengths, and states may still succumb to strategic errors. Good civil-military strategic assessment is a huge advantage, but no guarantee of international success.

Despite its prewar strengths, strategic assessment deteriorated significantly in Britain during the First World War as a result of changes in civil-military relations. Army leaders and Prime Minister Lloyd George clashed over the merits of a "Western" versus "Eastern" strategy. Divisions within the wartime coalition government and the army leadership's ability to mobilize support from conservatives, the military's ties to the media, and popular esteem within society at large vested it with substantial political power: civil-military relations were characterized by shared power and high preference divergence. Although formal prescriptions of civilian control were never in question, in practice the military enjoyed substantial leeway to challenge political prerogatives. In turn, contestation over the authorization process, manifested in competition over appointments and de facto rights of approval and veto, undermined Lloyd George's influence over military strategy. Strategic coordination was poor as army leaders resisted forthright discussion with political leaders about strategic issues and operational plans. Army leaders obscured and withheld important information about military activity during critical campaigns in the war. In fact, many of the dynamics in assessment evident in the wartime British case are remarkably resonant with those observed in Egypt in the 1960s, despite the vast differences in culture, region, historical time period, regime type, and many other factors.

Poor strategic assessment, in turn, undermined Britain's war effort. The internal assessment environment stymied debate about operational plans, such as about the devastating 1917 Battle of Passchendaele. Britain pursued plans for that operation even while Chief of the Imperial General Staff Robertson suppressed his doubts and Commander in Chief of the BEF Douglas Haig withheld information about his true ambitions in the battle. In turn, in the highly polarized civil-military setting Lloyd George stifled his concerns about his generals' operational methods, allowing the offensive to proceed. These dynamics, more broadly, did little to help overcome the vacuum of creativity and stagnation that afflicted British military activity during the war. Questions went unasked and faulty policies unaddressed. The decade of reform and improvements in strategic assessment in Britain that preceded the war thus gave way to highly politicized and problematic assessment during the conflict. Despite the stakes of a deadly world war, civil-military politics overrode the necessity of rationalizing strategic assessment.

While Britain benefited from relatively functional strategic assessment prior to the First World War, its continental counterpart, Wilhelmine Germany, experienced pronounced difficulties during the same time period. In particular, civil-military relations, characterized by shared power and low preference divergence, meant that while the military and the kaiser did not openly compete over institutional processes, default arrangements granted the military substantial, but not complete, autonomy in its relations with the political leadership. This generated flaws in strategic coordination: The military's coordination with the kaiser was idiosyncratic, while the interface between the diplomatic and military apparatus was poorly developed. These failings, in turn, meant that whatever tendencies the state had toward pathology, the flaws were unlikely to be recognized and analyzed comprehensively. The country pursued a war plan that required violating Belgian neutrality without ever analyzing its political implications for Germany's foremost diplomatic goal: keeping Britain out of a continental war. Ultimate lines of accountability and responsibility in deciding military activity were also ill-defined: The authorization process, although formally settled, was in practice ambiguous. This ambiguity complicated Austria-Hungary's efforts to "read" German preferences during the July 1914 crisis, reinforcing the former's belligerent strategy in the pivotal days before the outbreak of the war.

In Pakistan in the late 1990s, civil-military relations characterized by shared power and high preference divergence once again undermined strategic assessment. The efforts of Prime Minister Nawaz Sharif and his military chiefs to protect their prerogatives in decision making, manifested in disputes over the establishment of a National Security Council, undermining strategic coordination for the state as a whole. Consequently, the state lacked any effective structure for analyzing political-military strategy. Contestation over decision-making prerogatives also yielded an incoherent authorization process: It was unclear how decisions were being made about strategic-military issues during this critical period. Poor strategic assessment in turn rendered Pakistan vulnerable to destabilizing strategies in the country's international relations. In spring 1999 the Pakistani military implemented a tactical plan to invade Indian-held positions in the Kargil Heights. Not only was the plan completely at odds with Sharif's efforts to cooperate with India, it lacked clear political objectives. Ultimately Pakistan's disintegrated policy isolated it in the international community and lent credibility to India's claims for sympathy as its aggrieved neighbor.

In Turkey, military dominance and high civil-military preference divergence yielded "mixed" strategic assessment, with strengths in some attributes and weaknesses in others. The precariousness of Necmettin Erbakan's coalition and the military's unity and esteemed social position ensured a clear authorization process, with military chiefs retaining rights of approval and veto in decision making about security issues. Consequently, despite Prime Minister Erbakan's concerted efforts to enhance Turkey's ties to the Muslim world, the country's political-military policies remained remarkably integrated and consistent in their Western orientation. In addition, the clarity of the authorization process influenced the transparency of Turkey's signals to other states. In a little noted crisis between Turkey and Syria, the dominance of the Turkish military was widely observed and linked with the credibility of its threat to oust Kurdish rebels operating from Syrian soil. Despite these advantages, strategic coordination was poor: The political and military apparatuses of the state operated largely autonomously in security matters. The Turkish case, along with those of Egypt and Pakistan, thus shows how even in places with a tradition of military intervention in politics, the particular configuration of power and preferences in civil-military relations powerfully affects how the state engages in strategic assessment.

Finally, in the U.S. case political dominance and high preference divergence generated strengths, but also profound flaws in strategic assessment. In some respects, the process for evaluating political and military activity was functional. Prior to the 2003 Iraq War, Secretary of Defense Rumsfeld had ready access to information and could shape routines to privilege his control of it. Despite intense conflict with the military, a clear authorization process ensured he would retain rights to approve and veto initiatives in war planning. These prerogatives allowed Rumsfeld to promote a plan for the spring 2003 war that departed from extant operational approaches; it innovated in several key areas.

Nevertheless the pathologies in strategic assessment overshadowed these strengths. Like Egypt under Sadat, the U.S. case demonstrates how the methods leaders sometimes employ to insulate consultative processes from military "bias" can undermine strategic coordination. Here the consequences were profound. Rumsfeld's marginalization of officers whose views diverged from his own and appointment of like-minded officials to key positions truncated debate about critical assumptions regarding the postwar security environment in Iraq. They also limited the scope of debate about how many troops would be needed for the postconflict phase. Hence, the very assessment environment that allowed Rumsfeld to overcome the bureaucratic status quo and modify war plans also contributed to the tragic mistake not to plan adequately for the postwar security vacuum. In short, despite vast differences in the cases and in the ultimate international consequences of assessment, in both Egypt in the 1970s and the United States in 2002–2003, similar dynamics in civil-military relations produced similar weaknesses in assessment: In both, strategic coordination was undermined as the political leaders sought to insulate themselves from military leaders whose preferences over policy issues diverged from their own.

See table 8.1 for a summary of the international effects of strategic assessment.

262 CONCLUSION

Table 8.1
Strategic Assessment and International Outcomes in Empirical Cases

Case	SC	IS	AP	STC	Overall Quality of Assessment[1]	International Outcomes[2]
Egypt 1962–1967	–	–	–	–	Very poor	Multiple institutional weaknesses contribute to inflated capabilities estimates that fuel belligerent strategy in 1967; Israel responds with preemptive attack and war.
Pakistan 1997–1999	–	–	–	*	Poor	Poor strategic coordination contributes to failure to consider motivating assumptions and political ramifications of Kargil Heights invasion; undermines Pakistan's international position.
Britain 1914–1918	–	–	–	*	Poor	Poor strategic coordination and ambiguous authorization process perpetuate operational and tactical stagnation.
Germany 1888–1914	–	+	–	=	Poor	Poor strategic coordination contributes to military strategy that alienates Britain; ambiguity in decision making obscures German preferences and encourages Austrian belligerence.
Turkey 1996–1999	–	–[3]	+	=	Fair	Clear authorization process ensures consistency in political goals and military activity; also clarifies preferences, which render Turkey's threats credible to Syria in October 1998. Weaknesses in strategic coordination encourage disconnect in Kurdish policy/European ambitions.
United States 2002–2003	–	+	+	*	Fair (weaknesses arguably outweigh strengths)	Clear authorization process allows Rumsfeld to redefine war plan and "innovate" in several areas; successfully takes Baghdad but poor strategic coordination undermines postwar planning.

Table 8.1 (cont'd)
Strategic Assessment and International Outcomes in Empirical Cases

Case	SC	IS	AP	STC	Overall Quality of Assessment[1]	International Outcomes[2]
Egypt 1967–1981	−	+	+	+	Fair (strengths arguably outweigh weaknesses)	Clear authorization process allows Sadat to translate political objectives into military activity. Sadat achieves limited war, disengagement, peace treaty; however, some failures of strategic coordination yield bargaining weaknesses in peace process, which undermine domestic and international support for his grand strategy.
Britain 1902–1914	+	+	+	+	Good	Threat from Germany anticipated due to strengths of strategic coordination. Some military activity modified, but Britain still fails to prepare fully for major war in part because of exogenous, intracivilian conflict (see text).

Notes: SC = Strategic coordination
IS = Information sharing
AP = Authorization process
STC = Structural competence
+ : Civil-military relations have positive effect on attribute.
− : Civil-military relations have negative effect on attribute.
= : No theoretical prediction (see chapter 2).
* : No definitive finding; insufficient data to evaluate (see individual cases for explanation).

[1] Overall quality is a general reflection of strategic assessment at the political-military apex based on values of the listed attributes plus findings in the empirical chapters, which are summarized here. It is intended to give the reader a general sense of the outcome, not as a precise measure of assessment.

[2] International implications listed for reader's review, but recall that the dependent variable is strategic assessment (see chapter 1).

[3] IS is poor in Turkey but analytically inconsequential given logic of setting, so environment is summarized as fair, not poor (see chapter 2).

Dangerous States

One of the primary tasks of international relations scholarship is to help identify sources of war and instability in the international arena. This study contributes to that effort. It identifies a class of states that are special dangers to themselves and potentially to others: those in which military and political leaders share power in the state and systematically disagree over corporate or security matters.

In these situations political and military leaders have both the means and the motive to compete over how strategy is to be formulated and decided at the apex of the state. Each leader has a support base within society, and the military leadership is unified. This creates a domestic situation in which both political and military leaders have resources on which they can draw in bargaining with one another; neither can dictate the terms of interaction between them. In turn, as the leaders seek to advance their favored military strategies, policies, or corporate interests, they each try to establish processes that privilege their preferred outcomes in decision-making processes. Cumulatively this competition over institutional prerogatives undermines the state's processes for strategic assessment: It compromises how critical information about capabilities and the strategic environment is shared and analyzed, and how clearly and decisively the state can act upon that analysis.

Consequently, in the event of an interstate dispute, states with these civil-military relations have a hard time assessing their military standing and taking cues from their strategic environment. They are nearly incapable of formulating coherent political-military strategies and ensuring their consistent implementation. Like Egypt in 1967, they are apt to misestimate (and potentially overestimate) their military capabilities in an interstate crisis. They are prone to misread their adversaries and international environments and to take military actions that clash with political objectives, as did Pakistan in the summer of 1999. In turn, these misestimates and misjudgments can fuel provocations or overly ambitious demands of an adversary, thereby provoking crises and wars, as did both Egypt and Pakistan. For this reason these states are often dangers to themselves as well as to others.

States subject to this brand of political-military competition, moreover, represent a distinctly dangerous category apart from those in which the military dominates security policymaking.[1] As I argue throughout this book, when the military dominates, the process of assessment is essentially

---

[1] On the dangers of military dominance in decision making, see Sagan (1994, 1996/97), Van Evera (1991, 2001), Posen (1984).

internalized within the military organization; integration with the state's political and diplomatic apparatus is apt to be poor, and therefore the introduction of alternative perspectives in advisory processes is limited. Consequently, critical questions about the political ramifications of the use of force are apt to be neglected. However, military leaders are still capable, in principle, of making clearly defined decisions and exchanging the information available to them, which are two major advantages in the assessment process. In contrast, when military and political leaders are competing for control of procedural matters, not only are advisory processes politicized, the exchange of information is poor and strategy emerges from a dissolute authorization process, in which both sets of leaders are struggling to assert rights of veto and approval. In short, the structural problems for assessment induced by political-military competition are intense and wide-ranging.

Civil-Military Alienation

Civil-military competition, however, is not the only source of poor strategic assessment. Even when the military is subordinated to political authority, weaknesses in assessment institutions occur when political and military leaders clash intensely over strategic, corporate, or professional issues. Political dominance, or in the conventional lexicon civilian control, may be necessary, but it is not sufficient for good strategic assessment.

The problem originates in the incentives fostered by intense conflict between political and military leaders. As discussed in detail in chapter 2, when preferences over outcomes diverge, those conflicts revert to disputes over the processes that privilege some outcomes over others. Institutional disagreements flourish. Military leaders, for example, are motivated to shape conventions for presenting information in ways that protect their preferred policies. They are inclined to take actions that subvert the spirit if not the principle of political directives. Akin to a classical principal-agent problem, when they retain the power to do so, political leaders in turn will employ oversight methods that mitigate "bias" and enhance their access to information and otherwise minimize agency slack.[2] In turn, how specifically a political leader pursues oversight can prove enormously consequential for strategic assessment.

Among the methods available to political leaders are structuring advisory processes to lessen the impact of dissenting views and using selection processes to choose officers with whom their preferences converge. Political

[2] On principal-agent approaches and civil-military relations, see Feaver (2003) and Avant (1994); also see the discussion in chapter two.

leaders may restrict representation in consultative bodies or discount the information and advice supplied by military leaders. They may replace dissenters with like-minded officials. These are "rational" methods from the perspective of a political leader seeking to protect his or her access to information, analysis, and ability to translate political goals into military policy: Dissenters may not give due attention to some policy options; information may be suppressed or distorted; and military officials may take actions at odds with political preferences. Therefore, finding like-minded individuals to provide information and implement policy is necessary. Yet, it comes at a cost: The perspectives and opinions of those with unpopular views are not fully represented in debate and analysis. The civil-military dialogue is truncated.

These techniques are almost universally damaging to a leader's political-military strategies. They also appear to be quite pervasive. During 2002–2003 Donald Rumsfeld used these methods to insulate his goals from military leaders whom he viewed as hopelessly hidebound in their views of military reform. In so doing, the secretary of defense, in turn, abbreviated dialogue about postconflict planning for the 2003 Iraq War. In the 1970s Anwar Sadat also faced a military leadership at odds with him over military and security issues. He too tended to insulate himself from those in the military with whom he disagreed. Instead, he often relied on self-appointed, like-minded officials in advisory processes. He also marginalized dissenters in advisory processes, which lessened his exposure to critical views about some of his policies.

In fact, beyond the Rumsfeld and Sadat experiences, we can find evidence within diverse historical cases that suggests that dominant political leaders often use these methods to manage dissent over corporate and strategic issues. Adolf Hitler, for example, appeared to be quite adept at marginalizing those in his military command with whom he disagreed about Germany's prosecution of the Second World War. Yet, in so doing he created a corps of officials who put optimistic spins on information and limited his exposure to dissenting views from within his armed forces about the military balance between Nazi Germany and its adversaries.[3] Poor strategic assessment, originating in politicized advice, has, in turn, been linked to Germany's poor estimates of its capabilities in its ill-fated campaign against the Soviet Union in 1941 (Millett, Murray, and Watman 1988).

In the United States, President Lyndon Johnson's methods for managing his military chiefs are also evocative of these problems of managing military leaders with diverging views. During the Vietnam War, the president and his secretary of defense, Robert McNamara, viewed the country's

---

[3] On Hitler's management of his generals, see, for example, Addington (1994), Dupuy (1977), Murray (1984), Press (2005).

military chiefs as hopelessly parochial. Preferences diverged over strategic and operational issues in the war and whether to employ a graduated, limited use of force or commit to a substantial air campaign and deployment of ground forces. Consequently, Johnson employed a variety of "oversight" techniques with the effect of marginalizing his chiefs: He appointed individuals to key positions whose beliefs coincided with his own. He also limited access by his service chiefs to executive advisory forums. When the service chiefs, who themselves were mired in interservice rivalries[4] about how to prosecute the war, tried to offer guidance, their input was often heavily discounted and misrepresented, sometimes purposefully.[5] In general, the military chiefs' interface with representatives of political and diplomatic officials was poor.[6] In fact, rather than regularly seeking military input in the process of assessment, the chiefs were often consulted only after decisions had been made, and then in order to provide political cover for the administration (Gacek 1994: 190–91, 211–12).

Although certainly not the only cause of the failure in Vietnam, poor civil-military coordination certainly did not help, and some analysts suggest that it played a significant role, in the pathologies of U.S. policy during this period. As one critic of civil-military relations during the period argues, "Frank communication between the [Joint Chiefs of Staff] and the president might have permitted a reconciliation of their divergent perspectives and lent coherence to Vietnam planning" (McMaster 1997: 65). Yet such balanced exchanges were few and far between.[7] For Johnson, skeptical of military opinion and interested in protecting his priorities, insulating advisory processes from his uniformed chiefs made a great deal of sense. But it came at the expense of the overall quality of strategic assessment. In sum, even when political leaders dominate, recurrent and unyielding differences of opinion create incentives and unleash dynamics that can compromise strategic assessment.

---

[4] These interservice differences are in themselves unremarkable, given the strong organizational cultures both within and across the service branches and combat specialties in the United States. What is important is that there was little recognition of the need to try to reconcile divergent approaches to the use of force, in order to develop a principled and coherent military strategy. The chiefs themselves were not able to impose discipline on themselves (see Palmer 1984: 34, 35), which made the need for civilian questioning and investigation into the basis of these interservice differences all the more important. For illustrations of differences in the services approach to war, see (navy) Sharp (1978), (marines) Krulak (1984), (army) Summers (1982), and Krepinevich (1986).

[5] See, for example, the incidents cited in McMaster (1997: 99–103).

[6] For example, they were not invited to attend Johnson's famous Tuesday lunches in which he consulted with key advisers on domestic as well as national security matters; in fact, while the secretaries of state and defense and the national security advisor regularly attended, until 1967 no military officer was a regular member of this advisory group (after that the chairman of the Joint Chiefs of Staff was included).

[7] Also see Palmer (1984: 200–201), Gacek (1994: 211–16).

Herein lies another lesson of the book: These problems can afflict a variety of regime types—not least democracies, where "civilian control" of the military establishment is secure. Logically similar dynamics produce flaws in strategic coordination in both autocracies and democracies when political leaders dominate their military chiefs but their preferences over corporate or strategic issues diverge. Both regime types are prone to weaknesses in analyzing military activity and its integration with political objectives under these conditions.

Ideal Civil-Military Relations

Embedded here is also a lesson for our normative conception of "ideal" civil-military relations—a lesson that diverges from those implicit in the extant civil-military relations literature.

The existing scholarship, in fact, varies in its conclusions about when civil-military relations are healthiest. In his seminal work, *The Soldier and the State*, Samuel Huntington (1957), for example, argues that objective control, which implies that the military and political spheres should be divorced, maximizes military effectiveness. Military leaders should be left out of debate and dispute among politicians about political issues. However, once a political decision to use force has been made, they should be permitted to do their jobs as managers of the state's instruments of violence. In the ideal world, a clear division of labor between military and political activity is observed.

Other studies imply that active civilian intervention in military affairs is actually positive for civil-military relations: As Posen and others suggest, civilians, taking cues from the international environment, are best prepared to reform military activity and ensure its consistency with political goals and strategy.[8] Eliot Cohen (2002) also advocates active civilian involvement in wartime military activity. Following Clausewitz, he points out that the division of labor on which Huntington's objective control is premised is artificial: Military activity is inherently political, and there is no natural, inevitable separation between matters of policy and matters of warfare. His study of political leadership in wartime suggests that active involvement by political leaders in the details of military operations is a must.

This book suggests that both of these approaches are problematic in what they imply about when civil-military relations are "ideal" for strategic assessment. Briefly revisiting the U.S. case of planning for the 2003 Iraq War discussed in chapter 7 helps illustrate these shortcomings. Take, for

---

[8] This view is often implicit in scholarship that invokes organizational theory to explain military preferences.

example, what the perspectives prescribe for how civil-military relations might have been better in the United States, and consequently how planning might have improved in the months preceding the war. Huntington's implied remedy, a clear division of labor between political decisions and military activity, would have done little to ameliorate deficiencies in war-planning processes. In that event, the commander of Central Command, Tommy Franks, and his staff would have more or less unilaterally designed the war plan. Yet, given Franks's proclivities, it is not clear he would have invested more resources in Phase IV. There may have been more troops on the ground by virtue of the fact that he originally proposed more forces be deployed for use in combat operations, but this does not mean he would have invested in the conceptualization and prioritization of the postcombat phase of the war. Nor was civilian dominance and intervention enough to ensure rationalized strategic assessment. Secretary Rumsfeld clearly had the authority and inclination to intervene in military affairs, yet we still got the postconflict debacle. Assertive civilian control is insufficient for sound strategic assessment.

The U.S./Iraq case, and this research project more broadly, suggest a different lesson about when civil-military relations are at their normative ideal: The quality of debate between political and military leaders is the best measure of the healthiness of civil-military relations.[9] Political leaders may bring to the table their own biases and preexisting conceptions about military strategy and activity. Military leaders may also exhibit their own preconceived notions. Consequently, both must participate fully in comprehensive dialogue at the apex of decision making to expose flawed reasoning, hidden and contradictory assumptions, and alternative views in the analytical process. Both sides must share their private views and information and engage with open minds different arguments, even those that are marginal or unpopular, without prejudging their merits.[10] This does not mean that these conversations should always be harmonious. In fact, some friction is to be expected and even welcome in that it can encourage investment in search and analysis. Essential is whether it occurs in a structured environment with a clear authorization process so that conflicts cannot spin out of control. Also important is that underlying divergences in preferences are not so intense as to yield civil-military alienation and the perverse

---

[9] Note that, although the prominent theme in Eliot Cohen's book stresses the importance of civilian intervention in wartime decision-making, Cohen does also refer to the need for, as he puts it, an "unequal dialogue—a dialogue, in that both sides expressed their views bluntly, indeed, sometimes offensively, and not once but repeatedly—and unequal, in that the final authority of the civilian leader was unambiguous and unquestioned." See Cohen (2002: 247). This theme better captures the primary lesson of the Iraq case.

[10] For a similar conclusion, see Strachan (2006).

dynamics described above. Notably, in case after empirical case in which observers lament the state of civil-military relations, as in the United States under Defense Secretary Rumsfeld, it is the absence of this free-flowing dialogue to which they point. In sum, in the ideal world military and political leaders are actively engaged with one another.

Yet how can political leaders possibly achieve this ideal, given the structural factors often working against it? Some problems seem especially intractable, such as overcoming the dynamics that stem from shared power and high preference divergence between political and military leaders. Yet others may be more amenable to solving. One set of answers, in fact, is implicit in the previous section in which I describe the counterproductive effects some methods of oversight have on strategic assessment. One lesson of the principal-agent literature, on which I draw in that section, is that different "contracts" between actors (that is, principals and agents) are often possible (see, for example, Moe 1989; White 1991; Avant 1994; Feaver 2003).[11] By implication, when they dominate their military chiefs, political leaders may have some latitude in choosing the methods of oversight they impose on their subordinates. Certainly, appointing like-minded individuals to key positions is a powerful mechanism for promoting change (or the status quo) in a hierarchical organization like the military (Janowitz and Little 1974). Keeping dissenters at an arm's distance in advisory processes also prevents debate about unpopular initiatives from getting derailed. Political leaders have powerful incentives to employ these techniques. However, they might instead also select methods that still protect their goals but are less pathological for strategic coordination: that is, that allow for more of the rigorous dialogue prescribed above.

For example, rather than shutting out dissenters and privileging those with whom a leader generally agrees on issues, a political leader might encourage competition among all his or her military chiefs in order to force them to reveal information about each other's perspectives and participate in more rigorous debate.[12] The leader might increase the number of informal advisory forums, maintaining narrow representation in some, but in others giving those the leader is otherwise inclined to marginalize opportunities to voice their opinions. To encourage the latter to do so, the leader might deliberately maintain at least some officers with dissenting voices in

---

[11] In other words, the structure of oversight can differ. Moe (1989), for example, attributes such differences to the particular preferences of politicians, interest groups, and bureaucrats; Feaver (2003: 103, 190–93), to a variety of factors related to the costs of monitoring and payoffs for shirking; Avant (1994), to the number of principals (i.e., as engendered by political institutions) involved.

[12] On the utility of competition in managing agency problems specifically, see Knott and Miller (1987: 259). On competition's advantages, see Sapolsky (1997).

top positions and promote others, thereby lessening the perceived organizational and personal costs to speaking out.

Regardless of the methods employed, in situations where political-military preferences diverge it is unlikely that political leaders can altogether avoid pathologies in assessment given the tension between ensuring operational control in military activity and maintaining the "flexibility and attentiveness" essential to formulating strategy.[13] Yet, the hope is that perhaps they can mitigate some of the worst effects of some political oversight tactics. At the least, leaders might recognize their vulnerability to these flaws in civil-military assessment—they might realize that if they ignore those with whom they disagree, they may get the policies (they think) they want, but in the process shortchange their state's security and undermine their own goals.

Conceptualizing Domestic and International Linkage

Finally, this book has implications for how we conceptualize the relationship between states' internal and external relations. In recent years links between comparative and international politics have received growing theoretical attention.[14] Scholars have become interested in understanding how activities within states bear on their international relations and vice versa. This book advances that effort.

This study suggests three novel causal paths through which civil-military relations and international relations interact. One way is through leaders' information about their military capabilities. Estimates of military capabilities are central to the probability of battlefield success, failure, or stalemate, and the costs likely to be born by both sides in the event of war. They influence states' assessments of what they can expect to win and lose in the event of armed conflict, a critical component in the calculation of power that informs interstate bargaining both before and during war (for examples, see Fearon 1995; Blainey 1973; Wagner 2000). For both fighting wars and maintaining peace, estimates of military capabilities are critical.

Less understood are the sources of poor information about military capabilities. Why, after all, do leaders sometimes have wildly flawed estimates of their capabilities? Why do they believe themselves more powerful than they are, as did Egypt in the 1967 war with Israel? This book identifies one cause of those information failures: states' civil-military relations and their

---

[13] This tension is described in White (1991: 189–90). See also chapter 2.

[14] For a sampling of the variety of work in this area, see Rosecrance and Stein (1993), Trubowitz, Goldman, and Rhodes (1999), Goemans (2000), Bueno de Mesquita and Siverson (1995), Snyder (1991b), Solingen (1998), Spruyt (2005), Reiter and Stam (2002).

effects on the internal evaluation of military capabilities. This is a critical insight for scholars of international relations. If, after all, as Fearon (1995), Levy (1983), and Blainey (1973) argue, war is the result of states making overly ambitious demands of their adversaries when they have poor information about their capabilities, then the reasons they lack reliable information are implicated as causes of war. In other words, "whatever causes that contradictory optimism in nations must be classified as a cause of war itself" (Blainey 1973: 56). By affecting these calculations of power, civil-military relations are one potential cause of war.

This discussion suggests a second conduit through which states' civil-military relations might affect their international relations. As I argue in this book, where military and political leaders share power the authorization process is often rendered ambiguous: It is unclear who retains ultimate rights of approval and veto over security strategy and policy. One of the byproducts of that ambiguity is that it can be difficult for outsiders to "read" a state's decision-making processes and draw inferences about its preferences or resolve in international disputes. This proved a problem in Wilhelmine Germany when, in the final days of the July 1914 crisis, General Moltke sent his fateful telegram urging the Austrians on, even while the kaiser and his chancellor were pursuing a "Halt in Belgrade." The Austrians, faced with competing messages from Berlin, interpreted German preferences in a way that supported their aggressive policies. Conversely, as I described in chapter 6, in a little noted crisis in October 1998 the clarity of the decision-making process in Turkey helped reinforce the credibility of the country's threat to attack Syria if the latter did not end its support for Kurdish rebels. Thus, if influencing uncertainty about a state's own military capabilities is one way civil-military relations affect its international relations, a second is by magnifying (or reducing) uncertainty in other states about the content of its preferences in international crises.

Finally, the book generates insight into a third "problem" in international relations: when states adopt military strategies and take military actions that are poorly linked with their broader political goals. Numerous studies recount the dangers of states that pursue poorly integrated political-military strategies, and especially those that adopt ambitious goals in the international arena without the degree or configuration of military resources to support them. The latter invites a state's self-encirclement and imperial overextension; it catalyzes crises and wars and promotes losses on the battlefield (Snyder 1991b; Posen 1984; Avant 1994; Millett, Murray, and Watman 1988; Brooks 2007b).

Scholars have in the past looked to civil-military relations to explain why states adopt disintegrated policies. The scholarship on the "Cult of the Offensive," for example, focuses on the incentives inherent in offensive doctrines adopted by militaries, and the devastating wars those doctrines invite (Van Evera 1991; Snyder 1991a). Other studies detail the effects of logrolls of military services and atavistic social groups on the pursuit of overly ambitious political strategies (Snyder 1991b). Still others emphasize the impediments divided government or civilian culture clash pose to doctrinal change (Avant 1994; Kier 1997).

This book suggests that civil-military relations might generate disintegration through a different causal pathway. Civil-military relations affect the information about military capabilities and plans available to leaders in formulating their strategies. Where that information is poor and analysis weak, leaders are more likely to select political strategies at odds with their actual capabilities or international constraints. Disintegration can also occur when leaders lack the decision-making prerogatives to force military leaders to modify their activities in support of larger political objectives.

In sum, the book explains how the domestic dimension of civil-military relations, through its effects on how information is analyzed and policy decided within states, shapes their international strategies and relations. Through their effects on strategic assessment, civil-military relations ultimately condition interstate interaction.

REFERENCES

Abdel-Malek, Anouar. 1968. *Egypt: Military Society*. New York: Random House.
Abu Izzeddin, Nejla. 1975/1981. *Nasser of the Arabs: An Arab Assessment*. London: Third World Centre.
Abu-Lughod, Ibrahim, ed. 1970. *The Arab-Israeli Confrontation of June 1967: An Arab Perspective*. Evanston: Northwestern University Press.
Addington, Larry H. 1966. *From Moltke to Hitler: The Evolution of German Military Doctrine, 1865-1939*. Charleston, SC: The Citadel.
———. 1994 *Patterns of War since the Eighteenth Century*. Bloomington: Indiana University Press.
Aguero, Felipe. 1995. *Soldiers Citizens and Democracy: Post-Franco Spain in Comparative Perspective*. Baltimore: Johns Hopkins University Press.
Ajami, Fouad. 1982. "The Open Door Economy: Its Roots and Welfare Consequences." In *The Political Economy of Income Distribution in Egypt*, edited by Gouda Abdel-Kalek and Robert Tignor. London: Holmes and Meir.
Aker, Frank. 1985. *October 1973: The Arab Israeli War*. Hamden, CT: Archon Books.
Albertini, Luigi. 1953. *The Origins of the War of 1914*. Volume 2. London: Oxford University Press.
Ali, Rafaqat. 2000. " 'Hundreds of Soldiers Fell in Kargil': Army Kept Govt in Dark: Nawaz," *Dawn*, June 13.
Alterman, Jon B. 1998. *Sadat and His Legacy: Egypt and the World, 1977-1997*. Washington, DC: Washington Institute for Near East Policy.
Altunisik, Meliha Benli, and Ozlem Tur. 2005. *Turkey: Challenges of Continuity and Change*. London: Routledge.
Amir, Ayaz. 1999. "What Is the Political Leadership Up to." *Dawn*, July 2.
Amos, John W., III. 1979. *Arab-Israeli Political Military Relations: Arab Perceptions and the Politics of Escalation*. Oxford: Pergamon Press.
Ansari, Hamied. 1986. *Egypt: The Stalled Society*. Albany: State University of New York Press.
Aruri, Naseer H. 1975. *Middle East Crucible: Studies on the Arab-Israeli War of October 1973*. Wilmette, IL: Medina University Press.
Atkinson, Rick, and Thomas Ricks. 2003. "Audacious Mission, Awesome Risks." *Washington Post*, March 16.
Auda, Gehad. 1986. "The State of Political Control: The Case of Nasser, 1960-1967." *Arab Journal of the Social Sciences* 2, no. 1, 95–111.
Avant, Deborah D. 1994. *Political Institutions and Military Change*. Ithaca: Cornell University Press.
———. 1996-97. "Are the Reluctant Warriors Out of Control? Why the U.S. Military Is Averse to Responding to Post–Cold War Low Level Threats." *Security Studies* 6, no. 2 (Winter), 51–90.

Ayata, Sencer. 2004. "Changes in Domestic Politics and the Foreign Policy Orientation of the AK Party." In *The Future of Turkish Foreign Policy*, edited by Lenore G. Martin and Dimitris Keridis. Cambridge: MIT Press.

Aykan, Mahmut Bali. 1999. "The Turkish-Syrian Crisis of October 1998: A Turkish View." *Middle East Policy* 6, no. 4 (June), 174–91.

Ayubi, Nazih N. M. 1980. *Bureaucracy & Politics in Contemporary Egypt*. St. Anthony's Middle East Monographs, no. 10. London: Ithaca Press.

———. 1995. *Overstating the Arab State: Politics and Society in the Middle East*. London: I. B. Tauris.

Ayubi, Shaheen. 1994. *Nasser and Sadat*. Lanham, MD: University Press of America.

Bacevich, Andrew. 2004. "A Modern Major General." *New Left Review* 29 (September/October).

Bailey, Sydney D. 1985. *The Making of Resolution 242*. Boston: Martinus Nijhoff Publishers.

Baker, Raymond William. 1978. *Egypt's Uncertain Revolution under Nasser and Sadat*. Cambridge: Harvard University Press.

Bar-Joseph, Uri. 1996. "Rotem: The Forgotten Crisis on the Road to the 1967 War." *Journal of Contemporary History* 31, 547–66.

———. 2005. *The Watchman Fell Asleep: The Surprise of the Yom Kippur War*. Albany: State University of New York Press.

Barnett, Corelli. 1970. *Britain and Her Army, 1509–1970*. New York: William Morrow.

Barnett, Michael. 1992. *Confronting the Costs of War*. Princeton: Princeton University Press.

Bar-Siman-Tov, Yaacov. 1987. *Israel, the Superpowers and the War in the Middle East*. New York: Praeger.

———. 1991. "The Arab-Israeli War of October 1973." In *Avoiding War: Problems of Crisis Management*, edited by Alexander L. George. Boulder: Westview Press.

Bar-Zohar, Michael. 1970. *Embassies in Crisis: Diplomats and Demagogues Behind the Six-Day War*. Englewood Cliffs, NJ: Prentice Hall.

Baurah, Amit. 1998. "Karamat for a New Security Council." *The Hindu*, October 6.

Beattie, Kirk J. 1988. "Egypt: Thirty Five Years of Praetorian Politics." In *Military Disengagement from Politics*, edited by Constantine Danopoulos. London: Routledge.

———. 1994. *Egypt during the Nasser Years*. Boulder: Westview Press.

———. 2000. *Egypt during the Sadat Years*. London: Palgrave.

Becker, Gary S. 1983. "A Theory of Competition among Pressure Groups for Political Influence." *Quarterly Journal of Economics* 98, no. 3 (August), 371–400.

Beckett, Ian. 1991. "Frocks and Brasshats." In *The First World War and British History*, edited by Brian Bond. Oxford: Oxford University Press.

Be'eri, Eliezer. 1970. *Army Officers in Arab Politics and Society*. New York: Praeger.

———. 1976. "The Changing Role of the Military in Egyptian Politics." In *Military and State in Modern Asia*, edited by Harold Z. Schiffren. Jerusalem: Jerusalem Academic Press.

Beg, Mirza Aslam. 1999. "Kargil Withdrawal and 'Rogue Army' Image." *Defense Journal* 3, no. 8 (September).
Belkin, Aaron. 2005. *United We Stand? Divide and Conquer Politics and the Logic of International Hostility.* Albany: State University of New York Press.
Ben Meir, Yehuda. 1995. *Civil-Military Relations in Israel.* New York: Columbia University Press.
Bendor, J. A. Glazer, and T. Hammond. 2001. "Theories of Delegation." *Annual Review of Political Science* 4 (June), 235–69.
Bendor, Jonathan, Serge Taylor, and Roland Van Gaalen. 1987. "Politicians, Bureaucrats and Asymmetric Information." *American Journal of Political Science* 31, no. 4 (November): 796–828.
Bengio, Ofra. 2004. *The Turkish Israeli Relationship.* London: Palgrave.
Bensahel, Nora. 2006. "Mission Not Accomplished: What Went Wrong with Iraqi Reconstruction." *Journal of Strategic Studies* 29, no. 3 (June), 453–73.
Berghahn, Volker R. 1973. *Germany and the Approach of War in 1914.* London: Macmillan.
Betts, Richard K. 1991. *Soldiers, Statesmen and Cold War Crises.* 2d ed. New York: Columbia University Press.
Bhushan, Bharat. 1999. "In the 'Enemy's Country'." In *Guns and Yellow Roses: Essays on the Kargil War.* New Delhi: HarperCollins.
Biddle, Stephen. 2004. *Military Power: Explaining Victory and Defeat in Modern Battle.* Princeton: Princeton University Press.
Biddle, Stephen, and Robert Zirkle. 1996. "Technology, Civil-Military Relations, and Warfare in the Developing World: Conventional Proliferation and Military Effectiveness in Developing States." *Journal of Strategic Studies* 19, no. 2 (June), 171–212.
Bikbayev, Rafael, and Andrei Palaria. 1998. "Syria Denies Explosions on Its Territory Near Turkish Border." ITAR-TASS News Agency, October 11.
Binder. Leonard. 1978. *In a Moment of Enthusiasm.* Chicago: University of Chicago Press.
Birand, Mehmet Ali. 1991. *Shirts of Steel.* London: I. B. Tauris.
Blainey, Geoffrey. 1973. *The Causes of War.* New York: Free Press.
Bond, Brian. 1968. "Soldiers and Statesmen: British Civil-Military Relations in 1917." *Military Affairs* 32, no. 2 (October), 62–75.
———. 1996. "Introduction." In *Government and the Armed Forces in Britain, 1856–1990,* edited by Paul Smith. Rio Grande, OH: Hambledon Press.
Book of the International Symposium on the October 1973 War. Volume 1: *The Military Sector: [Proceedings].* 1976. Cairo, October 28–31, 1975.
Bourne, J. M. 1989. *Britain and the Great War: 1914–1918.* London: Edward Arnold.
Boyer, Peter J. 2002. "A Different War: Is the Army Becoming Irrelevant." *New Yorker,* July 1, 54–67.
Brady, Henry E., and David Collier. 2004. *Rethinking Social Inquiry.* Lanham, PA: Roman and Littlefield.
Brecher, Michael. 1975. *Decisions in Israel's Foreign Policy.* New Haven: Yale University Press.

Brinkley, Joel, and Eric Schmitt. 2003. "Iraqi Leaders Say US Was Warned of Disorder after Hussein, but Little Was Done." *New York Times*, November 30.

Brooks, Risa. 1998. *Political-Military Relations and the Stability of Arab Regimes*. Adelphi Paper, International Institute for Strategic Studies. Oxford: Oxford University Press.

———. 2000. "Institutions at the Domestic/International Nexus: The Political-Military Origins of Strategic Integration, Military Effectiveness and War." Ph.D. dissertation, University of California San Diego.

———. 2002. "Political Strategies of the Military in Democracies," manuscript.

———. 2006. "An Autocracy at War: Explaining Egypt's Military Effectiveness, 1967 and 1973." *Security Studies* 15, no. 3 (July–September), 396–430.

———. 2007a. "Conclusion." In *Creating Military Power: The Sources of Military Effectiveness*, edited by Risa A. Brooks and Elizabeth A. Stanley. Stanford: Stanford University Press.

———. 2007b. "Introduction: The Impact of Culture, Society, Institutions, and International Forces on Military Effectiveness." In *Creating Military Power: The Sources of Military Effectiveness*, edited by Risa A. Brooks and Elizabeth A. Stanley. Stanford: Stanford University Press.

———. 2007c. "Civil-Military Relations and Military Effectiveness: Egypt in the 1967 and 1973 Wars." In *Creating Military Power: The Sources of Military Effectiveness*, edited by Risa A. Brooks and Elizabeth A. Stanley. Stanford: Stanford University Press.

Brown, L. Carl. 1991. "Nasser and the June 1967 War: Plan or Improvisation." In *Quest for Understanding*, edited by S. Seikaly et al. Beirut: American University of Beirut.

Brumberg, Daniel. 1992. "Survival Strategies versus Democratic Bargains: The Politics of Economic Reform in Contemporary Egypt." In *The Politics of Economic Reform in the Middle East*, edited by Henri Barkey. New York: St. Martin's Press.

Bueno de Mesquita, Bruce, and Randolph M. Siverson. 1995. "War and the Survival of Political Leaders." *American Political Science Review* 89, no. 4 (December), 841–55.

Burke, John P., and Fred I. Greenstein. 1989. *How Presidents Test Reality: Decisions on Vietnam, 1954–1965*. New York: Russell Sage Foundation.

Celik, Yasemin. 1999. *Contemporary Turkish Foreign Policy*. Westport, CT: Praeger.

Cheema, Pervaiz Iqbal. 2002. *The Armed Forces of Pakistan*. New York: New York University Press.

Cheema, Zafar Iqbal. 2000. "Pakistan's Nuclear Use Doctrine and Command and Control." In *Planning the Unthinkable: How New Nuclear Powers Will Use Nuclear, Biological and Chemical Weapons*, edited by Peter R. Lavoy, Scott D. Sagan, and James J. Wirtz. Ithaca: Cornell University Press.

Cleveland, William L. 1994. *A History of the Modern Middle East*. Boulder: Westview Press.

Cloughley, Brian. 2000. *A History of the Pakistan Army*. Oxford: Oxford University Press.

Cohen, Eliot. 2002. *Supreme Command: Soldiers, Statesmen, and Leadership in Wartime*. New York: Free Press.

Cohen, Stephen. P. 1984. *The Pakistan Army*. Berkeley: University of California Press.

Colton, Timothy. 1979. *Commissars, Commanders, and Civilian Authority: The Structure of Soviet Military Politics*. Cambridge: Harvard University Press.

———. 1990. "Perspectives on Civil-Military Relations in the Soviet Union." In *Soldiers and the Soviet State*, edited by Timothy J. Colton and Thane Gustafson. Princeton: Princeton University Press.

Coogan, John W., and Peter F. Coogan. 1985. "The British Cabinet and the Anglo-French Staff Talks, 1905–1914: Who Knew What and When Did He Know it." *Journal of British Studies* 24, no. 1 (January), 110–31.

Cooper, Mark. 1979. "The Demilitarization of the Egyptian Cabinet." *International Journal of Middle East Studies* 14, no. 2 (May), 203–25.

Copeland, Dale. 2000. *The Origins of Major War*. Ithaca: Cornell University Press.

Cordesman, Anthony H. 2003. *The Iraq War: Strategy, Tactics and Military Lessons*. Washington, DC: Center for Strategic and International Studies.

Cordesman, Anthony H., and Abraham R. Wagner. 1990. *The Lessons of Modern War, Volume 1: The Arab Israeli Conflicts, 1973–1989*. Boulder: Westview Press.

Corrigan, Gordon. 2003. *Mud, Blood and Poppycock: Britain and the First World War*. London: Cassell.

Coryell, George. 2003. "Tampa's Schoomaker Picked to Head Army." *Tampa Tribune*, June 11.

Craig, Gordon A. 1955. *The Politics of the Prussian Army, 1640–1945*. Oxford: Oxford University Press.

Crane, Conrad C., and W. Andrew Terrill. 2003. *Reconstructing Iraq: Insights, Challenges, and Missions for Military Forces in a Post-Conflict Scenario*. Carlisle Barracks, PA: Strategic Studies Institute.

David, Edward. 1970. "The Liberal Party Divided, 1916–1918." *Historical Journal* 13, no. 3 (September), 509–32.

Dawisha, A. I. 1976. *Egypt in the Arab World*. London: Macmillan.

Deist, Wilhelm. 1982. "Kaiser Wilhelm II in the Context of His Military and Naval Entourage." In *Kaiser Wilhelm II: New Interpretations*, edited by John C. G. Rohl and Nicholaus Sombart. Cambridge: Cambridge University Press.

Dekmejian, R. Hrair. 1971. *Egypt under Nasser: A Study in Political Dynamics*. Albany: State University of New York Press.

———. 1982. "Egypt and Turkey: The Military in the Background." In *Soldiers, Peasants and Bureaucrats*, edited by Roman Kolkowicz and Andrzej Korbonski. London: George Allen and Unwin.

Desch, Michael C. 1999. *Civilian Control of the Military: The Changing Security Environment*. Baltimore: Johns Hopkins University Press.

Dessouki, Ali E. Hillal. 1991. "The Primacy of Economics in the Foreign Policy of Egypt." In *The Foreign Policies of Arab States*, edited by Bahgat Korany and Ali E. Hillal Dessouki. 2d ed. Boulder: Westview Press.

Deutsch, Harold C. 1986. "Military Planning and Foreign Policy: German Overtures to Two World Wars." In *Military Planning in the Twentieth Century, Proceedings of the Eleventh Military History Symposium, 10–12 October 1984*, edited by Harry R. Borowski. Colorado Springs: USAF Academy.

Diamond, Larry. 2004. "What Went Wrong in Iraq." *Foreign Affairs* 83 (September/October), 34–56.

Dixit, J. N. 2002. *India-Pakistan in War and Peace*. London: Routledge.

D'Ombrain, Nicholas. 1973. *War Machinery and High Politics: Defence Administration in Peacetime Britain*. Oxford: Oxford University Press.
Douglas, Roy. 2005. *Liberals: The History of the Liberal and Liberal Democrat Parties*. London: Hambledon and London.
Draper, Theodore. 1967. *Israel and World Politics: Roots of the Third Arab-Israeli War*. New York: Viking Press.
Dugger, Celia W. 1998. "Pakistani Premier Prevails in Clash with General." *New York Times*, October 20.
Dunn, Lewis A., Peter Lavoy, and Scott D Sagan. 2000. "Conclusions: Planning the Unthinkable." In *Planning the Unthinkable: How New Nuclear Powers Will Use Nuclear, Biological and Chemical Weapons*, edited by Peter R Lavoy, Scott D. Sagan, and James J. Wirtz. Ithaca: Cornell University Press.
Dupuy, Trevor. 1977. *A Genius for War: The German Army and the General Staff, 1807–1945*. London: MacDonald and Jane's.
———. 1978. *Elusive Victory: The Arab Israeli Wars, 1947–1974*. New York: Harper and Row.
Eban, Abba. 1977. *Abba Eban: An Autobiography*. New York: Random House.
———. 1992. *Personal Witness: Israel through My Eyes*. London: Jonathan Cape.
Eckstein, Harry. 1975. "Case Studies and Theory in Political Science." In *Handbook of Political Science*. Volume 7, edited by Fred Greenstein and Nelson Polsby. Reading, MA: Addison-Wesley.
Editorial Desk. 2001. "Making Way for Pentagon Reform." *New York Times*, August 20, A16.
Edmonson, George. 2002a. "Defense Overhaul Takes Plenty of Fire." *Atlanta Journal Constitution*, February 9.
———. 2002b. "F-22 Focus of Potential Cuts." *Atlanta Journal Constitution*, May 1, 12A.
Eits, Hermann. 1984. "Defense Planning in Egypt." In *Defense Planning in Less Industrialized States*, edited by Stephanie Neuman. Lexington MA: Lexington Books.
el-Badri, Hassan, Taha el Magdoub, and Mohammad dia el-din Zohdy. 1978. *The Ramadan War, 1973*. New York: Hippocrene Books.
el-Edroos, Syed Ali. 1980. *The Hashemite Arab Army 1908–1979*. Amman, Jordan: The Publishing Committee.
Eley, Geoff, and David Blackbourn. 1984. *The Peculiarities of German History*. Oxford: Oxford University Press.
el-Gamasy, Mohamed Abdel Ghani. 1993. *The October War: Memoirs of Field Marshal el-Gamasy of Egypt*. Cairo: American University in Cairo Press.
Elman, Colin. 2005. "Explanatory Typologies in Qualitative Studies of International Politics." *International Organization* 59, no. 2 (April), 293–326.
el-Shazly, Saad. 1980. *The Crossing of the Suez*. San Francisco: American Mideast Research.
el-Sherif, Ahmed Abou-Zeid. 1995. "The Pattern of Relations between Sadat's Regime and the Military Elite." M.A. thesis, American University in Cairo.
Engel, Mathew. 2003. "War in the Gulf: Scorned General's Tactics Proved Right: Profile Army Chief Sidelined by Rumsfeld." *Guardian*, March 29.

Eralp, Atila. 2004. "Turkey and the European Union." In *The Future of Turkish Foreign Policy*, edited by Lenore G. Martin and Dimitris Keridis. Cambridge: MIT Press.
Etzold, Thomas H. 1986. "JCS Strategic Planning and Vietnam: The Search for an Objective." In *Military Planning in the Twentieth Century, Proceedings of the Eleventh Military History Symposium*, edited by Harry R. Borowski. Colorado Springs: USAF Academy.
Evans, Richard J. 1983. "From Hitler to Bismarck: 'Third Reich' and Kaisserreich in Recent Historiography, Part I." *Historical Journal* 26, no. 2 (June), 485–97.
———. 1987. *Rethinking German History*. London: Allen and Unwin.
Fahmy, Ismail. 1983. *Negotiating for Peace*. Baltimore: Johns Hopkins University Press.
Fallows, James. 2004a. "Blind into Baghdad." *Atlantic Monthly*, January/February.
———. 2004b. Frontline special, "The Invasion of Iraq." Original air date February 26. Transcript available at http://www.pbs.org/wgbh/pages/frontline/programs/2004.html.
———. 2006. *Blind into Baghdad: America's War in Iraq*. New York: Vintage Books.
Farcau, Bruce W. 1994. *The Coup: Tactics in the Seizure of Power*. Westport, CT: Praeger.
———. 1996. *The Transition to Democracy in Latin America: The Role of the Military*. Westport, CT: Praeger.
Farid, Abdel Majid. 1994. *Nasser: The Final Years*. Reading, England: Ithaca Press.
Farrell, Theo. 2001. "Transnational Norms and Military Development: Constructing Ireland's Professional Army." *European Journal of International Relations* 7, no. 1 (March), 63–102.
Faruqui, Ahmad. 2002. "General Musharraf's Management of Pakistan's National Security." *RUSI Journal* 147, no. 1 (February).
———. 2003. *Rethinking the National Security of Pakistan: The Price of Strategic Myopia*. Ashgate.
Fearon, James D. 1995. "Rationalist Explanations for War." *International Organization* 49 (Summer), 379–414.
Feaver, Peter D. 1995. "Civil Military Conflict and the Use of Force." In *U.S. Civil-Military Relations: In Crisis or Transition*, edited by Don Snider and Miranda Carlton-Carew. Washington, DC: Center for Strategic and International Studies.
———. 2003. *Armed Servants: Agency, Oversight, and Civil-Military Relations*. Cambridge: Harvard University Press.
Feaver, Peter D., and Christopher Gelpi. 2004. *Choosing Your Battles*. Princeton: Princeton University Press.
Feaver, Peter D., and Richard H. Kohn. 2001. *Soldiers and Civilians: The Civil-Military Gap and American National Security*. Cambridge: MIT Press.
Ferguson, Niall. 1992. "Germany and the Origins of the First World War: New Perspectives." *Historical Journal* 35, no. 3 (September), 725–52.
Fernandez-Arnesto, Felipe. 1982. *Sadat and His Statecraft*. London: Kensal Press.
Feuchtwanger, Enger, and William J. Philpott. 1996. "Civil-Military Relations in a Period without Major Wars, 1855–85." In *Government and the Armed Forces in Britain, 1856–1990*, edited by Paul Smith. Rio Grande, OH: Hambledon Press.
Finer, Samuel. 1962. *The Man on Horseback*. Middlesex, England: Penguin Books.

Finklestone, Joseph. 1996. *Anwar Sadat: Visionary Who Dared*. London: Frank Cass.
Fischer, Fritz. 1975. *War of Illusions: German Policies from 1911 to 1914*. New York: W. W. Norton.
Fitch, J. Samuel. *The Armed Forces and Democracy in Latin America*. Baltimore: Johns Hopkins University Press, 1998.
Franks, Tommy. 2004. *American Soldier*. New York: Harper Collins.
Frantz, Douglas, 2001. "Military Bestrides Turkey's Path to the European Union." *New York Times*, January 14.
Fraser, Suzan. 1996. "Army-Islamist Rift Reflects Deep Divide in Turkey." Deutsche Presse-Agentur, March 29.
French, David. 1995. *The Strategy of the Lloyd George Coalition*. Oxford: Clarendon Press.
———. 1996. "'A One-Man Show'? Civil-Military Relations during the First World War." In *Government and the Armed Forces in Britain, 1856–1990*, edited by Paul Smith. Rio Grande, OH: Hambledon Press.
French, David, and Brian Holden Reid, eds. 2002. *The British General Staff: Reform and Innovation, 1890–1939*. London: Frank Cass.
Frieden, Jeffrey. 1999. "Actors and Preferences in International Relations." In *Strategic Choice and International Relations*, edited by David A. Lake and Robert Powell. Princeton: Princeton University Press.
Friedberg, Aaron L. 1988. *The Weary Titan: Britain and the Experience of Relative Decline, 1895–1905*. Princeton: Princeton University Press.
Friedlander, Melvin A. 1983. *Sadat and Begin: The Domestic Politics of Peacemaking*. Boulder: Westview Press.
Fry, Michael. 1988. "Political Changes in Britain, August 1914 to December 1916: Lloyd George Replaces Asquith: The Issues Underlying the Drama." *Historical Journal* 31, no. 3 (September): 609–27.
Gacek, Christopher. 1994. *The Logic of Force: The Dilemma of Limited War in American Foreign Policy*. New York: Columbia University Press.
Galvani, John, et al. 1973. "The October War: Egypt, Syria, Israel." *MERIP Reports*, no. 22 (November), 3–21.
Ganguly, Sumit. 2000. "Pakistan's Never Ending Story: Why the October Coup Was No Surprise." *Foreign Affairs* 79, no. 2 (March/April), 2–7.
———. 2001. *Conflict Unending: Indo-Pakistani Tensions since 1947*. New York: Columbia University Press.
Ganguly, Sumit, and Devin Hagerty. 2005. *Fearful Symmetry: India-Pakistan Crises in the Shadow of Nuclear Weapons*. Seattle: University of Washington Press.
Garner, Jay. 2003. Interview in Frontline special, "Truth, War and Consequences: What Went Wrong?" Original air date October 9. Transcript available at http://www.pbs.org/wgbh/pages/frontline/programs/2003.html.
Gartner, Scott. 1997. *Strategic Assessment in War*. New Haven: Yale University Press.
Gawrych, George W. 1987. "The Egyptian High Command in the 1973 War." *Armed Forces and Society* 13, no. 4 (Summer), 535–59.
———. 1991. "The Egyptian Military Defeat of 1967." *Journal of Contemporary History* 26, no. 2 (April), 277–310.

———. 1996. *The 1973 Arab-Israeli War: The Albatross of Decisive Victory*. Leavenworth Papers, no. 21. Fort Leavenworth, KS: U.S. Army Command and Staff College.

———. 2000. *The Albatross of Decisive Victory: War and Policy between Egypt and Israel in the 1967 and 1973 Arab-Israeli Wars*. Westport, CT: Greenwood Press.

Geddes, Barbara, and John Zaller. 1989. "Source of Popular Support for Authoritarian Regimes." *American Journal of Political Science* 33, no. 2 (May), 319–47.

Geiss, Imanuel. 1967. *July 1914: The Outbreak of the First World War*. New York: W. W. Norton.

———. 1976. *German Foreign Policy: 1871–1914*. London: Routledge & Kegan Paul.

George, Alexander. 1980. *Presidential Decision-making in Foreign Policy: The Effective Use of Information and Advice*. Boulder: Westview Press.

———. 1991. "Findings and Recommendations." In *Avoiding War: Problems of Crisis Management*, edited by Alexander George. Boulder: Westview Press.

George, Alexander L., and Andrew Bennett. 2004. *Case Studies and Theory Development in the Social Sciences*. Cambridge: BCSIA Studies in International Security, MIT Press.

Gibney, Frank. 2004. "The General Who Got It Right on Iraq." *Los Angeles Times*, December 26.

Gibson, Christopher P., and Don Snider. 1999. "Civil-Military Relations and the Potential to Influence: A Look at the National Security Decision-making Process." *Armed Forces and Society* 25, no. 2 (Winter), 193–218.

Ginor, Isabella, and Gideon Remez. 2007. *Foxbats over Dimona: The Soviet's Nuclear Gamble in the Six Day War*. New Haven: Yale University Press.

Goemans, H. E. 2000. *War and Punishment: The Cause of War Termination and the First World War*. Princeton: Princeton University Press.

Goerlitz, Walter. 1953. *History of the German General Staff, 1657–1945*. New York: Frederick A. Praeger.

Goertz, Gary, and Harvey Starr. 2003. *Necessary Conditions: Theory, Methodology and Applications*. Oxford: Roman and Littlefield.

Gooch, John. 1968. "The Maurice Debate 1918." *Journal of Contemporary History* 3, no. 4 (October), 211–228.

———. 1974. *The Plans of War: The General Staff and British Military Strategy c. 1900–1916*. London: Routledge and Kegan Paul.

———. 1994. "The Weary Titan: Strategy and Policy in Great Britain, 1890–1918." In *The Making of Strategy: Rulers, States, and War*, edited by Williamson Murray, Macgregor Knox, and Alvin Bernstein. Cambridge: Cambridge University Press.

———. 1995. "The Armed Services." In *The First World War in British History*, edited by Maurice W. Kirby and Mary B. Rose Stephen Constantine. London: Edward Arnold.

———. 1996. "Adversarial Attitudes: Servicemen, Politicians and Strategic Policy, 1899–1914." In *Government and the Armed Forces in Britain, 1856–1990*, edited by Paul Smith. Rio Grande, OH: Hambledon Press.

Gordon, Michael E. 2003. "A New Doctrine's Test." *New York Times*, April 1.

Gordon, Michael R. 2004. "The Strategy to Secure Iraq Did Not Foresee a Second War." *New York Times*, October 19.
Gordon, Michael R., and General Bernard E. Trainor. 2006. *COBRA II: The Inside Story of the Invasion and Occupation of Iraq*. New York: Pantheon.
Gorvett, Jon. 1998. "Turkish Broadside." *The Middle East*, November.
Gresh, Alain. 1998. "Turkish-Israeli-Syrian Relations and Their Impact on the Middle East." *The Middle East Journal* 52, no. 2 (Spring), 188–203.
Hagan, Joe D. 1993. *Political Opposition and Foreign Policy in Comparative Perspective*. London: Lynne Rienner.
Haggard, Stephan, and Robert Kaufman. 1995. *The Political Economy of Democratic Transitions*. Princeton: Princeton University Press.
Hale, William. 1994. *Turkish Politics and the Military*. London: Routledge.
———. 1999. "Foreign Policy and Domestic Politics." In *The Turkish Republic at 75 Years*, edited by David Shankland. Huntingdon, England: Eothen Press.
———. 2000. *Turkish Foreign Policy, 1774–2000*. London. Frank Cass.
———. 2003: "Human Rights, the European Union and the Turkish Accession Process." In *Turkey and the European Union*, edited by Ali Carkoglu and Barry Rubin. London: Frank Cass.
Hamer, W. S. 1970. *The British Army: Civil-Military Relations, 1885–1905*. Oxford: Oxford University Press.
Hammel, Eric. 1992. *Six Days in June*. New York: Scribner's.
Handel, Michael I. 1981. *The Diplomacy of Surprise: Hitler, Nixon, Sadat*. Cambridge: Harvard Center for International Affairs.
———. 1985. "Strategic Surprise: The Politics of Intelligence and Management of Uncertainty." In *Intelligence: Policy and Process*, edited by Alfred Maurer, Marion Tunstall, and James Keagle. Boulder: Westview Press.
———. 1989. *Leaders and Intelligence*. London: Frank Cass.
———. ed. 1976. *Perception, Deception and Surprise: The Case of the Yom Kippur War*. Jerusalem: Hebrew University, Leonard Davis Institute.
Haney, Patrick J. 2002. *Organizing for Foreign Policy Crises*. Ann Arbor: University of Michigan Press.
Hansen, Bent. 1969. *Economic Development in Egypt*. Santa Monica: Rand Corporation.
Haqqani, Husain. 2005. *Pakistan: Between Mosque and Military*. Washington DC: Carnegie Endowment.
Hart, Liddell. 1930. *Real War, 1914–1918*. Boston: Little, Brown.
Hazlehurst, Cameron. 1970. "Asquith as Prime Minister, 1908-1916." *English Historical Review* 85, no. 336 (July), 502–31.
Haykal, Muhammad. 1973. *The Cairo Documents*. New York: Doubleday.
———. 1975. *The Road to Ramadan*. London: William Collins Sons.
———. 1983. *Autumn of Fury*. London: Corgi.
———. 1996. *Secret Channels: The Inside Story of Arab-Israeli Peace Negotiations*. London: HarperCollins Publishers.
Heller, Mark. 1996. "Iraq's Army: Military Weakness, Political Utility." In *Iraq's Road to War*, edited by Amatzia Baram and Barry Rubin. New York: St. Martin's Press.

Heper, Metin, and Aylin Guney. 2000. "The Military and the Consolidation of Democracy: The Recent Turkish Experience." *Armed Forces and Society* 26, no. 4 (Summer), 635–58.

Hermann, Charles, Charles W. Kegley Jr ,and James N. Rosenau, eds. *New Directions in the Study of Foreign Policy*. Boston: Allen and Unwin.

Hersh, Seymour. 2003. "Offense and Defense; the Battle between Donald Rumsfeld and the Pentagon." *New Yorker*, April 7.

Herspring, Dale R. 2005. *The Pentagon and the Presidency*. Lawrence: University Press of Kansas.

Herwig, Holger H. 1988. "The Dynamics of Necessity: German Military Policy during the First World War." In *Military Effectiveness*. Volume 1: *The First World War*, edited by Allan R. Millett and Williamson Murray. Boston: Allen and Unwin.

———. 1994. "Strategic Uncertainties of a Nation-State: Prussia-Germany, 1871–1918." In *The Making of Strategy: Rulers, States, and War*, edited by Macgregor Knox and Williamson Murray Alvin Bernstein. Cambridge: Cambridge University Press.

———. 1997. *The First World War: Germany and Austria Hungary, 1914–1918*. London: Arnold.

———. 2003. "Germany." In *The Origins of World War I*, edited by Richard F. Hamilton and Holger H. Herwig. Cambridge: Cambridge University Press.

Hewitson, Mark. 2000. "German and France before the First World War: A Reassessment of Wilhelmine Foreign Policy." *English Historical Review* 115, no. 462 (June), 570–606.

Hewitson, Mark. 2004. *Germany and the Causes of the First World War*. Oxford: Berg.

Hinnebusch, Raymond A. 1985. *Egyptian Politics under Sadat*. Cambridge: Cambridge University Press.

———. 1991. "National Security." In *Egypt: A Country Study*, edited by Helen Metz. Washington, DC: Federal Research Division, Library of Congress.

Hirst, David, and Irene Beeson. 1981. *Sadat*. London: Faber and Faber.

Hofstadter, Dan. 1973. *Egypt and Nasser, 1967–72*. Volume 3. New York: Facts on File.

Hooker, Gregory. 2005. *Shaping the Plan for Operation Iraqi Freedom*. Washington, DC: Washington Institute for Near East Policy.

Howard, Michael. 1972. *The Continental Commitment*. London: Maurice Temple Smith

Hoyt, Timothy. 2001. "Pakistani Nuclear Doctrine and the Dangers of Strategic Myopia." *Asian Survey* 41, no. 6 (November/December), 956–77.

Hull, Isabel V. 1982. *The Entourage of Kaiser Wilhelm II: 1888–1918*. Cambridge: Cambridge University Press.

Hunter, Wendy. 1995. "Politicians against Soldiers: Contesting the Military in Postauthoritarian Brazil." *Comparative Politics* (July) 27, no. 4, 425–43.

Huntington, Samuel P. 1957. *The Soldier and the State*. Cambridge: Harvard University Press.

———. 1993. *The Third Wave: Democratization in the Late Twentieth Century*. Norman: University of Oklahoma Press.

Husain, Irfan. 2000. "Kargil: The Morning After." *Dawn*, April 29.

Indyk, Martin. 1984. *"To the Ends of the Earth": Sadat's Jerusalem Initiative.* Cambridge: Center for Middle Eastern Studies, Harvard University.
Insight Team of the London Sunday Times. 1974. *The Yom Kippur War.* Garden City, NY: Doubleday.
"Interviews: Kissinger Meets Haikal." 1974. *Journal of Palestine Studies* 3, no. 2, 210–30.
"Iraq: Translating Lessons into Future DoD Policies." 2005. Report and letter dated February 7 to Donald Rumsfeld by the RAND Corporation on lessons from the Iraq War.
Jackson, General Sir William, and Field Marshal Lord Bramall. 1992. *The Chiefs: The Story of the United Kingdom Chiefs of Staff.* London: Brassey's.
Jalland, Patricia, and John Stubbs. 1981. "The Irish Question after the Outbreak of War in 1914: Some Unfinished Party Business." *English Historical Review* 96, no. 381 (October): 778–807.
Janowitz, Morris. 1965. *The Professional Soldier: A Social and Political Portrait.* New York: Free Press.
———. 1977. *Military Institutions and Coercion in the Developing Nations.* 2nd ed. Chicago: University of Chicago Press.
Janowitz, Morris, and Roger W. Little. 1974. *Sociology and the Military Establishment.* Beverly Hills: Sage
Jarausch, Konrad. 1973. "Statesmen versus Structure: Germany's Role in the Outbreak of World War One Reexamined." *Laurentian University Review* 5, no. 3 (June), 133–60.
Jenkins, Gareth, 2001. *Context and Circumstance: The Turkish Military and Politics.* Adelphi paper 337. Oxford: Oxford University Press/International Institute for Strategic Studies.
Johnson, Franklyn Arthur. 1960. *Defence by Committee: The British Committee of Imperial Defence, 1885–1959.* London: Oxford University Press.
———. 1961. "The British Committee of Imperial Defense: Prototype of U.S. Security Organization." *Journal of Politics* 23, no. 2 (May), 231–61.
Joll, James. 1984. *The Origins of the First World War.* London: Longman.
Jones, Owen Bennett. 2002. *Pakistan: Eye of the Storm.* New Haven: Yale University Press.
Kagan, Frederick W. 2004. Frontline special, "The Invasion of Iraq." Original air date February 26. Transcript available at *http://www.pbs.org/wgbh/pages/frontline/programs/2004.html*.
Kaiser, David E. 1983. "Germany and the Origins of the First World War." *Journal of Modern History* 55, no. 3 (September), 442–74.
Kakutani, Michiko. 2006. "All the President's Books (Minding History's Whys and Wherefores)." *New York Times,* May 11.
Kanter, Arnold. 1975. *Defense Politics.* Chicago: University of Chicago Press.
Kamal, Nagib. 1982. "Views of the Egyptian Communists on Sadat's Policies." In *Political and Social Thought in the Contemporary Middle East,* edited by Kemal H. Karpat. Westport, CT: Praeger.
Kapur, Paul. 2004. "The Kargil Conflict and Nuclear Proliferation in South Asia." Paper prepared for the CISAC/US Army War College conference on South Asia and the Nuclear Future, Stanford University, June 4.

———. 2006. *Dangerous Deterrent: Nuclear Weapons Proliferation and Conflict in South Asia*. Stanford: Stanford University Press.
Karabelias, Gerasimos. 2000. "The Evolution of Civil-Military Relations in Postwar Turkey, 1980–95." In *Seventy Five Years of the Turkish Republic*, edited by Sylvia Kedourie. London: Frank Cass.
Karawan, Ibrahim. 1984. "Egypt's Defense Policy." In *Defense Planning in Less Industrialized States*, edited by Stephanie Neuman. Lexington MA: Lexington Books.
———. 1994. "Sadat and the Egyptian-Israeli Peace Revisited." *International Journal of Middle East Studies* 26, no. 2 (May), 249–66.
Kassem, Maye. 2004. *Egyptian Politics: The Dynamics of Authoritarian Rule*. Boulder: Lynne Rienner.
Kebschull, Harvey G. 1994. "Operation 'Just Missed': Lessons from Failed Coup Attempts." *Armed Forces and Society* 20, no. 4 (Summer), 565–79.
Keegan, John C. 1979. *World Armies*. New York: Facts on File.
———. 1999. *The First World War*. London: Pimlico.
———. 2004. *The Iraq War*. New York: Vintage Books
Kehr, Eckart. 1977. *Economic Interest, Militarism, and Foreign Policy: Essays on German History*. Berkeley: University of California Press.
Kennedy, Paul. 1980. *The Rise of the Anglo-German Antagonism*. London: George Allen and Unwin.
———. 1982. "The Kaiser and German Weltpolitik: reflections on Wilhelm II's Place in the Making of German Foreign Policy." In *Kaiser Wilhelm II: New Interpretations*, edited by John C. G. Rohl and Nicholaus Sombart. Cambridge: Cambridge University Press.
———. 1983. *Strategy and Diplomacy 1870–1945*. London: Allen and Unwin.
———. 1988. "Britain in the First World War." In *Military Effectiveness: Volume 1: The First World War*, edited by Allan R. Millett and Williamson Murray. Boston: Allen and Unwin.
Kerr, Malcom H. 1965. *The Arab Cold War, 1958–1964: A Study of Ideology in Politics*. London: Oxford University Press.
———. 1969. *The United Arab Republic: The Domestic Political and Economic Background of Foreign Policy*. Santa Monica: RAND Corporation.
Kier, Elizabeth. 1997. *Imagining War: French and British Military Doctrine between the Wars*. Princeton: Princeton University Press.
Kiewiet, D. Roderick, and Mathew D. McCubbins. 1991. *The Logic of Delegation*. Chicago: University of Chicago Press.
Kimche, David, and Dan Bawly. 1968. *The Sandstorm: The Arab Israeli War of June 1967: Prelude and Aftermath*. London: Secker and Warburg.
Kimche, Jon. 1974. "The Riddle of Sadat." *Midstream* 20, no. 4 (April), 7–28.
King, Gary, Robert Keohane, and Sidney Verba. 1994. *Designing Social Inquiry: Scientific Inference in Qualitative Research*. Princeton: Princeton University Press.
Kinzer, Stephen. 2001. *Crescent and Star*. New York: Farrar, Strauss and Giroux.
Kissinger, Henry. 1979. *White House Years*. Boston: Little, Brown.
———. 1982. *Years of Upheaval*. Boston: Little, Brown.
Kitchen, Martin. 1975. *A Military History of Germany*. Bloomington: Indiana University Press.

Knight, Jack. 1992. *Institutions and Social Conflict*. Cambridge: Cambridge University Press.
Knott, Jack H., and Gary J. Miller. 1987. *Reforming Bureaucracy: The Politics of Institutional Choice*. Englewood Cliffs, NJ: Prentice Hall.
Kochanski, Halik. 2002. "Planning for War in the Final Years for Pax Britannica." In *The British General Staff: Reform and Innovation, 1890–1939*, edited by David French and Brian Holden Reid. London: Frank Cass.
Kohn, Richard. 1993/94. "Out of Control: The Crisis in Civil-Military Relations," *National Interest*, no. 35 (Spring), 3–17.
Kohut, Thomas A. 1982. "Kaiser Wilhelm II and His Parents: An Inquiry into the Psychological Roots of German Policy towards England before the First World War." In *Kaiser Wilhelm II: New Interpretations*, edited by John C. G. Rohl and Nicholaus Sombart. Cambridge: Cambridge University Press.
Koonings, Kees, and Dirk Kruijt. 2002. *Political Armies: The Military and Nation Building in the Age of Democracy*. London: Zed Books.
Krasner, Stephen D. 1991. "Global Communications and National Power: Life on the Pareto Frontier." *World Politics* 43, no. 3 (April), 336–66.
Krepinevich, Andrew F. Jr. 1986. *The Army and Vietnam*. Baltimore: Johns Hopkins University Press.
———. 2003. "On Operation Iraqi Freedom: A First Blush Assessment," testimony before the House Armed Services Committee, October 21.
Krepon, Michael. 2005. "The Stability-Instability Paradox, Misperception, and Escalation-Control in South Asia." In *Prospects for Peace in South Asia*, edited by Rafiq Dossani and Henry S. Rowen. Stanford: Stanford University Press.
Krulak, Victor. 1984. *First to Fight*. Annapolis: Naval Institute Press.
Kubicek, Paul. 2001. "The Earthquake, Europe and Prospects for Political Change in Turkey." *Middle East Review of International Affairs* 5, no. 2 (Summer), 34–47.
Kukreja, Veena. 1985. *Military Intervention in Politics: A Case Study of Politics*. New Delhi: NBO Publishers.
———. 2003. *Contemporary Pakistan*. New Delhi: Sage.
Kumar, Dinesh. 1999. "Secret Tapes Bare the Strategy of a State within a State." *Times of India*, July 12.
Kupchan, Charles. A. 1994. *The Vulnerability of Empire*. Ithaca: Cornell University Press.
Lacouture, Jean. 1973. *Nasser: A Biography*. New York: Alfred A. Knopf.
Langdon, John W. 1991. *July 1914: The Long Debate, 1918–1990*. Oxford: Berg.
Laqueur, Walter. 1969. *The Road to War, 1967*. London: Penguin Books.
Larrabee, F. Stephen, and Ian O. Lesser. 2003. *Turkish Foreign Policy in an Age of Uncertainty*. Santa Monica: RAND Corporation.
Lavoy, Peter, Scott Sagan, and James J. Wirtz, eds. 2000. *Planning the Unthinkable: How New Powers Will Use Nuclear, Biological and Chemical Weapons*. Ithaca: Cornell University Press.
Lawrence, Tony. 1997. "Sharif's Election to Better Indo-Pakistani Ties." Agence France Presse, February 4.
Lebow, Richard Ned. 1981. *Between Peace and War: The Nature of International Crises*. Baltimore: Johns Hopkins University Press.

Legro, Jeffrey. 1995. *Cooperation under Fire: Anglo-German Restraint during World War II.* Ithaca: Cornell University Press.
Leng, Russell. J. 2000. *Bargaining and Learning in Recurring Crises.* Ann Arbor: University of Michigan Press.
Levy, Jack S. 1983. "Misperception and the Causes of War: Theoretical Linkages and Analytical Problems." *World Politics* 36, no. 1 (October), 76–99.
———. 1991. "The Role of Crisis Management in the Outbreak of World War I." In *Avoiding War: Problems of Crisis Management*, edited by Alexander George. Boulder: Westview Press.
Lieberman, Elli. 1994. "The Rational Deterrence Debate: Is the Dependent Variable Elusive?" *Security Studies* 3, no. 3 (Spring), 348–427.
———. 1995. "What Makes Deterrence Work? Lessons from the Egyptian-Israeli Enduring Rivalry." *Security Studies* 4, no. 4 (Summer), 851–910.
Lippman, Thomas. 1989. *Egypt after Nasser.* New York: Paragon House.
Lobell, Steven E. 1999. "Second Image Reversed: Britain's Choice of Free Trade or Imperial Preferences, 1903–1906, 1917–1923, 1930–1932." *International Studies Quarterly* 43, 671–694.
Lodhi, Maleena. 1999. "The Kargil Crisis: Anatomy of a Debacle." *Newsline* (July).
Loeb, Vernon, and Thomas Ricks. 2002. "Rumsfeld's Style, Goals Strain Ties in Pentagon." *Washington Post*, October 16.
Lombardi, Ben. 1997. "Turkey—the Return of the Reluctant Generals." *Political Science Quarterly* 112, no. 2 (Summer), 191–215.
Loveman, Brian. 1993. *The Constitution of Tyranny: Regimes of Exception in Spanish America.* Pittsburgh: University of Pittsburgh Press.
Luttwak, Edward N. 1968. *Coup d' Etat: A Practical Handbook.* Cambridge: Harvard University Press.
McDermott, Anthony. 1988. *Egypt from Nasser to Mubarak: A Flawed Revolution.* London: Croom Helm.
McDermott, J. 1979. "The Revolution in British Military Thinking from the Boer War to the Moroccan Crisis." In *The War Plans of the Great Powers*, edited by Paul Kennedy. Boston: Unwin Hyman.
McDermott, Rose. 2004. *Political Psychological in International Relations.* Ann Arbor: University of Michigan Press.
MacKintosh, John P. 1962. "The Role of the Committee of Imperial Defense before 1914." *English Historical Review* 77, no. 304 (July), 490–503.
McManus, Doyle, and Esther Schrader. 2003. "War with Iraq/Policy." *Los Angeles Times*, April 2.
McMaster, H. R. 1997. *Dereliction of Duty: Lyndon Johnson, Robert McNamara, the Joint Chiefs of Staff, and the Lies That Led to Vietnam.* New York: HarperCollins.
Mahmood, Zahid. 1985. "Sadat and Camp David Reconsidered." *Journal of Palestine Studies* 15, no. 1 (Autumn), 62–87.
Mahoney, James. 2003. "Strategies of Causal Assessment in Comparative Historical Analysis." In *Comparative Historical Analysis in the Social Sciences*, edited by James Mahoney and Dietrich Rueschemeyer. Cambridge: Cambridge University Press.
Mahoney, James, and Gary Goertz. 2006. "A Tale of Two Cultures: Contrasting Quantitative and Qualitative Research." Manuscript.

Mansoor, Menahem, ed. 1972. *Political and Diplomatic History of the Arab World, 1900–1967*. Volume 5: *1965–1967*. Madison: University Of Wisconsin Press.
March, James G., and Johan P. Olsen. 1984. "The New Institutionalism: Organizational Factors in Political Life." *American Political Science Review* 78, no. 3 (September), 734–49.
Maurice, Major-General Sir Frederick. 1972. "Intrigues of the War." In *The Maurice Case*, edited by Nancy Maurice. London: Leo Cooper.
Mazari, Shireen M. 2000. "Re-examining Kargil." *Defense Journal* 3, no. 11 (June).
Mazzetti, Mark, and Jim Rutenberg. 2006. "Pentagon Memo Aims to Counter Rumsfeld Critics." *New York Times*, April 16.
Mendenhall, Robert. 2005. *Pre-War Planning for a Post-War Iraq*. Carlisle Barracks, PA: U.S. Army War College.
Meital, Yoram. 1997. *Egypt's Struggle for Peace*. Gainesville: University Press of Florida.
Millett, Allan R., Williamson Murray, and Kenneth H. Watman. 1988. "The Effectiveness of Military Organizations." In *Military Effectiveness*. Volume 1: *The First World War*, edited by Allan R. Millett and Williamson Murray. Boston: Allen and Unwin.
Miller, Gary. 1992. *Managerial Dilemmas*. Cambridge: Cambridge University Press.
Moe, Terry M. 1989. "The Politics of Bureaucratic Structure." In *Can the Government Govern?* edited by John E. Chubb and Paul E. Peterson. Washington, DC: Brookings.
———. 1995. "The Politics of Structural Choice: Toward a Theory of Public Bureaucracy" In *Organization Theory: From Chester Barnard to the Present and Beyond*, edited by Oliver E. Williamson. Oxford: Oxford University Press.
———. 2005. "Power and Political Institutions." *Perspectives on Politics* 3, no. 2 (June), 215–33.
Mohi El Din, Khaled. 1995. *Memories of a Revolution, Egypt 1952*. Cairo: American University Press.
Mombauer, Annika. 2001. *Helmuth von Moltke and the Origins of the First World War*. Cambridge: Cambridge University Press.
———. 2002. *The Origins of the First World War: Controversies and Consensus*. London: Pearson Education.
———. 2005. "Of War Plans and War Guilt: The Debate Surrounding the Schlieffen Plan." *Journal of Strategic Studies* 28, no. 5 (October), 751–63.
Mommsen, Wolfgang J. 1973. "Domestic Factors in German Foreign Policy 1914." *Central European History* 6, no. 1, 3–43.
———. 1990. "Kaiser Wilhelm II and German Politics." *Journal of Contemporary History* 25, no. 2/3 (May–June), 289–316.
Mor, Bed D. 1991. "Nasser's Decision-making in the 1967 Middle East Crisis: A Rational Choice Explanation." *Journal of Peace Research* 28, 359–76.
Morrow, James D. 1994. "Modeling the Forms of International Cooperation: Distribution versus Information." *International Organization* 48, no. 3, 387–423.
Mufson, Steve. 1998. "Indian Tests Pose 'Difficult Choice' for Pakistan, Even in Nuclear Choice." *Washington Post*, May 18.

Muftuler-Bac, Meltem. 1999. "The Never-Ending Story: Turkey and the European Union." In *Turkey Before and After Ataturk: Internal and External Affairs*, edited by Sylvia Kedourie. Portland, OR: Frank Cass.

Murdock, Clark (principal investigator). 2004. *Beyond Goldwater-Nichols*. Washington DC: Center for Strategic and International Studies.

Murray, Williamson. 1984. *The Change in the European Balance of Power, 1938-1939*. Princeton: Princeton University Press.

Murray, Williamson, and Mark Grimsley. 1994. "Introduction: On Strategy." In *The Making of Strategy: Rulers, States and War*, edited by Williamson Murray, MacGregor Knox, and Alvin Bernstein. Cambridge: Cambridge University Press.

Nassif, Ramses. 1988. *U Thant in New York, 1961-1971*. London: C. Hurst.

Neff, Donald. 1988. *Warriors against Israel*. Vermont: Amana Books.

Newbold, Gregory. 2006. "Why Iraq Was a Mistake." *Time*, April 9.

Nordlinger, Eric A. 1977. *Soldiers in Politics: Military Coups and Governments*. Englewood Cliffs, NJ: Prentice Hall.

Nun, Jose. 1967. "The Middle Class Military Coup." In *The Politics of Conformity in Latin America*, edited by Claudio Veliz. Oxford: Oxford University Press.

Nutting, Anthony. 1972. *Nasser*. London: Constable.

Odell, John. S. 2006. "A Major Milestone with One Major Limitation." *Qualitative Methods* (Newsletter of APSA Organized Section), 4, no. 1 (Spring).

O'Donnell, Guillermo A. 1973. *Modernization and Bureaucratic-Authoritarianism: Studies in South American Politics*. Berkeley: Institute of International Studies, University of California.

O'Donnell, Guillermo A., Philippe C. Schmitter, and Laurence Whitehead, eds. 1986. *Transitions from Authoritarian Rule: Latin America*. Baltimore: Johns Hopkins University Press.

O'Hanlon, Michael E. 2004-05. "Iraq without a Plan." *Policy Review*, no. 128 (December/January).

Olson, Robert. 2001. "Turkey-Syria Relations, 1997-2000: Kurds, Water, Israel and 'Undeclared War'." *Orient* 42: 101-17.

Oneal, John R. 1982. *Foreign Policy-making in Times of Crisis*. Columbus: Ohio State University Press.

Oren, Michael B. 2002. *Six Days of War: June 1967 and the Making of the Modern Middle East*. New York: Oxford University Press.

Orren, Karen, and Stephen Skowronek. 1994. "Beyond the Iconography of Order: Notes for a New Institutionalism." In *The Dynamics of American Politics*, edited by L. C. Dodd and C. Jillson. Boulder: Westview Press.

Owen, Richard. 1978. "Military-Industrial Relations: Krupp and the Imperial Navy Office." In *Society and Politics in Wilhelmine Germany*, edited by Richard J. Evans. London: Croom Helm.

Ozbudun, Ergun. 2000. *Contemporary Turkish Politics*. Boulder: Lynne Rienner.

Ozcan, Gencer. 2001. "The Military and the Making of Foreign Policy." In *Turkey in World Politics: An Emerging Multiregional Power*, edited by Barry Rubin and Kemal Kirisci. Boulder: Lynne Rienner Press.

Pace, Eric, 1967a. "Egypt Releasing 1000 Arrested after '65 Plot." *New York Times*, November 11.

———. 1967b. "Nasser Says He Is Resigning, but Assembly Rejects Action; Forces of Israel Invade Syria." *New York Times*, June 10.
Packer, George. 2003. "War after the War." *New Yorker*, November 24.
Packer, George. 2005. *The Assassins' Gate: America in Iraq*. New York: Farrar, Straus and Giroux.
Packer, Ian. 1998. *Lloyd George*. New York: St. Martin's Press.
Palmer, Bruce. 1984. *The 25-Year War*. Lexington: University of Kentucky Press.
Palmer, Monte. 1960. "The United Arab Republic: An Assessment of Its Failure." *Middle East Studies* 20.
Palmer, Monte, Leila Ali, and Yasin al-Sayyid. 1988. *The Egyptian Bureaucracy*. Syracuse: Syracuse University Press.
Parker, Richard B. 1992a. "The June 1967 War: Some Mysteries Explored." *Middle East Journal* 46 (Spring), 177–98.
———. 1992b. "The June War: Whose Conspiracy?" *Journal of Palestine Studies* 21, no. 4 (Summer), 5–21.
———. 1993. *The Politics of Miscalculation in the Middle East*. Bloomington: Indiana University Press.
———. 1996. *The Six Day War, a Retrospective*. Gainesville: University Press of Florida.
———. 2001. *The October War: A Retrospective*. Gainesville: University Press of Florida.
Peceny, Mark, et al. 2002. "Dictatorial Peace?" *American Political Science Review* 96, no. 1 (March), 15–26.
Perlmutter, Amos. 1974. *Egypt: The Praetorian State*. New Brunswick: Transaction Books.
———. 1977. *The Military and Politics in Modern Times: On Professionals, Praetorians and Revolutionary Soldiers*. New Haven: Yale University Press.
Peterson, Steve W. 2004. "Central but Inadequate: The Application of Theory in Operation Iraqi Freedom." Manuscript, National War College, Washington, DC, available at http://handle.dtic.mil/100.2/ADA441663.
Phillips, David L. 2005. *Losing Iraq: Inside the Postwar Reconstruction Fiasco*. Boulder: Westview Press.
Phillips, Kate, Shane Lauth, and Eric Schenck. 2006. *U.S. Military Operations in Iraq: Planning, Combat and Occupation*. Carlisle Barracks, PA: U.S. Army War College Strategic Studies Institute.
Philpott, William J. 1996. "The Campaign for a Ministry of Defence, 1919–36." In *Government and the Armed Forces in Britain, 1856–1990*, edited by Paul Smith. Rio Grande, OH: Hambledon Press.
———. 2002. "The General Staff and the Paradoxes of Continental War." In *The British General Staff: Reform and Innovation, 1890–1939*, edited by David French and Brian Holden Reid. London: Frank Cass.
Pierson, Paul, and Theda Skocpol. 2002. "Historical Institutionalism in Contemporary Political Science." In *Political Science: The State of the Discipline*, edited by Ira Katznelson and Helen V. Milner. New York: W. W. Norton.
Pion-Berlin, David. 1992. "Military Autonomy in Emerging Democracies in South America." *Comparative Politics* 25, no. 1 (October), 83–102.

———. 1997. *Through Corridors of Power: Institutions and Civil-Military Relations in Argentina*. University Park: Pennsylvania State University Press.

———. ed. 2001. *Civil-Military Relations in Latin America: New Analytical Perspectives*. Chapel Hill: University of North Carolina Press.

Podeh, Elie, and Onn Winckler. 2004. *Rethinking Nasserism: Revolution and Historical Memory in Egypt*. Gainesville: University Press of Florida.

Pollack, Kenneth. 1998. "Egyptian National Security." In *Sadat and His Legacy: Egypt and the World, 1977–1997*, edited by Jon B. Alterman. Washington, DC: Washington Institute for Near East Policy.

———. 2002. *Arabs at War; Military Effectiveness 1948–1991*. Lincoln: University of Nebraska Press.

Posen, Barry. 1984. *The Sources of Military Doctrine*. Ithaca: Cornell University Press.

Powell Walter W., and Paul J. DiMaggio, eds. 1991. *The New Institutionalism in Organizational Analysis*. Chicago: University of Chicago Press.

Powell, Colin. 1992/93. "US Forces: Challenges Ahead." *Foreign Affairs* 71, no. 5 (Winter), 32–45.

Press, Daryl. 2005. *Calculating Credibility: How Leaders Evaluate Military Threats*. Ithaca: Cornell University Press.

Przeworski, Adam. 1991. *Democracy and the Market*. Cambridge: Cambridge University Press.

Pugh, Martin. 1988. *Lloyd George*. New York: Longman.

———. 1993. *The Making of Modern British Politics*. Oxford: Blackwell.

———. 1994. *State and Society: British Political and Social History, 1870–1992*. London: Edward Arnold.

———. 1995. "Domestic Politics." In *The First World War in British History*, edited by Maurice W. Kirby, Stephen Constantine, and Mary B. Rose. London: Edward Arnold.

Purdum, Todd S. 2003. "Rumsfeld's Imperious Style Turns Combative." *New York Times*, March 30.

———. 2004. Frontline special, "The Invasion of Iraq." Original air date February 26. Transcript available at *http://www.pbs.org/wgbh/pages/frontline/programs/2004.html*.

Qadir, Shaukat. 2002. "An Analysis of the Kargil Conflict 1999." *RUSI Journal* 17, no. 2 (April).

Quandt, William B. 1993. *Peace Process: American Diplomacy and the Arab-Israeli Conflict since 1967*. Washington, DC: Brookings Institution.

Rabin, Yitzak. 1979. *The Rabin Memoirs*. Boston: Little, Brown.

Rabinovich, Abraham. 2004. *The Yom Kippur War: The Epic Encounter That Transformed the Middle East*. New York: Schocken Books

Radu, Michael S., ed. 2003. *Dangerous Neighborhood: Contemporary Issues in Turkey's Foreign Relations*. New Brunswick, NJ: Transaction.

Rahmy, Ali Abdel Rahman. 1983. *Egyptian Policy in the Arab World: Intervention in Yemen 1962–67*. Washington, DC: University Press of America.

Rapoport, David C. "The Praetorian Army: Insecurity, Venality and Impotence." In *Soldiers, Peasants and Bureaucrats*, edited by Roman Kolkowicz and Andrzej Korbonski. London: Allen and Unwin.

Rashid, Ahmed. 1997. "Sharif Stages Constitutional Coup." *Daily Telegraph*, April 10.
———. 1999. "Pakistan's Coup: Planting the Seeds of Democracy." *Current History* 98, no. 632 (December), 409–14.
Rathmell, Andrew. 2005. "Planning Post-conflict Reconstruction in Iraq: What Can We Learn?" *International Affairs* 81, no. 5 (October), 1013–38.
Reich, Bernard. 1995. *Arab-Israeli Conflict and Conciliation*. Westport, CT: Greenwood Press.
Reiter, Dan. 2003. "Exploring the Bargaining Model of War." *Perspectives on Politics* 1, no. 1.
Reiter, Dan, and Allan Stam. 2002. *Democracies at War*. Princeton: Princeton University Press.
Rejwan. Nissim. 1974. *Nasserist Ideology: Its Exponents and Critics*. New York: John Wiley and Sons.
Remmer, Karen. 1989. *Military Rule in Latin America*. Boston: Unwin Hyman.
Reston, James. 1967. "Struggle for Control in Cairo Seen Behind Nasser's Move," *New York Times*, June 10, 1967, p. 1.
Riad, Mahmoud. 1981. *The Struggle for Peace in the Middle East*. London: Quartet Books.
Ricks, Thomas E. 2001a. "For Rumsfeld, Many Road-blocks." *Washington Post*, August 7.
———. 2001b. "Review Fractures Pentagon." *Washington Post*, July 14.
———. 2001c. "Rumsfeld, Joint Chiefs Spar over Roles in Retooling Military." *Washington Post*, May 25.
———. 2001d. "Rumsfeld on High Wire of Defense Reform." *Washington Post*, May 20.
———. 2001e. "Rumsfeld's Hands-on War." *Washington Post*, December 9.
———. 2002a. "Military Bids to Postpone Iraq Invasion." *Washington Post*, May 24.
———. 2002b. "Some Top Military Brass Favor Status Quo in Iraq." *Washington Post*, July 28.
Ricks, Thomas. 2003. "Rumsfeld Stands Tall after Iraq Victory." *Washington Post*, April 20.
———. 2004a. Interview in PBS Frontline special, "The Invasion of Iraq." Original air date February 26. Transcript available at *http://www.pbs.org/wgbh/pages/frontline/programs/2004.html*.
———. 2004b. Interview in PBS Frontline special, "Rumsfeld's War." Original air date October 26. Available at *http://www.pbs.org/wgbh/pages/frontline/programs/2004.html*.
———. 2005. "Pentagon Blamed for Lack of Postwar Planning in Iraq." *Washington Post*, April 1.
———. 2006. *Fiasco*. New York: Penguin Press.
Ricks, Thomas E., and Vernon Loeb. 2003. "Iraq Takes a Toll on Rumsfeld." *Washington Post*, September 14.
Rieff, David. 2003. "Blueprint for a Mess." *New York Times*, November 2.
Riker, William. 1980. "Implications from the Disequilibrium of Majority Rule for the Study of Institutions." *American Political Science Review* 74, 432–47.
Rikhye, Indar Jit. 1980. *The Sinai Blunder: Withdrawal of the United Nations Emergency Force Leading to the Six Day War of June 1967*. London: Frank Cass.

Ritter, Gerhard. 1970. *The Sword and the Scepter.* Miami: University of Miami Press.
———. 1958. *The Schlieffen Plan: Critique of a Myth.* New York: Praeger.
Rizvi, Hasan-Askari. 2000. *Military, State and Society in Pakistan.* New York: St. Martin's Press.
———. 2003. "The Pakistan Military: A Bibliographical Study." In *Pakistan at the Millennium,* edited by Charles H. Kennedy et al. Oxford: Oxford University Press.
Robins, Philip. 2003. *Suits and Uniforms: Turkish Foreign policy since the Cold War.* Seattle: University of Washington Press.
Roeder, Philip G. 1993. *Red Sunset: The Failure of Soviet Politics.* Princeton: Princeton University Press.
Rogowski, Ronald. 1989. *Commerce and Coalitions.* Princeton: Princeton University Press.
Rohl, John C. G. 1969. "Admiral von Muller and the Approach of War, 1911–1914." *Historical Journal* 12, no. 4 (December), 651–73.
———. 1994. *The Kaiser and His Court.* Cambridge: Cambridge University Press.
Rohl, John C. G., and Nicholaus Sombart, editors. 1982. *Kaiser Wilhelm II: New Interpretations.* Cambridge: Cambridge University Press.
Rosecrance, Richard, and Arthur A. Stein, eds. 1993. *The Domestic Bases of Grand Strategy.* Ithaca: Cornell University Press.
Rosen, Stephen Peter. 1996. *Societies and Military Power.* Ithaca: Cornell University Press.
———. 2005. *War and Human Nature.* Princeton: Princeton University Press.
Rouleau, Eric. 2000. "Turkey's Dream of Democracy." *Foreign Affairs* 79, no. 6 (November/December), 100–14.
"Rumsfeld Did Not Intimidate Joint Chiefs, Ex-Chairman Says." Associated Press, April 17, 2006.
Sadat, Anwar. 1978. *In Search of Identity.* New York: Harper and Row.
"Sadat's Power Base." *Journal of Palestine Studies* 7, no. 2 (Winter), 159–61.
Sadowski, Yahya. 1991. *Political Vegetables? Businessman and Bureaucrat in the Development of Egyptian Agriculture.* Washington, DC: Brookings Institution.
Safran, Nadav. 1969. *From War to War: The Arab-Israeli Confrontation, 1948–1967.* New York: Bobbs-Merrill.
Safty, Adel. 1991. "Sadat's Negotiations with the United States and Israel: From Sinai to Camp David." *American Journal of Economics and Sociology* 50, no. 3 (July), 285–98.
St. John, Robert. 1960. *The Boss: The Story of Gamal Abdel Nasser.* New York: McGraw Hill.
Sagan, Scott D. 1986. "1914 Revisited: Allies, Offense and Instability." *International Security* 11, no. 2 (Fall), 161–64.
———. 1994. "The Perils of Proliferation: Organization Theory, Deterrence Theory and the Spread of Nuclear Weapons." *International Security* 18, no. 4 (Spring), 66–107.
———. 1996–97. "Why Do States Build Nuclear Weapons: Three Models in Search of a Bomb." *International Security* 21, no. 3 (Winter), 54–86.
———. 2000. "The Origins of Military Doctrine and Command and Control Systems." In *Planning the Unthinkable: How New Nuclear Powers Will Use Nuclear,*

Biological and Chemical Weapons, edited by Peter R. Lavoy, Scott D. Sagan, and James J. Wirtz. Ithaca: Cornell University Press.

Sagan, Scott D., and Kenneth N. Waltz. 2003. *The Spread of Nuclear Weapons: A Debate Renewed.* New York: W. W. Norton.

Sakallioglu, Umit Cizre. 1997. "The Anatomy of the Turkish Military's Political Autonomy." *Comparative Politics* 29, no. 2 (January), 151–66.

Sapolsky, Harvey M. 1997. "Interservice Competition: The Solution, Not the Problem." *Joint Forces Quarterly*, no. 15 (Spring), 50–53.

Schepsle, Kenneth A. 1989. "Studying Institutions: Some Lessons from the Rational Choice Approach." *Journal of Theoretical Politics* 1, no. 2.

Schmidt, Gustav. 1990. "Contradictory Postures and Conflicting Objectives: The July Crisis." In *Escape into War?*, edited by Gregor Schollgen. Oxford: Berg.

Schofield, Julian. 2000. "Militarized Decision-making for War in Pakistan: 1947–1971." *Armed Forces in Society* 27, no. 1 (Fall), 131–48

Schollgen, Gregor. 1990. "Introduction: The Theme Reflected in Recent German Research." In *Escape into War?*, edited by Gregor Schollgen. Oxford: Berg.

Schultz, Kenneth A. 2001. *Democracy and Coercive Diplomacy.* Cambridge: Cambridge University Press.

Sechser, Todd. 2004. "Are Soldiers Less War Prone Than Statesmen?" *Journal of Conflict Resolution* (October).

Segev, Tom. 2007. *1967: Israel, the War, and the Year That Transformed the Middle East.* New York: Metropolitan Books.

Shafqat, Saeed. 1997. *Civil-Military Relations in Pakistan.* Boulder: Westview Press.

Shamir, Shimon. 1998. "Sadat's Strategy and Legacy." In *Sadat and His Legacy: Egypt and the World, 1977–1997*, edited by Jon B. Alterman. Washington, DC: Washington Institute for Near East Policy.

Shane, Scott. 2006. "Civilians Reign over U.S. Military by Tradition and Design." *New York Times*, April 16.

Shanker, Thom. 2004. "In Memoir, U.S. General Tells of Gaps in War Plans." *New York Times*, August 1.

Shanker, Thom, and Eric Schmitt. 2003. "Rumsfeld Seeks Consensus through Jousting." *New York Times*, March 19.

Sharp, U. S. Grant. 1978. *Strategy for Defeat.* San Rafael, CA: Presidio Press.

Shinseki, Eric. 2003. "The Fiscal Year 2004 Defense Budget." Testimony at Hearing of the Senate Armed Services Committee, February 25.

Shlaim, Avi . 1976. "Failures in National Intelligence Estimates: The Case of the Yom Kippur War." *World Politics* 28, no. 3 (April), 348–80.

Shoukri, Ghali. 1981. *Portrait of a President.* London: Zed Press.

Sicker, Martin. 2001. *The Middle East in the Twentieth Century.* Westport, CT: Praeger.

Simpson, Keith. 1991. "The Reputation of Sir Douglas Haig." In *The First World War and British History*, edited by Brian Bond. Oxford: Oxford University Press.

Singer, Stacey, and Christy McKerney. 2000. "Overseas Ballots Get Turn—Usually Overlooked—They Could Hold Key." *Pittsburgh Post Gazette*, November 17.

Singh, Jasit. 1999. *Kargil 1999: Pakistan's Fourth War for Kashmir.* New Delhi: Knowledge World.

Slevin, Peter, and Dana Priest. 2003., "Wolfowitz Concedes Iraq Errors." *Washington Post*, July 24.
Snider, Don, and Miranda Carlton-Carew, eds. 1995. *U.S. Civil-Military Relations: In Crisis or Transition*. Washington, DC: Center for Strategic and International Studies.
Snyder, Jack. 1991a. "Civil-Military Relations and the Cult of the Offensive, 1914 and 1984." In *Military Strategy and the Origins of the First World War*, edited by Steven E. Miller. Princeton: Princeton University Press.
———. 1991b. *Myths of Empire: Domestic Politics and International Ambition*. Ithaca: Cornell University Press.
Solingen, Etel. 1998. *Regional Orders at Century's End*. Princeton: Princeton University Press.
Spears, Sir Edward. 1972. "An Appreciation." In *The Maurice Case*, edited by Nancy Maurice. London: Leo Cooper.
Springborg, Robert. 1975. "Patterns of Association in the Egyptian Political Elite." In *Political Elites in the Middle East*, edited by George Lenczowski. Washington, DC: American Enterprise Institute.
———. 1979. "Patrimonialism and Policy Making in Egypt: Nasser and Sadat and the Tenure Policy for Reclaimed Lands." *Middle Eastern Studies* 15, no. 1 (January), 49–69.
Sprinz, Detlef, and Yael Wolinksy-Nahmias, eds. 2004. *Models, Numbers and Cases: Methods for Studying International Relations*. Ann Arbor: University of Michigan Press.
Spruyt, Hendrik. 2005. *Ending Empire: Contested Sovereignty and Territorial Partition*. Ithaca: Cornell University Press.
"Statement by Shams Badran on Events Preceding the June War of 1967." 1968. *Al-Ahram*, February 2. Reprinted *in International Documents on Palestine, 1969*, edited by Zuhari Diab. Beirut: Institute for Palestine Studies, 1971, documents 298, 319–22.
Stein, Janice Gross. 1980. "'Intelligence' and 'Stupidity' Reconsidered: Estimation and Decision in Israel, 1973." *Journal of Strategic Studies* 3, no. 1, 147–77.
———. 1991. "The Arab-Israeli War of 1967: Inadvertent War through Miscalculated Escalation." In *Avoiding War: Problems of Crisis Management*, edited by Alexander George. Boulder: Westview Press.
———. 1996. "Deterrence and Learning in an Enduring Rivalry: Egypt and Israel, 1948–73." *Security Studies* 6, no. 1 (Autumn), 104–52.
Stein, Janice Gross, and Raymond Tanter. 1980. *Rational Decision-making: Israel's Security Choices*. Columbus: Ohio State University Press.
Stein, Kenneth W. 1999. *Heroic Diplomacy: Sadat, Kissinger, Carter, Begin and the Quest for Arab-Israeli Peace*. New York: Routledge.
Steiner, Zara S., and Keith Neilson. 2003. *Britain and the Origins of the First World War*. 2d ed. Basingstoke: Palgrave Macmillan.
Steinmo, Sven, Kathleen Thelen, and Frank Longstreth. 1992. *Structuring Politics: Historical Institutionalism in Comparative Analysis*. Cambridge: Cambridge University Press.
Stepan, Alfred. 1988. *Re-Thinking Military Politics*. Princeton: Princeton University Press.

Stephens, Robert. 1971. *Nasser: A Political Biography.* New York: Simon and Schuster.
Stevenson, Charles A. 2006. *Warriors and Politicians: U.S. Civil-Military Relations under Stress.* London: Routledge.
Stevenson, David. 1997. *The Outbreak of the First World War.* New York: St. Martin's Press.
Stork, Joe. 1978. "Sadat's Desperate Mission." MERIP Reports no. 64 (February), 3–16.
Strachan, Hew. 1997. *The Politics of the British Army.* Oxford: Oxford University Press.
———. 2002. "The British Army, Its General Staff and the Continental Commitment." In *The British General Staff: Reform and Innovation, 1890–1939,* edited by David French and Brian Holden Reid. London: Frank Cass.
———. 2006. "Making Strategy: Civil-Military Relations after Iraq." *Survival* 48, no. 3 (Autumn), 59–82.
Summers, Harry. 1982. *On Strategy.* Novato, CA: Presidio Press.
Suttie, Andrew. 2005. *Rewriting the First World War.* Basingstoke: Palgrave Macmillan.
Sweetman, John. 1986. "Historical Perspective: From Waterloo to the Curragh." In *Sword and Mace,* edited by John Sweetman. London: Brassey's Defence Publishers.
———. 2002. " 'Selection by Disparagement': Lord Esher, the General Staff and the Politics of Command." In *The British General Staff: Reform and Innovation, c. 1890–1939,* edited by David French and Brian Holden Reid. London: Frank Cass.
Syed, Anwar H. 1998. "Pakistan in 1997." *Asian Survey* 38, no. 2 (February), 116–25.
Taylor, A.J.P. 1965. *Politics in Wartime and other essays.* New York: Atheneum.
Taylor, Brian. 2003. *Politics and the Russian Army: Civil-Military Relations, 1689–2000.* Cambridge: Cambridge University Press.
Tensoro, Jose Manuel, and Shahid Ur-Rehman. 1997. "The Watchers." *Asiaweek,* August 8, 41.
Terraine, J. 1963. *Douglas Haig: The Educated Soldier.* London: Cassell.
Thelen, Kathleen. 1999. "Historical Institutionalism in Comparative Politics." *The Annual Review of Political Science* 2:369–404.
Third Infantry Division After Action Report; Operation Iraqi Freedom. Accessed on June 15, 2005 at *http://www.globalsecurity.org/military/library/report/2003/3id-aar-jul03.pdf.*
Townshend, Charles. 1989. "Military Force and Civil Authority in the United Kingdom, 1914–1921." *Journal of British Studies* 28, no. 3 (July), 262–92.
Trachtenberg, Marc. 1991. *History and Strategy.* Princeton: Princeton University Press.
Tremblay, Reeta Chowdhari, and Julian Schofield. 2005. "Institutional Causes of the India-Pakistan Rivalry." In *The India-Pakistani Conflict,* edited by T. V. Paul. Cambridge: Cambridge University Press.
Trubowitz, Peter, Emily O. Goldman, and Edward Rhodes, eds. 1999. *The Politics of Strategic Adjustment: Ideas, Institutions and Interests.* New York: Columbia University Press.
Trubowitz, Peter. 1998. *Defining the National Interest.* Chicago: University of Chicago Press.

Trumpener, Ulrich. 1976. "War Premeditated?" *Central European History* 9, 58–85.
Tsouras, Peter. 1994. *Changing Orders: The Evolution of the World's Armies, 1945 to the Present*. New York: Facts on File.
Tuchman, Barbara. 1962. *The Guns of August*. New York: Macmillan.
Turner, John. 1988. "British Politics and the Great War." In *Britain and the First World War*, edited by John Turner. London: Unwin Hyman.
Turner, L.C.F. "The Edge of The Precipice: A Comparison between November 1912 and July 1914." *RMC Historical Journal* 3, 3–18.
———. 1965. "The Role of the General Staffs in 1914." *Australian Journal of Politics and History* 11, no. 3, 305–23.
Ulrich, Marybeth Peterson. 1999. *Democratizing Communist Militaries: The Cases of the Czech and Russian Armed Forces*. Ann Arbor: University of Michigan Press.
Van Evera, Stephen. 1991. "The Cult of the Offensive and the Origins of the First World War." In *Military Strategy and the Origins of the First World War*, edited by Steven Miller. Princeton: Princeton University Press.
———. 1997. *Guide to Methods for Students of Political Science*. Ithaca: Cornell University Press.
———. 2001. "More Causes of War: Misperception and the Roots of Conflict." Manuscript, Massachusetts Institute of Technology.
Van Riper, Paul. 2004. Frontline special, "Rumsfeld's War." Original air date October 26. Available at *http://www.pbs.org/wgbh/pages/frontline/programs/2004.html*.
Vatikiotis, Panayiotis J. 1968. "Some Political Consequences of the 1952 Revolution in Egypt." In *Political and Social Change in Modern Egypt*, edited by P. M. Holt. Oxford: Oxford University Press.
Wagner, Harrison R. 2000. "Bargaining and War." *American Journal of Political Science* 44, no. 3 (July), 469–84.
Walz, Jay. 1967a. "Amer May Face Egyptian Court." *New York Times*, September 5.
———. 1967b. "Security Arrests Put at 181 in Cairo." *New York Times*, September 20.
———. 1967c. "Story of the Plot against Nasser." *New York Times*, September 24.
———. 1967d. "Trials Promised in Cairo Plot Case." *New York Times*, September 14.
Waterbury, John. 1978. *Egypt: Burdens of the Past/Options for the Future*. Bloomington: Indiana University Press.
———. 1983. *The Egypt of Nasser and Sadat: The Political Economy of Two Regimes*. Princeton: Princeton University Press.
———. 1993. *Exposed to Innumerable Delusions*. Cambridge: Cambridge University Press.
Wayne, Leslie. 2006. "Air Force Jet Wins Battle in Congress." *New York Times*, September 28, 1.
Wehler, Hans Ulrich. 1985. *The German Empire, 1871–1918*. Leamington Spa, NH.
Weigley, Russell F. 1993. "The American Military and the Principle of Civilian Control from McClellan to Powell." *Journal of Military History* 57, no. 5 (October), 27–58.
Weingast, Barry R. 2002. "Rational Choice Institutionalism." In *Political Science: The State of the Discipline*, edited by Ira Katznelson and Helen V. Milner. New York: W. W. Norton.

Weinraub, Bernard, with Thom Shanker. 2003. "Rumsfeld's Design for War Criticized on the Battlefield." *New York Times*, April 1.
Weinroth, Howard. S. 1970. "The British Radicals and the Balance of Power, 1902–1914." *Historical Journal* 13, no. 4 (December), 653–82.
Welch, Claude E., Jr. 1987. *No Farewell to Arms: Military Disengagement from Politics in Africa and Latin America*. Boulder: Westview Press.
Welch, Claude E., Jr., and Arthur K. Smith. 1974. *Military Role and Rule: Perspectives on Civil-Military Relations*. North Scituate, MA: Duxbury Press.
Whetten, Lawrence L. 1974. *The Canal War: Four Power Conflicts in the Middle East*. Cambridge: MIT Press.
White, Harrison C. 1991. "Agency as Control." In *Principals and Agents: The Structure of Business*, edited by John W. Pratt and Richard Zeckhauser. 2d ed. Boston: Harvard Business School Press.
White, Thomas. 2004a. Interview in PBS Frontline special, "The Invasion of Iraq." Original air date February 26. Transcript available at *http://www.pbs.org/wgbh/pages/frontline/programs/2004.html*.
———. 2004b. Interview in PBS Frontline special, "Rumsfeld's War." Original air date October 26. Available at *http://www.pbs.org/wgbh/pages/frontline/programs/2004.html*.
"Who Really Runs Pakistan?" 1999. *Economist*, June 26.
Williams, Louis, ed. 1975. *Military Aspects of the Israeli-Arab Conflict*. Tel Aviv: University Publishing Service.
Williamson Jr., Samuel R., and Russell Van Wyk. July 1914: *Soldiers, Statesmen and the Coming of the Great War*. Boston: Bedford/St. Martin's.
Williamson, Oliver E. 1975. *Markets and Hierarchies: Analysis and Antitrust Implications*. New York: Free Press.
Williamson, Samuel R. Jr. 1969. *The Politics of Grand Stratgey: Britain and France Prepare for War, 1904–1914*. Cambridge: Harvard University Press.
Wilson, Keith. 1995. "Britain." In *Decisions for War, 1914*, edited by Keith Wilson. London: UCL Press.
———. 1995. *Decisions for War*. London: UCL Press.
Winter, Denis. 1991. *Haig: A Reassessment*. London: Viking.
Wolfowitz, Paul. 2003. Testimony at Hearing on Fiscal Year 2004 Defense Budget. House Budget Committee, February 27.
Wood, David. 2000. "Military Breaks Ranks with Non-Partisan Tradition; Many in Service Turn to Bush, Reject Political Correctness." *Plain Dealer* (Cleveland), October 22.
Woodward, Bob. 2004. *Plan of Attack*. New York: Simon and Schuster.
Woodward, David R. 1983. *Lloyd George and the Generals*. East Brunswick, NJ: Associated University Presses.
Xu Yuenai and Yang Shilong. 1997. "News Analysis: Security Panel Setup Unleashes Pandora's Box of Controversies." Xinhua News Agency, January 17.
Ya'ari, Ehud. 1980. "Sadat's Pyramid of Power." *Jerusalem Quarterly*, no. 14 (Winter), 110–21.
Yaphe, Judith S. 1997. "Turkey's Domestic Affairs." *Strategic Forum*, no. 121, Institute for National Strategic Studies, Fort McNair. Washington, DC: National Defense University.

Yavuz, M. Hakan. 1997. "Turkish-Israeli Relations through the Lens of the Turkish Identity Debate." *Journal of Palestine Studies* 27, no. 1 (Autumn), 22–37.

Yost, Charles W. 1968. "The Arab-Israeli War: How It Began." *Foreign Affairs* 46, no. 2 (January): 304–20.

Zegart, Amy. 1999. *Flawed by Design: The Evolution of the CIA, JCS, and NSC*. Stanford: Stanford University Press.

Zisk, Kimberly Marten. 1993. *Engaging the Enemy: Organization Theory and Soviet Military Innovation*. Princeton: Princeton University Press.

Zuber, Terence. 2002. *Inventing the Schlieffen Plan: German War Planning, 1871–1914*. Oxford: Oxford University Press.

INDEX

Agadir Crisis, 152
Agranat Commission 109n17. *See also* Israel; October War
al-Asad. *See* Asad, al-
al-Feki. *See* Feki, al-
Ali, Ahmed Ismail, 133, 139, 140; and October War 134–135
Ali, Kamal Hassan, 136, 137, 137n72
Amer, Abdel Hakim, 21, 63, 67, 68, 70; appointment of to chief of Egyptian military, 73; and closure of Straits of Tiran, 92, 95; and competition with Nasser over military appointments, 88–89; and control over Military Intelligence and General Intelligence, 80; and early relationship with Nasser, 77; as emissary to Syria, 77; as executive in fishing and transportation industries, 75; as executive within soccer federation, 75; and falling out with Nasser, 77; as first vice president of the regime, 75; formation of Ground Forces Command by, 89; and May 13 (1967) Soviet Report, 81, 90; and Nasser, arrested by, 112; —, attempts to contest Nasser's control over decision-making, 256; —, as holding different preferences than, 77–79; —, resistance to coordination with, 84; and Operation Dawn, 92; political positions held by, 74–75; and preference for confronting Israel, 78, 81; as protective of information on military, 80–81; purge of, 102n1, 112; resignation of, 111; role of in weakening military self-monitoring, 86; suicide of, 112; support base of, 73–75, 76; and troop deployment to Sharm al-Sheikh, 92; and UNEF redeployment request, 91. *See also* Egypt; Arab-Israeli War; Nasser, Gamal Abdel
Anderson, Robert B., 66, 66n10, 68n17
Arab-Israeli War (1967), 55, 57n68, 62; and Amer's interest in confrontation with Israel, 78, 81; background to, 63–67; Egyptian strategic assessment in, 79–94; Israel views of, 64–67, 68; and Israeli and Egyptian relative capabilities compared, 95–96; Nasser's strategy for, 93–98; —, and impact of Cold war atmosphere on, 97–98; and Operation Dawn, 78; role of Egyptian misestimate of military capabilities in, 95–97; role of poor intelligence in, 85–86; Soviet Union role in, 64, 81–82, 90; standard interpretations of origin of, 67–70. *See also* Egypt; Israel; Nasser
"Arab Cold War," 63
Arab Socialist Union (ASU), 75; electoral reforms of, 112. *See also* Youth Organization; Sabri, Ali
Asad, Hafez al-, 223, 224
Asquith, Herbert, 30, 146, 147, 153–155, 161, 163, 165, 167; and British entry into First World War, 164; formation of War Committee by, 166n37. *See also* Britain; First World War
Ataturk, Kemal, 210; influence on Turkish military of, 213–214
Austria-Hungary, 167, 189–90, 260, 272; and assassination of Archduke Ferdinand, 187; mobilization for war by, 193
authorization process: and Britain during First World War, 166–169, 259; in 1970s Egypt, 131–137, 138–139, 257; as attribute of strategic assessment, 4; clarity of and best case for strategic assessment, 44; defined, 39; evaluation of, 40–42; as key process in strategic assessment, 39–42; in late 1990s Turkey 214–217, 219, 222, 260–261; —, clarity of and threat credibility, 223–224; and mid-1960s Egypt, 88–92, 256; in Pakistan under Sharif, 202–203, 205–207, 260; in pre-World War I Britain, 148; role of veto in, 41; and United States during 2003 Iraq War, 235, 261; in Wilhelmine Germany, 189–191. *See also* strategic assessment

autocracy, and strategic assessment, 12
Avant, Deborah, 58, 265n2, 270n11

Badawi, Ahmed, 137
Badran, Shams, 86; and 1967 delegation to Soviet Union, 81–82, 82n46; as head of Amer's patronage network, 74; as minister of war, 80, 80n44
Baghdad, 240, 245, 246, 247, 251, 252, 254, 255
Balfour, Arthur, 151, 154
Balkan League, 184
Balkan wars (1912–1913), 184
Bar Lev line, 105, 124, 128
bargaining models (of war), 8. See also Fearon, James
Basra, 247n45. See also Iraq War (2003)

Batiste, John (major general), 231n9
Beattie, Kirk J., 111n23, 112n31, 115n40
Beg, Mirza Aslam, 199n7, 202, 202n15
Begin, Menachem, 65, 106, 142. See also Camp David Accords
Belgium, 186. See also Passchendaele; Schlieffen Plan
Ben-Gurion, David, 96n70
Berchtold (count), 191, 193
Betts, Richard, 16, 35n47, 39n50
Bir Gifgafa (airfield), 64, 92
Bismarck, Otto von, 180
Boer War, 144, 158; impact of on strategic coordination reform in pre–First World War Britain, 148–149
Bosnia, 234, 242, 243, 246
Brady, Henry E., and David Collier, 56n67
Britain, 30, 56, 60, 61, 260; and Cardwell reforms, 147; Committee of Imperial Defense (CID) of, 149, 149n13, 149–50, 151, 258; —, and Anglo-Russian relations, 151, 157; —, concern by over Germany, 152, 157; —, and links to General Staff, 150; —, and possible intervention in continental war, 151–155; —, as playing central role in pre–First World War strategic reorientation, 151–156; —, and preparations for First World War, 158; —, role in facilitating strategic coordination, 151–155; during First World War (1914–1918) 161–177; —, as having no clearly defined goals, 174; —, and civil-military relations, 163–165; —, coalition government during, 164; —, and contestation over authorization process, 166–169; —, conventional accounts of, 161–162; —, military support for "western" strategy, 163; —, and Passchendaele, 162, 169n45, 169–171, 259; —, problems of information sharing, 169–170; —, problems in strategic coordination, 170–174; —, and strategic assessment, 165–177, 259; —, and training doctrine, 159n24; General Staff of, 150, 151; —and pre-First World War strategic coordination, 151–156; —planning of military operations by, 154–155; and Liberal party, decline of, 163–164; —, internal division in, 163–164; —, opposition by to continental commitment, 145, 151–156, 159; —, opposition by to increasing size of army, 159; pre–First World War (1902–1914), 144–161; —, civil-military relations of, 146–147, 258, 260; —, conventional accounts of, 144–145; —; coordination with France, 155; —, and Curragh mutiny, 147n6; —, and debate over continental commitment, 145, 151–156; —, and domestic politics as constraint on strategy, 145–146, 153–154, 158; —, impact of Esher Report, 149, 150; —, international relations of, 156–161; —, Liberals and, 147; —, and preparations for war, 158–161, 176n58; —, and reform of strategic coordination after Boer War, 148–156; —, strategic assessment and, 148–161; —, strategic reorientation during, 156–158; and Schlieffen Plan, 176–177, 177n60, 186–7, 192; War Cabinet of, and Passchendaele, 170–171; —, and German offensive of 1918, 172; War Office of, 150. See also Boer War; First World War
British Expeditionary Force (BEF), 151, 152, 154, 157, 162. See also Britain; First World War; Haig, Douglas
Bush, George W., 24, 229, 233; administration of, 223, 234; —, as insulated, 229–230; —, and 2003 Iraq War, 229–230. See also United States; Iraq War (2003); Rumsfeld, Donald

Cadorna, Luigi, 168
Cambridge, Duke of, 149n10
Camp David, 127, 136, 138, 141

Camp David Accords, 102, 106–107. *See also* Carter, Jimmy; Egypt; Israel; Sadat, Anwar; Begin, Menachem
Campbell-Bannerman, Henry, 146, 147, 154
Carter, Jimmy, 106. *See also* Camp David Accords
case study methodology. *See under* research design
Central Command (CENTCOM). *See* Iraq War (2003)
Churchill, Winston, 153n20
civil-military relations: in 1970s Egypt, 111–122, 257; in 1990s Pakistan, 198–200, 260; in United States (2002–2003), 233–235; and Britain during the First World War, 259; in pre–First World War Britain, 146–147, 258; comparative politics approach to, 3, 22–23, 22n15; ideal type of, 268–271; and institutional theory, 19–23; in late 1990s Turkey, 212–214, 260–261; in mid-1960s Egypt, 256–257; and miscalculations of military capabilities, 271–272; as necessary cause of strategic assessment, 54; and objective control, 268; quality of debate as best measure of civil-military health, 269–270; role of class, regional, or ethnic composition in, 26; role of external threat and, 26; role of military culture in, 26; significance of for international relations, 11–12, 271–273; sources of conflict or agreement in, 26–27; standard accounts of, 268–269; and strategic assessment, 2, 3, 4, 265–256; in Wilhelmine Germany, 181–182, 260
Clausewitz, 268
Clinton, Bill, 24, 233; administration of, 30, 234; meeting with Sharif over Kargil, 208
Coalition Forces Land Component Command (CFLCC). *See* Iraq War (2003)
COBRA II, 228, 229n2, 244. *See also* Iraq War (2003)
Cohen, Eliot, 16, 228, 229, 269n9; on active civil involvement in military affairs, 268
comparative politics, and civil-military relations, 3, 22–23
Copeland, Dale, 178n62, 179n63, 188
Corekci, Ahmet, 214
Craig, Gordon A., 189n81, 190, 193, 194

cross-case comparisons. *See under* research design
"Cult of the Offensive," 272–273

dangerous states, 264–265
de Gaulle, Charles, 24
decision making (processes): distributional approach to, 16, 23; impact of policy making environment on, 16; and institutional theory, 15; and strategic assessment
democracy: and evaluation of international environment, 12; and strategic assessment, 12
Derby (lord), 166–167, 168
Desch, Michael C., 120n48
diachronic (cross-case) comparison. *See under* research design
distributional approach (to variations in strategic assessment), 16–23; definition of, 4; historical institutional dimension of, 19; rational choice dimension of, 19. *See also* strategic assessment

Eaton, Paul D. (major general), 231n9
Eban, Abba, 65, 69n22
Ecevit, Bulent, 211n32
ECLIPSE II. *See* Iraq War (2003)
Edmonds, Sir James, 160
Egypt, 60, 61, 261, 264, 271; alignment of with the West, 138; and Arab-Israeli War, 62, 257, 271 (*see also* Arab-Israeli War); —, decline in support for military after, 113; —, and evaluation of Israeli military capabilities, 128; —, military capability improvement following, 120; Arab Socialist Union of, 75; Council for Defense and National Security of, —establishment of, 201; —Sharif's abandonment of, 201; in 1970s, 102–142, 257–258; —, and 1974 Third Army Rebellion, 121; —, and 1979 peace treaty with Israel, 138 ; —, authorization process in, 131–137, 257; —, civil-military preference divergence during, 120–122; —, civil-military relations in, 113–122; —, composition of executive cabinet in, 118–119; —, economic opening of, 112–113, 114–115, 116; —, impact of Sadat's strategies on international relations of, 137–142; —, and information sharing under Sadat, 123–125, 257; —, and intelligence under Sadat, 123; —, and International

Egypt (cont'd)
Monetary Fund austerity measures, 116, 116n42; —, lack of military cohesion in, 117–118; —, and political liberalization under Sadat, 112–113, 115–116; —, professionalization of military in, 107–108, 129, 129n57; —, and public sector growth under Sadat, 115, 115n37; —, strategic assessment in, 123–137, 257–258; —, strategic coordination under Sadat, 126–128; —, structural competence in, 128–131, 257; Free Officer coup in, 71, 77; Liberation Rally and National Union of, 75; National Defense Council of, 83, 83n48; in mid-1960s, 62–100; —, civil-military relations in, 71–79, 111–113; —, division of power between Nasser and Amer, 76; —, information sharing in, 256; —, lack of strategic coordination in mid-1960s, 82–85; —, military capabilities in, 87; —, strategic assessment in, 79–92, 256–257; —, structural competence in, 85–88; Presidential Council of, 88; reasons for focusing on, 55, 58; and Revolutionary Command Council, 58, 71; Soviet military support of, 95; strategic and pathological quality of institutional outcomes in, 21; Supreme Council of the Armed Forces (SCAF), 123–124, 127, 132; and Yemeni civil war, 64, 79; and Youth Organization (YO), 75–76; view of state as autocratic, 110
el-Gamasy. *See* Gamasy
Elman, Colin, 51n58
Erbakan, Necmettin, 56, 211, 260–261; and accession to prime minister, 212; attempt by to advance Iran-Turkey relations, 214, 218, 219, 220; attempt by to establish Development Eight, 219; and attempts to promote Turkey's muslim identity, 214; and attempt to resist Turkish military's officer dismissals, 215–216; and "Campaign for Muslim Solidarity", 218–219; and divergence of preferences with Turkish military, 213–214; divisions in coalition government of, 212, 213; inability of to alter Turkish grand strategy, 218–222; interest in severing Turkish ties with Israel, 219–220, 220n61, 221; and National Security Council of Turkey, 215–217; opposition by to Turkish European Union entry, 222; pro-Muslim foreign policy of, 218–221; Turkish military's distrust of, 214; as politically weak, 212–213. *See also* Turkey
Erdogan, Recep Tayyip, 216n47
Esher (lord), 149, 150, 155
Esher Report, 149, 150. *See also* Britain
Eshkol, Levi, 65, 69, 69n22
European Union, 208, 210; Turkish interest in membership in, 218, 222, 223
Evans, Richard, 180
Evron, Ephraim, 66n12

Fahmy, Ismail, 142n77
Falkenhayn, Erich von, 179
Falluja, 254. *See also* Iraq War (2003)
Farid, Abdel Majid, 81, 98, 98n74
Farouk (king), 71, 77
Farrell, Theo, 26n24
Fawzi, Mohammed, 21, 65n9, 84, 89, 92, 121n49, 129n59; attempted coup by, 117–118
Fawzi, Mahmoud, 91n57
Fearon, James, 18n7, 272. *See also* bargaining theories (of war)
Feaver, Peter, 24n17, 26n25, 35n47, 265n2, 270n11
Feki, Ahmad Hassan al-, 69n21
Ferdinand, Archduke, 187
Finer, Samuel, 26n23, 31n38
First World War, 56, 60, 61; 1918 German offensive and, 172–174; Britain during, 259; British preparations for, 158–161, 176n88, 258; British use of cavalry in, 176; conventional explanations for origin of, 179–180; Gallipoli/Dardanelles campaign, 175; July 14 crisis and start of, 187–188; lack of British tactical innovation in, 176–177, 177n60; and Passchendaele, 162, 169–171, 259. *See also* Britain; Germany; George, Lloyd; Haig, Douglas; Robertson, William
Fischer, Fritz, 179, 185
Foch, Ferdinand, 176
Förster, Stig, 192n85
Förster thesis, 159n25
France, 145, 154, 184, 185; and Schlieffen Plan, 186. *See also* First World War
Franks, Tommy, 228, 236, 237n27, 239, 243, 247n43; and 2003 Iraq War, cancellation of follow on troops by, 251; —, combat planning by, 229n2; —, debate with Rumsfeld over troop deployment numbers, 248–249, 250, 251; —, lack of focus

on stability operations by, 242, 245–246; —, post-conflict planning and, 231n7, 248n46; and Rumsfeld, 229
French, Sir John, 155
Friedberg, Aaron L., 145, 145n3
Future of Iraq Project, 230

Gamasy, Mohammed Abdel, 127, 129, 130n60, 133, 134n66, 137n72; on disengagement after October War (1973), 140, 141
Ganguly, Sumit, 205n26
Garner, Jay (general), 247, 247n45, 253n54
Gawrych, George W. 89n53, 92n62, 104n2, 107n12, 110n20, 132
Gaza Strip, 62, 67
Generated Start, 229n2. *See also* Iraq War (2003)
George, Alexander, and Andrew Bennett, 55n64, 56n66, 60nn75 and 77, 61. *See also* research design
George, Lloyd, 30, 161, 161n26, 162, 165, 171, 259; and 1918 German offensive, 172–174; and Aleppo offensive, 172; appointment of to prime minister, 163n31, 164; attempts to control decision making by, 167–196; attempts by to establish unified command with France 168–169; attempts to subordinate military by, 167–169; concerns of during First World War, 174; and concern with British military's tactics, 175–176; constraints of coalition government on, 166–167; criticism of British military by, 170n46; difficulty in questioning of Haig's leadership by, 176; establishment of War Cabinet by, 166n37; and support for "eastern" strategy during First World War, 163, 167–168; and Passchendaele campaign, 170–171, 175
George V (king), support for military by, 167
Germany (Wilhelmine), 26, 31, 56, 58, 59n72, 177–194, 266, 272; 1918 offensives by during First World War, 172–174; British Committee of Imperial Defense and, 152, 157; civil-military relations of, 181–182, 260; and "Cult of the Offensive", 178; debate over war aims of, 179; and December 1912 war council, 184–185; difficulty in assessing preferences of, 193; information sharing in, 183; international relations of, 191–194; low level of civil-military preference divergence in, 181; military autonomy in, 183; and Pan-German League, 182; power of military in, 181–182; problems in authorization process in, 189–191, 260; and relationship with Britain, 185; and Schlieffen Plan, 186–188, 192; Social Democratic Party of, 182; strategic assessment in, 182–191; strategic coordination problems in, 183–189, 260; as strategically ineffective, 178; —, conventional explanations for, 178–180. *See also* First World War; Schlieffen Plan; Wilhelm II
Ginor, Isabella, and Gordon Remez, 64n2, 70n 23
Goemans, H. E., 161n27
Goertz, Gary, and Harvey Starr, 54n61
Golan Heights, 62, 67. *See also* Arab-Israeli War (1967); October War (1973)
Goma, Sharawy, 112n29
Gordon, Michael R., and General Bernard E. Trainor, 232, 241, 244, 248
Grechko, Andrei, 81–82
Grey, Sir Edward, 151n16, 153
Grierson (general), 155, 160
Group of Eight (G8), 208
Gulf War (1991), 240, 241n32

Haig, Douglas (general), 147, 162, 259; as commander in chief of British Expeditionary Force, 164; as controversial figure, 175–177; and disagreement with Lloyd George over war strategy, 167–169; and partnership with William Robertson, 164–165; and Passchendaele campaign, 169–171, 175; support for western front strategy in First World War, 163n32; use of calvary during First World War by, 176
Haldane (lord), 149, 151n16
Hankey (lord), 158, 168
Haykal, Mohammed. *See* Heikal, Mohammed
Heeringen, August von, 185
Heikal, Mohammed, 65n6, 70, 90, 90n55, 92, 92n62, 97n71, 121n49
Heller, Mark, 39n50
Hinnebusch, Raymond, 113–114, 141
historical institutionalism. *See* institutionalism
Hitler, Adolf, 24, 266

Hollweg, Bethmann, 179, 184, 186, 190, 191; and assassination of Archduke Ferdinand, 187–188; and attempts to improve Anglo-German relations, 185
Hotzendorff, Conrad von, 189, 191, 193
Hoyt, Timothy, 196
Hull, Isabel V., 180
Hunter, Wendy, 32
Huntington, Samuel, 269; emphasis on objective control of military, 268
Hussein, Saddam, 2, 226, 227, 229, 248, 251, 252, 253. *See also* Iraq War (2003)
Huweidy, Amin, 112n29

India, 151, 157, 260; and Kargil war (1999), 197, 206, 206n28, 207–209; and nuclear stability in South Asia, 196–197; rivalry with Pakistan, 197, 197n1; —, over Kashmir, 195
information: distributional conflict over, 17–18; military specialization and, 35; role in strategic assessment, 34–39. *See also* information sharing; strategic assessment
information sharing: in 1970s Egypt, 123–125, 138; as attribute of strategic assessment, 4; defined, 35; evaluation of, 35–36; as key process in strategic assessment, 35–36; in late 1990s Turkey, 218; in mid-1960s Egypt, 80–82, 256; in pre–World War I Britain, 148; most beneficial form of, 42–44; wartime Britain problems with, 169–174, 259; in United States during 2003 Iraq War, 236, 261; in Wilhelmine Germany, 183
institutional theory, 15; and civil-military relations, 19–23
institutions: as aggregate outcome of goal-seeking behavior, 19; distributional conflict in emergence and evolution of, 16–17; efficiency oriented approach to, 19–20, 20n12; historical approach to, 19; informal, 4n4; as mutable, 19, 19n9; principal-agent approaches to, 21–22; rational choice approach to, 19, 19n10; and shaping of outcomes, 16–17; strategic and pathological outcomes of, 21–23; as strategic outcomes, 20–23; suboptimality in, 19n10, 20
institutionalism: historical, 19; rational choice, 19, 19n10. *See also* institutions; institutional theory

International Court of Justice (ICJ), and Arab-Israeli War, 66n13
International Monetary Fund (IMF), 116, 116n42
international relations: and civil-military relations, 3; realist theories of, 57–58
international-domestic linkage, 271–273
interservice rivalry, 59
Iran, 210, 214, 219, 220, 221
Iraq: Kurds in, 221, 221n65; post-Iraq War (2003) situation in, 252–255; and Turkey, 220–221
Iraq War (2003), 2, 56; authorization process in, 235; cancellation of follow on troops for, 250–251; Central Command (CENTCOM) in, 231, 243–246; —, and post-conflict planning by, 243–247; Coalition Forces Land Component Command (CFLCC) in, 244–245, 247, 248n48, 250–251; and COBRA II, 228, 229n2, 244; and ECLIPSE II, 244–245; and Generated Start, 229n2; information sharing in, 236; international implications of, 252–255; and Joint Task Force IV, 246n9, 248n48; and OPLAN 1003, 240; and OPLAN 1003V, flaws in 243; post-conflict planning for, 227–228, 242–243, 243–250; —, as underdeveloped, 227; — as underresourced, 228; role of Office of Reconstruction and Humanitarian Assistance (ORHA) in, 230n6, 247, 247n42, 253, 253n54; role of Third Infantry Division in, 246; strategic coordination in, 236–239, 241–242, 243–251, 261; and too few troops sent, 248–250; United States post-conflict failures and, 226, 241–250; United States plans for, 227, 239–243, 269; —, conventional accounts of, 226, 228; —, problems with, 241–243. *See also* Franks, Tommy; Rumsfeld, Donald; United States
Islamism, 214. *See also* Erbakan, Necmettin; Turkey
Ismail, Ahmed Ali, 104n2, 126, 129
Israel, 55, 78, 124, 210, 256; and 1979 peace treaty with Egypt, 138; and Arab-Israeli War (1967), 1, 62, 64–67, 99–100, 257; —, and assessment of Egyptian capabilities by, 96; and Camp David Accords, 106–107; mid-1960s Egypt lack of intelligence on, 85–86; and October War (1973), 105, 105n4; —, intelligence fail-

ures in, 109, 109n17, 132n63; and placement of UNEF, 78; and Turkey, 218, 219–220, 221; —, military interest in deepening ties with, 214

Janowitz, Morris, 26, 31n40
Jenkins, Gareth, 211, 213
Joffe (general), 176
Johnson, Lyndon, 100nn79–80, 266–267, 267n6; administration of, 100, 100n80; military oversight efforts of, 267
Jones, Owen Bennett, 205n26, 206
Jordan, 26, 62
Junkers, 26, 182. See also, Germany

Karamat (general), 201–202, 202n15, 204
Kargil (Heights) war (1999), 197, 200, 203, 205–207; international implications of, 207–209; uncertainty over making of decision to launch, 205. See also India; Pakistan; Sharif, Nawaz
Kashmir, 195, 197, 205, 208. See also Kargil war; India; Pakistan
Kehr, Eckart, 182n68
Kemalism, 213, 214n39. See also Kemal, Ataturk; Turkey
Kerr, Malcom, 57n68, 63
Keys, Ronald (lt. general), 238
Khan, Ali Quli, 204
Kier, Elizabeth, 58, 213–214
Kilometer 101 talks, 106n9
King, Gary, Robert Keohane, and Sidney Verba, 56n67
Kissinger, Henry, 102, 109, 122, 140–141; negotiation for disengagement of forces after October War (1973), 106
Knott, Jack H., and Gary J. Miller, 17n6, 270n12
Kohut, Thomas A., 180
Koonings, Kees, and Dirk Kruijt, 29n35
Kosovo, 234, 242
Krasner, Stephen, 28n31
Kupchan, Charles A., 154
Kurdistan Workers party (PKK), 221, 224; and Syria, 224–225; and Turkey, 224–225
Kuwait, 247, 247n45

Lahore agreement (1999), 208
Lakatos, Imre, 54. See also research design
Latin America, 29, 31
Law, Bonar, 173
leaders: military, 3n3; political, 3n3

Lebow, Richard Ned, 178, 179
Leghari (president), 207
Legro, Jeffrey, 213–214
Levy, Jacob, 272
Liberal party. See Britain
Lichnowsky (prince), 184, 188
Libya, 219

Mahoney, James, 54n61, 60n77. See also research design
Marei, Sayed, 69n21
Marne, Battle of the, 176n58
Marse, Sir Ivor, 177n60
Maurice Debate, 172–174
Maurice, Sir Frederick, and 1918 German offensive 172–174
McKiernan, David (lt. general), 244, 245, 247n45; on force deployment, 250–251
McNamara, Robert, 266–267
military: and allocation of appointment and promotion rights, 41; and allocation of punishment and dismissal rights, 41; dominance of and strategic assessment, 51–53, 51n57; leadership cohesion and, 31–32; as political actor, 22–23; private information and, 35–36; and security policy, 23; sources of interests of, 26–27; ties to domestic society as source of power for, 29–31; veto rights of, 41
military capabilities: assessment of, 38; —, importance of structural competence for, 38; estimates of, 7–8; impact of poor strategic assessment on estimates of, 7–8; information on, 271–272; miscalculations of, 7–8; —, role of civil-military relations in, 271–272
military culture, 26
military effectiveness, 38n49
military oversight, 270, 265–267; Johnson's efforts at, 267; Rumsfeld's efforts at, 237–239, 266; Sadat's efforts at, 126–128, 129, 129n57, 131; Sharif's efforts at, 203–205
Mill (John Stuart), 60. See also research design
Miller, Gary, 22n14
Moe, Terry, 17n6, 19n11, 270n11
Mohieddin, Zakariya, 65n6, 66n13, 67n15, 76, 92
Moltke, Helmuth von, 159n25, 179, 184, 184n72, 185, 189, 190, 191, 192, 272; interest in rapid mobilization for war by,

Moltke, Helmuth von (*cont'd*) 190; on possibility for protracted war, 192–193; and Schlieffen Plan, 188–189
Monash, Sir Jon, 177n60
Morely (lord), 153
Motherland party, 212. *See also* Turkey
Mubarak, Hosni, 136, 137, 137n72, 139
Muller, Georg Alexander von, 185
Murtagi (general), 90n55, 92
Musharraf, Pervez, 201n14, 204, 205, 206n28
Muslim Brotherhood: and attempt to assassinate Nasser, 113; leaders of freed by Sadat, 115. *See also* Egypt
Myers, Richard (general), 232, 232n13, 236, 238

Nagib (general), 71
Nasser, Gamal Abdel, 1, 55, 58, 62–63, 64, 127, 256; and Arab Socialist Union, 75; and Arab-Israeli war (1967), 63–67, 257; —, conventional interpretations for role in provocation of, 67–70; —, strategy for, 93–98; Bir Gifgafa speech by, 64, 92; and Amer, arrest of by, 112; —, and divergence in preferences with, 77–79; and early relationship with, 77; and attempts to bolster support after Arab-Israeli war, 113; as charismatic leader, 110n22; death of, 102; and decision to close Straits of Tiran, 64–65, 92; efforts at establishing control over military appointments by, 88–89; efforts at establishing civilian support by, 71–73, 75–76; and elimination of Amer clique in military, 112, 112n29; establishment of Presidential Council by, 88; as insulated from internal military affairs, 80–81; and Operation Dawn, 92; poor strategic assessment by, 2; and post–Arab-Israeli war civilian reforms, 112–113; and post–Arab-Israeli war military reforms, 108, 108n13, 112; public support for, 111; resignation and reinstatement of, 111; and Sadat compared, 1–2, 110; and Suez conflict (1956), 63; sequestration under, 115, 115n38; and UNEF redeployment request, 78, 90–91, 91n57. *See also* Amer, Abdel Hakim; Arab-Israeli War; Egypt
National Defense Council. *See under* Egypt
national security councils, 41

Newbold, Gregory (marine lt. general), 231n9, 238, 241n33
North Atlantic Treaty Organization (NATO), 218, 244
nuclear deterrence, in South Asia, 196–197

Ocalan, Abdullah, 223, 224
October War (1973): analysis of, 105–106, 105n6; clarity of Egyptian authorization process in, 131–137; command decisions during, 133–136; conventional explanations of, 107–110; and disengagement agreements, 106, 136–137, 140; —, skepticism of, 140–142; Egyptian civil-military divergence in preferences over, 120–121; and Egyptian Third Army, 105, 105n5; and Egypt's Military Intelligence, 128; lessons from Arab-Israeli war and, 130; as limited war, 133–136; and Plan Badr, 133; planning of, 124–125, 129–130, 132–133; role of control over information sharing in, 125, 138; role of Israeli intelligence failures in, 109; role of strategic coordination in, 126, 138; Sadat's motives in launching, 107, 137; and Syria, 134, 134n67; and UN ceasefire, 105, 105n5. *See also* Egypt; Israel; Sadat, Anwar
Odell, John S., 55n63, 60n77
Office of Reconstruction and Humanitarian Assistance (ORHA). *See under* Iraq War (2003)
O'Hanlon, Michael, 229n2
Operation Dawn, 78, 78n39, 92. *See also* Arab-Israeli war (1967); Amer, Abdel Hakim; Egypt; Nasser, Gamal Abdel
Operation Poised Hammer, 218n54. *See also* Turkey
Operation Provide Comfort, 221n65
OPLAN 1003. *See under* Iraq War (2003)
OPLAN 1003V. *See under* Iraq War (2003)
Oren, Michael B., 78n39, 92n62, 95n66
oversight (military), 270, 265–267; Lyndon Johnson's efforts at, 267; Rumsfeld's efforts at, 237–239, 266; Sadat's efforts at, 123–124, 126–128, 129, 129n57, 131, 138–139; Sharif's efforts at, 203–205
Ozal, Turgut, 215n43

Pace, Peter (general), 232, 236
Pakistan, 29, 56, 58, 60, 61, 78, 261, 264; authorization process in, 260; Council for Defense and National Security of, 201;

military's role in politics, 198–199; Muslim League of, 198; National Security Council of, 260; and nuclear stability in South Asia, 196–197; as pivotal player in South Asia, 195; prominent role of military in civil society, 195; and rivalry with India over Kashmir, 195, 197; strategic coordination in, 260; under Nawaz Sharif (1997–1999), 196–209: —, authorization process, 202, 203, 205–207; —, civil-military relations in, 198–200, 260; —, and control over military appointments, 203–205; —, conventional interpretations of, 196–197; —, debate of establishment of National Security Council, 201, 201n14; —, and Kargil war (1999), 197, 203, 205–209, 260; —, and military's interest in economy, 199; —, and role of military in society and politics, 198, 199; —, shifts in military's support for, 199, 200, 202–204; —, and strategic assessment, 200–207; —, and strategic coordination, 200–202, 205–207; —, and Troika, 203, 203n20. *See also* Sharif, Nawaz

Palestine, 141–142, 172. *See also* Egypt

Passchendaele, 162, 169n45, 169–171, 259. *See also* Britain; First World War; Haig, Douglas

Pion-Berlin, David, 28n30

Plan Badr, 133. *See also*, October War (1973)

political leaders: defined, 3n3; and military oversight, 265–266; —, impact of on strategic assessment, 265–266; polices pursued by as indicator of support base, 32–33; social support base as source of power for, 32; sources of interests of, 26–27

Pollack, Kenneth, 38n49, 107n12

Posen, Barry, 264n1; on civilian intervention in military affairs, 268

Powell, Colin, 24n18, 30, 233

Powell Doctrine, 241n32

power: civil-military balance of, 4, 27–34; —, as continuous variable, 33; —, as factor in policy making environment, 17; —, impact of on strategic assessment, 28–29; —, measurement of, 29–33; —, role in distributional conflict, 17; configurations of, 33–34; military, 29–32

preferences: divergence of, 23–27; —, as continuous variable, 25; —, level of as exogenous, 27n27; —, measurement of, 25–27; —, and military strategy, 24; —, and state security goals, 24; —, and strategic assessment, 4; as factor in policy making environment, 17; role of in distributional conflict, 17

principal-agent approach, 49n53, 270; and institutions, 21–22

process-tracing. *See* George, Alexander, and Andrew Bennet; research design

Prussia, 182. *See also* Germany

Przeworski, Adam, and Henry Teune, 60

Rabin, Yitzak, 96

Ramadan War (1973). *See* October War (1973)

rational choice, and institutions, 19. *See also* institutionalism

Rawlinson, Sir Henry, 177n60

realism: and German threat to Britain, 157–158; and Six Day War, 57n68; and strategic assessment, 57

regime type, and strategic assessment, 60

Reiter, Dan, and Allan Stam, 28n49

research design, 53–61; and alternative explanations, 58–61; —, control for, 54, 56–60; —, intra-civilian divisions as; 58–59; —, interservice rivalry as, 59; —, presidential management style as, 59–60; —, realism/international stimuli as, 57–58; —, regime type as, 60; before and after approach to, 60; and case studies, 54, 55–61; —, and cross-case comparisons, 55; —, supplementary, 56–61; —, diachronic analysis of, 60; —, selection of, 55–56; 58–59; 60–61; —, synchronic analysis of, 60; —, and within case process-tracing, 54, 55–56, 61; method of agreement in, 60; method of difference in, 60; necessary causes in, 54; —, civil-military relations as, 54; role of qualitative methods in, 54–55; and two- versus three-corner tests, 54

Revolutionary Command Council. *See under* Egypt

Riad, Mahmoud, 65n9, 66, 97

Rice, Condoleeza, 230, 230n5. *See also* Iraq War (2003)

Rikhye (general), 90, 91

Robertson, William (general), 147, 160, 163n32, 259; changes in strategic vision of, 171; as chief of Imperial General

Robertson, William (cont'd)
  Staff, 164, 167; and disagreement with Lloyd George over war strategy, 167–169; and Maurice Debate, 173; and partnership with Douglas Haig, 164–165; and Passchendaele, 171. *See also* Britain; Haig, Douglas
Rosen, Stephen, 13n10, 26n22, 180
Rotem crisis (1960), 64, 64n4
Rumsfeld, Donald, 2, 59, 233, 226, 230, 255, 269, 270; ability to get information of, 236, 261; combative personality of, 228; decision making power of, 235; interest of in civilian control over military, 228; interest of in military transformation, 234–235, 242–243; military oversight efforts of, 237–239, 266; and planning for Iraq War (2003), 229n2, 240–241, 266; —, and cancellation of follow on troops, 251; —, and debates with Tommy Franks over number of troops, 248; —, interest in small combat force, 250, 251; —, post-conflict strategy, 230; poor relationship with military of, 237–238; —, retired generals' criticism of, 231–232; preference divergence with military, 232–234; and relationship with Tommy Franks, 229. *See also* Frank, Tommy; Iraq War (2003)
Russia, 145, 151, 157, 178, 184, 185, 188, 190, 221; Austria's mobilization for war against, 193; and relations with Britain, 151, 157; in Schlieffen Plan, 186. *See also* Britain; Germany

Sabri, Ali, 102n1; and Arab Socialist Union, 75; as challenge to Sadat, 117; dismissed by Sadat, 117
Sadat, Anwar, 55, 58–59, 65n9, 79, 92, 257, 261; and 1977 trip to Jerusalem, 106, 141; ability of to monitor military, 123–124, 129, 131, 138–139; access to military information, 123, 138; and attempt to align Egypt with the "West," 102, 138; and attempt to recover territory lost to Israel in Arab-Israeli War, 104; and Camp David Accords, 106–107, 127; civil-military relations under, 111–122; confrontation with Ali Sabri clique, 117–118; control over dissemination of information by, 125; dismissal of Ali Sabri, 117; and efforts at building support base, 113–116; encouragement of Islamic politics by, 115; expulsion of Soviet military advisors by, 127; grand strategy of, background to 104–107; —, conventional explanations of, 107–110; and IMF austerity measures, 116, 116n42; impact of foreign policy on military, 122; and Law 43, 114; military oversight efforts of, 266; and Egyptian economic liberalization, 114, 116; middle-class support for, 116; and Nasser compared, 1–2, 110, 124, 138; National Defense Council marginalized by, 127; on the need to distance Egypt from the Soviet Union, 122n51; and October war (1973), —, decision to aid Syria during, 134, 134n67; —, and disengagement from, 106, 126, 136–137, 140; —, motives for launching, 107, 137; —, conventional explanations of peace initiatives of, 109–110; —, planning of, 124; role of threat in cooperation with military in, 108n14; and Operation Spark, 104; and Palestinian issue, 141–142; and political liberalization, 115–116; promotion to power of, 102, 102n1; and restrictions placed on military's role in consultation, 126–128; role of learning in strategic choices of, 108–109; role of peasant background in decision making, 110n20; role of personality in decision making of, 109–110; role of regime type in successes, 110; seen as sacrificing national security, 140–142; strength at strategic assessment, 2; as unilateral decision maker, 111; use of Supreme Council of Armed Forces (SCAF) by, 123–124, 127; as weak, 258; worker discontent with, 116. *See also* Egypt; Nasser, Gamal Abdel; October War (1973)
Sadiq, Mohammed Ahmed, 117, 121, 129n59, 139; and opposition to October war (1973), 132
Sagan, Scott D., 53n59, 196–197, 264n1
Saudi Arabia, 63
Schlieffen Plan: and British continental intervention, 186–187; and clash of military and political objectives, 188–189, 192; conventional accounts of, 186–187. *See also* Germany
Schoomaker, Peter, 238
Second World War, 266
Segev, Tom, 96n70

INDEX 313

September 11, 235
Serbia, 190; and assassination of Archduke Ferdinand, 187–188
Sharaf, Sami, 112n29
Sharif, Nawaz, 56, 195, 260; amending of constitution by, 199–200; attempts at military oversight of, 203–205; civil-military reforms during tenure, 198–200; and conflicts with political establishment, 199–200; coup against, 205; and debate over establishment of National Security Council, 201–202; decline in support for, 199, 199n9, 200, 203–205; and establishment of Council for Defense and National Security, 201, 202; first stint as prime minister, 199–200, 200n5; and Kargil war (1999), 205–207; —, trip to United States to resolve, 203, 208; and relationship with military, 198–199; second appointment to prime minister, 198; support base of, 198. See also Pakistan; Kargil war (1999)
Sharm al-Sheikh, 64, 92
Sharon, Ariel, 106
Shazly, Saad, 133; dismissed by Sadat, 135n68; and October War (1973), 134, 135
Shinseki, Eric, 238, 244, 249–250; and Iraq War (2003) troop level recommendations, 245–250, 251
Sidqi, Mahmud 78n40, 84
Sinai I, 106; Egyptian military disagreement with, 121. See also Kissenger, Henry; October War (1973); Sadat, Anwar
Sinai II, 106, 127, 140. See also Kissenger, Henry; October War (1973); Sadat, Anwar
Sinai Peninsula, 1, 62, 64, 67, 78, 140, 141. See also October War (1973)
Six Day War. See Arab-Israeli War (1967)
Snyder, Jack, 59n74, 178, 179
Soldier and the State, The, 268
Somalia, 234, 242
Somme, Battle of the, 163n31, 170
South Asia, 195; nuclear stability in, 196–197
Soviet Union, 266; and Egyptian military support for relations with, 122, 122n21, and October War (1973), 105n5; role in setting off Arab-Israeli War (1967), 64, 81–82, 90; Sadat's attempts to get military aid from, 109n17; as source of military equipment for Egypt, 95; training of Egyptian military by, 122n21. See also Arab-Israeli War (1967); October War (1973)
Sprintz, Detlef, and Yael Wolinsky-Nahmias, 56n67
Spruyt, Hendrik, 60n76, 271n14
Stein, Janice Gross, 69n20, 95n67, 108n15
Strachan, Hew, 156, 159n24, 160
strategic assessment, 34–53; in 1970s Egypt, 123–137, 257–258; best civil-military conditions for, 5, 42–45; and civil-military relations, 2, 3, 4, 265–256; constituent attributes of, 4; defined, 34–35; distributional approach to variations in, 4, 16–23; domestic dimension of, 3; failures in, 7–9; —, and estimates of military capabilities, 7–8; —, and international outcomes, 9–11; fair, 48–53; —, political dominance and high preference divergence, 48–51; —, military dominance and high/low preference divergence, 51–53; hypotheses on, 42–53; impact of civil-military balance of power on, 28–29; institutions of as mutable, 19; international dimension of, 3; and interservice rivalry, 59; in late 1990s Turkey, 214–218, 261; and leader psychology, 59–60; and low civil-military preference divergence, 42; in mid-1960s Egypt, 9–92, 256–257; and oversight (of military), 265–267, 270; in Pakistan under Sharif, 200–207, 260; poor, 46–48; in pre–First World War Britain, 148–161, 258; problems of, 6–9; —, principal-agent problems and, 265–267; processes in, 35–42; and realist theories of international relations, 57–58; and regime type, 60, 268; role of authorization process in, 4, 39–42; role of civil-military balance of power in, 5; role of information sharing in, 4, 35–36; role of institutions in, 4, 4n4; role of preference divergence in, 4, 5; role of strategic coordination in, 4, 36–38; role of structural competence in, 4, 38–39; undermining of, 264–265; in United States, during 2003 Iraq War, 235–252, 261; —, during Vietnam War, 267; as vital to international peace and security, 2; as vital to state security, 2; variations in, 5–6; —, as independent of regime type, 12; in wartime Britain, 165–174, 259; in Wilhel-

strategic assessment (cont'd)
mine Germany, 182–191; worst civil-military conditions for, 5–6, 45–46. See also authorization process; information sharing; strategic coordination; structural competence
strategic coordination: in 1970s Egypt, 126–128, 139–142; as attribute of strategic assessment, 4; defined, 36; evaluation of, 37–38; as key proces in strategic assessment, 36–38; in late 1990s Turkey, 217, 219–221, 222, 261; in mid-1960s Egypt, 82–85; Nasser's poor attempts at, 2; in Pakistan under Sharif, 200–202, 260; in pre-First World War Britain, 148; routinization of as beneficial to strategic assessment, 44; Sadat's strengths at, 2; in United States, during 2003 Iraq War, 2, 236–239, 241–242, 243–251, 261; —, during Vietnam War, 267; in wartime Britain, 259; —, problems of, 170–174; in Wilhelmine Germany, 183–189, 260. See also strategic assessment
structural competence: in 1970s Egypt, 128–131, 138, 257; as attribute of strategic assessment, 4; defined, 38; evaluation of, 38–39; as key processes in strategic assessment, 38–39; in mid-1960s Egypt, 85–88, 256; in pre-First World War Britain, 148. See also strategic assessment
Suez Canal, 105, 124, 125, 128, 133, 140. See also Egypt
Suez conflict (1956), 63, 78. See also Egypt
Supreme Command, 228
Supreme Council of the Armed Forces (SCAF). See under Egypt
synchronic (cross-case) comparison. See under research design
Syria, 1, 210; and October War (1973), 134, 134n67; and Pakistan, 224–225; and Turkey, 223–225, 261, 272; withdrawal of from United Arab Republic, 77

Thant, U, 66n13
Thelen, Kathleen, 19n10
Tiran, Straits of, 1, 68, 84; closure of 64–65, 91–92. See also Arab-Israeli War (1967); Egypt; Nasser, Gamal Abdel
Tirpitz, Alfred von (admiral), 184, 185
Trachtenberg, Mark, 189
Turkey, 29, 56, 58, 60, 61, 184, 201n14; authorization process in, 260–261; —, clarity of and threat credibility, 223–224; civil-military relations in, 260–261; grand strategy of in mid-1990s, 218; and Kurds, 195, 218, 220–221, 222, 261; in late 1990s, 209–225; —, authorization process, 214–217, 219, 222; —, civil-military relations, 212–214; —, conventional accounts of, 210–211; —, and European Union, 209, 214, 218, 222; —, external assessment of Turkish security preferences, 221–222, 222n68; —, fragmentation of politics under Erbakan, 212; —, increases in Islamic support, 212; —, Kurdish rebellion, 222; —role of military in civilian politics, 210–211, 213; —, influence of military in National Security Council, 210, 215–217; —, information sharing, 218; —, international relations, 218–225; —, invasion of Iraq, 218; —, military distrust of Erbakan, 214; —, military dominance over appointments, 214–216; —, military's expulsion of pro-Islamist officers, 215–216; —, Operation Poised Hammer, 218n54; —, and relations with Israel, 218, 219–220, 221; —, and NATO, 218; —, power of military, 213, 221–222; —, preference divergence between military and Erbakan, 213–214, 215–217, 218–222; —, relations with Iraq, 220–221; —, strategic assessment, 214–218; —, strategic coordination 217, 219–221, 222; National Security Council of, 41, 215–217; prominent role of military in, 195; strategic assessment in, 261; strategic coordination in, 261; and Syria, 223–225, 224n74; 261, 272; under Turgut Ozal, 215n43; Welfare party (WP), 212, 214. See also Erbakan, Necmettin

United Nations, 1, 1n1; and Arab-Israeli War (1967), 64; and ceasefire for October War (1973), 105, 105n5
United Nations Emergency Forces, 64, 78; request for redeployment of by Egypt, 90–91
United States, 56, 58, 61; Arab-Israeli War (1967), 99–100, 99n78, 100n79, 138, 141; authorization process in, 235; civil-military preference divergence in, 234; civil-military relations in, 233–235, 261; —, and 2003 Iraq War, 2; —, during Vietnam War, 266–267; —, and strategic as-

sessment, 2; and Goldwater-Nichols reforms (1986), 232n13; increase in political influence of military in, 233; international implications of 2003 Iraq War for, 252–255; interservice rivalries in, 267, 267n4; military organization of, 237n27; National Security Council of, 41; and Operation Provide Comfort, 221n65; strategic assessment in, 235–252. *See also* Iraq War (2003); Rumsfeld Donald

Urquhat, Sir Brian, 91n59

Van Evera, Stephen, 54n60, 61, 264n1. *See also* research design
Vietnam War, 266–267; poor civil-military coordination in, 267.

War of Attrition (1969–1970), 126
Welfare party (WP). *See under* Turkey
West Bank, 62, 67, 141
Wilhelm I (kaiser), 180
Wilhelm II (kaiser), 59, 177, 179, 183, 189, 193; and assassination of Archduke Ferdinand, 187–188; base of support for, 182; identification of with military's interests, 181; psychological accounts of, 180. *See also* First World War; Germany
Wilhelmine Germany. *See* Germany (Wilhelmine)
Wilson, Henry (general), 152; commitment to western front strategy during First World War of, 169n45; as director of military operations, 155; and increasing size of military, 160; and Maurice Debate, 173. *See also* Britain
Wolfowitz, Paul, 249–250, 250n51
Wolseley (lord), 149n10
Woodward, Bob, 232, 248

Yilmaz, Masut, 211n32, 224
Yom Kippur war (1973). *See* October War (1973)
Yost, Charles, 62n1, 66, 97
Youth Organization *See under* Egypt

Zia-ul-Haq (general), 199
Ziauddin (general), 204, 205
Zinni, Anthony, 248n48
Zuber, Terence, 186n76

GPSR Authorized Representative: Easy Access System Europe - Mustamäe tee 50, 10621 Tallinn, Estonia, gpsr.requests@easproject.com

www.ingramcontent.com/pod-product-compliance
Lightning Source LLC
Chambersburg PA
CBHW031545300426
44111CB00006BA/181